3rd Workshop on Noisy User-generated Text (W-NUT 2017)

Copenhagen, Denmark
7 September 2017

ISBN: 978-1-5108-4753-8

W-NUT 2017

**The Third Workshop on
Noisy User-generated Text
(W-NUT 2017)**

Proceedings of the Workshop

September 7, 2017
Copenhagen, Denmark

Introduction

The W-NUT 2017 workshop focuses on a core set of natural language processing tasks on top of noisy user-generated text, such as that found on social media, web forums and online reviews. Recent years have seen a significant increase of interest in these areas. The internet has democratized content creation leading to an explosion of informal user-generated text, publicly available in electronic format, motivating the need for NLP on noisy text to enable new data analytics applications. The workshop is an opportunity to bring together researchers interested in noisy text with different backgrounds and encourage crossover. The workshop this year features a shared task on Emerging and Rare entity recognition.

The workshop received 27 main track submissions, 17 of which were accepted, in addition to 6 system description papers for the shared task and a task overview paper. There are 3 invited speakers, Bill Dolan, Dirk Hovy and Miles Osborne with each of their talks covering a different aspect of NLP for user-generated text. We would like to thank the Program Committee members who reviewed the papers this year. We would also like to thank the workshop participants.

Leon Derczynski, Wei Xu, Alan Ritter and Tim Baldwin
Co-Organizers

Organizers:

Leon Derczynski, The University of Sheffield
Wei Xu, The Ohio State University
Alan Ritter, The Ohio State University
Tim Baldwin, The University of Melbourne

Program Committee:

Anietie Andy (Howard University/UPenn)
Su Lin Blodgett (UMass Amherst)
Colin Cherry (National Research Council Canada)
Paul Cook (University of New Brunswick)
Marina Danilevsky (IBM Research)
Seza Doğruöz (Tilburg University)
Heba Elfardy (Columbia University)
Dan Garrette (Google Research)
Weiwei Guo (LinkedIn)
Masato Hagiwara (Duolingo)
Hua He (University of Maryland)
Yulan He (Aston University)
Dirk Hovy (University of Copenhagen)
Jing Jiang (Singapore Management University)
Nobuhiro Kaji (Yahoo! Research)
Piroska Lendvai (University of Göttingen)
Wuwei Lan (Ohio State University)
Jessy Li (UPenn / UT Austin)
Sujian Li (Peking University)
Jiwei Li (Stanford University)
Chen Li (University of Texas at Dallas)
Patrick Littell (Carnegie Mellon University)
Huan Liu (Arizona State University)
Zhiyuan Liu (Tsinghua University)
Wei-Yun Ma (Academia Sinica)
Héctor Martínez Alonso (INRIA)
Chandra May (Johns Hopkins University)
Rada Mihalcea (University of Michigan)
Preslav Nakov (Qatar Computing Research Institute)
Eric Nichols (Honda Research Institute)
Brendan O'Connor (Umass Amherst)
Naoaki Okazaki (Tohoku University)
Siddharth Patwardhan (Apple)
Ellie Pavlick (University of Pennsylvania)
Bryan Perozzi (Google Research)
Barbara Plank (University of Groningen)
Daniel Preoţiuc-Pietro (University of Pennsylvania)
Preethi Raghavan (IBM Research)
Afshin Rahimi (The University of Melbourne)
Roi Reichart (Technion)

Alla Rozovskaya (City University of New York)
Mugizi Rwebangira (Howard University)
Djamé Seddah (University Paris-Sorbonne)
Hiroyuki Shindo (NAIST)
Richard Sproat (Google Research)
Veselin Stoyanov (Facebook)
Jeniya Tabassum (Ohio State University)
Marlies van der Wees (University of Amsterdam)
Svitlana Volkova (Pacific Northwest National Laboratory)
Byron Wallace (Northeastern University)
Diyi Yang (Carnegie Mellon University)
Yi Yang (Georgia Tech)
Guido Zarrella (MITRE)

Invited Speakers:

Bill Dolan, Microsoft Research
Dirk Hovy, University of Copenhagen
Miles Osborne, Bloomberg

Conference Program

September 7

9:00–9:05   **Opening**

9:05–9:50   **Invited Talk: Common Sense Knowledge as an Emergent Property of Neural Conversational Models (Bill Dolan)**

9:50–10:35   **Oral Session I**

9:50–10:05   *Boundary-based MWE segmentation with text partitioning*
Jake Williams

10:05–10:20   *Towards the Understanding of Gaming Audiences by Modeling Twitch Emotes*
Francesco Barbieri, Luis Espinosa Anke, Miguel Ballesteros, Juan Soler and Horacio Saggion

10:20–10:35   *Churn Identification in Microblogs using Convolutional Neural Networks with Structured Logical Knowledge*
Mourad Gridach, Hatem Haddad and Hala Mulki

10:35–11:00   **Coffee Break**

11:00–12:30   **Oral Session II**

11:00–11:15   *To normalize, or not to normalize: The impact of normalization on Part-of-Speech tagging*
Rob van der Goot, Barbara Plank and Malvina Nissim

11:15–11:30   *Constructing an Alias List for Named Entities during an Event*
Anietie Andy, Mark Dredze, Mugizi Rwebangira and Chris Callison-Burch

11:30–11:45   *Incorporating Metadata into Content-Based User Embeddings*
Linzi Xing and Michael J. Paul

11:45–12:00   *Simple Queries as Distant Labels for Predicting Gender on Twitter*
Chris Emmery, Grzegorz Chrupała and Walter Daelemans

12:00–12:15   *A Dataset and Classifier for Recognizing Social Media English*
Su Lin Blodgett, Johnny Wei and Brendan O'Connor

12:15–12:30   *Evaluating hypotheses in geolocation on a very large sample of Twitter*
Bahar Salehi and Anders Søgaard

12:30–14:00   Lunch

14:00–14:45   Invited Talk: Tweets in Finance (Miles Osborne)

14:45–14:55   Lightning Talks

The Effect of Error Rate in Artificially Generated Data for Automatic Preposition and Determiner Correction
Fraser Bowen, Jon Dehdari and Josef Van Genabith

An Entity Resolution Approach to Isolate Instances of Human Trafficking Online
Chirag Nagpal, Kyle Miller, Benedikt Boecking and Artur Dubrawski

Noisy Uyghur Text Normalization
Osman Tursun and Ruket Cakici

Crowdsourcing Multiple Choice Science Questions
Johannes Welbl, Nelson F. Liu and Matt Gardner

A Text Normalisation System for Non-Standard English Words
Emma Flint, Elliot Ford, Olivia Thomas, Andrew Caines and Paula Buttery

Huntsville, hospitals, and hockey teams: Names can reveal your location
Bahar Salehi, Dirk Hovy, Eduard Hovy and Anders Søgaard

Improving Document Clustering by Removing Unnatural Language
Myungha Jang, Jinho D. Choi and James Allan

Lithium NLP: A System for Rich Information Extraction from Noisy User Generated Text on Social Media
Preeti Bhargava, Nemanja Spasojevic and Guoning Hu

14:55–15:30   Shared Task Session

14:55–15:10   *Results of the WNUT2017 Shared Task on Novel and Emerging Entity Recognition*
Leon Derczynski, Eric Nichols, Marieke van Erp and Nut Limsopatham

15:10–15:20   *A Multi-task Approach for Named Entity Recognition in Social Media Data*
Gustavo Aguilar, Suraj Maharjan, Adrian Pastor López Monroy and Thamar Solorio

15:20–15:30   *Distributed Representation, LDA Topic Modelling and Deep Learning for Emerging Named Entity Recognition from Social Media*
Patrick Jansson and Shuhua Liu

Multi-channel BiLSTM-CRF Model for Emerging Named Entity Recognition in Social Media
Bill Y. Lin, Frank Xu, Zhiyi Luo and Kenny Zhu

Transfer Learning and Sentence Level Features for Named Entity Recognition on Tweets
Pius von Däniken and Mark Cieliebak

Context-Sensitive Recognition for Emerging and Rare Entities
Jake Williams and Giovanni Santia

A Feature-based Ensemble Approach to Recognition of Emerging and Rare Named Entities
Utpal Kumar Sikdar and Björn Gambäck

xii

15:30–16:30   **Poster Session**

16:30–17:15   **Invited Talk: Modeling Language as a Social Construct (Dirk Hovy)**

17:15–17:30   **Closing and Best Paper Awards**

Boundary-Based MWE Segmentation With Text Partitioning

Jake Ryland Williams
Drexel University
30 N. 33rd Street
Philadelphia, PA 19104
jw3477@drexel.edu

Abstract

This work presents a fine-grained, text-chunking algorithm designed for the task of multiword expressions (MWEs) segmentation. As a lexical class, MWEs include a wide variety of idioms, whose automatic identification are a necessity for the handling of colloquial language. This algorithm's core novelty is its use of non-word tokens, i.e., boundaries, in a bottom-up strategy. Leveraging boundaries refines token-level information, forging high-level performance from relatively basic data. The generality of this model's feature space allows for its application across languages and domains. Experiments spanning 19 different languages exhibit a broadly-applicable, state-of-the-art model. Evaluation against recent shared-task data places text partitioning as the overall, best performing MWE segmentation algorithm, covering all MWE classes and multiple English domains (including user-generated text). This performance, coupled with a non-combinatorial, fast-running design, produces an ideal combination for implementations at scale, which are facilitated through the release of open-source software.

1 Introduction

Multiword expressions (MWEs) constitute a mixed class of complex lexical objects that often behave in syntactically unruly ways. A unifying property that ties this class together is the lexicalization of multiple words into a single unit. MWEs are generally difficult to understand through grammatical decomposition, casting them as types of minimal semantic units. There is variation in this non-compositionality property (Bannard et al., 2003), which in part may be attributed to differences in MWE types. These range from multi-word named entities, such as *Long Beach, California*, to proverbs, such as *it takes one to know one*, to idiomatic verbal expressions, like *cut* it *out* (which often contain flexible gaps). For all of their strangeness they appear across natural languages (Jackendoff, 1997; Sag et al., 2002), though generally not for common meanings, and frequently with opaque etymologies that confound non-native speakers.

1.1 Motivation

There are numerous applications in NLP for which a preliminary identification of MWEs holds great promise. This notably includes idiom-level machine translation (Carpuat and Diab, 2010); reduced polysemy in sense disambiguation (Finlayson and Kulkarni, 2011); keyphrase-refined information retrieval (Newman et al., 2012); and the integration of idiomatic and formulaic language in learning environments (Ellis et al., 2008). Parallel to these linguistically-focused applications is the possibility that MWE identification can positively affect machine learning applications in text analysis. Regardless of algorithm complexity, a common preliminary step in this area is tokenization. Having the "correct" segmentation of a text into words and MWEs results in a meaning-appropriate tokenization of minimal semantic units. Partial steps in this direction have been taken through recent work focusing on making the bag of phrases framework available as a simple improvement to the bag of words. However, that work (Handler et al., 2016) utilized only noun phrases, leaving the connection between MWEs and a comprehensive bag of phrases framework yet to be acknowledged. With the specific focus of MWEs on idiomaticity, a comprehensive bag of words and phrases framework would be possible, provided the MWE identification task is resolved.

1.2 Task description

Despite the variety that exist, studies often only focus on a few MWEs classes, or on only specific lengths (Tsvetkov and Wintner, 2011). In fact,

1

Proceedings of the 3rd Workshop on Noisy User-generated Text, pages 1–10
Copenhagen, Denmark, September 7, 2017. ©2017 Association for Computational Linguistics

named entity extraction may be thought of as satisfying the MWE identification task for just this one MWE class. The problem has a broader framing when all classes of MWEs are considered. Furthermore, since a mixed tokenization of words and phrases as minimal semantic units is a desired outcome, it is helpful to consider this task as a kind of fine-grained segmentation. Thus, this work refers to its task as **MWE segmentation**, and not identification or extraction. In other words, the specific goal here is to delimit texts into the smallest possible, independent units of meaning. Schneider et al. (2014b) were the first to treat this problem as such, when they created the first data set comprehensively annotated for MWEs. From this data set, an exemplar annotated record is:[1]

$$\text{My wife had } taken_1 \;\boxed{\text{her } 07'_2 \text{ Ford}_2 \text{ Fusion}_2}\; in_1$$
$$\text{for a routine } oil_3 \; change_3.$$

whose segmentation is an example of the present focus of this work. Note that the present study focuses only on MWE tokens, does not aim to approach the task of MWE class identification, and does not attempt to disambiguate MWE meanings. For detailed descriptions of these other MWE-related tasks, Baldwin and Kim (2010) provide an extensive discussion.

1.3 Existing work

The identification of MWEs and collocations is an area of study that has seen notable focus in recent years (Seretan, 2008; Pecina, 2010; Newman et al., 2012; Ramisch, 2015; Schneider et al., 2014a), and has a strong history of attention (both directly and through related work) in the literature (Becker, 1975; Church and Hanks, 1990; Sag et al., 2002). It has become commonplace for approaches to leverage well-studied machine learning algorithms such as structured perceptrons (Schneider et al., 2014a) and conditonal random fields (Constant and Sigogne, 2011; Hosseini et al., 2016). The flexibility of these algorithms allow researchers to mix a variety of feature types, ranging from tokens to parts of speech to syntax trees. Juxtaposed to these relatively-complex models exist the simpler and more-heuristic (Cordeiro et al., 2015). Some rely singularly on MWE dictionaries, while others incorporate multiple measures or are rule-based, like

those present in the suite available through mwe-toolkit (Ramisch, 2015) or jMWE (Kulkarni and Finlayson, 2011).

MWEs have been the focus of considerable attention for languages other than English, too. Hungarian MWE corpora focusing on light verb constructions have been under development for some time (T. et al., 2011). In application to the French language, part-of-speech tagging has seen benefit (Constant and Sigogne, 2011) through awareness and relativity to MWEs. Recently, Savary et al. (2017) conducted a shared task for the identification of verbal MWEs with a data set spanning 18 languages (excluding English). While extending this area of work to a large variety of languages, this task saw notable multilingual algorithmic developments (Saied and Candito, 2017), but did not approach the identification of all MWE classes, comprehensively. On the other hand, a SemEval 2016 shared task (Schneider et al., 2016) covered English domains and all MWE classes, bearing the greatest similarity to the present work. In general, these shared tasks have all highlighted a need for the improvement of algorithms.

2 Algorithms

2.1 Text partitioning

Text partitioning is a physical model developed recently (Williams et al., 2015) for fine-grained text segmentation. It treats a text as a dichotomous squence, alternating between word (w_i) and non-word (b_i) tokens:

$$(\cdots, b_{i-1}, w_i, b_i, w_{i+1}, b_{i+1} \cdots)$$

The key feature of text partitioning is its treatment of non-word, i.e., "boundary", tokens. Acting like glue, these may take one of two distinct states, $s \in \{0, 1\}$, identifying if a non-word token is bound (b_i^1) or broken (b_i^0). **A non-word token in the bound state binds words together.** Thus, a text partitioning algorithm is a function that determines the states of non-word tokens.

In its original development, text partitioning was studied simplistically, with space as the only non-word token. In that work, a threshold probability, q, was set. For each space, b_i, in a text, a uniform random binding probability, q_i, would be drawn. If $q_i > q$, b_i would be bound, and otherwise it would be broken. As a parameter, q thus allowed for the tuning of a text into its collection of words ($q = 1$), clauses ($q = 0$), or, for any value,

---

[1] Note that color/indices redundantly indicate separate MWEs, with the colored box highlighting an MWE's gap, and black, unnumbered text tokenized simply as words.

$q \in (0, 1)$, a randomly-determined collection of N-grams. While non-deterministic, this method was found to preserve word frequencies, (unlike the sliding-window method), and made possible the study of Zipf's law for mixed distributions of words and N-grams.

The present work utilizes the parameter q to develop a supervised machine learning algorithm for MWE segmentation. A threshold probability, q, is still set, and the supervised component is the determination of the binding probabilities (q_i) for a text's non-word tokens. Provided a gold-standard, MWE-segmented text:

$$(\cdots, b_{i-1}^{s_{i-1}}, w_i, b_i^{s_i}, w_{i+1}, b_{i+1}^{s_{i+1}} \cdots)$$

let $f(w_i, b_i^{s_i}, w_{i+1})$ denote the frequency at which a boundary b_i is observed between w_i and w_{i+1} in the state s_i. Provided this, a binding probability is defined as:

$$q_i = \frac{f(w_i, b_i^1, w_{i+1})}{f(w_i, b_i^1, w_{i+1}) + f(w_i, b_i^0, w_{i+1})}.$$

This basic, 2-gram text partitioning model makes the binding probabilities a function of boundaries and their immediately-surrounding words. In principle, this might be extended to a more-nuanced model, with binding probabilities refined by larger-gram information.

2.1.1 Extensions

Some MWEs consist of non-contiguous spans of words. These varieties are often referred to as "gappy" expressions, an example of which is shown in Sec. 1.2. Text partitioning may easily be extended to handle gappy MWEs by instituting a unique boundary token,[2] e.g.,

$$b = \_\_\text{GAP}\_\_$$

that indicates the presence of a gap. For example, to handle the gappy MWE *out of control* in the statement:

The situation was out$_1$ of$_1$ their control$_1$.

a binding probability for b (as above) between words $w_5 = of$ and $w_7 = control$ would be computed from the state frequencies $f(w_5, b^{\{0,1\}}, w_7)$. Since gappy MWEs are relatively sparse as compared to other MWEs, a single gap-boundary token is used for all gap sizes. This is designed

for a flexible handling of variable gap sizes, given the relatively small amount of gold-standard data that is presently available. However, this may in principle be refined to particular gap-sized specifications, possibly ideal for higher precision in the presence of larger quantities of gold-standard data.

A number of MWE types, such as named entities, are entirely open classes. Often occurring only once, or as entirely emergent objects, these pose a significant challenge for MWE segmentation, along with the general sparsity and size of the current gold-standards. For their inclusion in the gold-standard datasets and the general quality of automated taggers, part-of-speech (POS) information may generally be leveraged to increase recall. These data are utilized in a parallel text partitioning algorithm, swapping tokens for tags,[3] so that binding probabilities, $q_{i,\text{tok}}$ and $q_{i,\text{POS}}$, are computed for both data types. Two thresholds are then used to determine states via a logical disjunction, i.e., b_i binds if $q_{i,\text{tok}} > q_{\text{tok}} \lor q_{i,\text{POS}} > q_{\text{POS}}$.

Algorithm 1 Pseudocode for the longest first defined (LFD) algorithm. Here, a candidate MWE's tokens are pruned from left to right for the longest referenced in a training lexicon, *lex*. When no form is found in *lex*, the first token is automatically pruned, (accepting it as an expression), leaving the algorithm to start from the next. Note that the "$\frown$" symbol indicates a concatenation operation in line 10, where the current *form* is placed onto the end of the *lexemes* array.

```
 1:  procedure LFD(tokens)
 2:      lexemes ← (·)
 3:      N ← length(tokens)
 4:      while N do
 5:          indices ← (N + 1) : 1
 6:          for i in indices do
 7:              form ← join(tokens[0 : i])
 8:              remaining ← tokens[i : N]
 9:              if form ∈ lex or not i − 1 then
10:                  lexemes ← lexemes ⌢ form
11:                  if length(tokens) = 1 then
12:                      tokens ← (·)
13:                  else
14:                      tokens ← remaining
15:                  break
16:          N ← length(tokens)
17:      return lexemes
```

---

[2] Note that the exact form for b that is used to indicate a gap is not important, but that it just needs to be unique to compute state frequencies and binding probabilities.

[3] Note that this requires the inclusion of a special POS tag, e.g., "SP", for the space character.

2.2 The longest first defined

In the presented form, text partitioning only focuses on information immediately local to boundaries (surrounding word pairs). This has positive effects for recall, but can result in lower precision, since there is no guarantee that a sequence of bound tokens is an MWE. For example, if presented with the text:

"I go for take out there, frequently."

the segment *take out there* might be bound, since *take out* and *out there* are both known MWE forms, potentially observed in training. To balance this, a directional, lookup-based algorithm is proposed. Referred to as the **longest first defined** (LFD) algorithm (see Alg. 1), this algorithm prunes candidates by clipping off the longest known (MWE) references along the reading direction of a language. This requires knowledge of MWE lexica, which may be derived from both gold-standard data and external sources (see Sec. 3). Continuing with the example, if the text partitioning algorithm outputs the candidate, *take out there*, it would next be passed to the LFD. The LFD would find *take out there* unreferenced, and check the next-shortest (2-word) segments, from left to right. The LFD would immediately find *take out* referenced, output it, and continue on the remainder, *there*. With only one term remaining, the word *there* would then be trivially output and the algorithm terminated. While this algorithm will likely fail when confronted with pathological expressions, like those in "garden path" sentences, e.g., "The prime number few.", directionality is a powerful heuristic in many languages that may be leveraged for increased precision.

3 Materials

3.1 Gold standard data

Treating MWE segmentation as a supervised machine learning task, this work relies on several recently-constructed MWE-annotated data sets. This includes the business reviews contained in the Supersense-Tagged Repository of English with a Unified Semantics for Lexical Expressions, annotated by Schneider et al. (2014b; 2015). These data were harmonized and merged with the Ritter and Lowlands data set of supersense-annotated tweets (Johannsen et al., 2014) for the SemEval 2016 shared task (#10) on Detecting Minimal Semantic Units and their Meanings (DIMSUM),

conducted by Schneider et al. (2016). The DIMSUM data set additionally possesses token lemmas and gold-standard part of speech (POS) tags for the 17 universal POS categories. In addition to the shared task training data of business reviews and tweets, the DIMSUM shared task resulted in the creation of three domains of testing data, which spanned business reviews, tweets, and TED talk transcripts. All DIMSUM data are comprehensive in being annotated for all MWE classes.

To evaluate against a diversity of languages this work also utilizes data produced by the multinational, European Cooperation in Science and Technology's action group: PARSing and Multiword Expressions within a European multilingual network (PARSEME) (Savary et al., 2015). In 2017, the PARSEME group conducted a shared task with data spanning 18 languages[4] (Savary et al., 2017), focusing on several classes of verbal MWEs. So, while the PARSEME data are not annotated for all MWEs classes, they do provide an assessment against multiple languages. However, the resources gathered for the 18 languages exhibit a large degree of variation in overall size and numbers of MWEs annotated, leading to observable differences in identifiability.

The gold standard data sets were produced with variations in annotation formats. The DIMSUM data set utilizes a variant of the beginning inside outside (BIO) scheme (Ramshaw and Marcus, 1995) used for named entity extraction. Additionally, their annotations indicate which tokens are linked to which, as opposed to the PARSEME data set, which simply identifies tokens to indexed MWEs. Note that this has implications to task evaluation: the PARSEME evaluations can only assess tokens' presence inside of specific MWEs, while the DIMSUM evaluations can focus on specific token-token attachments/separations. Evaluations against the DIMSUM datasets are therefore more informative of segmentation, than identification. Additionally, the DIMSUM data sets use lowercase BIO tags to indicate the presence

---

[4] While the shared task was originally planned to cover 21 languages, corpus release was only achieved for Bulgarian (BG), Czech (CS), German (DE), Greek (EL), Spanish (ES), Farsi (FA), French (FR), Hebrew (HE), Hungarian (HU), Italian (IT), Lithuanian (LT), Maltese (MT), Polish (PL), Brazilian Portuguese (PT), Romanian (RO), Slovene (SL), Swedish (SV), and Turkish (TR). No sufficiently available native annotators were found for English (EN), Yiddish (YI), and Croatian (HR). High-level data (including POS tags) were provided for all of the 18 languages, except BG, HE, and LT.

of tokens inside of the gaps of others. However, the DIMSUM data sets provide no information on the locations of spaces in sentences, unlike the PARSEME data sets, which do. Since the present work relies on knowledge of spaces to identify token-token boundaries for segmentation, the DIMSUM data sets had to first be pre-processed to infer the locations of spaces. This is done in such a way as to preserve comparability with the work others, (discussed in Sec. 4.1).

3.2 Support data

The gold-standard data sets (DIMSUM, and PARSEME) exhibit variations in size, domain, language, and in the classes of annotated MWEs. Ideally, each of these data sets would cover all MWE classes. Since the English data sets do, and many are open classes (e.g., the named entity class readily accepts new members), gold standards cannot be expected to cover all MWE forms. So, to produce segmentations that identify rare MWEs, like those that occur once in the gold standard data, this work relies on support data. Note that because the PARSEME data set covers a restricted set of MWE types (verbal MWEs, only), type-unrestricted lexical resources, such as Wiktionary and Wikipedia, can be expected to substantially hurt precision while helping recall. Thus, the support data described below are only used for the English language experiments, i.e., the DIMSUM data sets. Enhancement by support data for the PARSEME task and extension to the identification of MWE types are thus left for future development, together.

Since this work approaches the problem as a segmentation task, information is needed on MWE edge-boundaries. Thus, support data must present MWEs in their written contexts, and not just as entries in a lexicon. Example usages of dictionary entries provide this detail, and are leveraged from Wiktionary (data accessed 1/11/16) and Wordnet (Miller, 1995). These exemplified dictionary entries help to fill gold standard data gaps, but still lack many noun compounds and named entities. Outside of dictionaries, MWEs such as these may be found in encyclopedias. Thus, the Wikipedia hyperlinks present in all Wikipedia (data accessed 5/1/16) articles are utilized. Specifically, the exact hyperlink targets are used (not the displayed text), and without using any term extraction measures for filtering, as opposed to the data produced by

Hartmann et al. (2012). This results in data that are noisy, with many entities that may not actually be classifiable as MWEs. However, their availability and broad coverage offset these negative properties, which is exhibited by this work's evaluation.

4 Methods

4.1 Pre-processing

None of the gold standard data sets explicitly identify the locations of spaces in their annotations. This is a challenge for the present work, since it focuses on word-word boundaries (of which space is the most common) to identify the separations between segments. This turns out to not be an issue with the PARSEME data sets, which indicate when a given token is not followed by a space. However for the DIMSUM data sets, the locations of spaces had to be inferred. To resolve this issue, a set of heuristic rules are adopted with a default assumption of space on both sides of a tokens. Exceptions to this default include, group openings (e.g., brackets and parentheses) and odd-indexed quotes (double, single, etc.), for which space is only assumed at left; and punctuation tokens (e.g., commas and periods), group closures (e.g., brackets and parentheses), and even-indexed quotes (double, single, etc.), for which space is only assumed at right. While these heuristics will certainly not correctly identify all instances of space, they make the data sets more faithful to their original texts. Furthermore, since the annotations and evaluation procedures only focus on links between non-space tokens, the data may be re-indexed during pre-processing so as to allow for any resulting evaluation to be comparable to those of the data set authors' and shared task participants'. Thus, the omission of space characters and their inference in this work only negatively impacts text partitioning's evaluation. In other words, if this work were applied to annotated data that properly represents space, higher performance might be exhibited.

4.2 Evaluation

It is reasonably straightforward to measure precision, recall, and F_1 for exact matches of MWEs. However, this strategy is unreasonably coarse, failing to represent partial credit when algorithms get only portions of MWEs correct. Thus, the developers of the different gold standard data sets have established other evaluation metrics that are more flexible. Utilizing these partial credit MWE evaluation metrics provides refined detail into the performance of algorithms. However, these are not the same across the gold standard data sets. So, to maintain comparability of the present results, this work uses the specific strategies associated to each shared task.

In application to the PARSEME data sets, precision, recall, and F_1 describe tokens' presence in MWEs. Alternatively, DIMSUM-style metrics measure link/boundary-based evaluations. Specifically, this strategy checks if the links between tokens are correct. Note that this latter (DIMSUM) evaluation is better aligned to the formulation of text partitioning, but leaves the number evaluation points at one fewer per MWE than the PARSEME scheme. Thus, PARSEME evaluations favor longer MWEs more heavily.

4.3 Experimental design

The basic text partitioning model relies on the single threshold parameter, q, and integration of POS tags relies on a second. So, optimization ultimately entails the determination of parameters for both tokens, q_{tok}, and POS tags q_{POS}. To balance both precision and recall, these parameters are determined through optimization of the F_1 measure. In the absence of the LFD, F_1-optimal pairs, $(q_{\text{tok}}, q_{\text{POS}})$, are first determined via a full parameter scan over

$$(q_{\text{tok}}, q_{\text{POS}}) \in \{0, 0.01, \cdots, 0.99, 1\}^2.$$

For a given threshold pair, LFD-enhancement can then only increase precision, while decreasing recall. So, subsequent optimization with the LFD is accomplished through scanning values of q_{tok} and q_{POS} in the parameter space no less than those previously determined for basic, non-LFD model.

The different experiments were conducted in accordance with the protocols established by the designers of data sets and shared tasks, and in all cases, an eight-fold cross-validation was conducted for optimization. Exact comparability was achieved for the DIMSUM and PARSEME experiments as a result of the precise configurations of training and testing data from the shared tasks. Moreover, since an evaluation script was provided for each, metrics reported for DIMSUM and PARSEME experiments are in complete accord with the results of the shared tasks. For the DIMSUM experiments, results should be com-pared to the open track (external data was utilized), and for the PARSEME experiments, results should be compared to the closed track (no external data was utilized).

5 Results

Evaluations spanning the variety of languages (19, in total) showed high levels of performance, especially in application to English, where there was a diversity of domains (business reviews, Tweets, and TED talk transcripts), along with comprehensive MWE annotations. Moreover, these results were generally observed for text partitioning both with, and without the LFD. As expected, application of the LFD generally led to increased precision. While integration of POS tags was found to generally improve MWE segmentation in all English experiments, this was frequently not the case in applications to other languages. However, this observation should be taken with consideration for the restriction to the fewer MWE classes (verbal MWEs, only) annotated in the PARSEME (non-English) shared task languages, and additionally the fact that no external data were used. Detailed results for all DIMSUM and PARSEME experiments are recorded in Tab. 1.

For the DIMSUM experiments, final parameterizations were determined as $(q_{\text{tok}}, q_{\text{POS}}) = (0.5, 0.71)$ for text partitioning, alone, and $(q_{\text{tok}}, q_{\text{POS}}) = (0.74, 0.71)$ for the LFD-enhanced model. Comparing the base and LFD-enhanced models, higher overall performance was always achieved with the LFD (increasing F_1 by as many as 12 points). Including text partitioning in the shared-task rankings (for a total of 5 models) placed the LFD-enhanced model first at all domains but Twitter, for which third was reached (though within 3 F_1-points of first). However, combining all three domains into a single experiment placed the LFD-enhanced text partitioning algorithm as first, making it the best-performing algorithm, overall. In application to the user-reviews domain, text partitioning maintained first-place status, even without the LFD enhancement. For all other domains the base model ranked third.

For the PARSEME experiments, final parameterizations varied widely. This is not surprising, considering the significant variation in data set annotations and domains across the 18 languages. Additionally, POS tags were found to be of less-consistent value to the text partition-

Experiment	LFD	q_{tok}	q_{POS}	P	R	F_1	Rank	F_1-range
DIMSUM								
EN	N	0.5	0.71	0.5396	0.5507	0.5451	3/5	0.1348 – 0.5724
EN	Y	0.74	0.71	0.6538	0.5606	0.6036	1/5	-
Tweets	N	0.5	0.71	0.5897	0.5226	0.55542	3/5	0.1550 – 0.6109
Tweets	Y	0.74	0.71	0.6667	0.5185	0.5833	3/5	-
Reviews	N	0.5	0.71	0.5721	0.5584	0.5626	1/5	0.0868 – 0.5408
Reviews	Y	0.74	0.71	0.6742	0.5823	0.6249	1/5	-
TED	N	0.5	0.71	0.3984	0.6108	0.4823	3/5	0.2011 – 0.5714
TED	Y	0.74	0.71	0.5810	0.6228	0.6012	1/5	-
PARSEME								
BG	N	0.79	N/A	0.7071	0.5141	0.5954	2/3	0.5916 – 0.6615
BG	Y	0.83	N/A	0.8534	0.4309	0.5727	3/3	-
CS	N	0.73	0.0	0.7849	0.6655	0.7203	3/5	0.2352 – 73.65
CS	Y	0.9	0.59	0.8363	0.6324	0.7202	3/5	-
DE	N	0.82	0.0	0.5582	0.2788	0.3719	4/6	0.283 – 0.4545
DE	Y	0.98	0.78	0.6892	0.2010	0.3112	5/6	-
EL	N	0.78	0.0	0.3931	0.3815	0.3872	5/6	0.3871 – 0.4688
EL	Y	0.99	0.66	0.5755	0.3314	0.4206	4/6	-
ES	N	0.64	0.71	0.7473	0.4098	0.5293	2/6	0.3093 – 0.5839
ES	Y	0.99	0.71	0.7526	0.4371	0.5530	2/6	-
FA	N	0.57	0.68	0.7040	0.8313	0.7624	3/3	0.8536 – 0.9020
FA	Y	0.93	0.68	0.7028	0.8266	0.7597	3/3	-
FR	N	0.73	0.0	0.6589	0.3836	0.4849	4/7	0.1 – 0.6152
FR	Y	0.88	0.0	0.9045	0.3592	0.5142	3/7	-
HE	N	0.78	N/A	0.5969	0.2107	0.3115	2/3	0.0 – 0.313
HE	Y	1.0	N/A	0.9714	0.1812	0.3056	2/3	-
HU	N	0.97	0.66	0.7221	0.6612	0.6903	2/6	0.6226 – 0.7081
IIU	Y	0.97	0.66	0.7208	0.6568	0.6873	3/6	-
IT	N	0.85	0.0	0.5497	0.3174	0.4024	2/5	0.1824 – 0.4357
IT	Y	0.97	0.92	0.6503	0.2804	0.3919	2/5	-
LT	N	0.79	N/A	0.6567	0.1803	0.2830	1/3	0.0 – 0.2533
LT	Y	1.0	N/A	0.6471	0.1352	0.2237	2/3	-
MT	N	0.86	0.0	0.1591	0.1538	0.1564	2/5	0.0 – 0.1629
MT	Y	0.98	0.0	0.2126	0.1138	0.1483	2/5	-
PL	N	0.66	0.0	0.8962	0.5966	0.7164	2/5	0.0 – 0.7274
PL	Y	0.66	0.0	0.9623	0.5966	0.7366	1/5	-
PT	N	0.79	0.0	0.7518	0.4921	0.5948	4/5	0.3079 – 0.7094
PT	Y	0.95	0.0	0.8717	0.4605	0.6027	3/5	-
RO	N	0.71	0.0	0.8350	0.7850	0.8092	3/5	0.7799 – 0.8358
RO	Y	0.87	0.0	0.8766	0.7832	0.8272	2/5	-
SL	N	0.7	0.0	0.6606	0.4504	0.5356	1/5	0.3320 – 0.4655
SL	Y	0.76	0.0	0.7192	0.3959	0.5107	1/5	-
SV	N	1.0	0.95	0.0949	0.7771	0.1691	5/5	0.2669 – 0.3149
SV	Y	1.0	0.95	0.1013	0.7751	0.1792	5/5	-
TR	N	0.87	0.0	0.3852	0.3706	0.3778	5/5	0.4550 – 0.5528
TR	Y	0.9	0.91	0.3814	0.4037	0.3922	5/5	-

Table 1: Evaluation results, including data sets (Experiment); the LFD's application (**LFD**); token (q_{tok}) and POS (q_{POS}) thresholds; precision (P), recall (R), and F-measure (F_1); shared-task rank (**Rank**); and shared task F_1 ranges (**F_1-Range**). DIMSUM experiments spanned three domains: Twitter (Tweets), business reviews (Reviews), and TED talk transcripts (TED), with combined evaluation under EN. PARSEME language experiments are identified by ISO 639-1 two-letter codes.

ing algorithm, particularly when the LFD was not applied. Indeed, cross-validation of the base model resulted in $q_{\text{POS}} = 0$ as optimal for 11 out of the 15 languages where POS tags were made available. However, cross-validation of the LFD-enhanced algorithm resulted in only 6 parameterizations having $q_{\text{POS}} = 0$ as optimal. First place status was achieved for three out of the 18 languages (LT, PL, and SL), and for all languages aside from SV and TR, mid-to-high ranking F_1 values were achieved.[5] In contrast to the DIM-

---

[5] Note that anomalous MWEs were observed in the DE HU data sets, where large portions of the annotated MWEs consisted of only a single token. While the PARSEME annotation scheme includes multiword components that span a single token, e.g., "don't" in *don't talk the talk*, those observed in DE and HU were found outside of the annotation

SUM data sets, application of the LFD improved F_1 scores in only roughly half of the experiments.

6 Discussion

Evaluation against the comprehensively-annotated English data sets has shown text partitioning to be the current highest overall ranking MWE segmentation algorithm. This result is upheld for two out of the three available test domains (business reviews and TED talk transcripts), with a close third place achieved against data from Twitter. This exhibits the algorithms general applicability across domains, and especially in the context of noisy text. Combined with the algorithm's fast-running and non-combinatorial nature, this makes text partitioning ideal for large-scale applications to the identification of colloquial language, often found on social media. For these purposes, the presented algorithms have been made available as open-source tools as the Python "Partitioner" module, which may be accessed through Github[6] and the Python Package Index[7] for general use.

Unfortunately, the PARSEME experiments did not provide an evaluation against all types of MWEs. However, they did exhibit the general applicability of text partitioning across languages. So, while the PARSEME data are not sufficient for comprehensive MWE segmentation, trained models have also been made available for the 18 non-English languages through the Python Partitioner module. Across the 18 PARSEME shared-task languages text partitioning's F_1 values were found to rank as mid to high, with the notable exception of SV. While the SV data is peculiar in being quite small (with its training set smaller than its testing set), models entered into the PARSEME shared task achieved roughly twice the F_1 score for SV, indicating the possibility that text partitioning requires some critical mass of training data in order to achieve high levels of performance. Thus, for general increases in performance and for extension to comprehensive MWE segmentations, future directions of this work will likely do well to seek the

collection of larger and more-comprehensive data sets.

As defined, text partitioning is subtly different from a 2-gram model: it focuses on non-word boundary tokens, as opposed to just word-word pairs. Because this algorithm relies on knowledge of boundary token states, it cannot be trained well on MWE lexica, alone. Fort this model to achieve high precision, boundaries commonly occurring as broken must be observed as such, even if they are necessary components of known MWEs. Thus, the use of boundary-adjacent words for prediction is a limitation of the present model. This may possibly be overcome through use of more distant words and boundaries. However, since gold-standard data are still relatively small, they will likely require significant expansion before such models may be effectively implemented. Thus, future directions with more nuanced text partitioning models highlight the importance of generating more gold standard data, too.

Acknowledgments

The author thanks Sharon Williams for her ongoing support and thoughtful conversations, Chaomei Chen for his early inspiration of the project, Andy Reagan for his collaboration on the Python Partitioner module, Giovanni Santia for his thoughtful conversations, and the anonymous reviewers for their thoughtful comments. The author gratefully acknowledges research support from the University of California, Berkeley's School of Information, along with Drexel University's Department of Information Science and College of Computing and Informatics.

References

Timothy Baldwin and Su Nam Kim. 2010. Muiltiword expressions. In *Handbook of Natural Language Processing*. CRC Press, Boca Raton, USA, pages 267–292.

Colin Bannard, Timothy Baldwin, and Alex Lascarides. 2003. A statistical approach to the semantics of verb-particles. In *Proceedings of the ACL 2003 Workshop on Multiword Expressions: Analysis, Acquisition and Treatment - Volume 18*. pages 65–72.

Joseph D. Becker. 1975. The phrasal lexicon. In *Proceedings of the 1975 Workshop on Theoretical Issues in Natural Language Processing*. TINLAP '75, pages 60–63.

---

format. This included 27.2% of all MWEs annotated in the DE test records and 64.8% of all in the HU test records. Since text partitioning identifies segment boundaries, it cannot handle these anomalous MWEs, unlike the models entered into the PARSEME shared task. So to accommodate these and maintain comparability, a separate algorithm was employed. This simply placed lone MWE tags on tokens that were observed as anomalous 50% or more of the time in training.

[6] https://github.com/jakerylandwilliams/partitioner

[7] https://pypi.python.org/pypi/partitioner

Marine Carpuat and Mona Diab. 2010. Task-based evaluation of multiword expressions: A pilot study in statistical machine translation. In *Human Language Technologies: The 2010 Annual Conference of the North American Chapter of the Association for Computational Linguistics*. HLT '10, pages 242–245.

Kenneth W. Church and Patrick Hanks. 1990. Word association norms, mutual information, and lexicography. *Computational Linguistics* 16(1):22–29. Http://dl.acm.org/citation.cfm?id=89086.89095.

Matthieu Constant and Anthony Sigogne. 2011. Mwu-aware part-of-speech tagging with a crf model and lexical resources. In *Proceedings of the Workshop on Multiword Expressions: From Parsing and Generation to the Real World*. MWE '11, pages 49–56.

Silvio Ricardo Cordeiro, Carlos Ramisch, and Aline Villavicencio. 2015. Token-based mwe identification strategies in the mwetoolkit. In *Proceedings of the PARSEME 4th general meeting*.

Nick C. Ellis, Rita Simpson-Vlach, and Carson Maynard. 2008. Formulaic Language in Native and Second Language Speakers: Psycholinguistics, Corpus Linguistics, and TESOL. *TESOL Quarterly: A Journal for Teachers of English to Speakers of Other Languages and of Standard English as a Second Dialect* 42(3):375–396.

Mark Alan Finlayson and Nidhi Kulkarni. 2011. Detecting multi-word expressions improves word sense disambiguation. In *Proceedings of the Workshop on Multiword Expressions: From Parsing and Generation to the Real World*. MWE '11, pages 20–24.

Abram Handler, Matthew J. Denny, Hanna Wallach, and Brendan OConnor. 2016. Bag of what? simple noun phrase extraction for text analysis. In *Proceedings of the Workshop on Natural Language Processing and Computational Social Science*. pages 114–124.

Silvana Hartmann, György Szarvas, and Iryna Gurevych. 2012. Mining multiword terms from wikipedia pages 226–258.

Mohammad Javad Hosseini, Noah A. Smith, and Su-In Lee. 2016. UW-CSE at SemEval-2016 Task 10: Detecting multiword expressions and supersenses using double-chained conditional random fields. In *Proceedings of SemEval*.

Ray S. Jackendoff. 1997. *The Architecture of the Language Faculty*. MIT Press.

Anders Johannsen, Dirk Hovy, Hctor Martinez, Barbara Plank, and Anders Sgaard. 2014. More or less supervised super-sense tagging of twitter. In *The 3rd Joint Conference on Lexical and Computational Semantics*.

Nidhi Kulkarni and Mark Alan Finlayson. 2011. jmwe: A java toolkit for detecting multi-word expressions. In *Proceedings of the Workshop on Multiword Expressions: From Parsing and Generation to the Real World*. MWE '11, pages 122–124.

George A. Miller. 1995. Wordnet: A lexical database for english. *Commun. ACM* 38(11):39–41.

David Newman, Nagendra Koilada, Jey Han Lau, and Timothy Baldwin. 2012. Bayesian text segmentation for index term identification and keyphrase extraction. In *Proceedings of the 9th Workshop on Multiword Expressions*. pages 139–144.

Pavel Pecina. 2010. Lexical association measures and collocation extraction. *Language Resources and Evaluation* 44(1-2):137–158. Http://dx.doi.org/10.1007/s10579-009-9101-4. https://doi.org/10.1007/s10579-009-9101-4.

Carlos Ramisch. 2015. *Multiword Expressions Acquisition: A Generic and Open Framework*. Springer Publishing Company, Incorporated. https://doi.org/10.1007/978-3-319-09207-2.

Lance A. Ramshaw and Mitchell P. Marcus. 1995. Text chunking using transformation-based learning. In *Proceedings of the Third ACL Workshop on Very Large Corpora*. pages 82–94.

Ivan A. Sag, Timothy Baldwin, Francis Bond, Ann Copestake, and Dan Flickinger. 2002. *Multiword Expressions: A Pain in the Neck for NLP*. Springer, Berlin, Heidelberg. https://doi.org/10.1007/3-540-45715-1_1.

Hazem Al Saied and Marie Candito. 2017. The atilf-llf system for parseme shared task: a transition-based verbal multiword expression tagger. In *Proceedings of the 13th Workshop on Multiword Expressions*. pages 127–132.

Agata Savary, Carlos Ramisch, Silvio Cordeiro, Federico Sangati, Veronika Vincze, Behrang Qasem-iZadeh, Marie Candito, Fabienne Cap, Voula Giouli, Ivelina Stoyanova, and Antoine Doucet. 2017. The parseme shared task on automatic identification of verbal multiword expression. In *Proceedings of the 13th Workshop on Multiword Expressions*. pages 31–47.

Agata Savary, Manfred Sailer, Yannick Parmentier, Michael Rosner, Victoria Rosén, Adam Przepiórkowski, Cvetana Krstev, Veronika Vincze, Beata Wójtowicz, Gyri Smørdal Losnegaard, Carla Parra Escartín, Jakub Waszczuk, Matthieu Constant, Petya Osenova, and Federico Sangati. 2015. PARSEME – PARSing and Multiword Expressions within a European multilingual network. In *7th Language & Technology Conference: Human Language Technologies as a Challenge for Computer Science and Linguistics (LTC 2015)*.

Nathan Schneider, Emily Danchik, Chris Dyer, and Noah A. Smith. 2014a. Discriminative lexical semantic segmentation with gaps: Running the mwe gamut. *Transactions of the Association for Computational Linguistics* 2:193–206.

Nathan Schneider, Dirk Hovy, Anders Johannsen, and Marine Carpuat. 2016. SemEval-2016 Task 10: Detecting Minimal Semantic Units and their Meanings (DiMSUM). In *Proceedings of SemEval*.

Nathan Schneider, Spencer Onuffer, Nora Kazour, Emily Danchik, Michael T. Mordowanec, Henrietta Conrad, and Noah A. Smith. 2014b. Comprehensive annotation of multiword expressions in a social web corpus. In *Proceedings of the Ninth International Conference on Language Resources and Evaluation (LREC'14)*. pages 455–461.

Nathan Schneider and Noah A. Smith. 2015. A corpus and model integrating multiword expressions and supersenses. In *Proceedings of the 2015 Conference of the North American Chapter of the Association for Computational Linguistics: Human Language Technologies*. The Association for Computational Linguistics, pages 1537–1547.

V. Seretan. 2008. *Collocation Extraction Based on Syntactic Parsing*. Ph.D. thesis, University of Geneva.

István Nagy T., Gábor Berend, György Móra, and Veronika Vincze. 2011. Domain-dependent detection of light verb constructions. In *RANLP Student Research Workshop*. pages 1–8.

Yulia Tsvetkov and Shuly Wintner. 2011. Identification of multi-word expressions by combining multiple linguistic information sources. In *Proceedings of the Conference on Empirical Methods in Natural Language Processing*. EMNLP '11, pages 836–845.

Jake Ryland Williams, Paul R. Lessard, Suma Desu, Eric M. Clark, James P. Bagrow, Chris M. Danforth, and Peter Sheridan Dodds. 2015. Zipf's law holds for phrases, not words. *Scientific Reports* 5.

Towards the Understanding of Gaming Audiences
by Modeling Twitch Emotes

Francesco Barbieri◇ **Luis Espinosa-Anke**◇ **Miguel Ballesteros**♠
Juan Soler-Company ◇ **Horacio Saggion**◇

◇ Large Scale Text Understanding Systems Lab, TALN Group
Universitat Pompeu Fabra, Barcelona, Spain
♠IBM T.J Watson Research Center, U.S
{name.surname}@upf.edu, miguel.ballesteros@ibm.com

Abstract

Videogame streaming platforms have become a paramount example of noisy user-generated text. These are websites where gaming is broadcasted, and allows interaction with viewers via integrated chatrooms. Probably the best known platform of this kind is Twitch, which has more than 100 million monthly viewers. Despite these numbers, and unlike other platforms featuring short messages (e.g. Twitter), Twitch has not received much attention from the Natural Language Processing community. In this paper we aim at bridging this gap by proposing two important tasks specific to the Twitch platform, namely (1) *Emote* prediction; and (2) Trolling detection. In our experiments, we evaluate three models: a BOW baseline, a logistic supervised classifiers based on word embeddings, and a bidirectional long short-term memory recurrent neural network (LSTM). Our results show that the LSTM model outperforms the other two models, where explicit features with proven effectiveness for similar tasks were encoded.

1 Introduction

Understanding the language of social media is a mature research area in Natural Language Processing (NLP) and Artificial Intelligence. Not only for the challenges it poses from a linguistic perspective, but also for being a task with a direct impact in relevant sectors like politics, stock market or health (Small, 2011; Bollen et al., 2011; Culotta, 2010). The notion of *understanding* in social media contexts may be divided in more specific AI tasks, including, among others, Sentiment Analysis (Pang and Lee, 2008), Irony Detection (Reyes et al., 2013b), or Event Summarization via Twitter Streams (Chakrabarti and Punera, 2011), as well as other subtasks such as Event (Weng and Lee, 2011) or Stance Detection (Mohammad et al., 2016) in Twitter.

While the study of language in social media typically involves blog posts, comments or product reviews, one of the most interesting areas of research concerns those highly restrictive platforms, e.g. enforcing character limits in each message. One of these platforms, Twitter, has attracted much attention due to its large user base as well as the linguistic idiosyncrasies of its language. It is interesting, therefore, to focus on another growing platform (in number of users) which shares some of the features that made Twitter popular in NLP. This platform is TWITCH.TV (henceforth, Twitch), the largest videogame video streaming service, currently a subsidiary of Amazon. Inc.

Twitch is used by a large community of individual *gamers* to broadcast themselves playing a game (Smith et al., 2013), but also by companies to broadcast live videogame and *electronic sports* (competitive video gaming) events, as well as releasing footage of new products, such as consoles or games. An outstanding feature of Twitch broadcasts is that they run alongside a permanent chat platform. Properly analyzing the content of Twitch chat messages can be useful for understanding the opinion of the community towards any industry product or stakeholder, in addition to its industrial relevance (Kaytoue et al., 2012). Moreover, analyzing this platform is fundamental for informing a number of AI-related applications such as behaviour prediction or Information Retrieval.

Interpreting Twitch language, however, is a challenging problem, as it features a vast amount of *Internet memes*, slang and gaming-related

11

Proceedings of the 3rd Workshop on Noisy User-generated Text, pages 11–20
Copenhagen, Denmark, September 7, 2017. ©2017 Association for Computational Linguistics

lingo. In addition, Twitch language is characterized by combining short text messages with small pictures known as *emotes*. These emotes generally serve a different communicative purpose than most visual aids (e.g. Twitter *emojis*), and therefore require specific modeling.

In this paper, we put forward an approach for the understanding of Twitch messages by means of modeling the underlying semantics of Twitch emotes, and a dataset of Twitch chat messages. Building up on previous research on predicting paralinguistic elements (e.g. emojis) (Barbieri et al., 2017), we target the *Emote Prediction* problem, i.e. the task of, given a collection of chatroom messages, predicting which *emote* the user is more likely to use. Second, *Trolling Detection*, which we reformulate as the task to detect a specific set of emotes which are broadly used by Twitch users in troll messages. For both tasks, we evaluate models which consider sequences of words (bidirectional recurrent neural networks (Graves and Schmidhuber, 2005)), and compare against order-agnostic baselines which have proven to be highly competitive in similar tasks.

2   Twitch Language

An essential feature in a Twitch live broadcast is the chatroom alongside the gameplay. This component enables interaction among viewers and between viewers and streamers. This interaction is in general expressed via short messages, although in larger channels with higher activity, the majority of users may only use *emotes* in their messages for conveying emotions (Olejniczak, 2015). While not entirely arbitrary, the language and the content of conversations are remarkably diverse. In a very short time span, users may comment on the game that is being played, make an out-of-context joke, or discuss an unrelated event like a football game.

2.1   Twitch Emotes

Twitch messages can be enhanced with Twitch *emotes*, "small pictorial glyphs that fans pepper into text"[1]. These emotes range from the more regular *smiley* faces, to others such as game-specific, channel-specific, or even sponsored emotes which are introduced to the platform during the promotion of an event or a videogame. They constitute a core element in Twitch language

and therefore their interpretation is essential to fully understand a message.

2.2   The *kappa* emote as a trolling indicator

The most used Twitch emote is known as 'Kappa' ([emote])[2]. It is a black and white emote based on the face of a former Twitch employee, and is freely available to any registered user (unlike other emotes, which are behind a paywall). There is wide agreement in the online community that this emote "represents sarcasm, irony, puns, jokes, and trolls alike"[3].

3   Tasks

In this section we describe the two tasks we propose. Similarly to Barbieri et al. (2017) we focus on, given a Twitch message, predicting its associated emote. We argue that predicting the emote is similar to understanding the intended meaning of the message (Hogenboom et al., 2013, 2015; Castellucci et al., 2015), regardless of how it was phrased.

3.1   Predicting Twitch Emotes

This is a generic task, consisting in predicting any of the 30 most used emotes in our Twitch dataset. Our aim is to classify messages that only include one and only one type of emote, even if it appears repeatedly, and which constitutes the classification label.

3.2   Trolling Detection

The availability and general usage of the 'kappa' emote enables a potential test bed for performing experiments on detecting troll messages in Twitch chatrooms. We approach this task under the assumption that adding 'kappa' at the end of a message has a similar effect as it would be to add `#irony` or `#sarcasm` at the end of a Twitter message (see (Davidov et al., 2010; Reyes et al., 2013b; Barbieri and Saggion, 2014) for extensive research on irony and sarcasm detection in Twitter under this assumption). Thus, for the trolling prediction experiments, we benefit from this particularity and construct an evaluation dataset where messages are split by considering presence or absence of this emote. In an additional experiment, we further investigate the properties of derivations

---

Dataset	Chars	Tokens	Mentions
30 emotes	28,7M (57.4)	5,5M (10.9)	58M (0.12)
M-Kappa	22,7M (45.6)	4,4M (8.9)	68,5M (0.13)

Table 1: Statistics of the two datasets used in the emote prediction experiments.

of the 'kappa' emote, e.g. 'keepo' , 'kappaross' or 'kappapride' .

4 Data Gathering and Preprocessing

Our Twitch corpus was gathered thanks to a crawler of chat messages applied in the 300 most popular Twitch channels from September 2015 to February 2016. From this initial corpus, we only keep messages from the streams of the five most popular Twitch games[4] at the time (by viewer numbers).

For preprocessing, we benefit from a modified version of the CMU TWEET TOKENIZER (Gimpel et al., 2011), and removed all hyperlinks and non-ASCII characters, and also lower cased all textual content in order to reduce noise and sparsity. We also removed messages that where sequentially repeated (a common spamming practice in Twitch). We also remove messages with less than four tokens. This process yields a corpus of 62 million messages (Counter-Strike 15M, Dota 6M, Hearthstone 15M, League 20M, and World of Worcraft 6M).

We restrict our dataset to chat messages with one and only one emote.

The final dataset used in the experiments is obtained by keeping only those messages including one of the 30 most frequent emotes. From this large corpus, two datasets were derived for the experiments we report in this paper. The first one (30 Emote Dataset) is composed of 100,000 messages per game that have only one type of emote, resulting in 500,000 messages in total. Messages were randomly selected to avoid topic bias. The second dataset (Multi Kappa dataset) is composed of 100,000 messages per game that contain 'kappa' emotes, hence a total of 500,000 messages. Due to the similarity of some emotes to 'kappa' we considered five different emotes as 'kappa', namely 'kappa', 'kappapride', 'keepo', 'kappaross' and 'kappaclaus'.

Table 1 displays statistics of the datasets. For each dataset we show the total number of characters, the total number of tokens, the total number of user mentions, and for each statistics we also show in parenthesis the ratio per message. We can see that the 30 Emotes Dataset includes slightly longer messages (with in average 57.4 chars against 45.6 chars).

5 Models Description

In this section we describe the methodology followed to construct the three models we evaluate, namely (1) a bidirectional LSTM; (2) a BOW-based classifier; and (3) a Skipgram classifier based on vector average.

5.1 Bi-Directional LSTMs

Given the proven effectiveness of recurrent neural networks in different tasks (Chung et al., 2014; Vinyals et al., 2015; Bahdanau et al., 2014, inter-alia), which also includes modeling of tweets (Dhingra et al., 2016; Barbieri et al., 2017), our Emote prediction model is based on RNNs, which are modeled to learn sequential data. We use the word based B-LSTM architecture by Barbieri et al. (2017), designed to model emojis in Twitter.

The forward LSTM reads the message from left to right and the backward one reads the message in the reverse direction.[5] The learned vector of each LSTM, is passed through a component-wise rectified linear unit (ReLU) nonlinearity (Glorot et al., 2011); finally, an affine transformation of these learned vectors is passed to a softmax layer to give a distribution over the list of emotes that may be predicted given the Twitch chat message.

The inputs of the LSTMs are word embeddings (100 dimensions). We use a lookup table to learn word representations. For out-of-vocabulary words (OOVs), the system uses a fixed vector that is handled as a separate word. In order to train the fixed representation for OOVs, we stochastically replace (with $p = 0.5$) each word that occurs only once in the training data with the fixed representation in each training iteration.

5.2 Baselines

Two baselines were compared to the performance of the B-LSTM model. We chose two common algorithms for text classification, which unlike

---

[4]These games are: *Counter Strike: Global Offensive, Dota 2, Hearthstone: Heroes of Warcraft, League of Legends* and *World of Warcraft.*

[5]LSTM hidden states are of size 100, and each LSTM has two layers.

LSTMs, do not take into account the entire sequence of words.

5.2.1 Bag of Words

We designed a Bag-of-Words (Bow) classifier as such model has been successfully employed in several classification tasks, like sentiment analysis and irony detection (Davidov et al., 2010; Gonzalez-Ibanez et al., 2011; Reyes et al., 2013a). We represent each message with a vector of the most informative tokens (punctuation marks are included as well). Words are selected using term frequency-inverse document frequency (TF-IDF), which is intended to reflect how important a word is to a document (message) in the corpus. After obtaining a vector for each message we classify with a L2-regularized logistic regression classifier to make the predictions[6] with ε equal to 0.001.

5.2.2 Skip-Gram Vector Average

We employ the Skip-gram model (Mikolov et al., 2013) learned from the 62M Twitch dataset (where testing instances have been removed) to learn Twitch semantic vectors. Then, we build a model (henceforth, Vec-AVG) which represents each message as the average of the vectors corresponding to each word included in a given Twitch message. After obtaining a representation of each message, we train a L2-regularized logistic regression classifier, (with ε equal to 0.001).

6 Experimental Results

In this section, we describe the experimental setup for each of the tasks, and present the results of our proposed model.

6.1 Predicting Twitch Emotes

This is a multilabel classification task, where each label corresponds to the 30 emotes listed in Table 3. We compare three models, namely the BoW and Vec-AVG baselines and the B-LSTM model. We report the performance of the models in Table 2, where we also show the results of a majority baseline (where all the prediction are equal to "kappa" in this case).

We further investigate the behavior of the B-LSTM model by analyzing its *emote*-wise performance. Results are summarized in Table 3, where we report Precision, Recall and F-Measure for

---

[6]We used the MatLab implementation of Multicore LIBLINEAR https://www.csie.ntu.edu.tw/~cjlin/libsvmtools/multicore-liblinear/

Model	P	R	F1
Majority	0.06	0.25	0.10
BOW	0.35	0.33	0.29
Vec-AVG	0.46	0.38	0.32
B-LSTM	**0.47**	**0.42**	**0.39**

Table 2: Precision, Recall and F-Measure of the two models in the 30 emotes prediction experiment.

each *emote*, along with their Ranking and occurrences in the test set. The Ranking is the average number of *emotes* with higher probability than the gold emote in the probability distribution (in each prediction) provided by the classifiers (softmax). For example, a Ranking equal to 3.0 means that the gold *emote* is selected, in average, as the third option (the Ranking goes from 1 to X where X is the number of emotes).

6.2 Trolling Detection

We perform two tasks. First, a *Trolling VS Non-Trolling* experiment, which we frame as a classification problem consisting in discriminating between messages with any of the 'kappa'-related emotes, and those without. Second, in the *Multi-Kappa* experiment, we aim at performing a finergrained classification among similar but different ways of trolling, which Twitch users perform by consciously selecting a specific variation of the 'kappa' emote.

6.2.1 Trolling VS Non-Trolling

We compare the performance of the three competing models, namely BoW, Vec-AVG and B-LSTMs. However, for the purpose of this experiment, we perform modifications in the label set. Our aim is to explicitly perform a coarse and a fine-grained experiment on trolling detection by clustering together labels which are generally used for the same trolling purpose (all 'kappa'-related emotes). Note that the aim of the task is in all cases the same, discerning between trolling and non-trolling messages. The resulting label sets and their associated datasets are:

- **D1** This is the original dataset, with the original 30 emote label set. In this configuration, a true positive occurs when the model correctly assigns any 'kappa' label to a message with a 'kappa'-related emote. Similarly, true negatives come from correctly predicting the

Emo	Name	P	R	F1	Rank	Te	Tr
	kappa	0.38	0.78	0.52	1.78	25	127
	4head	0.38	0.14	0.21	3	9.2	45
	pogchamp	0.42	0.44	0.43	3.01	9.2	46
	elegiggle	0.43	0.44	0.43	3.34	8.9	43
	biblethump	0.39	0.36	0.37	4.41	5.3	25
	dansgame	0.41	0.31	0.35	4.21	4.8	24
	kreygasm	0.3	0.19	0.23	6.37	4.2	21
	failfish	0.44	0.17	0.25	5.17	3.6	19
	swiftrage	0.57	0.4	0.47	5.61	3.3	15
	wutface	0.62	0.14	0.22	7.26	2.4	14
	keepo	1	0	0.01	9.79	2.2	11
	residentsleeper	0.54	0.3	0.38	7.66	2.2	10
	kappapride	0.48	0.26	0.34	8.54	2.1	11
	trihard	0.75	0.49	0.6	5.79	2.1	10
	kappaross	0.61	0.2	0.3	8.38	1.7	8
	babyrage	0.54	0.28	0.37	8.16	1.6	9
	notlikethis	0.53	0.13	0.21	10.33	1.5	8
	opieop	0.71	0.11	0.19	9.15	1.4	7
	smorc	0.69	0.47	0.56	7.93	1.4	7
	anele	0.42	0.57	0.49	6.38	1.2	6
	seemsgood	0.75	0.33	0.46	9.83	1.2	6
	brokeback	0.8	0.16	0.27	13.85	1.2	5
	osfrog	0.7	0.48	0.57	8.36	1	6
	mrdestructoid	0.64	0.42	0.5	9.98	0.7	4
	heyguys	0.72	0.21	0.32	16.07	0.6	3
	kappaclaus	0.92	0.21	0.34	14.42	0.6	3
	datsheffy	0.72	0.48	0.57	9.65	0.5	2
	coolcat	0.89	0.38	0.53	13.34	0.4	2
	osrob	1	0.91	0.95	2.91	0.3	2
	pjsalt	0.67	0.12	0.21	19.57	0.3	2

Table 3: Detailed results for each class in the Emote prediction experiment. We report the results of the B-LSTMs model. We report Precision, Recall, F-Measure, Rank and thousand of occurrences in the Test (Te) and in the Train (Tr) for each emote.

D	Model	Class	P	R	F1
-	Majority	Avg	0.47	0.68	0.56
D1	BoW	Iro	0.41	0.73	0.53
		Non-Iro	0.81	0.52	0.63
		Avg	0.68	0.59	0.60
	Vec-AVG	Iro	0.41	0.89	0.56
		Non-Iro	0.89	0.40	0.55
		Avg	0.73	0.55	0.55
	B-LSTM	Iro	0.47	0.79	**0.59**
		Non-Iro	0.86	0.59	0.70
		Avg	0.74	0.66	0.67
D2	BoW	Iro	0.41	0.78	0.53
		Non-Iro	0.82	0.47	0.60
		Avg	0.69	0.57	0.58
	Vec-AVG	Iro	0.39	0.92	0.55
		Non-Iro	0.91	0.34	0.49
		Avg	0.74	0.52	0.51
	B-LSTM	Iro	0.45	**0.85**	**0.59**
		Non-Iro	**0.88**	0.53	0.66
		Avg	**0.75**	0.63	0.64
D1	BoW	Iro	0.44	0.29	0.35
		Non-Iro	0.72	**0.83**	0.77
		Avg	0.63	0.66	0.64
	Vec-AVG	Iro	0.72	0.91	0.80
		Non-Iro	0.52	0.22	0.31
		Avg	0.66	0.69	0.65
	B-LSTM	Iro	**0.58**	0.49	0.53
		Non-Iro	0.78	**0.83**	**0.81**
		Avg	0.72	**0.72**	**0.72**

Table 4: Results of the trolling prediction experiments. The classes are two, trolling and non-trolling.

absence of a non 'kappa' label in a message.

- **D2** In this case, we replace all 'kappa' emotes with an umbrella *super-'kappa'* emote, thus forcing the model to learn a coarser-grained class. Negative examples are the same as in D1.

- **D3** This is the coarsest of the three configurations, where we train with a *super-'kappa'* positive class, and a superclass for negative cases (clustering all the non-'kappa' emotes into a dummy negative label).

6.2.2 Multi-'Kappa'

'Kappa'-related emotes are used to express irony or sarcasm and in general troll alike messages. We are interested in investigating if there is a fine-grained pattern in the usage of any of these emotes, as the community does not seem to use them interchangeably. Thus, we perform a *multi-'kappa'* experiment, i.e. an experiment designed to discern among nuanced ironic messages.

In Table 5 we show comparative results of the models under evaluation for this task, in terms of Precision, Recall and F-Measure of the five classes ordered by frequency, from the most frequent ('kappa') to the rarest ('kappaclaus'). Similarly as

15

Model	Class	P	R	F1
Majority	Avg	0.60	0.78	0.68
BoW	kappa	0.81	0.98	0.88
	kappapride	0.67	0.28	0.39
	keepo	0.20	0.01	0.02
	kappaross	0.60	0.19	0.28
	kappaclaus	0.51	0.14	0.22
	Avg	0.73	0.79	0.74
Vec-AVG	kappa	0.80	0.99	0.89
	kappapride	0.76	0.23	0.36
	keepo	1.00	0.01	0.02
	kappaross	0.68	0.10	0.18
	kappaclaus	0.77	0.16	0.27
	Avg	**0.81**	0.80	0.74
B-LSTM	kappa	0.81	0.99	0.89
	kappapride	0.78	0.32	0.46
	keepo	0.00	0.00	0.00
	kappaross	0.84	0.24	0.38
	kappaclaus	0.82	0.20	0.32
	Avg	0.75	**0.81**	**0.76**

Table 5: Results of the multi 'kappa' prediction experiment.

in the previous experiment, the B-LSTM method outperformed the baselines, this time, however, with a smaller difference. We can see that the three systems show similar F1 in the 'kappa' prediction (0.74, 0.74 and 0.76). However the B-LSTM works better on the other kappa emotes, suggesting that the B-LSTM model is better at modeling the inner semantic of the kappa emotes.

6.3 Discussion

In the first experiment, *Predicting Twitch Emotes*, our B-LSTM model notably outperforms the baselines, showing a 10 point difference. Further analysis on the behavior of our model can be found in Table 3. We observed that the emotes which are best recognized (highest F-Measure) are not necessarily the most frequent. For example, the best predicted emotes are 'osrob', 'osfrog' and 'datsheffy', with F-Measure scores of 0.95, 0.57 and 0.57 respectively. In contrast, the most difficult emote to identify is 'keepo' (F-Measure of 0.01), probably due to its semantic overlap with 'kappa'. On the other hand, specific emotes such as 'trihard'[7], 'mrdestructoid'[8] or 'smorc'[9] are easier to

---

[7]It refers to the idea of 'trying hard', i.e. putting maximum effort in a task.

[8]General robot emoticon.

[9]Used in scenarios where 'Orc' characters are present.

predict, due to their stronger bound to a specific topic and the univocity of their meaning.

However, we found that the model often prioritizes the most frequent emotes. We look into this observation by computing Pearson Correlation (PC) between frequency and Ranking, which yields -0.6, hence, if an emote shows high frequency, it has low Ranking, and vice versa. However, in terms of Recall and F-Measure, these do not show any correlation with frequency (PC of 0.3 and 0.1 respectively), nor Ranking. Finally, let us highlight the fact that Precision is inversely correlated to frequency, with a PC score of -0.54. Again, the model may have high confidence in rare emotes only in very specific cases, and it is then when they are selected.

We provide a visualization of the model's performance with a confusion matrix (Figure 1). As mentioned earlier, the B-LSTM has a bias towards 'kappa', the most frequent emote in Twitch. It is also clear that 'biblethump', 'elegiggle', 'kreygasm' and 'pogchamp' are also very frequent in Twitch language due to the large number of confusions involving these emotes. 'Elegiggle' and 'failfish' are often confused. The main reason behind this confusion might be that they are both used in situations where the streamer has failed ('faifish'), and the audience finds this funny. Interestingly, '4head', one of the most frequent emotes, seems to not be the source of wrong predictions. The reason behind that is that the usual usage of '4Head' is to substitute the word forehead, which clearly restricts the communicative contexts available for it being used. The emote 'pogchamp', moreover, is wrongly selected with notable frequency. We have observed that the use of 'pogchamp' and 'kreygasm' emotes is fairly interchangeable, as in gaming, the notion of positive surprise ('pogchamp') and ecstasy ('kreygasm') are more strongly related to the same events or reactions.

Table 4 shows the performance of our model on the task of differentiating between ironic and non-ironic messages using three different training strategies and comparing these performances with a two baselines. It can be observed that once again our model outperforms the baselines in every case and that it achieves very competitive performance when the system is trained by labeling every message with a 'kappa' emote as trolling and every message with a non-kappa emote as non-trolling.

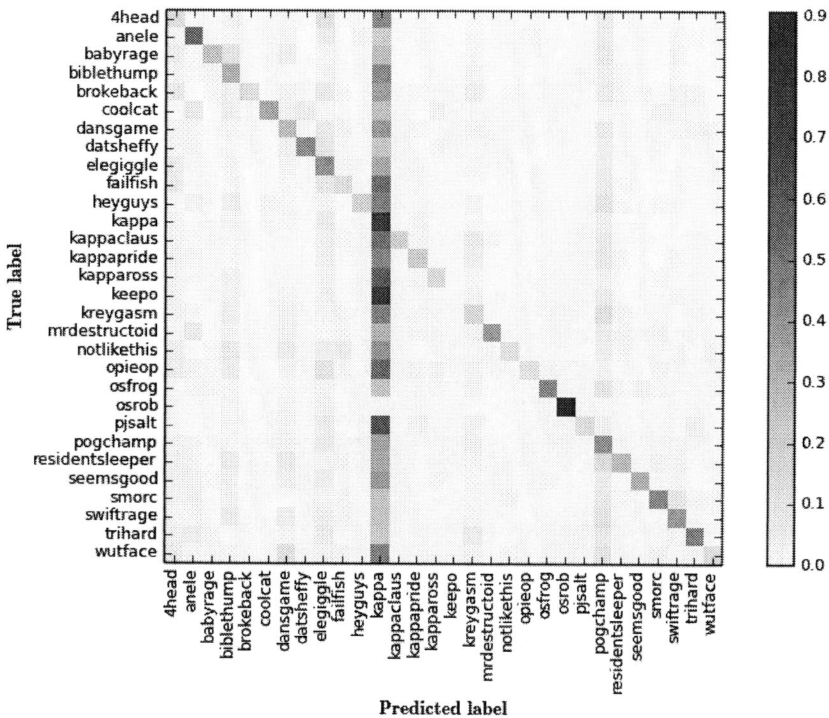

Figure 1: Confusion Matrix of B-LSTMs of the 30 emotes prediction experiment

Even in the first two training strategies, where the messages are labeled with a higher amount of emotes (and as a result, the system can confuse emotes that are used in similar scenarios), the performance is high.

Once we differentiated between trolling and non-trolling messages, we further explored a finer grained classification process over the 'kappa' derivations. Table 5 presents the results in the classification of 'kappa' emotes of our system compared again with the two baselines. From our results, it seems that there are indeed differences in the usage of certain emotes. The emote 'kappa' is a sort of generalisation of each one of its other derivations. Note that there are three cases where the usage of emotes that are not 'kappa' have patterns that are not equivalent: 'kappaclaus', which is a version of kappa with a christmas theme, 'kappapride' which is a kappa face with the characteristic colors of the rainbow flag of the LGBT movement and 'kappaross', which is a Twitch homage to the painter Bob Ross. Even if the underlying intention of the mentioned emotes is trolls alike, it is clear that their intended meaning is not the same as 'kappa'. On the other hand, 'keepo', the

'kappa' emote with cat ears, is always confused with 'kappa', and thus we can conclude that both emotes are used interchangeably.

7 Related Work

The most similar communicative phenomena to emotes are *emojis*. Emojis are used by the vast majority of Social Media services and instant messaging platforms (Jibril and Abdullah, 2013; Park et al., 2013, 2014). Emojis (like the older emoticons) give the possibility to express a variety of ideas and feelings in a visual, concise and appealing way that is perfectly suited for the informal style of Social Media. Several recent works studied Emojis, focusing on emojis' semantics and usage (Aoki and Uchida, 2011; Barbieri et al., 2016a,b,c; Eisner et al., 2016; Ljubesic and Fiser, 2016; Ai et al., 2017; Miller et al., 2017), and sentiment (Novak et al., 2015; Hu et al., 2017). Finally, (Barbieri et al., 2017) presented an emoji prediction model for Twitter, where they use a char based B-LSTM to detect the 20 most frequent emojis.

Most work on irony and sarcasm detection in

Twitter has employed *hashtags* as labels for detecting irony. This approach was introduced by Tsur et al. (Tsur et al., 2010) and (Gonzalez-Ibanez et al., 2011), who used the *#sarcasm* hashtag to retrieve sarcastic tweets. This technique was later validated by various studies (Wang, 2013; Sulis et al., 2016), which analyze the language associated to the use of irony-related *hashtags* (such as *#irony*, and *#not*). Recent years have seen an increase in models for detecting *#irony* and *#sarcasm*. Many of these models adopted hand crafted features (amoung others (Reyes et al., 2013a; Barbieri and Saggion, 2014; Liu et al., 2014; Joshi et al., 2015)), and others employed pretrained word embeddings or deep learning systems such as CNN or LSTMs (Joshi et al., 2016; Ghosh and Veale, 2016; Poria et al., 2016; Amir et al., 2016).

8 Conclusions and Future Work

In this paper we have addressed the problem of modeling the usage of Twitch emotes. This is an important problem in social media text understanding, as the inherent noisy nature of these messages can be alleviated by having robust systems that interpret the semantics of visual aids such as Twitter emojis or Twitch emotes.

Emote understanding is approached in this paper via different approaches, namely a BOW system, a logistic regression classifier based on embedding average, and a bidirectional LSTM. The main conclusion that we draw from our experiments is that the RNN model is more capable to predict Twitch emotes than its competing baselines. In addition, we performed an analysis on the usage of different trolling emotes and studied their usage patterns and differences.

As future work we plan to incorporate more context to the model, providing a representation of previous chat messages where the emote appears. This would allow us to tackle the problem of the emote detection as a sequence modeling task, and this will be more natural as it is not easy to predict an emote of a message with no context. Finally, as Barbieri et al. (2017) we plan to investigate character-based approaches to represent words (Ling et al., 2015; Ballesteros et al., 2015) and/or messages (Dhingra et al., 2016) since Twitch data contain noisy text.

Acknowledgments

We thank the three anonymous reviewers for their time and their useful suggestions. Francesco, Luis and Horacio acknowledge support from the TUNER project (TIN2015-65308-C5-5-R, MINECO/FEDER, UE) and the Maria de Maeztu Units of Excellence Programme (MDM-2015-0502).

References

Wei Ai, Xuan Lu, Xuanzhe Liu, Ning Wang, Gang Huang, and Qiaozhu Mei. 2017. Untangling emoji popularity through semantic embeddings. In *International AAAI Conference on Web and Social Media, ICWSM*. pages 2–11.

Silvio Amir, Byron C Wallace, Hao Lyu, and Paula Carvalho Mário J Silva. 2016. Modelling context with user embeddings for sarcasm detection in social media. *arXiv preprint arXiv:1607.00976* .

Sho Aoki and Osamu Uchida. 2011. A method for automatically generating the emotional vectors of emoticons using weblog articles. In *Proc. 10th WSEAS Int. Conf. on Applied Computer and Applied Computational Science, Stevens Point, Wisconsin, USA*. pages 132–136.

Dzmitry Bahdanau, Kyunghyun Cho, and Yoshua Bengio. 2014. Neural machine translation by jointly learning to align and translate. *CoRR* .

Miguel Ballesteros, Chris Dyer, and Noah A. Smith. 2015. Improved transition-based parsing by modeling characters instead of words with lstms. In *Proceedings of the 2015 Conference on Empirical Methods in Natural Language Processing*. Association for Computational Linguistics, Lisbon, Portugal, pages 349–359. http://aclweb.org/anthology/D15-1041.

Francesco Barbieri, Miguel Ballesteros, and Horacio Saggion. 2017. Are Emojis Predictable? In *European Chapter of the Association for Computational Linguistics, EACL*. ACL, Valencia, Spain.

Francesco Barbieri, Luis Espinosa Anke, and Horacio Saggion. 2016a. Revealing Patterns of Twitter Emoji Usage in Barcelona and Madrid. In *19 th International Conference of the Catalan Association for Artificial Intelligence*. Barcelona, Spain, pages 326–332.

Francesco Barbieri, German Kruszewski, Francesco Ronzano, and Horacio Saggion. 2016b. How Cosmopolitan Are Emojis? Exploring Emojis Usage and Meaning over Different Languages with Distributional Semantics. In *Proceedings of the 2016 ACM on Multimedia Conference*. ACM, Amsterdam, Netherlands, pages 531–535.

Francesco Barbieri, Francesco Ronzano, and Horacio Saggion. 2016c. What does this emoji mean? a vector space skip-gram model for twitter emojis. In *Language Resources and Evaluation conference, LREC*. Portoroz, Slovenia, pages 526–534.

Francesco Barbieri and Horacio Saggion. 2014. Modelling Irony in Twitter. In *Proceedings of the EACL Student Research Workshop*. ACL, Gothenburg, Sweden, pages 56–64. http://www.aclweb.org/anthology/E14-3007.

Johan Bollen, Huina Mao, and Xiaojun Zeng. 2011. Twitter mood predicts the stock market. *Journal of Computational Science* 2(1):1–8.

Giuseppe Castellucci, Danilo Croce, and Roberto Basili. 2015. Acquiring a large scale polarity lexicon through unsupervised distributional methods. In *Natural Language Processing and Information Systems*, Springer, pages 73–86.

Deepayan Chakrabarti and Kunal Punera. 2011. Event summarization using tweets. *International AAAI Conference on Web and Social Media, ICWSM* 11:66–73.

Junyoung Chung, Çaglar Gülçehre, KyungHyun Cho, and Yoshua Bengio. 2014. Empirical evaluation of gated recurrent neural networks on sequence modeling. *CoRR* .

Aron Culotta. 2010. Towards detecting influenza epidemics by analyzing twitter messages. In *Proceedings of the first workshop on social media analytics*. ACM, pages 115–122.

Dmitry Davidov, Oren Tsur, and Ari Rappoport. 2010. Semi-supervised recognition of sarcastic sentences in twitter and amazon. In *Proceedings of the Fourteenth Conference on Computational Natural Language Learning*. Association for Computational Linguistics, pages 107–116.

Bhuwan Dhingra, Zhong Zhou, Dylan Fitzpatrick, Michael Muehl, and William W. Cohen. 2016. Tweet2vec: Character-based distributed representations for social media. In *Proceedings of the ACL*.

Ben Eisner, Tim Rocktaschel, Isabelle Augenstein, Matko Bosnjak, and Sebastian Riedel. 2016. emoji2vec: Learning emoji representations from their description. In *Proceedings of The Fourth International Workshop on Natural Language Processing for Social Media*. Association for Computational Linguistics, Austin, TX, USA, pages 48–54.

Aniruddha Ghosh and Tony Veale. 2016. Fracking sarcasm using neural network. In *WASSA@ NAACL-HLT*. pages 161–169.

Kevin Gimpel, Nathan Schneider, Brendan O'Connor, Dipanjan Das, Daniel Mills, Jacob Eisenstein, Michael Heilman, Dani Yogatama, Jeffrey Flanigan, and Noah A Smith. 2011. Part-of-speech tagging for twitter: Annotation, features, and experiments. In *Proceedings of the 49th Annual Meeting of the Association for Computational Linguistics: Human Language Technologies: short papers-Volume 2*. Association for Computational Linguistics, pages 42–47.

Xavier Glorot, Antoine Bordes, and Yoshua Bengio. 2011. Deep sparse rectifier neural networks. In *Proceedings of the Conference on Artificial Intelligence and Statistics (AISTATS)*.

Roberto Gonzalez-Ibanez, Smaranda Muresan, and Nina Wacholder. 2011. Identifying sarcasm in twitter: a closer look. In *NAACL*.

Alex Graves and Jürgen Schmidhuber. 2005. Framewise phoneme classification with bidirectional LSTM networks. In *Proceedings of the International Joint Conference on Neural Networks (IJCNN)*.

Alexander Hogenboom, Daniella Bal, Flavius Frasincar, Malissa Bal, Franciska de Jong, and Uzay Kaymak. 2013. Exploiting emoticons in sentiment analysis. In *Proceedings of the 28th Annual ACM Symposium on Applied Computing*. ACM, pages 703–710.

Alexander Hogenboom, Daniella Bal, Flavius Frasincar, Malissa Bal, Franciska De Jong, and Uzay Kaymak. 2015. Exploiting emoticons in polarity classification of text. *J. Web Eng.* 14(1&2):22–40.

Tianran Hu, Han Guo, Hao Sun, Thuyvy Thi Nguyen, and Jiebo Luo. 2017. Spice up your chat: The intentions and sentiment effects of using emoji. *arXiv preprint arXiv:1703.02860* .

Tanimu Ahmed Jibril and Mardziah Hayati Abdullah. 2013. Relevance of emoticons in computer-mediated communication contexts: An overview. *Asian Social Science* 9(4):201.

Aditya Joshi, Prayas Jain, Pushpak Bhattacharyya, and Mark Carman. 2016. Who would have thought of that!': A hierarchical topic model for extraction of sarcasm-prevalent topics and sarcasm detection. *arXiv preprint arXiv:1611.04326* .

Aditya Joshi, Vinita Sharma, and Pushpak Bhattacharyya. 2015. Harnessing context incongruity for sarcasm detection. In *ACL (2)*. pages 757–762.

Mehdi Kaytoue, Arlei Silva, Loïc Cerf, Wagner Meira Jr, and Chedy Raïssi. 2012. Watch me playing, i am a professional: a first study on video game live streaming. In *Proceedings of the 21st international conference companion on World Wide Web*. ACM, pages 1181–1188.

Wang Ling, Chris Dyer, Alan Black, and Isabel Trancoso. 2015. Two/too simple adaptations of word2vec for syntax problems. In *Proceedings of the North American Chapter of the Association for Computational Linguistics (NAACL)*.

Peng Liu, Wei Chen, Gaoyan Ou, Tengjiao Wang, Dongqing Yang, and Kai Lei. 2014. Sarcasm detection in social media based on imbalanced classification. In *International Conference on Web-Age Information Management*. Springer, pages 459–471.

Nikola Ljubesic and Darja Fiser. 2016. A global analysis of emoji usage. In *Proceedings of the 10th Web as Corpus Workshop and the EmpiriST Shared Task*. Association for Computational Linguistics, Berlin, Germany, pages 82–89.

Tomas Mikolov, Quoc V Le, and Ilya Sutskever. 2013. Exploiting similarities among languages for machine translation. *arXiv preprint arXiv:1309.4168*.

Hannah Jean Miller, Daniel Kluver, Jacob Thebault-Spieker, Loren G Terveen, and Brent J Hecht. 2017. Understanding emoji ambiguity in context: The role of text in emoji-related miscommunication. In *International AAAI Conference on Web and Social Media, ICWSM*. pages 152–161.

Saif M Mohammad, Svetlana Kiritchenko, Parinaz Sobhani, Xiaodan Zhu, and Colin Cherry. 2016. Semeval-2016 task 6: Detecting stance in tweets. In *Proceedings of the International Workshop on Semantic Evaluation, SemEval*. volume 16.

Petra Kralj Novak, Jasmina Smailovic, Borut Sluban, and Igor Mozetic. 2015. Sentiment of emojis. *PloS one* 10(12):e0144296.

Jedrzej Olejniczak. 2015. A linguistic study of language variety used on twitch.tv: Descriptive and corpus-based approaches. In *Proceedings of Redefining Community in Intercultural Context (RCIC15.*

Bo Pang and Lillian Lee. 2008. Opinion mining and sentiment analysis. *Foundations and trends in information retrieval* 2(1-2):1–135.

Jaram Park, Young Min Baek, and Meeyoung Cha. 2014. Cross-cultural comparison of nonverbal cues in emoticons on twitter: Evidence from big data analysis. *Journal of Communication* 64(2):333–354.

Jaram Park, Vladimir Barash, Clay Fink, and Meeyoung Cha. 2013. Emoticon style: Interpreting differences in emoticons across cultures. In *International AAAI Conference on Web and Social Media, ICWSM*.

Soujanya Poria, Erik Cambria, Devamanyu Hazarika, and Prateek Vij. 2016. A deeper look into sarcastic tweets using deep convolutional neural networks. *arXiv preprint arXiv:1610.08815* .

Antonio Reyes, Paolo Rosso, and Tony Veale. 2013a. A multidimensional Approach for Detecting Irony in Twitter. *Language Resources and Evaluation* pages 1–30.

Antonio Reyes, Paolo Rosso, and Tony Veale. 2013b. A multidimensional approach for detecting irony in twitter. *Language resources and evaluation* 47(1):239–268.

Tamara A Small. 2011. What the hashtag? a content analysis of canadian politics on twitter. *Information, Communication & Society* 14(6):872–895.

Thomas Smith, Marianna Obrist, and Peter Wright. 2013. Live-streaming changes the (video) game. In *Proceedings of the 11th european conference on Interactive TV and video*. ACM, pages 131–138.

Emilio Sulis, Delia Irazú Hernández Farías, Paolo Rosso, Viviana Patti, and Giancarlo Ruffo. 2016. Figurative messages and affect in twitter: differences between# irony,# sarcasm and# not. *Knowledge-Based Systems* .

Oren Tsur, Dmitry Davidov, and Ari Rappoport. 2010. Icwsm-a great catchy name: Semi-supervised recognition of sarcastic sentences in online product reviews. In *International AAAI Conference on Web and Social Media, ICWSM*.

Oriol Vinyals, Lukasz Kaiser, Terry Koo, Slav Petrov, Ilya Sutskever, and Geoffrey Hinton. 2015. Grammar as a foreign language. In *Proc. ICLR*.

Po-Ya Angela Wang. 2013. #irony or #sarcasma quantitative and qualitative study based on twitter. *27th Pacific Asia Conference on Language, Information, and Computation* .

Jianshu Weng and Bu-Sung Lee. 2011. Event detection in twitter. *International AAAI Conference on Web and Social Media, ICWSM* 11:401–408.

Churn Identification in Microblogs using Convolutional Neural Networks with Structured Logical Knowledge

Mourad Gridach

Department of Computer Science
High Institute of Technology
Ibn Zohr University, Agadir
Morocco
m.gridach@uiz.ac.ma

Hatem Haddad

Department of Computer and Decision
Engineering, Université Libre de Bruxelles
Belgium
Hatem.Haddad@ulb.ac.be

Hala Mulki

Department of Computer Engineering
Selcuk University, Konya
Turkey
hallamulki@gmail.com

Abstract

For brands, gaining new customer is more expensive than keeping an existing one. Therefore, the ability to keep customers in a brand is becoming more challenging these days. Churn happens when a customer leaves a brand to another competitor. Most of the previous work considers the problem of churn prediction using CDRs. In this paper, we use micro-posts to classify customers into churny or non-churny. We explore the power of CNNs since they achieved state-of-the-art in various computer vision and NLP applications. However, the robustness of end-to-end models has some limitations such as the availability of a large amount of labeled data and uninterpretability of these models. We investigate the use of CNNs augmented with structured logic rules to overcome or reduce this issue. We developed our system called *Churn_teacher* by using an iterative distillation method that transfers the knowledge, extracted using just the combination of three logic rules, directly into the weight of Deep Neural Networks (DNNs). Furthermore, we used weight normalization to speed up training our convolutional neural networks. Experimental results showed that with just these three rules, we were able to get state-of-the-art on publicly available Twitter dataset about three Telecom brands.

1 Introduction

Customer churn may be defined as the process of losing a customer that recently switches from a brand to another competitor. The churn problem can be tackled from different angles: most of the previous work used Call Detail Records (CDRs) to identify churners from non-churners (Zaratiegui et al., 2015). More recently, with more data became available on the web, brands can use customers opinionated comments via social networks, forums and especially Twitter to detect churny from non-churny customers. We used the churn dataset developed by (Amiri and Daumé III, 2015). This dataset was collected from Twitter for three telecommunication brands: Verizon, T-Mobile, and AT&T.

In recent years, deep learning models have achieved great success in various domains and difficult problems such as computer vision (Krizhevsky et al., 2012) and speech recognition (Dahl et al., 2012; Hinton et al., 2012). In natural language processing, much of the work with deep learning models has involved language modeling (Bengio et al., 2003; Mikolov et al., 2013), sentiment analysis (Socher et al., 2013), and more recently, neural machine translation (Cho et al., 2014; Sutskever et al., 2014). Furthermore, these models can use backpropagation algorithm for

Proceedings of the 3rd Workshop on Noisy User-generated Text, pages 21–30
Copenhagen, Denmark, September 7, 2017. ©2017 Association for Computational Linguistics

training (Rumelhart et al., 1988).

Regardless of the success of deep neural networks, these models still have a gap compared to human learning process. While the success came from the high expressiveness, it leads them to predict results in uninterpretable ways, which could have a negative side effects on the whole learning process (Szegedy et al., 2013; Nguyen et al., 2015). In addition, these models require a huge amount of labeled data, which is considered as time consuming for the community since it requires human experts in most applications (natural language and computer vision). Recent works tackled this issue by trying to bridge this gap in different applications: in supervised learning such as machine translation (Wu et al., 2016) and unsupervised learning (Bengio et al., 2015).

In the Natural Language Processing (NLP) community, there has been much work to augment the training process with additional and useful features (Collobert et al., 2011) which proved its success in various NLP applications such as Named Entity Recognition (NER) and Sentiment Analysis. The majority of these works used pretrained word embeddings obtained from unlabeled data to initialize their word vectors, which allow them to improve the performance. Another solution came from integrating logical rules extracted from the data directly into the weights of neural networks. (Hu et al., 2016) explored a distillation framework that transfers structured knowledge coded as logic rules into the weights of neural networks. (Garcez et al., 2012) developed a neural network from a given rule to do reasoning.

In this paper, we combine the two ideas: firstly, we used unsupervised word representations to initialize our word vectors. We explored three different pretraiend word embeddings and compared the results with a randomly sampled one. Secondly, we used three main logic rules, which were proven to be useful and crucial. The "but" rule was explored by (Hu et al., 2016) in sentiment analysis and we add two new rules: "switch to" and "switch from". (Amiri and Daumé III, 2016) showed that the last two rules have a remarkable influence into the churn classification problem.

Moreover, in order to accelerate training our model on churn training dataset, we conduct an investigation of using weight normalization (Salimans and Kingma, 2016), which is a new recently developed method to accelerate training deep neural networks.

Experiments on Twitter dataset built from a large number of tweets about three Telecommunication brands show that we were able to obtain state-of-the-art results for churn classification in microblogs. Our system, called $Churn\_teacher$, is constructed by using a structured logical knowledge expressed into three logic rules transferred into the weights of convolutional neural networks. We outperform the previous models based on hand engineering features or also using recurrent neural networks combined with minimal features. Our system is philosophical close to (Hu et al., 2016), which showed that combining deep neural networks with logic rules performed well on two NLP tasks: NER and Sentiment Analysis.

The rest of this paper is structured as follows: in section 2, we discuss the related work done in churn prediction application. In section 3, we present our churn prediction approach which is based on structured logical knowledge transferred into the weights of Convolutional Neural Networks (CNNs). In section 4, we discuss the impact of pretrained word embeddings on the churn classification. The experimental results are presented in section 5. Finally, we present the conclusion with the future work in section 6.

2   Related Work

Churn prediction is an important area of focus for sentiment analysis and opinion mining. In the 2009, ACM Conference on Knowledge Discovery and Datamining (KDD) hosted a competition on predicting mobile network churn using a large dataset posted by Orange Labs, which makes churn prediction, a promising application in the next few years. We can divide the previous work on Customer churn prediction in two research groups: the first group uses data from companies such as Telecom providers, banks, or other organizations. More recently, with the explosion of social networks, researchers are interested to use social networks such as Twitter to predict churners.

Using data from banks, (Keramati et al., 2016) developed a system for a customer churn in electronic banking services. They used a decision tree algorithm to build their classification model. The main goal of this paper is studying the most relevant features of churners in banking services such as demographic variables (age, gender, career, etc.), transaction data through electronic banking portals (ATM, mobile bank, telephone bank, etc.), and others. They used a method called CRISP-DM which contains six phases: Business understanding, Data understanding, Data preprocessing, Modeling, Evaluation and Deployment. At the final stage, they used a decision tree method to model the previous phases.

(Backiel et al., 2016) studied the impact of incorporating social network information into churn prediction models. The authors used three different machine learning (ML) techniques: logistic regression, neural networks and Cox proportional hazards. To extract features to use with these ML techniques, they built a call graph, which allowed them to extract the relevant features.

(Li et al., 2016) developed a model based on stacked auto-encoder as a feature extractor to detect the most influential features in Telecom churn prediction. In addition, they proposed a second model where they augmented the previous model with a Fishers ration analysis called Hybrid Stack Auto-Encoder (HSAE). The models were evaluated on Orange datasets. Experimental results showed that the HSAE model outperformed all the other models including Principal Component Analysis (PCA).

More recently, researchers tackle the churn prediction problem using data collected from microblogs. (Amiri and Daumé III, 2015) developed a system for churn prediction in microblogs. They investigated the machine learning models such as support vector machines, and logistic regression with the combination of extracted features. Furthermore, they investigated the use of three different churn indicators: demographic, content, and context indicators. Experimental results showed that the combination of the three indicators lead to the best performance.

(Amiri and Daumé III, 2016) used the power of Recurrent Neural Networks (RNN) as a representation learning models in order to learn micropost and churn indicator representations. The experiments on publicly available Twitter dataset showed the efficiency of the proposed method in classifying customers in churners and non-churners. Moreover, authors showed that the churn classification problem is different from classical sentiment analysis problem since the previous state-of-the-art sentiment analysis systems failed to classify churny/non-churny customers.

In this work, we focus on churn prediction in microblogs where we use a publicly available Twitter dataset provided by (Amiri and Daumé III, 2015) to evaluate our system.

3 The Proposed System

In this section, we introduce our system that enables a convolutional neural network to learn simultaneously from logic rules and labeled data in order to classify customers as churners and non-churners. The general architecture of our system can be seen as the combination of the knowledge distillation (Hinton et al., 2015) and the posterior regularization method (Ganchev et al., 2010). (Hu et al., 2016) explored this combination to build two systems for English sentiment analysis and named entity recognition. We show that this framework can also be applied to customer churn prediction by deriving more logic rules and transfer the structured logical knowledge into the weights of a convolutional neural network.

3.1 Problem Formulation

For the purpose of this paper, let us assume we have $x \in \mathcal{X}$ is the input variable and $y \in \mathcal{Y}$ is the target variable. Let us consider the training data $\mathcal{D} = \{(x_n, y_n)\}_{n=1}^{N}$ which is a set of instantiations of (x, y) and N is the number of training examples in our dataset. For the purpose and the clarity of this paper, we focus on classification problem where the target y is a one-hot encoding of the class labels. We consider a subset of the training data $(X, Y) \subset (\mathcal{X}, \mathcal{Y})$ as a set of instances of (x, y). A neural network defines a conditional probability $p_\theta(y|x)$ parameterized by θ.

3.2 Neural Network with Structured Logical Knowledge

In this section, we describe the distillation method that allowed our system to transfer the structured logical knowledge into the weights of convolutional neural networks to classify customers as churners and non-churners.

Let us define the set of constraint functions f_l such that: $f_l \in \mathcal{X} \times \mathcal{Y} \rightarrow \mathcal{R}$, where l is the index of a specific constraint function. In our problem, the set of functions will be represented as logical rules where the overall truth values are in the interval $[0, 1]$. These functions will allow us to encode the structured logical knowledge where the goal is to satisfy (i.e., maximize by optimizing the predictions y) with confidence weights $\lambda_l \in \mathcal{R}$.

The construction of a structure-enriched teacher network q at each iteration from the neural network parameters is obtained by solving the following optimization problem:

$$\min_{q \in \mathcal{P}} KL(q(Y)\|p_\theta(Y|X)) - C \sum_l \lambda_l \, \mathbb{E}_q[f_l(X, Y)] \tag{1}$$

where $\mathcal{P}$ denotes the appropriate distribution space; and C is the regularization parameter. In this paper, the teacher is called $Churn\_teacher$ where its main goal is to teach the model to classify customers from churners and non-churners. The closeness between our $Churn\_teacher$ and p_θ, which represents the conditional probability obtained by the softmax output layer of the convolutional neural network, is measured using the Kullback-Leibler (KL) divergence where the aim is minimizing it. We note that problem (1) is convex and has a closed-form solution given by the following:

$$q^*(Y) \propto p_\theta(Y|X) \exp \left\{ C \sum_l \lambda_l f_l(X, Y) \right\} \tag{2}$$

It should be noted that the normalization term can be computed efficiently through direct enumeration of the chosen rule constraints. At each iteration, the probability distribution of the neural network p_θ is updated using the distillation objective (Hinton et al., 2015) that balances between imitating soft predictions of our $Churn\_teacher$ q and predicting true hard labels:

$$\theta^{(t+1)} = arg \min_{\theta \in \Theta} \frac{1}{N} \sum_{n=1}^{N} (1 - \pi) l(y_n, \sigma_\theta(x_n))$$
$$+ \pi l(sp_n^{(t)}, \sigma_\theta(x_n)) \tag{3}$$

where l denotes the cross entropy loss function that we used in this paper; N is the training size; $\sigma_\theta(x)$ is the softmax output of p_θ on x; sp_n is the soft prediction vector of the $Churn\_teacher$ q on training point x_n at iteration t and π is the imitation parameter calibrating the relative importance of the two objectives. In addition to their teacher

q, (Hu et al., 2016) tested their results using a student network p. Related to their experimental results, the teacher q always gives better results than the student p. We decide to only use the teacher network q called in our work the $Churn\_teacher$.

3.3 Neural Network Architecture

In this section, we give an overview of the convolutional neural network used in our work. The main architecture of our CNN is depicted in Figure 1. We followed the convolutional neural network architecture as proposed by (Kim, 2014).

In the first step, we initialize each word in a sentence T with length n with pretrained word representations learned from unannotated corpora. Then, we add padding whenever it is necessary for the model. T is represented as the following:

$$v_1^n = v_1 \oplus v_2 \oplus ... \oplus v_n \tag{4}$$

where v_i represents the word vector of the $i-th$ word in the sentence T and $\oplus$ represents the concatenation operator. We use successive filters w to obtain multiples feature map. Each filter is applied to a window of m words to get a single feature map: $F_i = \phi(w.v_i^{i+m-1} + b)$ where b is the bias and ϕ denotes an elementwise nonlinearity where we used ReLU (Rectified Linear Unit). In the next step, we applied a max-over-time pooling operation (Collobert et al., 2011) to the feature map and take the maximum value. The results are fed to a fully connected softmax layer to get probabilities over the sentences. Figure 1 illustrates the architecture of our system where we consider the system is classifying the input sentence: "Damn thats crud. You should switch to Verizon".

3.4 Logic Rules

In the early stages of the expansion of artificial intelligence, (Minsky, 1983) argued that the cognitive process of human beings learn from two different sources: examples as deep neural networks are doing these days and also from rich experiences and general knowledge. For this reason, we will use both of the sources for churn prediction in microblogs where the convolutional neural network learns from examples and logic rules add structured knowledge into the weights of CNN by playing a role of a regularizer in the learning process.

In this section, we present the three logic rules that we used in our churn prediction system. We

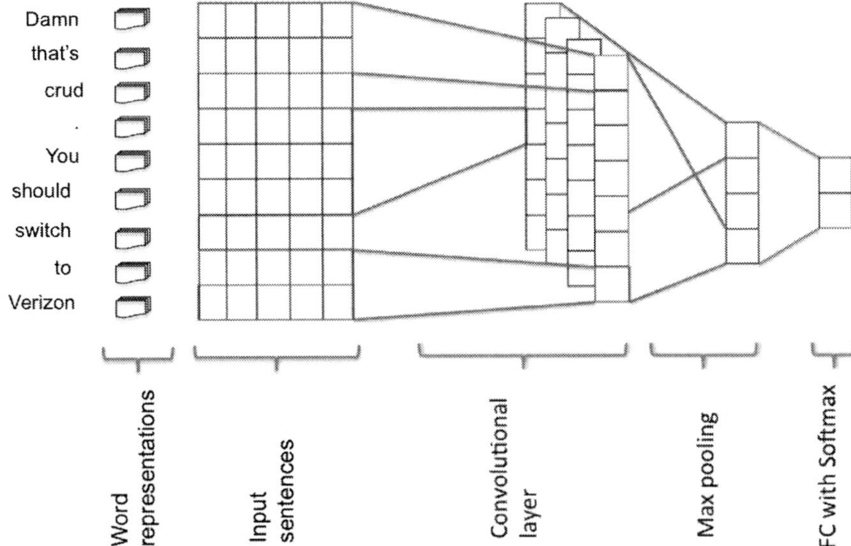

Figure 1: The system architecture. The word vectors are initialized with pretrained word representations from one of the three models: GloVe, Skip-Gram or CBOW. We feed these word vectors to the convolutional neural network as input sentences followed by a max-pooling overtime followed by a fully-connected layer and softmax to get probabilities (FC with Softmax)

borrow the first logic rule from sentiment analysis literature by using the conjunction word "but". It has been shown that "but" played a vital role in determining the sentiment of a sentence where the overall sentiment is dominated by the clauses following the word "but" (Jia et al., 2009; Dadvar et al., 2011; Hogenboom et al., 2011; Hu et al., 2016). For a given sentence with "$C1$ but $C2$", we assume that the sentiment of the whole sentiment will take the polarity of clause $C2$.

The second logic rule that we used is "switch from" considered as a target-dependent churn classification rule. (Amiri and Daumé III, 2016) showed that "switch from" can have an important role to classify if the customer will be churner or non-churner. The last logic rule that we explored in our work is similar to the second rule for being target dependent churn classification where we substitute the preposition "from" to be the preposition "to" to obtain "switch to". For a given sentence with the form "$C1$ switch to $C2$", it is clear that the customer will choose to switch to the brand present in clause $C2$.

Consider the two examples from the training data:

- Damn thats crud. You should switch to Verizon.

- Gonna switch from bad @verizon internet to @comcast. @VerizonFiOS will never be in my area and i bet @googlefiber will get here first.

In the first example, the customer will switch to the brand "Verizon" while for the second example, the customer will leave the brand "Verizon" to another competitor. Consequently, with respect to the brand "Verizon", the first tweet is classified as "Non-churny" and the second tweet is classified as "Churny".

To encode these rules, we used soft logic (Bach et al., 2015) where we can represent truth values from the interval [0, 1]. The main Boolean operators are formulated as the following (Foulds et al., 2015):

$$X \& Y = max\{X + Y - 1, 0\}$$
$$X \vee Y = min\{X + Y, 1\}$$
$$X_1 \wedge ... \wedge X_N = \sum_i \frac{X_i}{N} \quad (5)$$
$$\neg X = 1 - X$$

This logic rule "but" is written as follows:

$$has \text{ "C1-but-C2" } structure(S) \implies$$
$$[1(y = +) \implies \sigma_\theta(C2)_+ \wedge \sigma_\theta(C2)_+ \implies \quad (6)$$
$$1(y = +)]$$

In the equation above, $1(.)$ represents an indicator function that can take two values: 1 if the argument is true, and 0 otherwise. Class "+" represents "positive"; and $\sigma_\theta(C2)_+$ is the element of $\sigma_\theta(C2)$ for class "+". Following the Equation 5, when S has the "C1- but-C2" structure, the truth value of the above logic rule equals to $(1 + \sigma_\theta(C2)_+)/2$ when y = "+", and $(2 - \sigma_\theta(C2)_+)/2$ otherwise.

For the two other logic rules "switch to" and "switch from", we followed the same structure of the "but" rule with a slightly different settings:

$$has \text{ "C1-switch to/from-C2" } structure(S) \implies$$
$$[1(y = +) \implies \sigma_\theta(C2)_+ \wedge \sigma_\theta(C2)_+ \implies$$
$$1(y = +)]$$
$$(7)$$

For the logic rule "switch to", if we are classifying the sentence S with respect to a brand in the clause $C2$, then the argument will be true which gives the formula: $(1 + (\sigma_\theta(C2)_+)/2$. The logic rule "switch from" plays an opposite role where if a brand is in clause $C2$, the overall sentiment will be negative with respect to this brand, so we use this formula: $(2 - \sigma_\theta(C2)_+)/2$.

3.5 Training Details

Training is done using stochastic gradient descent over mini-batches with the Adadelta update rule (Zeiler, 2012). Word vectors are initialized using pretrained word embeddings and fine-tuned throughout training. At each iteration of the training process, we enumerate the rule constraints (or a set of rules if we use them all at once) in order to compute the soft predictions of our $Churn\_teacher$ q by using the equation 2. During the experiments, we choose the imitation parameter to be $\pi(t) = 1 - 0.85t$ and the regularization parameter to be $C = 100$. We set the confidence levels of rules to be $\lambda_l = 1$. It should be noted that we used the model results on development set in order to select the best hyperparameters. The training procedure is summarized in algorithm 1.

Algorithm 1: Churn prediction using CNN with logic rules

Input: The training data $\mathcal{D} = \{(x_n, y_n)\}_{n=1}^N$

The rule set $R = \{(R_l, \lambda_l)\}_{l=1}^3$
Parameters: π - imitation parameter
$\quad\quad\quad\quad C$ regularization strength
Initialize neural network parameters
Choose the rule Rl or a set of rules
do
    Sample a minibatch (X, Y) $\subset \mathcal{D}$
    Build the $Churn\_teacher$ network using Equation 2
    Update p_θ using Equation 3
while not converged

Output: Churn_teacher q

3.6 The Effect of Weight Normalization

It should be noted that we use weight normalization which is a new method introduced by (Salimans and Kingma, 2016) to reparameterize the weight vectors in a deep neural network in order to decouple the length of those weight vectors from their direction. Using this method, the authors showed that they were able to improve the conditioning of the optimization problem and speed up convergence of stochastic gradient descent. This method followed earlier work by (Ioffe and Szegedy, 2015) where they introduced batch normalization trying to normalize each neuron output by the mean and standard deviation of the outputs computed over a minibatch of examples. More recently, this method was widely used in deep learning architectures such as deep convolutional neural networks, deep reinforcement learning, generative adversarial networks (GANs) and others (Smith and Topin, 2016; Gehring et al., 2017). Using weight normalization in training our convolutional neural network allowed us to accelerate convergence of stochastic gradient descent.

4 Input Word Embeddings

The research in representations of words as continuous vectors has a long history where many ideas were proposed (Hinton et al., 1985). More recently, (Bengio et al., 2003) proposed a model architecture based on feedforward neural networks for estimating neural network language model. The most popular model for word representations was developed by (Mikolov et al., 2013) called word2vec where they used either of two model architectures to produce a distributed representation of words: continuous bag-of-words (CBOW) model or Skip-Gram (SG) model. Another popular model for word representations developed by (Pennington et al., 2014) called "GloVe" (Global Vectors). The main difference between

Base NN	Word Embeddings Model	F1 score
CNN	Random embeddings	77.13
CNN	Continuous bag-of-words	79.89
CNN	Skip-Gram	79.55
CNN	GloVe	80.67

Table 1: Results with different choices of pre-trained word embeddings with a comparison with randomly initialized ones on churn predicition in microblogs

Brand	Churny	Non-Churny
Verizon	447	1543
T-Mobile	95	978
AT&T	402	1389

Table 2: Statistics and details about the churn microblog dataset.

this model and word2vec models is the representations of a word in vector space: word2vec models use a window approach while GloVe uses the global statistics of word-word co-occurrence in the corpus to be captured by the model.

(Hisamoto et al., 2013) used word embeddings features for English dependency parsing where they employed flat (non-hierarchical) cluster IDs and binary strings obtained via sign quantization of the vectors. For chunking, (Turian et al., 2010) showed that adding word embeddings allows the English chunker to increase its F1-score. (Huang et al., 2014) showed that adding word embeddings as features for English part-of-speech (POS) tagging task helped the model to increase its performance. (Bansal et al., 2014) argued that using word embeddings in parsing English text improved the system performance. For English sentiment analysis, (Kim, 2014) showed that using pretrained word embeddings helped their system to improve its accuracy.

As in (Collobert et al., 2011), in order to test the importance of pretrained word embeddings in churn prediction for microblogs, we performed experiments with different sets of publicly published word embeddings, as well as a random sampling method, to initialize word vectors in our model. We investigate three different pretrained word embeddings: Skip-Gram, continuous bag-of-words and Stanford's GloVe model. Table 1 gives the performance of three different word embeddings, as well as the randomly sampled one. It should be noted that the random embeddings are uniformly sampled from range $[-\sqrt{\frac{3}{dim}}, +\sqrt{\frac{3}{dim}}]$, where dim is the dimension of embeddings. According

Models	Precision	Recall	F1
CNN	75.36	79	77.13
CNN + pretrained	79.28	82.11	80.67
CNN-pre + but	80.84	83.09	81.95
CNN-pre + switch from	79.74	82.14	80.92
CNN-pre + switch to	80.89	84.39	82.60
CNN-pre + all the 3 rules	82.56	85.18	83.85

Table 3: Results with the three logic rules compared to the without and with word embeddings. We test the model by using each rule independently and after that we combine them in one experiment.

to the results in Table 1, we see that using pretrained word embeddings obtain a significant improvement, about 3.54% in F1 score as opposed to the ones using random embeddings. This is consistent with results reported by previous work done in other NLP tasks (Collobert et al., 2011; Huang et al., 2015; Chiu and Nichols, 2015).

For different pretrained embeddings, Stanford's GloVe 300 dimensional embeddings achieves best results, about 1.12% better than Skip-gram model and 0.78% better than continuous bag-of-words model. One possible reason that Word2Vec is not as good as the Stanford's GloVe model is because of vocabulary mismatch, since Word2Vec embeddings were trained in case-sensitive manner, excluding many common symbols such as punctuations and digits. Because we do not use any kind of data pre-processing to deal with such common symbols or rare words, it might be an issue for using Word2Vec.

5 Experimental Results

For the evaluation of our model, we use the dataset provided by (Amiri and Daumé III, 2015). The authors collected the data from twitter for three telecom brands: Verizon, T- Mobile, and AT&T. Table 2 presents the details about the entries of this dataset. We divide the experimental process into two stages: the first stage concerns running the experiments using the convolutional neural network without and with different logic rules in order to select the best achieved results. In the second stage, we compare our best settings with the previous state-of-art system in churn prediction in microblogs.

Table 3 shows the churn classification results. The first row represents the baseline where we use only the convolutional neural network. In the second row, we initialize our word vectors using

Rule	Number of rules in the training set	Number of rules in the test set
But	358	83
Switch to	321	71
Switch from	62	11
Total	741	165

Table 4: Statistics about the three rules (but, switch to and switch from) in the training and test set.

Models	F1 score
Unigram + Nb (Amiri and Daumé III, 2015)	73.42
(Amiri and Daumé III, 2016)	78.30
Churn_teacher	83.85

Table 5: Comparison of our system with two previous systems.

pretrained word vectors using GloVe model since it gives us the best results among the other pretrained word vectors. We get an improvement around 2.5% in F1-score. We refer to this model by "CNN-pre". This results is consistent with the fact that these pretrained word vectors are universal feature extractors that shown an important results in different NLP applications such as sentiment analysis, named entity recognition and Part-of-speech tagging.

By transferring the knowledge extracted using the "but" logic rule into the weights of the convolutional neural network, we were able to improve the F1-score over the CNN-pre model by 1.28 points in F1-score. For the "switch from" logic rule, we get a slight improvement over the CNN-pre model by 0.25 points in F1-score. The biggest improvement among the three logic rules was obtained by the "switch to" rule where we were able to improve the performance over the CNN-pre model by 1.93 points in F1-score. The last row in Table 3 concerns the results that we obtained by using all the three logic rules where logically we achieved best results and outperformed the CNN-pre model by 3.18 points in F1-score.

While we do not have a complete explanation why we got better results with "switch to" rule, we believe that it is caused by the fact that there 321 sentences in the training data containing this rule which represents around 8% sentences contains the word "switch to". Moreover, it will be clear that customer will leave a specific brand to another new brand. For the "switch from" rule, we get slight improvement over the CNN-pre model because few sentences containing this rule (around 2% sentences contains the word "switch from").

Table 4 shows the statistics about the presence of the three rules in the training data. For "but" rule, we also get an important improvement over the CNN-pre model which confirms the results obtained by (Hu et al., 2016) using the same rule in sentiment analysis. We note that around 9% sentences contains the word "but". In the last row, we combine all the three rules and we were able to obtain the best performance. We refer to this model as "$Churn\_teacher$". This is consistent with the argument by (Hu et al., 2016) where they argued that more rules will allow the system to improve its performance over the base convolutional neural network.

We test our model using this dataset and compare the obtained results with two other systems. The state-of-the-art results were produced by (Amiri and Daumé III, 2016) where they achieved 78.30% in F1 score. They used a combination of Bag of Words features and Recurrent Neural Networks. The second system referenced here as "Unigram + Nb" developed by (Amiri and Daumé III, 2015) used different N-grams ($n = 1, 2, 3$) and their combination on both of the word and character levels.

By adding three rules to the convolutional neural networks, we outperformed the "Unigram + Nb" system by a large margin (10.43 points in F1-score). Furthermore, our model also outperformed the system developed by (Amiri and Daumé III, 2016) by a good margin (5.55 points in F1-score). Table 5 shows a brief presentation of the experimental results and the comparison with the two other systems.

6 Conclusion

In this paper, we explored the problem of target-dependent churn classification in microblogs. We combine the power of convolutional neural networks with structured logic knowledge by constructing a churn teacher capable of classifying customers into churners and non-churners. In addition, we confirm that initializing word vectors with pretrained word embeddings trained on unannotated corpora improved the system performance.

A key aspect of our system is that it explores the transfer of the structured knowledge of logic rules into the weights of convolutional neural networks for churn classification problem. By combining three logic rules, our model largely outperformed all the previous models on publicly available Twitter dataset. We showed that "but" rule is also useful for churn prediction to confirm the results obtained for sentiment classification problem. We consider the two other rules ("switch to" and "switch from") as target-specific rules for churn classification problem which helped the system to improve its performance.

In the future work, we will explore the use of character-level embeddings where we will represent word in a sentence by a word vector representing the concatenation of two embeddings: its equivalent word embeddings obtained from the lookup table and the embeddings obtained from its characters. Furthermore, we will explore the use of named entity recognition to recognize different organizations where we will focus on brands which we believe could help us to a better churn classification.

Acknowledgments

We thank the anonymous reviewers for their valuable comments. We would like to thank Doctor Hadi Amiri and Doctor Hal Daume III for providing us with Twitter dataset for churn prediction in microblogs.

References

Hadi Amiri and Hal Daumé III. 2015. Target-dependent churn classification in microblogs. In *AAAI*. pages 2361–2367.

Hadi Amiri and Hal Daumé III. 2016. Short text representation for detecting churn in microblogs. In *AAAI*. pages 2566–2572.

Stephen H Bach, Matthias Broecheler, Bert Huang, and Lise Getoor. 2015. Hinge-loss markov random fields and probabilistic soft logic. *arXiv preprint arXiv:1505.04406* .

Aimée Backiel, Bart Baesens, and Gerda Claeskens. 2016. Predicting time-to-churn of prepaid mobile telephone customers using social network analysis. *Journal of the Operational Research Society* 67(9):0.

Mohit Bansal, Kevin Gimpel, and Karen Livescu. 2014. Tailoring continuous word representations for dependency parsing. In *ACL (2)*. pages 809–815.

Yoshua Bengio, Réjean Ducharme, Pascal Vincent, and Christian Jauvin. 2003. A neural probabilistic language model. *Journal of machine learning research* 3(Feb):1137–1155.

Yoshua Bengio, Dong-Hyun Lee, Jorg Bornschein, Thomas Mesnard, and Zhouhan Lin. 2015. Towards biologically plausible deep learning. *arXiv preprint arXiv:1502.04156* .

Jason PC Chiu and Eric Nichols. 2015. Named entity recognition with bidirectional lstm-cnns. *arXiv preprint arXiv:1511.08308* .

Kyunghyun Cho, Bart Van Merriënboer, Dzmitry Bahdanau, and Yoshua Bengio. 2014. On the properties of neural machine translation: Encoder-decoder approaches. *arXiv preprint arXiv:1409.1259* .

Ronan Collobert, Jason Weston, Léon Bottou, Michael Karlen, Koray Kavukcuoglu, and Pavel Kuksa. 2011. Natural language processing (almost) from scratch. *Journal of Machine Learning Research* 12(Aug):2493–2537.

Maral Dadvar, Claudia Hauff, and FMG De Jong. 2011. Scope of negation detection in sentiment analysis .

George E Dahl, Dong Yu, Li Deng, and Alex Acero. 2012. Context-dependent pre-trained deep neural networks for large-vocabulary speech recognition. *IEEE Transactions on Audio, Speech, and Language Processing* 20(1):30–42.

James Foulds, Shachi Kumar, and Lise Getoor. 2015. Latent topic networks: A versatile probabilistic programming framework for topic models. In *International Conference on Machine Learning*. pages 777–786.

Kuzman Ganchev, Jennifer Gillenwater, Ben Taskar, et al. 2010. Posterior regularization for structured latent variable models. *Journal of Machine Learning Research* 11(Jul):2001–2049.

Artur S d'Avila Garcez, Krysia Broda, and Dov M Gabbay. 2012. *Neural-symbolic learning systems: foundations and applications*. Springer Science & Business Media.

Jonas Gehring, Michael Auli, David Grangier, Denis Yarats, and Yann N Dauphin. 2017. Convolutional sequence to sequence learning. *arXiv preprint arXiv:1705.03122* .

GE Hinton, DE Rumelhart, and RJ Williams. 1985. Learning internal representations by back-propagating errors. *Parallel Distributed Processing: Explorations in the Microstructure of Cognition* 1.

Geoffrey Hinton, Li Deng, Dong Yu, George E Dahl, Abdel-rahman Mohamed, Navdeep Jaitly, Andrew Senior, Vincent Vanhoucke, Patrick Nguyen, Tara N Sainath, et al. 2012. Deep neural networks for acoustic modeling in speech recognition: The shared views of four research groups. *IEEE Signal Processing Magazine* 29(6):82–97.

Geoffrey Hinton, Oriol Vinyals, and Jeff Dean. 2015. Distilling the knowledge in a neural network. *arXiv preprint arXiv:1503.02531* .

Sorami Hisamoto, Kevin Duh, and Yuji Matsumoto. 2013. An empirical investigation of word representations for parsing the web. In *Proceedings of ANLP*. pages 188–193.

Alexander Hogenboom, Paul Van Iterson, Bas Heerschop, Flavius Frasincar, and Uzay Kaymak. 2011. Determining negation scope and strength in sentiment analysis. In *Systems, Man, and Cybernetics (SMC), 2011 IEEE International Conference on*. IEEE, pages 2589–2594.

Zhiting Hu, Xuezhe Ma, Zhengzhong Liu, Eduard Hovy, and Eric Xing. 2016. Harnessing deep neural networks with logic rules. *arXiv preprint arXiv:1603.06318* .

Fei Huang, Arun Ahuja, Doug Downey, Yi Yang, Yuhong Guo, and Alexander Yates. 2014. Learning representations for weakly supervised natural language processing tasks. *Computational Linguistics* 40(1):85–120.

Zhiheng Huang, Wei Xu, and Kai Yu. 2015. Bidirectional lstm-crf models for sequence tagging. *arXiv preprint arXiv:1508.01991* .

Sergey Ioffe and Christian Szegedy. 2015. Batch normalization: Accelerating deep network training by reducing internal covariate shift. *arXiv preprint arXiv:1502.03167* .

Lifeng Jia, Clement Yu, and Weiyi Meng. 2009. The effect of negation on sentiment analysis and retrieval effectiveness. In *Proceedings of the 18th ACM conference on Information and knowledge management*. ACM, pages 1827–1830.

Abbas Keramati, Hajar Ghaneei, and Seyed Mohammad Mirmohammadi. 2016. Developing a prediction model for customer churn from electronic banking services using data mining. *Financial Innovation* 2(1):10.

Yoon Kim. 2014. Convolutional neural networks for sentence classification. *arXiv preprint arXiv:1408.5882* .

Alex Krizhevsky, Ilya Sutskever, and Geoffrey E Hinton. 2012. Imagenet classification with deep convolutional neural networks. In *Advances in neural information processing systems*. pages 1097–1105.

Ruiqi Li, Peng Wang, and Zonghai Chen. 2016. A feature extraction method based on stacked autoencoder for telecom churn prediction. In *Asian Simulation Conference*. Springer, pages 568–576.

Tomas Mikolov, Ilya Sutskever, Kai Chen, Greg S Corrado, and Jeff Dean. 2013. Distributed representations of words and phrases and their compositionality. In *Advances in neural information processing systems*. pages 3111–3119.

Marvin Minsky. 1983. *Learning meaning*. Artificial Intelligence Laboratory, Massachusetts Institute of Technology.

Anh Nguyen, Jason Yosinski, and Jeff Clune. 2015. Deep neural networks are easily fooled: High confidence predictions for unrecognizable images. In *Proceedings of the IEEE Conference on Computer Vision and Pattern Recognition*. pages 427–436.

Jeffrey Pennington, Richard Socher, and Christopher D Manning. 2014. Glove: Global vectors for word representation. In *EMNLP*. volume 14, pages 1532–1543.

David E Rumelhart, Geoffrey E Hinton, and Ronald J Williams. 1988. Learning representations by backpropagating errors. *Cognitive modeling* 5(3):1.

Tim Salimans and Diederik P Kingma. 2016. Weight normalization: A simple reparameterization to accelerate training of deep neural networks. In *Advances in Neural Information Processing Systems*. pages 901–901.

Leslie N Smith and Nicholay Topin. 2016. Deep convolutional neural network design patterns. *arXiv preprint arXiv:1611.00847* .

Richard Socher, Alex Perelygin, Jean Y Wu, Jason Chuang, Christopher D Manning, Andrew Y Ng, Christopher Potts, et al. 2013. Recursive deep models for semantic compositionality over a sentiment treebank. In *Proceedings of the conference on empirical methods in natural language processing (EMNLP)*. volume 1631, page 1642.

Ilya Sutskever, Oriol Vinyals, and Quoc V Le. 2014. Sequence to sequence learning with neural networks. In *Advances in neural information processing systems*. pages 3104–3112.

Christian Szegedy, Wojciech Zaremba, Ilya Sutskever, Joan Bruna, Dumitru Erhan, Ian Goodfellow, and Rob Fergus. 2013. Intriguing properties of neural networks. *arXiv preprint arXiv:1312.6199* .

Joseph Turian, Lev Ratinov, and Yoshua Bengio. 2010. Word representations: a simple and general method for semi-supervised learning. In *Proceedings of the 48th annual meeting of the association for computational linguistics*. Association for Computational Linguistics, pages 384–394.

Yonghui Wu, Mike Schuster, Zhifeng Chen, Quoc V Le, Mohammad Norouzi, Wolfgang Macherey, Maxim Krikun, Yuan Cao, Qin Gao, Klaus Macherey, et al. 2016. Google's neural machine translation system: Bridging the gap between human and machine translation. *arXiv preprint arXiv:1609.08144* .

Jaime Zaratiegui, Ana Montoro, and Federico Castanedo. 2015. Performing highly accurate predictions through convolutional networks for actual telecommunication challenges. *arXiv preprint arXiv:1511.04906* .

Matthew D Zeiler. 2012. Adadelta: an adaptive learning rate method. *arXiv preprint arXiv:1212.5701* .

To Normalize, or Not to Normalize:
The Impact of Normalization on Part-of-Speech Tagging

Rob van der Goot   Barbara Plank   Malvina Nissim
Center for Language and Cognition, University of Groningen, The Netherlands
{r.van.der.goot,b.plank,m.nissim}@rug.nl

Abstract

Does normalization help Part-of-Speech (POS) tagging accuracy on noisy, non-canonical data? To the best of our knowledge, little is known on the actual impact of normalization in a real-world scenario, where gold error detection is not available. We investigate the effect of automatic normalization on POS tagging of tweets. We also compare normalization to strategies that leverage large amounts of unlabeled data kept in its raw form. Our results show that normalization helps, but does not add consistently beyond just word embedding layer initialization. The latter approach yields a tagging model that is competitive with a Twitter state-of-the-art tagger.

1 Introduction

Non-canonical data poses a series of challenges to Natural Language Processing, as reflected in large performance drops documented in a variety of tasks, e.g., on POS tagging (Gimpel et al., 2011; Hovy et al., 2014), parsing (McClosky, 2010; Foster et al., 2011) and named entity recognition (Ritter et al., 2011). In this paper we focus on POS tagging and on a particular source of non-canonical language, namely Twitter data.

One obvious way to tackle the problem of processing non-canonical data is to build taggers that are specifically tailored to such text. A prime example is the ARK POS tagger, designed especially to process English Twitter data (Gimpel et al., 2011; Owoputi et al., 2013), on which it achieves state-of-the-art results. One drawback of this approach is that non-canonical data is not all of the same kind, so that for non-canonical non-Twitter data or even collections of Twitter samples from

JJ	NN	NN	NNS
new	pix	comming	tomoroe
JJ	NNS	VBG	NN
new	pictures	coming	tomorrow

Figure 1: Example tweet from the test data, raw and normalized form, tagged with Stanford NLP.

different times, typically a new specifically dedicated tool needs to be created.

The alternative route is to take a general purpose state-of-the-art POS tagger and adapt it to successfully tag non-canonical data. In the case of Twitter, one way to go about this is *lexical normalization*. It is the task of detecting "ill-formed" words (Han and Baldwin, 2011) and replacing them with their canonical counterpart. To illustrate why this might help, consider the following tweet: "new pix comming tomoroe". An off-the-shelf system such as the Stanford NLP suite[1] makes several mistakes on the raw input, e.g., the verb 'comming' as well as the plural noun 'pix' are tagged as singular noun. Instead, its normalized form is analyzed correctly, as shown in Figure 1.

While being a promising direction, we see at least two issues with the assessment of normalization as a successful step in POS tagging non-canonical text. Firstly, normalization experiments are usually carried out assuming that the tokens to be normalized are already detected (*gold error detection*). Thus little is known on how normalization impacts tagging accuracy in a real-world scenario (*not* assuming gold error detection). Secondly, normalization is one way to go about processing non-canonical data, but not the only one (Eisenstein, 2013; Plank, 2016). Indeed, alternative approaches leverage the abundance of *unlabeled data* kept in its raw form. For instance,

---

[1] http://nlp.stanford.edu:8080/parser/index.jsp, accessed June 1, 2017.

Proceedings of the 3rd Workshop on Noisy User-generated Text, pages 31–39
Copenhagen, Denmark, September 7, 2017. ©2017 Association for Computational Linguistics

such data can be exploited with semi-supervised learning methods (Abney, 2007). The advantage of this approach is that portability could be successful also towards domains where normalization is not necessary or crucial. These observations lead us to the following research questions:

Q1 In a real-world setting, without assuming gold error detection, does normalization help in POS tagging of tweets?

Q2 In the context of POS tagging, is it more beneficial to normalize input data or is it better to work with raw data and exploit large amounts of it in a semi-supervised setting?

Q3 To what extent are normalization and semi-supervised approaches complementary?

To answer these questions, we run a battery of experiments that evaluate different approaches. Specifically:

1. We study the impact of normalization on POS tagging in a realistic setup, i.e., we compare normalizing only unknown words, or words for which we know they need correction; we compare this with a fully automatic normalization model (Section 3).

2. We evaluate the impact of leveraging large amounts of unlabeled data using two approaches: a) deriving various word representations, and studying their effect for model initialization (Section 4.1); b) applying a bootstrapping approach based on self-training to automatically derive labeled training data, evaluating a range of a-priori data selection mechanisms (Section 4.2).

3. We experiment with combining the most promising methods from both directions, to gain insights on their potential complementarity (Section 5).

2 Experimental Setup

We run two main sets of POS tagging experiments. In the first one, we use normalization in a variety of settings (see Section 3). In the second one, we leverage large amounts of unlabeled data that does not undergo any normalization but is used as training in a semi-supervised setting (Section 4). For all experiments we use existing datasets as well as newly created resources, cf. Section 2.1. The POS model used is described in Section 2.2.

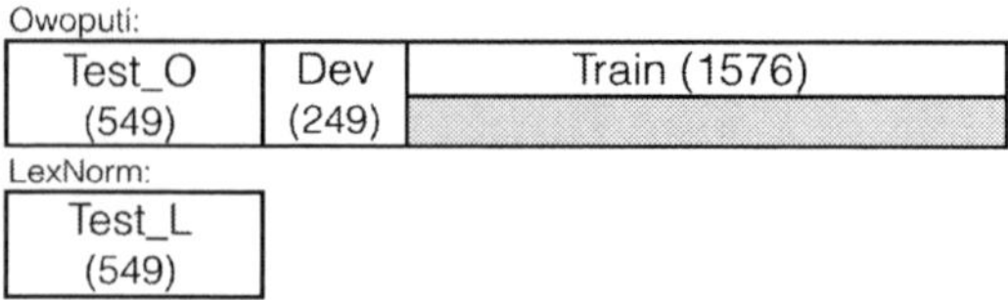

Figure 2: Labeled data for POS and normalization. Gray area: no gold normalization layer available.

2.1 Data

The annotated datasets used in this study originate from two sources: Owoputi et al. (2013) and Han and Baldwin (2011), which we will refer to as OWOPUTI and LEXNORM, respectively. All datasets used in this study are annotated with the 26 Twitter tags as described in (Gimpel et al., 2011).[2] OWOPUTI was originally annotated with POS labels, whereas LEXNORM was solely annotated for normalization. Li and Liu (2015) added a POS tag layer to the LEXNORM corpus, and a normalization layer to 798 Tweets from OWOPUTI, which we split into a separate DEV and TEST part of 249 and 549 Tweets, respectively, keeping the original POS labels. We use DEV throughout all experiments during development, and test our final best system on the held-out test sets (both containing 549 tweets). An illustration of the data is given in Figure 2.

For the different improvements to our baseline tagger, we need raw data from the target domain (Twitter). In addition, the normalization model needs unlabeled canonical data. We use a snapshot of English Wikipedia as unlabeled canonical data source. To get raw data for the social media domain, we collected Tweets during the whole year of 2016 by means of the Twitter API. We only collected Tweets containing one of the 100 frequent words in the Oxford English Corpus[3] as a rough language filter. This resulted in a dataset of 760,744,676 English Tweets. We do some very basic pre-processing in which we replace urls and usernames by <URL> and <USERNAME>, and remove duplicate tweets. Because of different casing strategies, we always apply a simple postprocessing step to 'rt' (retweet) tokens.

---

[2] Some tags are rare, like M and Y. In fact, M occurs only once in TEST_L; Y never occurs in DEV and only once in TEST_L and three times in TEST_O. Therefore our confusion matrices (over DEV and TEST_O, respectively) have different number of labels on the axes.

[3] https://en.wikipedia.org/wiki/Most_common_words_in_English

2.2 Model

We use BILTY, an off-the-shelf bi-directional Long Short-Term Memory (bi-LSTM) tagger which utilizes both word and character embeddings (Plank et al., 2016). The tagger is trained on 1,576 training tweets (Section 2.1). We tune the parameters of the POS tagger on the development set to derive the following hyperparameter setup, which we use throughout the rest of the experiments: 10 epochs, 1 bi-LSTM layer, 100 input dimensions for words, 256 for characters, σ=0.2, `constant` embeddings initializer, `Adam` trainer, and updating embeddings during backpropagation.[4]

3 To Normalize

First we evaluate the impact of normalization on the POS tagger.

3.1 Model

We use an in-house developed normalization model (van der Goot and van Noord, 2017).[5] The model is based on the assumption that different normalization problems require different handling. First, since unintentional disfluencies can often be corrected by the use of a spell checker, the normalization model exploits Aspell[6]. Second, since intentional disfluencies typically have a much larger edit distance, the normalization system uses word embeddings (Mikolov et al., 2013);[7] words close to the non-canonical word in the vector space are considered potential normalization candidates. On top of that, the model uses a lookup list generated from the training data, which works especially well for slang.

Features originating from the ranking are combined with uni- and bi-gram probabilities from Wikipedia data as well as from raw Tweets (Section 2.1). A random forest classifier (Breiman, 2001) is then used to rank the candidates for each word. Note that the original word is also a candidate; this enables the model to handle error detection, which is not always the case in models of previous work.

We train the normalization model on 2,577 tweets from Li and Liu (2014). Our model (van der Goot and van Noord, 2017) achieves state-of-art performance on the erroneous tokens (using gold error detection) on the LexNorm dataset (Han and Baldwin, 2011) as well as state-of-art on another corpus which is usually benchmarked without assuming gold error detection (Baldwin et al., 2015). We refer the reader to the paper (van der Goot and van Noord, 2017) for further details.

To obtain a more detailed view of the effect of normalization on POS tagging, we investigate four experimental setups:

- normalizing only unknown words;

- considering all words: the model decides whether a word should be normalized or not;

- assuming gold error detection: the model knows which words should be normalized;

- gold normalization; we consider this a theoretical upper bound.

Traditionally, normalization is used to make the test data more similar to the train data. Since we train our tagger on the social media domain as well, the normalization of only the test data might actually result in more distance between the train and test data. Therefore, we also train the tagger on normalized training data, and on the union of the normalized and the original training data.

3.2 Results

The effects of the different normalization strategies on the DEV data are shown in Table 1. Throughout the paper we report average accuracies over 5 runs including standard deviation.

The first row shows the effect of normalization at test-time only. From these results we can conclude that normalizing all words is beneficial over normalizing only unknown words; this shows that normalization has a positive effect that goes beyond changing unknown words.

The results of using the gold normalization suggest that there is still more to gain by improving the normalization model. In contrast, the results for gold error detection (GOLDED) show that error detection is not the main reason for this difference, since the performance difference between ALL and GOLDED is relatively small compared to the gap with GOLD.

---

[4]`Adam` was consistently better than `sgd` on this small training dataset. More LSTM layers lowered performance.

[5]Available at: `https://bitbucket.org/robvanderg/monoise`

[6]`www.aspell.net`

[7]Using the tweets from Section 2.1 and the following parameters: `-size 400 -window 1 -negative 5 -sample 1e-4 -iter 5`

↓ **Train** → **Test**	RAW	UNK	ALL	GOLDED	GOLD
RAW	82.16 (±.33)	83.44 (±.25)	**84.06** (±.32)	84.67 (±.23)	86.71 (±.25)
ALL	80.42 (±.71)	81.99 (±.64)	83.87 (±.28)	84.05 (±.31)	86.11 (±.14)
UNION	81.54 (±.27)	83.11 (±.31)	84.04 (±.34)	84.42 (±.24)	86.35 (±.17)

Table 1: Results of normalization (N) on DEV (macro average and stdev over 5 runs). RAW: no normalization, ALL: automatic normalization, UNK: normalize only unknown words, GOLDED: use gold error detection, GOLD: use gold normalization (Oracle). Row: whether training data is normalized. UNION stands for the training set formed by the union of both normalized and original raw data.

Considering the normalization of the training data, we see that it has a negative effect. The table suggests that training on the raw (non-normalized) training data works best. Adding normalized data to raw data (UNION) does not yield any clear improvement over RAW only, but requires more training time. For the test data, normalization is instead always beneficial.

To sum up, normalization improved the base tagger by 1.9% absolute performance on the development data, reaching 84.06% accuracy. Overall, our state-of-art normalization model only reaches approximately 50% of the theoretical upper bound of using gold normalization. We next investigate whether using large amounts of unlabeled data can help us to obtain a similar effect.

4 Or Not to Normalize

An alternative option to normalization is to leave the text as is, and exploit very large amounts of raw data via semi-supervised learning. The rationale behind this is the following: provided the size of the data is sufficient, a model can be trained to naturally learn the POS tags of noisy data.

4.1 Effect of Word Embeddings

An easy and effective use of word embeddings in neural network approaches is to use them to initialize the word lookup parameters.

We train a skip-gram word embeddings model using word2vec (Mikolov et al., 2013) on 760M tweets (as described in Section 3.1). We also experiment with structured skip-grams (Ling et al., 2015), an adaptation of word2vec which takes word order into account. It has been shown to be beneficial for syntactically oriented tasks, like POS tagging. Therefore we want to evaluate structured skip-grams as well.

The normalization model uses word embeddings with a window size of 1; we compare this with the default window size of 5 for structured skip-grams.

Results Table 2 shows the results of using the different skip-gram models for initialization of the word embeddings layer. Structured skip-grams perform slightly better, confirming earlier findings. Using a smaller window is more beneficial, probably because of the fragmented nature of Twitter data.

Structured skip-grams of window size 1 result in the best embedding model. This results in an improvement from 82.16% (Table 1) to 88.51% accuracy. This improvement is considerably larger than what obtained by normalization (82.16).

4.2 Effect of Self-training

We work with a rather small training set, which is all that is available to us in terms of gold data. This is due to the use of an idiosyncratic tagset (Gimpel et al., 2011). Adding more data could be beneficial to the system. To get an idea of how much effect extra annotated data could potentially have on POS tag accuracy, we plot the performance using smaller amounts of gold training data in Figure 3. We can see that there is still a slight upward trend; however, even when adding manually annotated data, the performance sometimes drop, especially after adding 55% of the training data.

To create more training data, we use an iterative indelible self-training setup (Abney, 2007) to obtain automatically labeled data. Specifically: 100

	WINDOW SIZE	
	1	5
SKIPG.	88.14 (±.30)	87.56 (±.08)
STRUCT.SKIPG.	**88.51** (±.24)	88.11 (±.49)

Table 2: Accuracy on raw DEV: various pretrained skip-gram embeddings for initialization.

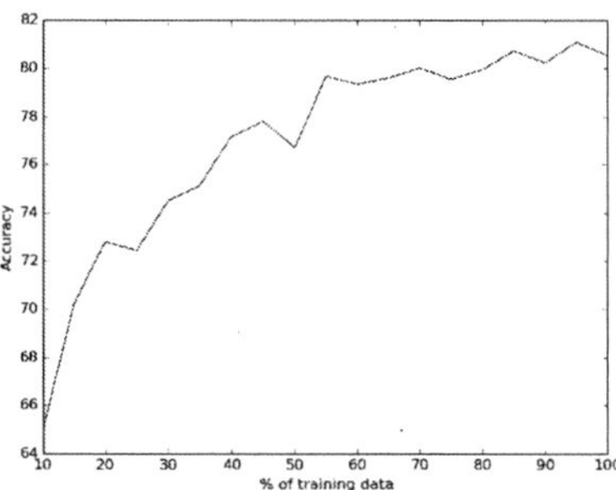

Figure 3: Effect of increasing amounts of training data (100% training data == 1,576 tweets).

tweets are tagged, they get added to the training data, and after this a new model is trained.

While we do not adopt any filtering strategy on the predictions (e.g., confidence thresholds), we do explore different strategies of *a-priori* data selection, from two corpora: raw tweets (Section 3.1), and the English Web Treebank (Petrov and McDonald, 2012).

For the English Web Treebank (EWT), we directly use raw text. Moreover, because the texts in the EWT are distributed by domains, i.e., *answers, emails, weblogs, newsgroups*, and *reviews*, we preserve this information and keep the data separate according to their domain to see whether adding data from the different domains can provide a more useful signal.

For the raw tweets, we compare different strategies of sampling. In addition to selecting random tweets, we experimented with selections aimed at providing the tagger with specific information that we knew was missing or confusing in the original training data. One strategy thus was to include tweets that contained words occurring in the development data but not in the training data. Note that this would result in a very slow tagger in a real-world situation, since the tagger needs to be retrained for every new unknown word. Another strategy was based on a preliminary analysis of errors on the development data: from the confusion matrix we observed that a frequently confounded tag was proper noun. Considering named entities as adequate proxies for proper nouns in this context, we also experimented with adding tweets that contained named entities. The detection of named entities was performed using a Twitter-specific named entity recognizer (Ritter et al., 2011). For control and comparison, we also collect additional

training data where only tweets that do *not* contain named entities are selected. Hence, we end up with the following four sampling strategies:

- random sampling
- tweets containing words which occur in the development data, but not in the training data
- tweets containing named entities
- tweets not containing named entities

Results Adding more automatically-labeled data did not show any consistent improvement. This holds for both selection methods regarding named entities (presence/absence of NERs) and different domains of the Web treebank. Therefore we do not elaborate further here. We hypothesize that post-selection based on e.g., confidence sampling, is a more promising direction. We consider this future work.

5 Normalizing and Not Normalizing

In the previous sections, we explored ways to improve the POS tagging of Tweets. The most promising directions were initializing the tagger with pre-trained embeddings and using normalization. Self-training was not effective. In this Section, we report on additional experiments on the development data aimed at obtaining insights on the potential of combining these two strategies.

5.1 Consequences of Normalization

	BILTY	+NORM	+VECS	+COMB
CANONICAL	86.1	85.6	91.2	90.1
NON-CANON.	50.8	70.3	71.1	78.5

Table 3: Effect of different models on canonical/non-canonical words.

Table 3 shows the effect of the two approaches on the two subsets of tokens (canonical/non-canonical) on the DEV set. Word embeddings have a higher impact on standard, canonical tokens. It is interesting to note that word embeddings and normalization both have a similar yet complementary effect on the words to be normalized (non-canonical). The improvements on non-canonical words seem to be complementary. The combined model additionally improves on words which need normalization, whereas it scores almost 1% lower on canonical words. This suggests that both strategies have potential to complement each other.

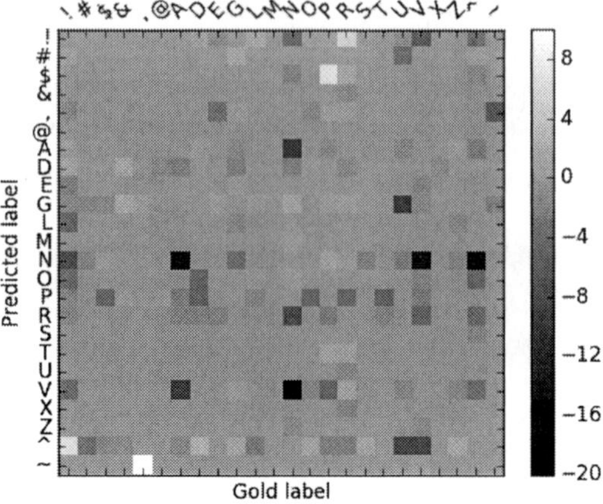

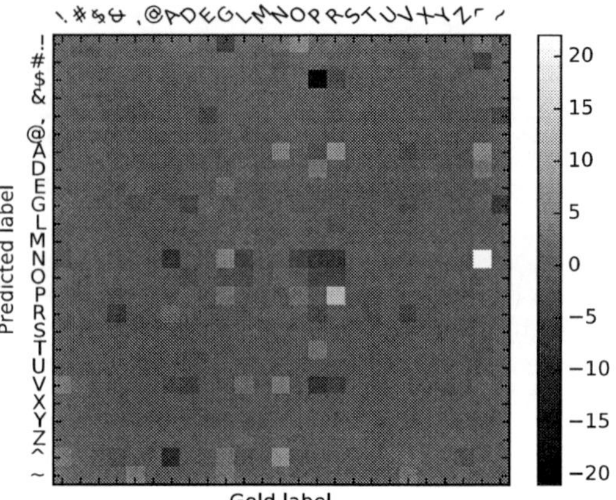

Figure 4: Differences in numbers of errors on development data between best normalization setting and best word embeddings. Dark means normalization makes more errors.

Figure 5: Comparison of errors per POS between our best model and the ARK tagger on TEST_O; darker means our system performs better.

5.2 Performance per POS

We compare the type of errors made by the best normalization setting versus the best word embeddings setting in a confusion matrix which displays the difference in errors in Figure 4. To recall: the best normalization setting was to use the raw training data, normalizing all words at test time; the best word embeddings model was a structured skip gram embeddings model with a window of 1.

In the confusion graph it becomes clear that normalization results in over-predicting nouns (N), which often get confused with verbs (V), adjectives (A) and proper nouns (^). Normalization is better at recognizing prepositions (P), which it confuses less with numerals ($) compared to the embedding model. This is due to normalizing '2' and '4'. Instead, the embedding model has better predictions for proper nouns, nouns and verbs, presumably due to the higher coverage.

6   Evaluation

In this section we report results on the test data, as introduced in Section 2.1.

Our main aim is to compare different approaches for successfully applying a generic state-of-the-art POS tagger to Twitter data. Therefore we have to assess the contribution of the two methods we explore (normalization and using embeddings) and see how they fare, not only to each other but also in comparison to a state-of-the-art Twitter tagger. We use the ARK tagger (Owoputi et al., 2013) and retrain it on our dataset for direct comparison with our models. The ARK system is a conditional random fields tagger, which exploits clusters, lexical features and gazetteers.

Table 4 shows the performance of our best models and the ARK tagger on the test datasets.

Embeddings work considerably better than normalization, which confirms what we found on the DEV data. The combined approach yields the highest accuracy over all evaluation sets, however, it significantly differs from embeddings only on TEST_L. This can be explained by our earlier observation (cf. Table 3), which shows that COMB yields the highest improvement on non-canonical tokens, but the same does not hold for canonical tokens. Notice that TEST_L does indeed contain the highest proportion of non-canonical tokens.

Our best results on all datasets are comparable to the state-of-the-art results achieved by the ARK tagger. In Figure 5 we compare the errors made by our system (COMB in Table 4) and ARK on TEST_O, which is the test set on which both tag-

	DEV	TEST_O	TEST_L
% non-canonical tokens	11.75%	10.95%	12.09%
BILTY	82.16 (±.33)	83.81 (±.23)	80.78 (±.32)
+NORM	84.06 (±.32)	84.73 (±.19)	84.61 (±.21)
+EMBEDS	**88.51** (±.24)	**90.02** (±.35)	88.53 (±.41)
+COMB	**88.89** (±.25)	**90.25** (±.19)	**89.63** (±.13)
ARK	89.08	90.65	89.67

Table 4: Results on test data (average over 5 runs) compared to ARK-tagger (Owoputi et al., 2013). Bold: best result (in case of multiple: no stat.significant difference according to randomization test).

gers obtain the highest performance.

The ARK tagger has difficulties with prepositions (P), which are mistagged as numerals ($). These are almost all cases of '2' and '4', which represent Twitter slang for 'to' and 'for', respectively. Our system performs a lot better on these, due to the normalization model as already observed earlier. Still regarding prepositions, ARK is better at distinguishing them from adverbs (R), which is a common mistake for our system. Our tagger makes more mistakes on confusing proper nouns (ˆ) with nouns (N) in comparison to ARK.

7 Related Work

Theoretically, this works fits well within the debate on normalization vs domain adaptation (Eisenstein, 2013). For a practical comparison, the work most related to ours is that of Li and Liu (2015). They propose a joint model for normalization and POS tagging. The candidate lists of six different normalization models, including spell checkers and machine translation systems, are combined with all their possible POS tags as found by the ARK Twitter POS tagger. Note that they use gold error detection, while we perform fully automatic normalization. These combined units of words and POS tags are then used to build joint Viterbi decoding (Viterbi, 1973). The optimal path in this decoding does not only contain a sequence of normalized tokens, but also a sequence of POS tags. This joint model proves to be beneficial for both tasks.

Work on normalization for improving POS tagging has also been done on other languages. For example, Ljubešić et al. (2017) show that performing normalization, in addition to using external resources, can remove half of the errors of a standard POS tagger for South Slavic languages. Quite surprisingly, instead, of all systems participating in shared tasks on POS tagging of Twitter data for both Italian (Bosco et al., 2016) and German (Beißwenger et al., 2016), none of the participating systems incorporated any normalization strategy before performing POS tagging.

Finally, normalization for POS tagging is certainly not limited to non-canonical data stemming from social media. Indeed, another stream of related work is focused on historical data, usually originating from the 15th till the 18th century. The motivation behind this is that in order to apply current language processing tools, the texts need to be normalized first, as spelling has changed through time. Experiments on POS tagging historical data that was previously normalized have been investigated for English (Yang and Eisenstein, 2016), German (Bollmann, 2013), and Dutch (Hupkes and Bod, 2016; Tjong Kim Sang, 2016). In this latter work, different methods of 'translating' historical Dutch texts to modern Dutch are explored, and a vocabulary lookup-based approach appears to work best.[8] In this paper we focused on normalization and POS tagging for Twitter data only.

8 Conclusion

We investigated the impact of normalization on POS tagging for the Twitter domain, presenting the first results on automatic normalization and comparing normalization to alternative strategies. We compared a generic tagger to a tagger specifically designed for Twitter data.

Regarding Q1, we can conclude that normalization does help. However, using large amounts of unlabeled data for embedding initialization yields an improvement that is twice as large as the one

---

[8]Interestingly, this work also resulted in a shared task on normalization of historical Dutch, in which the secondary evaluation metric was POS tagging accuracy: `https://ifarm.nl/clin2017st/`.

obtained using normalization (Q2).

Combining both methods (Q3) does indeed yield the highest scores on all datasets. This suggests that the two approaches are complementary, also because in isolation their most frequent errors differ. However, the contribution of normalization on top of embeddings alone is relatively small and only significant on one test set, which was specifically developed for normalization and contains the largest proportion of non-canonical tokens.

Overall, our best model is comparable to the ARK tagger. As a general direction, our results suggest that exploiting large amounts of unlabeled data of the target domain is preferable. However, if the data is expected to include a large proportion of non-canonical tokens, it is definitely worth applying normalization in combination with embeddings.

Our investigation was limited by the amount of available training data. Adding data via self-training did not help. We observed mixed results for different types of a-priori filtering, but none of them yielded a steady improvement. A more promising direction might be post-selection, based on confidence scores or agreement among different taggers. Obviously another way to go is to add manually labeled data, some of which is available for more canonical domains. This would require a mapping of tagsets, and might be another good testbed to assess the contribution of normalization, which we leave for future work.

All code and distributable data used in this paper are available at `https://github.com/bplank/wnut-2017-pos-norm`.

Acknowledgments

We want to thank Héctor Martínez Alonso and Gertjan van Noord for valuable comments on earlier drafts of this paper. We are also grateful to the anonymous reviewers. This research has been supported by the Nuance Foundation and the University of Groningen High Performance Computing center.

References

Steven Abney. 2007. *Semisupervised learning for computational linguistics*. CRC Press.

Timothy Baldwin, Marie-Catherine de Marneffe, Bo Han, Young-Bum Kim, Alan Ritter, and Wei Xu. 2015. Shared tasks of the 2015 workshop on noisy user-generated text: Twitter lexical normalization and named entity recognition. In *Proceedings of the Workshop on Noisy User-generated Text*, pages 126–135, Beijing, China. Association for Computational Linguistics.

Michael Beißwenger, Sabine Bartsch, Stefan Evert, and Kay-Michael Würzner. 2016. Empirist 2015: A shared task on the automatic linguistic annotation of computer-mediated communication and web corpora. In *Proceedings of the 10th Web as Corpus Workshop (WAC-X) and the EmpiriST Shared Task. Berlin, Germany*, pages 44–56.

Marcel Bollmann. 2013. POS tagging for historical texts with sparse training data. In *Proceedings of the 7th Linguistic Annotation Workshop and Interoperability with Discourse, LAW-ID@ACL 2013, August 8-9, 2013, Sofia, Bulgaria*, pages 11–18. The Association for Computer Linguistics.

Cristina Bosco, Fabio Tamburini, Andrea Bolioli, and Alessandro Mazzei. 2016. Overview of the evalita 2016 part of speech on twitter for italian task. In *Proceedings of Third Italian Conference on Computational Linguistics (CLiC-it 2016) & Fifth Evaluation Campaign of Natural Language Processing and Speech Tools for Italian. Final Workshop (EVALITA 2016). Associazione Italiana di Linguistica Computazionale (AILC)*.

Leo Breiman. 2001. Random forests. *Machine learning*, 45(1):5–32.

Jacob Eisenstein. 2013. What to do about bad language on the internet. In *Proceedings of the 2013 Conference of the North American Chapter of the Association for Computational Linguistics: Human Language Technologies*, pages 359–369, Atlanta, Georgia. Association for Computational Linguistics.

Jennifer Foster, Özlem Cetinoglu, Joachim Wagner, Joseph Le Roux, Joakim Nivre, Deirdre Hogan, and Josef van Genabith. 2011. From news to comment: Resources and benchmarks for parsing the language of web 2.0. In *Proceedings of the 5th International Joint Conference on Natural Language Processing (IJCNLP)*.

Kevin Gimpel, Nathan Schneider, Brendan O'Connor, Dipanjan Das, Daniel Mills, Jacob Eisenstein, Michael Heilman, Dani Yogatama, Jeffrey Flanigan, and Noah A. Smith. 2011. Part-of-speech tagging for twitter: Annotation, features, and experiments. In *Proceedings of the 49th Annual Meeting of the Association for Computational Linguistics: Human Language Technologies*, pages 42–47, Portland, Oregon, USA. Association for Computational Linguistics.

Rob van der Goot and Gertjan van Noord. 2017. Monoise: Modeling noise using a modular normalization system. *Computational Linguistics in the Netherlands Journal*, 7.

Bo Han and Timothy Baldwin. 2011. Lexical normalisation of short text messages: Makn sens a #twitter. In *Proceedings of the 49th Annual Meeting of the Association for Computational Linguistics: Human Language Technologies*, pages 368–378, Portland, Oregon, USA. Association for Computational Linguistics.

Dirk Hovy, Barbara Plank, and Anders Søgaard. 2014. When pos data sets don't add up: Combatting sample bias. In *Proceedings of the Ninth International Conference on Language Resources and Evaluation (LREC-2014)*, pages 4472–4475.

Dieuwke Hupkes and Rens Bod. 2016. Pos-tagging of historical dutch. In *Proceedings of the Tenth International Conference on Language Resources and Evaluation (LREC 2016)*, Paris, France. European Language Resources Association (ELRA).

Chen Li and Yang Liu. 2014. Improving text normalization via unsupervised model and discriminative reranking. In *Proceedings of the ACL 2014 Student Research Workshop*, pages 86–93, Baltimore, Maryland, USA. Association for Computational Linguistics.

Chen Li and Yang Liu. 2015. Joint POS tagging and text normalization for informal text. In *Proceedings of the Twenty-Fourth International Joint Conference on Artificial Intelligence, IJCAI 2015, Buenos Aires, Argentina, July 25-31, 2015*, pages 1263–1269.

Wang Ling, Chris Dyer, Alan W Black, and Isabel Trancoso. 2015. Two/too simple adaptations of word2vec for syntax problems. In *Proceedings of the 2015 Conference of the North American Chapter of the Association for Computational Linguistics: Human Language Technologies*, pages 1299–1304, Denver, Colorado. Association for Computational Linguistics.

Nikola Ljubešić, Tomaž Erjavec, and Darja Fišer. 2017. Adapting a state-of-the-art tagger for south slavic languages to non-standard text. In *Proceedings of the 6th Workshop on Balto-Slavic Natural Language Processing*, pages 60–68, Valencia, Spain. Association for Computational Linguistics.

David McClosky. 2010. *Any domain parsing: automatic domain adaptation for natural language parsing*. Ph.D. thesis, Brown University.

Tomas Mikolov, Kai Chen, Greg Corrado, and Jeffrey Dean. 2013. Efficient estimation of word representations in vector space. *arXiv preprint arXiv:1301.3781*.

Olutobi Owoputi, Brendan O'Connor, Chris Dyer, Kevin Gimpel, Nathan Schneider, and Noah A. Smith. 2013. Improved part-of-speech tagging for online conversational text with word clusters. In *Proceedings of the 2013 Conference of the North American Chapter of the Association for Computational Linguistics: Human Language Technologies*,

pages 380–390, Atlanta, Georgia. Association for Computational Linguistics.

Slav Petrov and Ryan McDonald. 2012. Overview of the 2012 shared task on parsing the web. In *Notes of the First Workshop on Syntactic Analysis of Non-Canonical Language (SANCL)*, volume 59.

Barbara Plank. 2016. What to do about non-standard (or non-canonical) language in NLP. In *KONVENS*.

Barbara Plank, Anders Søgaard, and Yoav Goldberg. 2016. Multilingual part-of-speech tagging with bidirectional long short-term memory models and auxiliary loss. In *Proceedings of the 54th Annual Meeting of the Association for Computational Linguistics (Volume 2: Short Papers)*, pages 412–418, Berlin, Germany. Association for Computational Linguistics.

Alan Ritter, Sam Clark, Mausam, and Oren Etzioni. 2011. Named entity recognition in tweets: An experimental study. In *Proceedings of the 2011 Conference on Empirical Methods in Natural Language Processing*, pages 1524–1534, Edinburgh, Scotland, UK. Association for Computational Linguistics.

Erik Tjong Kim Sang. 2016. Improving Part-of-Speech Tagging of Historical Text by First Translating to Modern Text. In *2nd IFIP International Workshop on Computational History and Data-Driven Humanities*. Springer Verlag.

A. Viterbi. 1973. Error bounds for convolutional codes and an asymptotically optimum decoding algorithm. *IEEE Trans. Inform. Theory*, 13(2):260–269.

Yi Yang and Jacob Eisenstein. 2016. Part-of-speech tagging for historical english. In *Proceedings of the 2016 Conference of the North American Chapter of the Association for Computational Linguistics: Human Language Technologies*, pages 1318–1328, San Diego, California. Association for Computational Linguistics.

Constructing an Alias List for Named Entities during an Event

Anietie Andy
aandy@seas.upenn.edu
University of Pennsylvania

Mark Dredze
mdredze@cs.jhu.edu
Johns Hopkins University

Mugizi Rwebangira
rweba@scs.howard.edu
Howard University

Chris Callison-Burch
ccb@cis.upenn.edu
University of Pennsylvania

Abstract

In certain fields, real-time knowledge from events can help in making informed decisions. In order to extract pertinent real-time knowledge related to an event, it is important to identify the named entities and their corresponding aliases related to the event. The problem of identifying aliases of named entities that spike has remained unexplored. In this paper, we introduce an algorithm, *EntitySpike*, that identifies entities that spike in popularity in tweets from a given time period, and constructs an alias list for these spiked entities. *EntitySpike* uses a temporal heuristic to identify named entities with similar context that occur in the same time period (within minutes) during an event. Each entity is encoded as a vector using this temporal heuristic. We show how these entity-vectors can be used to create a named entity alias list. We evaluated our algorithm on a dataset of temporally ordered tweets from a single event, the 2013 Grammy Awards show. We carried out various experiments on tweets that were published in the same time period and show that our algorithm identifies most entity name aliases and outperforms a competitive baseline.

1 Introduction

Twitter captures a large volume of discussions and messages related to events and topics, in real-time. Knowledge has been extracted from these data streams in different domains to gain various insights, for example, election results (Tumasjan et al., 2010), democratic movements (Starbird and Palen, 2012), tracking illnesses over time (Paul and Dredze, 2011; Guo et al., 2013) and making crucial real-time decisions such as earthquake detection (Sakaki et al., 2010).

Twitter is an informal forum that imposes a limit on the number of characters per tweet, hence, the vocabulary used to express tweets are diverse. This results in the prevalence of abbreviated or misspelled words in tweets and aliases used to represent named entities. Entity name variation poses a challenge to determining what or who a name refers to (Andrews et al., 2014); identifying name variations has been shown to help in different domains such as community question answering systems (Andy et al., 2016b,a) and automatic paraphrase acquisition (Shinyama et al., 2002). For example, given the following tweets that occurred in a 5-minute time period during an event:

- #Veep's Julia Louis-Dreyfus wins for Lead Actress in a Comedy Series #Emmys
- At least Selina Meyer is amazing at winning #Emmys. #Veep
- How does Elaine keep winning these awards?! #Emmys
- Is JLD ever NOT going to win for Veep?#Emmys

where the actress *Julia Louis-Dreyfus* is referred to as *Selina Meyers* — from her character in the show, *Veep*, *Elaine* — from her character in the show, *Seinfield*, and *JLD* — the abbreviation of her name. Identifying these entity name variations can be challenging; however, the context in which the entities occurred and temporal information can be used to determine the aliases of named entities. The goal of our research is to construct an alias list for entities that spike in popularity in a given time period during a single event, by using a temporal heuristic to cluster entities with similar context. This paper makes the following contributions:

- We formulate a temporal heuristic to identify

Proceedings of the 3rd Workshop on Noisy User-generated Text, pages 40–44
Copenhagen, Denmark, September 7, 2017. ©2017 Association for Computational Linguistics

entities with similar context that occur in the same time period during an event.

- We develop a novel algorithm, *EntitySpike*, that uses this temporal heuristic to encode entities as vectors and creates an alias list, if one exists, for entities that spike in popularity in a given time period.
- We present detailed experiments demonstrating that using temporal information identifies most named entity aliases.

2 Background and Preliminaries

In tweets collected during an on going event, there is a small window in time in which entities spike in popularity, though they have occurrences during the whole event (Dredze et al., 2016).

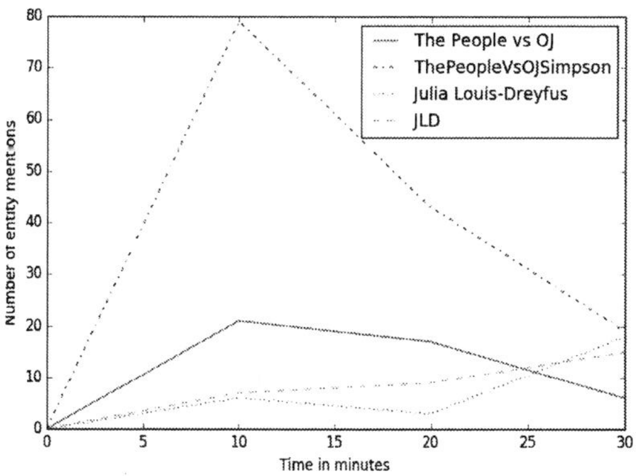

Figure 1: Name variations of entities that spike in popularity at the same time in 10 minute bins during the 2016 Emmy awards show

To investigate the validity of creating an alias list for entities that spike, we use the Twitter streaming API to collect 50,000 timestamped and temporally ordered tweets and re-tweets containing *#emmys*, while the 2016 Emmy Awards show was going on (we intend to make this dataset available to the research community). We selected tweets that occurred in a randomly selected 30 minutes time period and split these tweets into bins of 10 minute time periods i.e. each bin contained tweets that occurred in a 10 minute time interval. Figure 1 shows the entities that spiked the most in this time period and their name variations. We observed that when an entity spikes in popularity in a given time period, some of its aliases spike in popularity as well. Based on these observations, we propose an algorithm, *EntitySpike*, that creates an alias list for entities that spike in a given time period.

Task Definition: Given a sequence of tweets and entity mentions, denoted by $\mathbf{X}$ $= (\{e_1, S_1\}, \{e_2, S_2\}, ... \{e_n, S_n\})$, where e_i represents a named entity that spikes in popularity in a given time period e.g. *Julia Louis-Dreyfus*, and S_i represents the set of tweets that make reference to this named entity, e_i, during this specified time period; the task is to create an alias list for each e_i, if one exists.

Candidate Entity Identification: Following previous work in entity linking (Liu et al., 2013; Guo et al., 2013), we define an entity as a Wikipedia title page. An entity mention is a sequence of tokens in a tweet that can potentially link to an entity. The Grammy Awards show is mostly about famous people and so we focus only on entities belonging to the *Person* category. In order to construct a Wikipedia lexicon, we collect 1.5 million English Wikipedia title pages referring to *Person* named entities and extracted the backlinks (incoming links to the Wikipedia title page) from each of these Wikipedia title pages (we intend to make this dataset available to the research community).

Given a set of tweets $\{t_1, t_2, ..., t_n\}$ that occur in a given time period (within minutes) during the Grammy awards show, we extract all *k-grams* of size $\leq k$, from each tweet; we selected $k = 3$. We select a *k-gram* as a candidate entity mention if it is either an exact match of a Wikipedia title page or backlink or if it is contained in a Wikipedia title page or backlink, for example "Carrie" is contained in "Carrie Underwood".

3 Our Algorithm: *EntitySpike*

During an event, such as an award show, a large volume of tweets related to the event are generated by users, per minute. Most of these tweets contain named entities and their aliases. Our algorithm, *EntitySpike* identifies named entities that spike at a certain time period and constructs an alias list for these entities by using a temporal heuristic.

Exploiting Temporal Information about entities: While the award show is going on, artists and celebrities - some of which have nicknames, are showcased walking on the red carpet, performing on stage, presenting awards, or sitting in the audience. On social media platforms, such as twitter, people publish tweets related to these events, in real-time. Most of the generated tweets refer to people or entities in the same context e.g. their outfit, performance, actions etc. Some tweets make reference to named entities by their aliases, some of which look similar to their corresponding named entity e.g. *"Jay Z"* and *"Jay-Z"* and some look different e.g. *"Taylor Swift"* and *"Tswizzle"*. Given tweets that occur at a certain time period (within minutes), the context of most of the tweets will be similar. For example, one may see a burst of tweets published in the same 5-minute time period that say: *"X just won a Grammy"* or *"Y won her first Grammy"*. This suggests that *X* and *Y* refer to the same person, regardless of how different the names are. Based on this intuition, we propose the *Temporal Entity Similarity* heuristic:

Temporal Entity Similarity: *In tweets (related to an event), collected sequentially, named entities that occur at the same time period and have a similar context are referring to the same named entity.*

This temporal entity similarity heuristic helps capture the temporal context in which entities are mentioned and clusters entities that occur in a similar context. In figure 2, we present an outline of *EntitySpike* which uses the temporal entity similarity to create an alias list for named entities that spike in popularity in a given time period during an event. To measure the similarity between the named entities, we represent each entity as a vector. To create the vector for each entity, we select all the unique words in the *EntitySpike*, $(\{e_1, s_1\}, \{e_2, s_2\}, ..., \{e_n, s_n\})$ and count the frequency of occurrence of each word in tweets, S_i related to a named entity e_i. Two named entities refer to the same entity if the cosine similarity of their vectors is greater than a threshold.

4 Experiments

4.1 Data

For our experiments, we evaluated *EntitySpike* on the 2013 Grammy Awards Show dataset described

---

Algorithm 1 EntitySpike

Given $\mathbf{X} = (\{e_1, s_1\}, \{e_2, s_2\}, ..., \{e_n, s_n\})$, were $\mathbf{X}$ satisfies the temporal entity similarity heuristic

Output Alias list for e_i

1: **procedure** ENTITYSPIKE($\mathbf{X}$)
2:     **for** each entity e in $\mathbf{X}$ **do**
3:        *create temporal vector, V_e*
4:     **for** each v in $\mathbf{V_{e,...,n}}$ **do**
5:        *Cosine Similarity(v, $V_{e,...,n}$)*
6:        **if** *Cosine Similarity $>$ threshold* **then**
7:          *Insert into Aliaslist(V_e)*
8:     Return Aliaslist(V_e)

Figure 2: Temporal Entity Similarity Algorithm

in Dredze et al. (2016). The show lasted for approximately three and a half hours generating a lot of tweets, most of which made reference to artists, celebrities, and famous people - with entries in Wikipedia, by their names and nicknames (Dredze et al., 2016). To create this dataset, Dredze et al. (2016) used the Twitter streaming API to collect 10,736 temporally ordered and unique tweets written in English containing *grammy* (case insensitive, and including *#grammy*) during the event. Although these tweets were temporally ordered, their timestamps were not saved, hence, we split the dataset into equal size temporal bins (11 bins), with each bin containing 976 temporally ordered tweets. We represented each entity as a vector by collecting the frequency of occurrence of each entity in each bin i.e. each entity was represented as a vector of size 11.

4.2 Baseline

Before carrying out experiments for *EntitySpike*, we conducted preliminary experiments to show that entities that frequently co-occur together should have a high cosine similarity. The intuition here is that entities with a cosine similarity above a threshold could be referring to the same entity. Based on this intuition, we represented each entity as a vector by collecting the frequency of its occurrence in each bin. We calculated the cosine similarity between all of the named entities and ranked them. For each entity, we select the 10 highest ranked similar entities. For evaluation of this algorithm, we selected and labelled 40 named entities and their known aliases in our dataset. On these named entities and their aliases, this algorithm had a precision of *68.25%* and a recall of *43.1%*.

This algorithm shows that some entities that frequently occur in the same context at different time periods are referring to the same entity. We use this algorithm as our baseline.

Word2Vec Experiments: Given a named entity, we used *word2vec* as implemented by Mikolov et al. (2013) to find the top 10 most similar entities to the given entity. We observed that *word2vec* found related words and entities to a given entity, however, it found few entity aliases, some of which are misspelled words and abbreviations. Table 1 shows the top 2 related entities found by *word2vec* for some named entities.

Named Entity	Related Entities
Justin Timberlake	Timberlake, Beyonce
Adam Levine	Maroon 5, Rob Thomas
Taylor Swift	Miley Cyrus, Justin Bieber
JayZ	Music Beats, Young Joc

Table 1: Some named entities and related entities identified by *word2vec*

4.3 *EntitySpike* Experiments

As stated in section 4.1, we split our dataset into 11 equal size bins. In each bin, we calculated the frequency of occurrence of each entity and selected the top u most frequently occuring entities. We chose $u = 15$ because we wanted to compare a relatively small set of entities. We represented each of these entities using the method described in section 3 and calculated the cosine similarity between these entities. We selected an entity as an alias to another entity if they had a cosine similarity greater than a threshold (0.95). We evaluated *EntitySpike* on the named entities that spiked in each of the 11 bins. We labelled the aliases of these spiked entities - that were found in the dataset. We used the algorithm described in section 4.2 as a baseline. Table 2 shows the precision and recall (with respect to the spiked entities and their aliases) of *EntitySpike* and the baseline.

Algorithm	Precision	Recall
EntitySpike	73%	65%
Baseline	65%	69%

Table 2: Precision and recall of *EntitySpike and baseline*

Table 3 shows aliases of the named entities from table 1, that *EntitySpike* identified. It can be seen that *EntitySpike* found more aliases.

Named Entity	Alias
Justin Timberlake	Justin T, Timberlake
Adam Levine	Adam Levin, Adam
Taylor Swift	Taylor S,Taylor
JayZ	Jay Z, Jay-Z

Table 3: Some named entities and their aliases identified by our method

EntitySpike identified entities that spiked in a given time period and created an alias list for these entities. We conducted experiments that varied this time period i.e. we combined bins, and we observed that some spiked entities persisted across bins and combining two adjoining bins gave optimal results.

EntitySpike also identified related words. For each entity that spiked, we used *EntitySpike* to calculate the cosine similarity between them. Two entities were related if they had a cosine similarity above a threshold (0.89). For each spiked entity, we compared the results from this experiment with *word2vec* and *Entity Spike* found some of the related entities in *Word2vec*. For example, it identified that during the show, *Jayz* and *Beyonce* were related and also, *Chris Brown* and *Rihanna*. During the event, some entities were more related than usual; for example, *Jay Z* and *Justin Timberlake* preformed together during the show and a lot of tweets - referring to both of them were generated at this time period. *EntitySpike* was able to identify that these two entities were related at this particular time period. *EntitySpike* also identified some named entities that did not occur in Wikipedia e.g. "Kelly C" for "Kelly Clarkson" and "Rih" for "Rihanna".

5 Conclusion and future work

In conclusion, we proposed an algorithm that creates an alias list for entities that spike. We conducted experiments to show that our algorithm finds most entity aliases by using a temporal heuristic. In the future, we will research using temporal information to detect how relationships between entities change over a period of time.

References

Nicholas Andrews, Jason Eisner, and Mark Dredze. 2014. Robust entity clustering via phylogenetic inference. In *ACL (1)*. pages 775–785.

Anietie Andy, Mugizi Rwebangira, and Satoshi Sekine. 2016a. An entity-based approach to answering recurrent and non-recurrent questions with past answers. *OKBQA 2016* page 39.

Anietie Andy, Satoshi Sekine, Mugizi Rwebangira, and Mark Dredze. 2016b. Name variation in community question answering systems. *WNUT 2016* page 51.

Mark Dredze, Nicholas Andrews, and Jay DeYoung. 2016. Twitter at the grammys: A social media corpus for entity linking and disambiguation. In *Proceedings of the 4th Workshop on Natural Language Processing and Social Media*. pages 20–25.

Stephen Guo, Ming-Wei Chang, and Emre Kiciman. 2013. To link or not to link? a study on end-to-end tweet entity linking. In *HLT-NAACL*. pages 1020–1030.

Xiaohua Liu, Yitong Li, Haocheng Wu, Ming Zhou, Furu Wei, and Yi Lu. 2013. Entity linking for tweets. In *ACL (1)*. pages 1304–1311.

Tomas Mikolov, Kai Chen, Greg Corrado, and Jeffrey Dean. 2013. Efficient estimation of word representations in vector space. *arXiv preprint arXiv:1301.3781* .

Michael J Paul and Mark Dredze. 2011. You are what you tweet: Analyzing twitter for public health. *Icwsm* 20:265–272.

Takeshi Sakaki, Makoto Okazaki, and Yutaka Matsuo. 2010. Earthquake shakes twitter users: real-time event detection by social sensors. In *Proceedings of the 19th international conference on World wide web*. ACM, pages 851–860.

Yusuke Shinyama, Satoshi Sekine, and Kiyoshi Sudo. 2002. Automatic paraphrase acquisition from news articles. In *Proceedings of the second international conference on Human Language Technology Research*. Morgan Kaufmann Publishers Inc., pages 313–318.

Kate Starbird and Leysia Palen. 2012. (how) will the revolution be retweeted?: information diffusion and the 2011 egyptian uprising. In *Proceedings of the acm 2012 conference on computer supported cooperative work*. ACM, pages 7–16.

Andranik Tumasjan, Timm Oliver Sprenger, Philipp G Sandner, and Isabell M Welpe. 2010. Predicting elections with twitter: What 140 characters reveal about political sentiment. *ICWSM* 10(1):178–185.

Incorporating Metadata into Content-Based User Embeddings

Linzi Xing and **Michael J. Paul**
University of Colorado, Boulder, CO 80309
{Linzi.Xing,Michael.J.Paul}@colorado.edu

Abstract

Low-dimensional vector representations of social media users can benefit applications like recommendation systems and user attribute inference. Recent work has shown that user embeddings can be improved by combining different types of information, such as text and network data. We propose a data augmentation method that allows novel feature types to be used within off-the-shelf embedding models. Experimenting with the task of friend recommendation on a dataset of 5,019 Twitter users, we show that our approach can lead to substantial performance gains with the simple addition of network and geographic features.

1 Introduction

A variety of social media tasks benefit from having dense vector representations of users. For example, "who to follow" recommendations can be done by calculating cosine similarity between user vectors. Recent work has experimented with neural embeddings of social media users, most commonly based on text content (Amir et al., 2016; Wan et al., 2016), with some work combining input features from other metadata, including social network information (Li et al., 2015; Benton et al., 2016; Yang et al., 2016).

Since social media like Twitter provide different types of data (e.g., text, network, location), constructing user embeddings with appropriate features can improve the performance based on the target task's requirements. For instance, for recommending tweets a user may be interested in, the user's text content will be a crucial feature. For recommending users to follow, information about the user's current follow graph is likely to be important.

How to efficiently integrate diverse types of features into user representations is a challenge we address in this work. While "multiview" models that combine different feature types have been proposed for user embeddings, there is cost in adapting any particular model to a multiview setting. As an alternative, we propose a simple solution that treats all discrete features as "words," but preprocesses the data in a way that removes word order effects from non-textual features. This approach can be applied to most models of text content, such as the popular *paragraph2vec* model (Le and Mikolov, 2014), allowing diverse features without constructing specialized models.

Our primary contributions are as follows:

- We describe a preprocessing step that allows the inclusion of non-textual discrete features (e.g., followers, locations) into off-the-shelf text embedding methods. Our method is easy to use, requiring no special implementation.

- We introduce a novel type of feature for user embeddings—the geographic locations of users' friends—and show that this improves performance over standard text and network features on a new Twitter dataset.

- We find that jointly modeling all types of features improves performance over combining independent models of different feature sets, offering evidence that there are informative interactions between text content and metadata, and demonstrating that simply combining independent models is insufficient.

2 Previous Work

A number of recent studies have proposed models for constructing social media user embeddings.

Proceedings of the 3rd Workshop on Noisy User-generated Text, pages 45–49
Copenhagen, Denmark, September 7, 2017. ©2017 Association for Computational Linguistics

Amir et al. (2016) generated user embeddings capture users' individual word usage patterns with a model similar to paragraph2vec. In this method, only users' tweets are taken into account. Wan et al. (2016) proposed two neural network models, also based on paragraph2vec, to obtain users' vector representations from word representations obtained previously. Since their task was recommending tweets to users, only text was considered to construct user embeddings.

Other work has considered multiple types of features, or "views." Benton et al. (2016) proposed an approach based on Weighted Generalized Canonical Correlation Analysis (WGCCA) to turn several aspects of user information into low-dimensional vectors, including tweets and social network information. Before applying the WGCCA model, each type of information is first converted into an appropriate vector representation. Yang et al. (2016) considered text, social relationships and mentioned entities as features for user embeddings. This work used different models for learning each feature type. While trained separately, once a representation was learned for each feature type, a final user representation was learned with a composition model that included additional parameters to learn interactions between feature types. Li et al. (2015) proposed a similar approach, which uses different models for different types of user information, which are then linearly combined into a full model. During training, the parameters are learned jointly.

The multiview models above all used different view-specific models to capture the feature types. In contrast, we use a simple input representation that can be plugged into a single model.

3   Social Media Dataset

To motivate our methods, we will first describe our dataset of over 5,000 Twitter users. We randomly sampled users who follow American universities. Specifically, we collected the usernames of up to 5,000 followers of 25 universities (the top 25 undergraduate programs ranked by US News). Among the 5,000 followers of each university, we randomly sampled 400 users, for a total of 10,000 users. After removing accounts that were private or non-English (according to the tweet `lang` attribute), we were left with 5,019 users.

From each user, we collected their 200 most recent tweets (collected January 2017), as well as the usernames and locations of up to 100 followees by collecting the profiles of 100 randomly sampled accounts that are followed by the user. Our dataset contained an average of 155.4 tweets per user (with an average of 6.7 tokens per tweet, after pre-processing), and an average of 91.9 followees per user (with an average of 32.0 followees for whom we resolved a location).

3.1   Types of Metadata

In this work, we will train embeddings using two types of features in addition to the tweet content of each user: the **users** they follow, and the geographic **locations** of the users they follow. These features were selected to support our experimental task of friend recommendation (Section 5).

The motivation for the first type of feature is that if two users' followee lists have substantial overlap, then it indicates they are more likely to have a connection. We implement this by including the usernames of the accounts that each user follows.

The motivation for the second type of feature, with which we opted to use the locations of each user's followees rather than the the user's own location, is perhaps less obvious. First, this attribute is sparse (fewer than half of the users had a valid location), so including their followees' locations provides more information. Second, in many cases, friends' locations may be a more informative predictor of relationships. For example, suppose Users A, B, and C live in Kansas. Many of A and B's friends are located in California, but most C's friends are from New York. In this scenario, A and B may be more likely to have a relationship than C, while if we only used the users' own locations, then location would not differentiate them.

To extract high-precision locations, we extracted only locations from user profiles of the form "City, State", where the state had to match a dictionary of US states. We used the dictionary to rewrite state names in a canonical form (e.g., "California" $\rightarrow$ "CA").

4   User Embedding Model

This work uses paragraph2vec (Le and Mikolov, 2014) as our content embedding model. This is an unsupervised model that encodes text sequences (canonically, paragraphs) as low-dimensional vectors. The model is related to word2vec (Mikolov et al., 2013), with a modification that each paragraph is given a unique paragraph token at the be-

Figure 1: We augment text features by concatenating each user's input string with username and location features, padded with "dummy" tokens to prevent word order effects for non-textual features. Since each token's probability in paragraph2vec depends on the k tokens before and k tokens after it, we separate the username and location tokens with k dummy 'USR' and 'LOC' tokens so that no usernames or locations will appear in the same window.

ginning, which is treated like other tokens in the paragraph to help predict words. The result is a vector for each paragraph, in addition to the word vectors for each word. In our setting, we treat each user's concatenated stream of tweets as a single "paragraph" and apply the model as is. The training objective for each user u under this model is:

$$\frac{1}{M} \sum_{i=1}^{M} \log P(w_i | u, w_{i-k}, \cdots, w_{i+k}) \quad (1)$$

where M is the number of tokens in the user stream and k is the window size. u is the vector representation of the "paragraph" token that uniquely corresponds to the user, and w are the word tokens in the tweet stream.

4.1 Incorporating Metadata

We propose to add additional metadata features by simply appending the text sequences (the user tweet streams) with additional tokens for each username and each location string, representing the features described in Section 3.1. However, doing this naively will not work as intended, because the order of the word tokens within each window affects the probabilities, which is not appropriate for features that have no ordering.

To address this, we format the text such that two metadata features never appear within the same window. We pad the features with "dummy" tokens that appear before and after each username ('USR') or location ('LOC'). There are $2 \times k$ dummy tokens in between each feature, where k is the window size, as illustrated in Figure 1.

A side effect of this approach is that there will be redundant metadata features from different window positions that will always co-occur (e.g., "LOC Seattle LOC" and "LOC LOC Seattle"). This creates colinearity in the model, but this does not diminish the predictive performance, nor is this unusual when applying machine learning to text (e.g., including different length n-grams).

5 Experiments

To evaluate our proposed approach, we experiment with different vector representations of our dataset for the task of friend recommendation (Liben-Nowell and Kleinberg, 2007; Lo and Lin, 2006; Backstrom and Leskovec, 2011).

5.1 Implementation Details

We preprocessed the text to remove punctuation, stop words, hyperlinks, and usernames. All tweets were concatenated into one string. Additional features were concatenated to the same string using the padding procedure described in Section 4.1.

We used the paragraph2vec implementation from the Python package, Gensim (Řehůřek and Sojka, 2010), called `doc2vec`. The window size and vector dimensionality were set to 3 and 100.

5.2 Experimental Design

For friend recommendation, we calculate the cosine similarity between all pairs of users based on their vector representation. For each user, we select the top k users with the highest similarity. Using the user's followee list as ground truth, we measure the precision, recall, and mean reciprocal rank for k in $\{10, 20, 30, 40, 50\}$.

Similar to the design of (Benton et al., 2016), we used the most popular accounts as our test set. Specifically, we selected 58 users who were followed by more than 50 users in our dataset for evaluation. These users were excluded when generating the username features described in 3.1.

We experimented with our paragraph2vec-based embedding models with different feature sets. We consider the model with only text features to be our primary baseline, which we compare against models that add username features as well as both username and location features.

For our full model with all three feature types, we compared three different approaches for combining the features. In addition to training a single paragraph2vec model on all features jointly, as we

	k = 10			k = 20			k = 30			k = 40			k = 50		
	P	R	MRR	P	R	MRR	P	R	MRR	P	R	MRR	P	R	MRR
Random	.022	.003	.056	.030	.010	.070	.046	.014	.083	.029	.019	.052	.021	.018	.053
TF-IDF	.174	**0.019**	.192	.160	.033	.152	.137	.039	**0.131**	.120	.046	**0.118**	.110	.051	.104
Text only (T)	.133	.013	.205	.121	.027	.159	.116	.033	.127	.111	.042	.116	.108	.051	.104
Text+Users (T+U)	.168	.016	.210	.158	.031	.166	.148	.042	.129	.140	.053	.108	.135	.065	.108
T+U+L (Addition)	.131	.013	.135	.121	.027	.123	.131	.038	.092	.115	.042	.087	.120	.057	.077
T+U+L (Concat.)	.150	.014	.160	.146	.031	.112	.132	.038	.110	.128	.050	.088	.121	.061	.078
T+U+L (Joint)	**.193**†‡	**.019**†	**.227**‡	**.171**†‡	**.033**†	**.174**‡	**.162**†‡	**.046**†	.120‡	**.153**†‡*	**.059**†*	.114†‡	**.150**†‡*	**.071**†‡*	**.110**†‡
T+U+L (No padding)	.165	.015	.203	.159	.029	.160	.150	.042	.115	.146	.052	.105	.138	.064	.102

Table 1: Overview of results with precision (P), recall (R), and mean reciprocal rank (MRR) at k. This compares our non-embedding baselines with our embedding model using various feature sets: text only (T), text and usernames (T+U), and text with usernames and locations (T+U+L), either jointly modeled or independently combined by addition or concatenation. Markers indicate if the results of our joint T+U+L model are significantly different ($p<0.05$) from the text only ($\dagger$), concatenated T+U+L ($\ddagger$), or TF-IDF ($*$) models.

proposed in Section 4.1, we also trained three separate paragraph2vec models on the three feature types and then combined them, by adding the vectors in one version and by concatenating the three vectors in another. Since some prior work trained independent models for different views (Section 2), it is important to understand how joint versus independent training affects performance.

To understand the importance of padding the metadata features with dummy tokens, we also measured the performance of the full joint model without using extra tokens, labeled as "No padding" in the table.

Finally, we add two other baselines to put our results in context. First is a random baseline that randomly chooses k users in the ranking, which gives an approximate lower bound on performance. Second, we compare to a high-dimensional bag-of-words representation of text with TF-IDF weighting.

We measured the statistical significance of the results using a paired t-test to compare our full model to the baselines with close performance.

5.3 Results and Discussion

Results are shown in Table 1. The full joint model outperforms all others at precision and recall in all cases, and at MRR in a majority of cases.

There is a substantial improvement in the embedding model using all three feature types compared to the model using only text. The differences in precision and recall are highly significant, with p-values <0.001 in all cases. This demonstrates that our proposed features are useful for friend recommendation, and that our simple method for encoding them is effective. We also find that train-

ing a representation using all three feature types jointly gives significantly better performance than combining independently trained representations. Finally, we find that metadata features do improve performance even without padding, but not as well as when using padding.

While our full model outperformed the TF-IDF baseline in most cases, most differences were not significant, and the TF-IDF baseline outperformed the paragraph2vec model using only text. We believe the strong performance of TF-IDF relative to the paragraph2vec representations may be due to the fairly small size of our dataset. Since our goal was to investigate how to improve the quality of embeddings, we primarily focus on the comparison other embedding models rather than TF-IDF, but we present these results to show how the different representation types compare on this dataset.

6 Conclusion

We have described and evaluated a simple method for adding non-textual discrete features into a text embedding model for constructing embeddings of social media users. We constructed a novel geographic feature—the locations of a user's friends—and showed that the addition of network and geographic features significantly improves precision and recall over a text-only baseline up to 0.06 and 0.02, respectively. We also showed that including all feature types in one model leads to significantly better performance than combining independently trained models of different features. Our approach is based on modifying the input rather than the model, therefore requiring no special implementation and can be easily adapted to other embedding models or feature types.

References

Silvio Amir, Byron C. Wallace, Hao Lyu, Paula Carvalho, and Mario J. Silva. 2016. Modelling context with user embeddings for sarcasm detection in social media. arXiv preprint arXiv:1607.00976.

Lars Backstrom and Jure Leskovec. 2011. Supervised random walks: Predicting and recommending links in social networks. In *Fourth ACM International Conference on Web Search and Data Mining (WSDM)*.

Adrian Benton, Raman Arora, and Mark Dredze. 2016. Learning multiview embeddings of twitter users. Proceedings of the 54th Annual Meeting of the Association for Computational Linguistics, pages 14–19.

Quoc V. Le and Tomas Mikolov. 2014. Distributed representations of sentences and documents. Proceedings of The 31st International Conference on Machine Learning, pages 1188–1196.

Jiwei Li, Alan Ritter, and Dan Jurafsky. 2015. Learning multi-faceted representations of individuals from heterogeneous evidence using neural networks. arXiv preprint arXiv: 1510.05198.

David Liben-Nowell and Jon Kleinberg. 2007. The link-prediction problem for social networks. *Journal of the American Society for Information Science and Technology* 58(7):1019–1031.

Shuchuan Lo and Chingching Lin. 2006. WMR– a graph-based algorithm for friend recommendation. In *IEEE/WIC/ACM International Conference on Web Intelligence*.

Tomas Mikolov, Ilya Sutskever, Kai Chen, Greg Corrado, and Jeff Dean. 2013. Distributed representations of words and phrases and their compositionality. Advances in neural information processing systems, pages 3111–3119.

Radim Řehůřek and Petr Sojka. 2010. Software Framework for Topic Modelling with Large Corpora. In *Proceedings of the LREC 2010 Workshop on New Challenges for NLP Frameworks*. pages 45–50.

Xiaojun Wan, Yang Yu, and Xinjie Zhou. 2016. User embedding for scholarly microblog recommendation. Proceedings of the 54th Annual Meeting of the Association for Computational Linguistics, pages 449–453.

Yi Yang, Ming-Wei Chang, and Jacob Eisenstein. 2016. Toward socially-infused information extraction: Embedding authors, mentions, and entities. Proceedings of the 2016 Conference on Empirical Methods in Natural Language Processing, pages 1452–1461.

Simple Queries as Distant Labels for Predicting Gender on Twitter

Chris Emmery[1,2] and **Grzegorz Chrupała**[1] and **Walter Daelemans**[2]
[1]TiCC, Tilburg University, 5000 LE Tilburg, The Netherlands
[2]CLiPS, University of Antwerp, Prinsstraat 13, B-2000 Antwerpen, Belgium
`{c.d.emmery, g.a.chrupala}@uvt.nl`
`walter.daelemans@uantwerpen.be`

Abstract

The majority of research on extracting missing user attributes from social media profiles use costly hand-annotated labels for supervised learning. Distantly supervised methods exist, although these generally rely on knowledge gathered using external sources. This paper demonstrates the effectiveness of gathering distant labels for self-reported gender on Twitter using simple queries. We confirm the reliability of this query heuristic by comparing with manual annotation. Moreover, using these labels for distant supervision, we demonstrate competitive model performance on the same data as models trained on manual annotations. As such, we offer a cheap, extensible, and fast alternative that can be employed beyond the task of gender classification.

1 Introduction

The popularity of social media that rely on rich self-representation of users (e.g. Facebook, LinkedIn) make them a valuable resource for conducting research based on demographic information. However, the volume of personal information users provide on such platforms is generally restricted to their personal connections only, and therefore off-limits for scientific research. Twitter, on the other hand, allows only a restricted amount of structured personal information by design. As a result, their users tend to connect with people outside of their social circle more frequently, making many profiles and communication publicly accessible. A wide variety of research has long picked up on the interesting characteristics of this microblogging service, which is well facilitated by the Twitter REST API.

The applied Natural Language Processing (NLP) domain of author profiling aims to infer unknown user attributes, and is therefore broadly used to compensate for the lack thereof on Twitter. While previous research has already proven to be quite effective at this task using predictive models trained on manual annotations, the process of hand-labelling profiles is costly. Even for the ostensibly straight-forward task of annotating gender, a large portion of Twitter users purposefully avoids providing simple indicators such as real names or profile photos including a face. Consequently, this forces annotators to either dive deep into the user's timeline in search for linguistic cues, or to make decisions based on some personal interpretation, for which they have shown to often incorrectly apply stereotypical biases (Nguyen et al., 2014; Flekova et al., 2016).

We show that running a small collection of ad-hoc queries for self-reports of gender once ("I'm a male, female, man, woman" etc.) — provides distant labels for 6,610 profiles with high confidence in one week worth of data. Employing these for distant supervision, we demonstrate them to be an accurate signal for gender classification, and form a reliable, cheap method that has competitive performance with models trained on costly human-labelled profiles. Our contributions are as follows:

- We demonstrate a simple, extensible method for gathering self-reports on Twitter, that competes with expensive manual annotation.

- We publish the IDs, manual annotations, as well as the distant labels for 6.6K Twitter profiles, spanning 16.8M tweets.

The data, labels, and our code to collect more data and reproduce the experiments is made available open-source at `https://github.com/cmry/simple-queries`.

50

Proceedings of the 3rd Workshop on Noisy User-generated Text, pages 50–55
Copenhagen, Denmark, September 7, 2017. ©2017 Association for Computational Linguistics

2   Related Work

Author profiling applies machine learning to linguistic features within a piece of writing to make inferences regarding its author. The ability to make such inferences was first discussed for gender by Koppel et al. (2002), and initially applied to blogs (Argamon et al., 2007; Rosenthal and McKeown, 2011; Nguyen et al., 2011). Later, the work extended to social media — encompassing a wide variety of attributes such as gender, age, personality, location, education, income, religion, and political polarity (Eisenstein et al., 2011; Alowibdi et al., 2013; Volkova et al., 2014; Plank and Hovy, 2015; Volkova and Bachrach, 2016). Apart from relevancy in marketing, security and forensics, author profiling has shown to positively influence several text classification tasks (Hovy, 2015).

Gender profiling research on Twitter generally takes a data-driven, open-vocabulary approach using bag of words, or bag of n-gram features (Alowibdi et al., 2013; Ciot et al., 2013; Verhoeven et al., 2016), applying supervised classification using manually annotated profiles. However, distant supervision has as of yet only looked at non-textual cues for this task, unlike for example age, personality, and mental health (e.g. Al Zamal et al., 2012; Plank and Hovy, 2015; Coppersmith et al., 2015). For gender, Burger et al. (2011) and Li et al. (2014) collect links to external profiles, whereas Al Zamal et al. (2012) and Li et al. (2015) use a list with gender-associated names. Both of these approaches rely on continuous monitoring of streaming data, and utilize indicators that are typically easy cues for annotators, thereby omitting profiles that would be costly to annotate. In contrast, our method only has to be repeated once a week, and includes a different set of users where sampling is not influenced by external resources.

3   Data Collection

To empirically compare distant labels (i.e. obtained using heuristics) with manual annotations, we require both data containing self-reports, and corpora with hand-labelled Twitter profiles for comparison.

Distant Labels   The profiles in our corpus were collected on March 6th, 2017 — using the Twitter Search API[1] to query for messages self-

filter	N hand	F	F+R
none	1,456	.806	.806
rt	1,109	.873	.887
rt + "	1,059	.882	.896
rt + :	1,091	.887	.891
rt + " + :	1,045	.885	**.900**

Table 1: Several filter rules applied to the distant labels (effectively removing those matching the rules), their impact on both data reduction (N hand-labelled) and agreement increase. Agreement is specified for: only applying these filters (F), and in combination with the rules from Table 2 (F+R), and reflects the amount of correct distant labels compared to the manual labels.

reporting gender: e.g. {I' / I a}m a {man, woman, male, female, boy, girl, guy, dude, gal}. For each retrieved tweet, the timeline of the associated author was collected (up to 3,200 tweets) between Match 6th and 8th. Note that the maximum retrieval history for the Search API is limited to tweets from the past week. Hence, our set of queries collected 19,307 profiles spanning results for one week only.

This method has some inherent advantages in addition to the ones mentioned in Section 2: it guarantees to a large extent that the profiles gathered are primarily English (95% of all associated tweets), collects data from active users (average of 2,500 tweets per timeline), and generally avoids bots, or other spam profiles (0,2%[2] of all profiles). Finally, with gender profiling being considered a binary male/female classification task for much of the previous research and corpora, it also prevents including users that might not identify with the binary framework in which gender is typically cast.[3]

Manual Evaluation   To evaluate the accuracy of our distant labels, a random sub-sample was manually labelled for gender by two annotators using a full profile view ($\kappa = 0.78$), resulting in 1,456 agreed on labels. Based on the initial results (see Table 1), several rules were constructed to filter (thereby removing) any profiles the query tweet matched to. First, we observed that many tweets (31%) contained rt — indicating a retweet. Similar to tweets containing quotes (5%), or colons

---

[1]https://dev.twitter.com/rest/public/search

[2]Bots were identified during annotation.

[3]Accordingly, this method could be applied in future research tackling this long-standing issue by collecting and using self-reported non-binary representations of gender.

Location	Rule set
anywhere	according to, deep down
before query	feel like, where, (as) if, hoping, assume(s/d) (that), think, expect (that), then, (that) means, implying, guess, think(s), tells me

Table 2: Rules applied to the distant labels to flip the assumed gender. Their location can be *anywhere* in the tweet, or right *before* the *query* (e.g. "Sometimes I think I'm a girl").

	Volkova	Plank	Query
users	4,620	1,391	6,610
tweets	12,226,859	3,568,265	16,788,612
female	32,367	10,613	61,736
male	26,708	6,739	32,900
train	47,298	13,827	75,918
test	11,777	3,525	18,718

Table 3: Various metrics of the Twitter corpora annotated with gender used in this research. The train and test sizes reflect the amount of batches of 200 tweets.

(2%), these are generally not self-reports (e.g. "random guy: I'm a man... "), and were therefore removed. Overall, the filters increased agreement with our manual annotations, simultaneously causing a decrease to 6,610 profiles. This method however ensures a high accuracy of the distant labels, which should outweigh the amount of data.

In addition to these filters, several rules were constructed to deal with linguistic cues that make it highly likely for the gender to be the opposite of the literal report (see Table 2) — thus indicating the label should be flipped. Examples include "according to the Internet, I'm a girl", and "Don't just assume I'm a guy". For a detailed overview of their effect on the overall agreement, see F+R in Table 1. The ad-hoc list presented here improved agreement about .015. Note that despite being constructed by manual inspection of the mismatches between annotations and the distant labels, our filters, rules, and even the initial query can be extended with some creativity.

Preparation To compare our distant labels to annotated alternatives, we include Volkova et al. (2014)'s crowd-sourced corpus, and the manually labelled corpus by Plank and Hovy (2015). Henceforth, these external corpora will be referred to as Volkova and Plank respectively. The timelines of their provided user IDs where gathered between April 1st and 7th 2017 (see Table 3 for further details on their sizes).

The timelines for all corpora—including our Query corpus—were divided in batches of 200 tweets, as most related work follows this setup. Afterwards, each batch is provided with either a distant, or manual label, depending on the set of origin. This implies that users with less than 200 tweets were excluded, as well as any consecutive tweets that would not exactly fit into a batch of 200. The corpora were divided between a (gender

stratified) train and a test set by user ID. This guarantees that there is no bleed of batches from any user between any of the splits (refer to Table 3 for the final split sizes). Other than tokenisation using spaCy (Honnibal and Johnson, 2015), no special preprocessing steps were taken. We removed primarily non-English batches using langdetect[4] (Shuyo, 2010), as well as the original query tweets containing self-reports. The latter was done to avoid our queries being most characteristic for some batches.

4 Experiment

For document classification, fastText[5] (Joulin et al., 2016) was employed; a simple linear model with one hidden embedding layer that learns sentence representations using bag of words or n-gram input, producing a probability distribution over the given classes using the softmax function. It therefore follows the same architecture as the continuous bag of words model from Mikolov et al. (2013), replacing the middle word with a label. Joulin et al. (2016) demonstrate the model performs well on both sentiment and tag prediction tasks, significantly speeding up training and test time compared to several recent models.

Gender predictions were made using a typical set of n-gram features as input; token uni-grams and bi-grams, and character tri-grams. We incorporate only those grams that occur more than three times during training. As the corpora are quite small, we use embeddings with only 30 dimensions, a learning rate of 0.1, and a bucket size of 1M. All models are trained for 10 epochs. Given that fastText uses Hogwild (Recht et al., 2011)

---

[4] https://github.com/Mimino666/langdetect
[5] https://github.com/facebookresearch/fastText

		Majority	Lexicon	Train		
				Volkova	**Plank**	**Query**
Test	Volkova	.556	.796	**.822** (0.001)	.701 (0.007)	.771 (0.007)
	Plank	.659	.740	**.741** (0.005)	.723 (0.003)	.724 (0.009)
	Query	.674	.668	.730 (0.007)	.689 (0.005)	**.756** (0.002)
	Average	.630	.735	.764	.704	.750

Table 4: Individual accuracy scores and averages for majority baseline (Majority), the lexicon of Sap et al. (2014), and the three models (trained on Volkova, Plank, and our dataset respectively) evaluated on the test set for each corpus. Standard deviation is reported after repeating the same experiment 20 times.

for parallelising Stochastic Gradient Descent, randomness in the vector representations cannot be controlled using a seed. To estimate the standard deviation in the results, we ran each experiment 20 times. To evaluate how our distantly supervised model compares to using manual annotations, we trained all models in this same configuration for all three corpora. Each model was then evaluated on the test set for each corpus.

5 Results

Table 4 shows accuracy scores for this 3x3 experimental design, as well as a majority baseline score (always predicting female), and an average over the three test sets for each model. We closely reproduced the results from Volkova and Bachrach (2016); despite the difference in user[6] and tweet samples, exact split order, and their use of more features including style and part-of-speech tags, our performance approaches their reported .84 accuracy score. Plank and Hovy (2015) do not provide classification results for gender on their data. For comparison to state-of-the-art gender classification for English, the lexicon of Sap et al. (2014) is included in the results. Their work also compares with Volkova et al. (2014), and reports a higher score (.90) for their random sample setup than reproduced in our batch evaluation (.80).

Despite the fact that the model trained on the Volkova corpus performs best on both annotated corpora (Volkova and Plank), the difference is fairly small compared to our distantly supervised model — the latter of which somewhat expectedly performs best on its associated test set. On average, the Query and Volkova trained models only differ .014 in accuracy score, and the Query model outperforms the lexicon approach by .015. However, the more significant comparison is the out of sample performance for these two models and

the lexicon model on the Plank test set. Here, results are comparable between Query and Volkova, with a .017 difference, and higher standard deviation. However, here the lexicon approach outperforms the Query model with .016. Not only does this show our distant labels to be be comparable with hand labels, our models also seems to yield favourable performance over state of the art.

6 Conclusion

We use simple queries for self-reports to train a gender classifier for Twitter that has competitive performance to those trained on costly hand-annotated labels — showing minimal differences. These should be considered in light of the manual effort put into gathering the annotations, however. Labelling Twitter users with our set of queries yields up to 45,000 hits per 15 minutes (API rate limits considered), and therefore finishes in several minutes. Retrieving the timelines for the initial 19,307 users took roughly 21 hours. Including preprocessing (3 hours) and running `fastText` (a few minutes) the entire pipeline is encouragingly cheap, even considering time, and can feasibly be repeated on a weekly basis.

Hence, through manual analysis, as well as experimental evidence, we demonstrate our distantly supervised method to be a reliable and cheap alternative. Moreover, we pose several ways of improving this method by extending the queries, and further fine-tuning the applied filters and rules for a correct interpretation of the reports. By altering the queries to match other types of self-reports, it offers the possibility of quickly exploring its effectiveness for inferring other user attributes with little effort. We hope to facilitate this for the research community by providing our implementation. Our further work will focus on intelligently expanding the queries and evaluating this method on a larger scale with more attributes.

---

[6]We could only retrieve 4,620 of the reported 4,998.

References

Faiyaz Al Zamal, Wendy Liu, and Derek Ruths. 2012. Homophily and latent attribute inference: Inferring latent attributes of twitter users from neighbors. *ICWSM* 270.

Jalal S Alowibdi, Ugo A Buy, and Philip Yu. 2013. Empirical evaluation of profile characteristics for gender classification on twitter. In *Machine Learning and Applications (ICMLA), 2013 12th International Conference on*. IEEE, volume 1, pages 365–369.

Shlomo Argamon, Moshe Koppel, James W Pennebaker, and Jonathan Schler. 2007. Mining the blogosphere: Age, gender and the varieties of self-expression. *First Monday* 12(9).

John D Burger, John Henderson, George Kim, and Guido Zarrella. 2011. Discriminating gender on twitter. In *Proceedings of the Conference on Empirical Methods in Natural Language Processing*. Association for Computational Linguistics, pages 1301–1309.

Morgane Ciot, Morgan Sonderegger, and Derek Ruths. 2013. Gender inference of twitter users in non-english contexts. In *EMNLP*. pages 1136–1145.

Glen Coppersmith, Mark Dredze, Craig Harman, and Kristy Hollingshead. 2015. From adhd to sad: Analyzing the language of mental health on twitter through self-reported diagnoses. *NAACL HLT 2015* page 1.

Jacob Eisenstein, Noah A Smith, and Eric P Xing. 2011. Discovering sociolinguistic associations with structured sparsity. In *Proceedings of the 49th Annual Meeting of the Association for Computational Linguistics: Human Language Technologies-Volume 1*. Association for Computational Linguistics, pages 1365–1374.

Lucie Flekova, Jordan Carpenter, Salvatore Giorgi, Lyle Ungar, and Daniel Preotiuc-Pietro. 2016. Analyzing biases in human perception of user age and gender from text. In *Proceedings of the 54th Annual Meeting of the Association for Computational Linguistics, ACL*. pages 843–854.

Matthew Honnibal and Mark Johnson. 2015. An improved non-monotonic transition system for dependency parsing. In *Proceedings of the 2015 Conference on Empirical Methods in Natural Language Processing*. Association for Computational Linguistics, Lisbon, Portugal, pages 1373–1378.

Dirk Hovy. 2015. Demographic factors improve classification performance. In *ACL*. pages 752–762.

Armand Joulin, Edouard Grave, Piotr Bojanowski, and Tomas Mikolov. 2016. Bag of tricks for efficient text classification. *arXiv preprint arXiv:1607.01759* .

Moshe Koppel, Shlomo Argamon, and Anat Rachel Shimoni. 2002. Automatically categorizing written texts by author gender. *Literary and Linguistic Computing* 17(4):401–412.

Jiwei Li, Alan Ritter, and Eduard H Hovy. 2014. Weakly supervised user profile extraction from twitter. In *ACL (1)*. pages 165–174.

Jiwei Li, Alan Ritter, and Dan Jurafsky. 2015. Learning multi-faceted representations of individuals from heterogeneous evidence using neural networks. *arXiv preprint arXiv:1510.05198* .

Tomas Mikolov, Kai Chen, Greg Corrado, and Jeffrey Dean. 2013. Efficient estimation of word representations in vector space. *arXiv preprint arXiv:1301.3781* .

Dong Nguyen, Noah A Smith, and Carolyn P Rosé. 2011. Author age prediction from text using linear regression. In *Proceedings of the 5th ACL-HLT Workshop on Language Technology for Cultural Heritage, Social Sciences, and Humanities*. Association for Computational Linguistics, pages 115–123.

Dong-Phuong Nguyen, RB Trieschnigg, A Seza Doğruöz, Rilana Gravel, Mariët Theune, Theo Meder, and FMG de Jong. 2014. Why gender and age prediction from tweets is hard: Lessons from a crowdsourcing experiment. Association for Computational Linguistics.

Barbara Plank and Dirk Hovy. 2015. Personality traits on twitter—or—how to get 1,500 personality tests in a week. In *Proceedings of the 6th Workshop on Computational Approaches to Subjectivity, Sentiment and Social Media Analysis*. pages 92–98.

Benjamin Recht, Christopher Re, Stephen Wright, and Feng Niu. 2011. Hogwild: A lock-free approach to parallelizing stochastic gradient descent. In *Advances in Neural Information Processing Systems*. pages 693–701.

Sara Rosenthal and Kathleen McKeown. 2011. Age prediction in blogs: A study of style, content, and online behavior in pre-and post-social media generations. In *Proceedings of the 49th Annual Meeting of the Association for Computational Linguistics: Human Language Technologies-Volume 1*. Association for Computational Linguistics, pages 763–772.

Maarten Sap, Gregory Park, Johannes C Eichstaedt, Margaret L Kern, David Stillwell, Michal Kosinski, Lyle H Ungar, and H Andrew Schwartz. 2014. Developing age and gender predictive lexica over social media .

Nakatani Shuyo. 2010. Language detection library for java. *Retrieved Jul* 7:2016.

Ben Verhoeven, Walter Daelemans, and Barbara Plank. 2016. Twisty: a multilingual twitter stylometry corpus for gender and personality profiling. In *Proceedings of the 10th Annual Conference on Language Resources and Evaluation (LREC 2016)*. ELRA, ELRA, Portorož, Slovenia.

Svitlana Volkova and Yoram Bachrach. 2016. Inferring perceived demographics from user emotional tone and user-environment emotional contrast. In *Proceedings of the 54th Annual Meeting of the Association for Computational Linguistics, ACL*.

Svitlana Volkova, Glen Coppersmith, and Benjamin Van Durme. 2014. Inferring user political preferences from streaming communications. In *ACL (1)*. pages 186–196.

A Dataset and Classifier for Recognizing Social Media English

Su Lin Blodgett[*] **Johnny Tian-Zheng Wei**[†] **Brendan O'Connor**[*]

University of Massachusetts Amherst, Amherst, MA

[*]{blodgett, brenocon@cs.umass.edu} [†]jwei@umass.edu

Abstract

While language identification works well on standard texts, it performs much worse on social media language, in particular dialectal language—even for English. First, to support work on English language identification, we contribute a new dataset of tweets annotated for English versus non-English, with attention to ambiguity, code-switching, and automatic generation issues. It is randomly sampled from all public messages, avoiding biases towards pre-existing language classifiers. Second, we find that a demographic language model—which identifies messages with language similar to that used by several U.S. ethnic populations on Twitter—can be used to improve English language identification performance when combined with a traditional supervised language identifier. It increases recall with almost no loss of precision, including, surprisingly, for English messages written by non-U.S. authors.

Our dataset and identifier ensemble are available online.[1]

1 Introduction and Related Work

Language identification is the task of determining the major world language a document is written in. A range of supervised classification methods—often based on character n-gram features—achieve excellent performance for this problem on long, monolingual documents (Hughes et al., 2006). But short documents are much more challenging, such as Twitter messages (Lui and Baldwin, 2012, 2014; Bergsma et al., 2012; Williams and Dagli, 2017).

Compounding the challenge is domain mismatch: the types of casual language, dialectal language, and Internet-specific constructs found in social media are often not present in the standardized genres of training data for existing language identifiers. This is potentially especially problematic for language by minority dialect speakers—for example, Blodgett et al. (2016) found that current language identification models had lower recall for tweets written in African-American English (AAE) than those in standard English. This is not surprising given the domain mismatch—a survey of recent language identifiers shows that common sources of training data are Wikipedia, newswire (e.g. the Leipzig corpora), and government and legal documents such as EuroGov, EuroParl, or the Universal Declaration of Human Rights (Lui and Baldwin, 2012; King and Abney, 2013; Jaech et al., 2016; Kocmi and Bojar, 2017; Lui and Cook, 2013).

A language identification system typically aims to classify messages as one of a few hundred major world languages, which are generally well-resourced mainstream language varieties with officially recognized status by major political entities; these language varieties typically have official ISO 639 codes assigned to them (which are returned by language identification software APIs).[2] Given the high linguistic diversity of messages in social media, it is tempting to imagine fine-grained dialect identification (for example, identifying messages written in AAE), but at the same time, the traditional task of identifying major world languages will continue to be useful (for example, an AAE message could be reasonably analyzed with general English language technologies). In this work we maintain the paradigm of treating English as a broad language category, but propose that the texts

---

[1]http://slanglab.cs.umass.edu/TwitterLangID

[2]For example, langid.py, CLD2, Microsoft Azure, IBM Watson, and Google Translation API all offer ISO-returning language identification software or services.

56

Proceedings of the 3rd Workshop on Noisy User-generated Text, pages 56–61
Copenhagen, Denmark, September 7, 2017. ©2017 Association for Computational Linguistics

that match it ought to be broadened to include non-standard, social media, and dialectal varieties of English.

If there was abundant language-annotated Twitter data, it would be straightforward to train an in-domain language identifier. But very little exists, since it is inherently time-consuming and expensive to annotate. Datasets are typically small, or semi-automatically tagged (Bergsma et al., 2012), which may bias them towards pre-existing standardized language.

A promising approach is to leverage large quantities of non-language-labeled tweets to help adapt a standard identifier to perform better on social media. If the messages are treated as unlabeled, this could be framed as unsupervised domain adaptation problem, for which a number of approaches are available (Blitzer et al., 2006, 2007; Plank, 2009; Yang and Eisenstein, 2016).

We focus on a unique, and different, large-scale training signal—U.S. neighborhood-level demographics. There is considerable linguistic diversity within the U.S., and its geographic patterns have some rough correlation with different ethnic and race populations. Blodgett et al. analyzed them with a mixed membership model—for which messages written by authors living in areas heavy in a particular demographic group were more likely to use a unigram language model associated with that group—in order to focus on AAE. But they note their model found that non-English language tended to gravitate towards one of the latent language models, which was useful to better identify English spoken within the U.S. that a standard identifier missed.

We hypothesize that this generalizes beyond specific dialect populations within the U.S., testing whether this soft signal from the demographic model actually gives a better model of overall social media English. We evaluate as fairly and completely as possible; we first annotate a new dataset of uniformly sampled tweets for whether they are English versus non-English (§2). In §3, we apply Blodgett et al.'s model to infer U.S. demographic language proportions in new tweets, finding that when added as an ensemble to a pre-existing identifier, performance improves—including when paired with feature-based, neural network, and proprietary identifiers. Such ensembles perform better than in-domain training with the largest available annotated Twitter dataset, and also better than a self-training domain adaptation

Label	Full Count	Evaluation Count
English	5086	3758
Not English	4646	4608
Ambiguous	770	0
Total	10502	8366

Table 1: Dataset statistics for each language label; the evaluation count refers to the subset used for evaluation.

Label	Count
Code-Switched	162
Ambiguous due to Named Entities	132
Automatically Generated	1371

Table 2: Dataset statistics for additional labels.

approach on the same dataset used to construct the demographic language model—and the accuracy increases for English messages from many different countries around the world.

2 Dataset and Annotation

We sampled 10,502 messages from January 1, 2013 to September 11, 2016 from an archive of publicly available geotagged tweets. We annotated the tweets with three mutually exclusive binary labels: *English*, *Not English*, and *Ambiguous*. These tweets were further annotated with descriptive labels:

- *Code-switched*: Tweets containing both text in English and text in another language.

- *Ambiguous due to named entities*: Tweets containing only named entities, such as *Vegas!*, and therefore whose language could not be unambiguously determined.

- *Automatically generated*: Tweets whose content appeared to be automatically generated, such as *I just finished running 15.21 km in 1h:17m:32s with #Endomondo #endorphins https://t.co/bugbJOvJ31*.

We excluded any usernames and URLs in a tweet from the judgment of the tweet's language, but included hashtags. Tables 1 and 2 contain the statistics for these labels in our annotated dataset. For all our experiments, we evaluate only on the subset of messages in the dataset not labeled as ambiguous or automatically generated, which we call the evaluation dataset.

3 Experiments

3.1 Training Datasets

We investigate the effect of in-domain and extra out-of-domain training data with two datasets. The first is a dataset released by Twitter of 120,575 tweets uniformly sampled from all Twitter data, which were first labeled by three different classifiers (Twitter's internal algorithm, Google's Compact Language Detector 2, and *langid.py*), then annotated by humans where classifiers disagreed.[3] We reserve our own dataset for evaluation, but use this dataset for in-domain training. This dataset is only made available by tweet ID, and many of its messages are now missing; we were able to retrieve 74,259 tweets (61.6%). For the rest of this work, we call this the Twitter70 dataset (since it originally covered about 70 languages).

In addition, following Jaech et al. (2016), we supplemented Twitter70 with out-of-domain Wikipedia data for 41 languages,[4] sampling 10,000 sentences from each language.

3.2 Classifiers

We tested a number of classifiers on our annotated dataset trained on a variety of domains, and in some cases retrained.

- CLD2: a Naive Bayes classifier with a pretrained model from a proprietary corpus; it offers no support for re-training.

- Twitter: the output of Twitter's proprietary language identification algorithm.

- *langid.py*: a Naive Bayes classifier for 97 languages with character n-gram features, including a pretrained model based on text from JRC-Acquis, ClueWeb 09, Wikipedia, Reuters, and Debian i18n (Lui and Baldwin, 2012).

- Neural model: a hierarchical neural classifier that learns both character and word representations. It provides a training dataset with 41,250 Wikipedia sentence fragments in 33 languages (Jaech et al., 2016).[5]

Self-training We experimented with one simple approach to unsupervised domain adaptation: self-training with an unlabeled target domain corpus

(Plank, 2009) by using *langid.py* to label the corpus of tweets–released by Blodgett et al.[6] and the same one used to train their demographic model– then collecting those tweets classified with posterior probability greater than or equal to 0.98. We downsampled tweets classified as English to 1 million, yielding a total corpus of 2.2 million tweets. Since we did not have access to *langid.py*'s original training data, we trained a new model on this data, then combined it as an ensemble with the original model, where a tweet was classified as English if either component classified it as English.

Demographic prediction ensemble Blodgett et al. describes applying a U.S. demographically-aligned language model as an ensemble classifier, using a mixed membership model trained over four demographic topics (African-American, Hispanic, Asian, and white). For this classifier, tweets are first classified by an off-the-shelf classifier; if it is classified as English, the classification is accepted. Otherwise, the off-the-shelf classifier is overriden and the tweet classified as English if the total posterior probability of the African-American, Hispanic, and white topics under the demographic model was at least 90%. Table 3 lists these ensembles as "+ Demo". Blodgett et al. found the classifier seemed to improve recall, but this work better evaluates the approach with the new annotations.

3.3 Length-Normalized Analysis

From manual inspection, we observed that longer tweets are significantly more likely to be correctly classified; we investigate this length effect by grouping messages into five bins (shown in Table 6) according to the number of words in the message. We pre-processed messages by fixing HTML escape characters and removing URLs, @-mentions, emojis, and the "RT" token. For each bin, we calculate recall of the *langid.py* and the demographic ensemble classifier with *langid.py*.

4 Results and Discussion

We evaluated on the 8,366 tweets in our dataset that were not annotated as ambiguous or automatically generated. Table 3 shows the precision and recall for each experiment. We focus on recall, as Blodgett et al.'s analysis indicates that while precision is largely consistent across experiments, there is a significant gap in recall performance across different varieties of English.

---

[3] https://blog.twitter.com/2015/ evaluating-language-identification-performance

[4] https://sites.google.com/site/rmyeid/projects/polyglot

[5] Kocmi and Bojar (2017) offer an alternative neural model for language identification.

[6] http://slanglab.cs.umass.edu/TwitterAAE

Model	Training	Precision	Recall
CLD2	(1) Pre-trained	0.948	0.863
	(2) + Demo.	0.946	0.924 (+ 6.1%)
Tw. internal	(3) Pre-trained	0.979	0.866
	(4) + Demo.	0.974	0.925 (+ 5.9%)
langid.py	(5) Pre-trained	0.923	0.886
	(6) + Vocab.	0.472	0.993
	(7) Self-trained	0.924	0.894
	(8) + Demo.	0.923	0.930 (+ 3.6%)
	(9) Twitter70	0.927	0.940
	(10) + Demo.	0.923	0.957 (+ 1.7%)
	(11) Tw70 and Wiki.	0.946	0.903
	(12) + Demo.	0.943	0.946 (+ 4.3%)
Neural	(13) Pre-trained	0.973	0.415
	(14) + Demo.	0.976	0.773 (+ 35.8%)
	(15) Twitter70	0.949	0.840
	(16) + Demo.	0.946	0.892 (+ 5.2%)

Table 3: English classification results on not ambiguous, not automatically generated tweets. "+ Demo." indicates including in an ensemble with the demographics-based English classifier.

Country	En	~En	*langid.py* Recall	Ens. Recall
USA	2368	80	0.968	0.982
Brazil	42	945	0.833	0.833
Indonesia	161	707	0.764	0.767
Turkey	13	304	0.769	0.846
Japan	14	340	0.929	1.0
United Kingdom	401	18	0.962	0.980
Malaysia	90	174	0.833	0.833
Spain	28	263	0.75	0.821
Argentina	10	291	0.7	0.7
France	26	206	0.846	0.846
Mexico	25	162	0.76	0.76
Philippines	91	86	0.934	0.945
Thailand	14	111	0.643	0.786
Russia	9	129	0.667	0.778
Canada	96	7	0.979	0.990

Table 4: Language counts for countries with at least 100 non-ambiguous, non-automatically generated messages (out of 129 countries total), with English recall for the best-performing *langid.py* model and that model in an ensemble classifier.

Tweet
*@username good afternoon and Happy Birthdayyyyyyyyyy *Turns on music* Time to partyyyyy*
I miss you! #vivasantotomas #ust #goUST #igers #igdaily #igersasia #igersmanila #instagood
Sooo fucked yuuuuppp bouuutta start a figgght
catch mines you catch yours we both happy...
Go follow me on Instagram @username and like 5 pics for a goodmorningg post
Think me & my baddies getting rooms dis weekend!
@username HML if u do B
@username @username FR LIKE I CANT EVEN DEAL WITH PEOPLE LIKE THIS
I k you dont like me lowkey but hey
@username I DORN WVEN WTCH GIRL MEETS WORLDBUT IM WATCHINF THAT EPISODE

Table 5: Sample of tweets which were mis-classified as non-English by *langid.py* but correctly classified by the demographic ensemble. @-mentions are shown as @username for display in the table.

Unsurprisingly, we found that training on Twitter data improved classifiers' English recall, compared to their pre-trained models. In our experiments, we found that recall was best when training on the subset of the Twitter70 dataset containing only languages with at least 1,000 tweets present in the dataset. We also found that the additional information provided by the demographic model's predictions still adds to the increased performance from training on Twitter data. Notably, precision decreased by no more than 0.4% when the demographic model is added.

We also noted that pre-processing improved recall by 1 to 5%.

Proprietary algorithms We found that neither CLD2 nor Twitter's internal algorithm was competitive with *langid.py* out of the box, in line with previous findings, but combining their predictions with demographic predictions did increase recall.[7]

langid.py Self-training *langid.py* produced little change compared to the original pre-trained model (rows (5) vs. (7)), despite its use of 2.2 million new tweets from self-training step. We observed that even tweets that *langid.py* classified as non-English with more than 0.98 posterior probability were, in fact, generally English. This suggests that tweets are sufficiently different from standard training data that it is difficult for self-training to be effective. In contrast, simple in-domain training was effective: retraining it with the Twitter70 dataset achieved substantially better recall with a

---

[7] We tried several times to run the Google Translate API's language identifier, but it returned an internal server error for approximately 75% of the tweets.

5.4% raw increase compared to its out-of-domain original pretrained model (rows (5) vs. (9)).

In all cases, regardless of the data used to train the model, *langid.py*'s recall was improved with the addition of demographic predictions; for example, the demographic predictions added to the pre-trained model brought recall close to the model trained on Twitter70 alone, indicating that in the absence of in-domain training data, the demographic model's predictions can make a model competitive with a model that does have in-domain training data (rows (8) vs. (9)). Of course, in-domain labeled data only helps more (10).

Neural model Finally, the neural model performed worse than *langid.py* when trained on the same Twitter70 dataset (rows (9) vs. (15)), and its performance lagged when trained on its provided dataset of Wikipedia sentence fragments.[8] As with the other models, demographic predictions again improve performance.

Table 5 shows a sample of ten tweets misclassified as non-English by *langid.py* and correctly classified by the demographic ensemble as English. Several sources of potential error are evident; many non-conventional spellings, such as *partyyyyy* and *watchinf*, do not challenge an English reader but might reasonably challenge character n-gram models. Similarly, common social abbreviations such as *hml* and *fr* are challenging.

4.1 Improving English Recall Worldwide

We further analyzed our English recall results according to messages' country of origin, limiting our analysis to countries with at least 100 non-ambiguous, non-automatically generated messages in our dataset. For each country's messages, we compared the recall from best standalone *langid.py* model (trained on Twitter70) and the recall from same model combined with demographic predictions, as shown in Table 4. Surprisingly, for ten of the fifteen countries we found that using demographic predictions improved recall performance, suggesting that the additional soft signal of "Englishness" provided by the demographic model aids performance across tweets labeled as English globally. In future work, we would like to investigate linguistic properties of these non-U.S. English tweets.

---

[8]Unfortunately, we were unable to train it on the same Wikipedia data as in (11), which is a bit larger.

	Message Length	*langid.py* Recall	Ensemble Recall
English	$t \leq 5$	80.7	91.9
	$5 < t \leq 10$	88.8	92.4
	$10 < t \leq 15$	91.9	93.0
	$15 < t \leq 20$	96.1	96.7
	$t \geq 20$	97.2	97.5
Non-English	$t \leq 5$	90.0	99.9
	$5 < t \leq 10$	95.2	99.5
	$10 < t \leq 15$	95.6	99.9
	$15 < t \leq 20$	95.2	1.0
	$t \geq 20$	95.2	1.0

Table 6: Percent of the messages in each bin classified correctly as English or non-English by each classifier; t is the message length for the bin.

4.2 Improving Recall for Short Tweets

Our results from the length-normalized analysis, shown in Table 6, demonstrate that recall on short tweets, particularly short English tweets, is challenging; unsurprisingly, recall increases as tweet length increases. More importantly, for short tweets the demographic ensemble classifier greatly reduces this gap; while the difference in *langid.py*'s recall performance between the shortest and longest English tweets is 16.5%, the difference is only 5.6% for the ensemble classifier. The gap is similarly decreased for non-English tweets. We note also that precision is consistently high across all bins for both *langid.py* and the ensemble classifier. The experiment indicates that the demographic model's signal of "Englishness" may aid performance not only for global varieties of English, but also for short messages of any kind.

5 Conclusion

In this work, we presented a fully human-annotated dataset and evaluated a range of language identification models in a series of experiments across training datasets and in-domain and domain adaptation settings. We find that predictions from a partially supervised demographic model aids in recall performance across tweets labeled as English drawn from a range of countries, particularly in the absence of in-domain labeled data; we hope that our dataset will aid research in international varieties of English (Trudgill and Hannah, 2008). In future work, we would like to investigate other domain adaptation approaches; in addition, we would like to adapt the demographic model to other languages where dialectal variation might present similar challenges.

References

Shane Bergsma, Paul McNamee, Mossaab Bagdouri, Clayton Fink, and Theresa Wilson. 2012. Language identification for creating language-specific twitter collections. In *Proceedings of the second workshop on language in social media*, pages 65–74. ACL.

John Blitzer, Mark Dredze, Fernando Pereira, et al. 2007. Biographies, Bollywood, boom-boxes and blenders: Domain adaptation for sentiment classification. In *ACL*, volume 7, pages 440–447.

John Blitzer, Ryan McDonald, and Fernando Pereira. 2006. Domain adaptation with structural correspondence learning. In *Proceedings of EMNLP*. ACL.

Su Lin Blodgett, Lisa Green, and Brendan O'Connor. 2016. Demographic dialectal variation in social media: A case study of African-American English. In *Proceedings of EMNLP*, Austin, Texas. ACL.

Baden Hughes, Timothy Baldwin, Steven Bird, Jeremy Nicholson, and Andrew MacKinlay. 2006. Reconsidering language identification for written language resources. In *Proceedings of LREC*. European Language Resources Association.

Aaron Jaech, George Mulcaire, Shobhit Hathi, Mari Ostendorf, and Noah A. Smith. 2016. Hierarchical character-word models for language identification. In *Proceedings of EMNLP*, Austin, TX, USA. ACL.

Ben King and Steven P Abney. 2013. Labeling the languages of words in mixed-language documents using weakly supervised methods. In *Proceedings of NAACL-HLT*.

Tom Kocmi and Ondřej Bojar. 2017. Lanidenn: Multilingual language identification on character window. *To appear in Proceedings of EACL*.

Marco Lui and T. Baldwin. 2012. langid. py: An off-the-shelf language identification tool. In *Proceedings of the 50th Annual Meeting of the Association for Computational Linguistics (ACL 2012), Demo Session, Jeju, Republic of Korea*.

Marco Lui and Timothy Baldwin. 2014. Accurate language identification of twitter messages. In *Proceedings of the 5th workshop on language analysis for social media (LASM)@ EACL*, pages 17–25.

Marco Lui and Paul Cook. 2013. Classifying english documents by national dialect. In *Proceedings of the Australasian Language Technology Association Workshop (ALTA)*.

Barbara Plank. 2009. A comparison of structural correspondence learning and self-training for discriminative parse selection. In *Proceedings of the NAACL HLT Workshop on Semi-supervised Learning for NLP*. ACL.

Peter Trudgill and Jean Hannah. 2008. *International English: A guide to varieties of Standard English*. Routledge.

Jennifer Williams and Charlie Dagli. 2017. Twitter language identification of similar languages and dialects without ground truth. In *Proceedings of the Fourth Workshop on NLP for Similar Languages, Varieties and Dialects (VarDial)*. ACL.

Yi Yang and Jacob Eisenstein. 2016. Part-of-speech tagging for historical English. In *Proceedings of NAACL-HLT*, San Diego, California. ACL.

Evaluating hypotheses in geolocation on a very large sample of Twitter

Bahar Salehi and **Anders Søgaard**
`bahar.salehi@gmail.com soegaard@di.ku.dk`
Department of Computer Science
University of Copenhagen

Abstract

Recent work in geolocation has made several hypotheses about what linguistic markers are relevant to detect where people write from. In this paper, we examine six hypotheses against a corpus consisting of all geo-tagged tweets from the US, or whose geo-tags could be inferred, in a 19% sample of Twitter history. Our experiments lend support to all six hypotheses, including that spelling variants and hashtags are strong predictors of location. We also study what kinds of common nouns are predictive of location after controlling for named entities such as *dolphins* or *sharks*.

1 Introduction

Geolocation is interesting for several reasons. It has applications to personalization, event extraction, fraud detection, criminology, privacy, etc.; but it is also a method for studying how location affects language use, as well as how linguistic change interacts with geography.

The growth of social media has made large-scale geolocation studies possible, and most recent work on geo-location use social media data, primarily from Twitter. On Twitter about 1% of tweets are geo-tagged by the media users (Cheng et al., 2010), and while this is a tiny fraction of the full corpus, it enables us to query for millions of geo-tagged tweets.

Geolocation models rely on various intuitions about what linguistic constructions are predictive of location. Specifically, many authors have used city and country names as features for geolocation, as well as Twitter hashtags and spelling variations.

In this paper, we study names, hashtags, spelling variants, as well as a wide range of other features, and evaluate their usefulness in geolocation at a *very large scale*. We discuss different feature groups and show, for example, what common nouns are more predictive of location. One example of such a noun could be *earthquake*, which is a commonly used noun that refers to a natural disaster, but obviously within a given time frame, such natural disasters hit in very specific places, where people are more likely to tweet about them.

This paper does not introduce a novel geolocation model, but uses more data than previous studies to examine the research hypotheses that have guided recent work in the field.

Contributions (a) We evaluate common hypotheses about language and location on a much larger scale than previously done. (b) We show, as expected, that place names and hashtags are predictive of location. (c) We also show that spelling variation, out of vocabulary and non-standard words such as *feelinn* are indicative of location, even more so than the standard (in dictionary) words. This seems to hold for British spelling (in the US), abbreviations and phonologically motivated spelling. (d) We also analyze what classes of common nouns are indicative of location, discussing the problem of controlling for named entities that are frequent members of some of these classes. In social media, for example, animal words such as *dolphins* and *sharks*, may refer to cities' sport teams. Best predictors after controlling for named entities include natural phenomena, occupations, and organizations. (e) We show that the same findings also apply to geolocation of users around the world.

2 Related work

In text-based geolocation, researchers have used KL divergence between the distribution of a users words and the words used in geographic regions

62

Proceedings of the 3rd Workshop on Noisy User-generated Text, pages 62–67
Copenhagen, Denmark, September 7, 2017. ©2017 Association for Computational Linguistics

(Wing and Baldridge, 2011; Roller et al., 2012), regional topic distributions (Eisenstein et al., 2010; Ahmed et al., 2013; Hong et al., 2012), or feature selection/weighting to find words indicative of location (Priedhorsky et al., 2014; Han et al., 2012a, 2014; Wing and Baldridge, 2014).

Han et al. (2012b) showed that information gain ratio is a useful metric for measuring how location-indicative words are. They used a sample of 26 million tweets in their study, obtained through the public Twitter API.

Salehi et al. (2017) evaluate nine name entity types. Using various metrics, they find that GEO-LOC, FACILITY and SPORT-TEAM are more informative for geolocation than other NE types.

Chi et al. (2016) specifically study the contributions of city and country names, hashtags, and user mentions, to geolocation. Their results suggested that a combination of city and country names, as well as hashtags, are good location predictors. They used a sample of 9 million tweets in their study, obtained through the public Twitter API.

Pavalanathan and Eisenstein (2015) investigate the potential demographic biases of using non-standard words and entities. They show that younger users are more likely to use geographically specific non-standard words, while old men tend to use more location revealing entities.

In this study, we use more data than previous studies to examine the research hypotheses and linguistic features established in previous works on geolocation. In addition, in order to examine the generalizability of our findings we examine them on a more geographically diverse dataset covering tweets from all around the world.

3   Gathering Data

Our dataset is a fraction of a 19% random sample of the entire history of Twitter (the union of two independent 10% samples), up until early 2016. We consider the fraction of geo-located tweets with US geo-coordinates, as well as tweets with low-entropy location strings, for which we infer geotagged fractional counts:

If a location string s is used more than n times, we compute its distribution $P(s \mid county)$ over US counties. Non-geotagged instances of tweets associated with s are then attributed to counties based on this distribution as fractional counts. The final corpus consists of roughly 120 billion tweets

and around 450 million of these had geo-tags. Using the inference methodology, were able to attribute roughly 10 billion tweets.

We look at the distribution of words over US counties in this corpus, limiting ourselves to the most frequent 100,000 words. This is important to ensure support, but also makes geolocation harder, since rare words are generally more predictive of location. On the other hand, the fact that we rely on relatively frequent words makes our analysis more widely applicable.

The corpus has 4.5B tokens of the 100,000 most frequent words. So, on average we have 45,000 occurrences of each word. The minimum frequency is 612 tokens; the most frequent word occurs 138M times. The median is 1,742 occurrences.

4   Metrics

In this section, we introduce two metrics we use to examine the degree of location informativeness of words. Entropy and KL divergence.

KL divergence   The Kullback-Leibler divergence (KLD) (also known as information gain) is used to measure the similarity between two distributions. We use KLD to measure the similarity between the distribution of a word (P) with the distribution of all words (Q) across counties.

$$\text{KLD}(P_{word}, Q) = \sum_{c \in counties} P_{word}(c) \, \log \frac{P_{word}(c)}{Q(c)}.$$

Higher KLD shows less similarity to the distribution of all words and as a result higher location predictiveness.

Entropy   In information theory, entropy measures the unpredictability, where low entropy indicates high predictability. In this study, we compute entropy of each word as below:

$$\text{H}(word) = - \sum_{c \in counties} P_{word}(c) \log P_{word}(c)$$

where $P_{word}(c)$ is the probability of observing $word$ in the county c. This is computed by dividing the frequency of that word in that county by the total number of words in that county.

5   Experiments

5.1   Location Indicative Words

In this section, we examine the following 6 hypotheses using entropy and KLD metrics:

Hypothesis (">" = "more predictive than")	Ent1	Ent2	KLD1	KLD2	p-value
#0 Dictionary words > stopwords	**5.67**	7.74	**0.74**	0.12	< 0.001
#1 US English < British	5.59	**5.13**	0.63	**0.94**	< 0.05
#2 Dictionary words < geonames	5.67	**4.62**	0.74	**1.79**	< 0.001
#3 Dictionary words < OOV words	5.67	**4.61**	0.74	**1.52**	< 0.001
#4 Dictionary words < hashtags	5.67	**4.25**	0.74	**1.82**	< 0.001
#5 Dictionary words < emoticons	5.67	**5.07**	0.74	**1.03**	< 0.001
#6 Non-standard words > their normalized version	**5.27**	7.52	**0.92**	0.17	< 0.001

Table 1: Evaluating hypotheses by comparing average entropy/KLD scores of first group's words (Ent1/KLD1) with the words in second group (Ent2/KLD2). Lower entropy and higher KLD show higher predictability. P-value shows the significance of the differences.

0. Stopwords are not good predictors compared to other dictionary words.

1. British English is more location-specific than American English (in the US).

2. Geonames are better predictors compared to dictionary words.

3. Words not in dictionary (OOV) are better predictors than words in dictionary.

4. Hashtags are better predictors than dictionary words.

5. Emoticons are better predictors than dictionary words.

6. Non-standard spelling variants are better predictors than their standard spellings.

The results are shown in Table 1. The rest of this section investigates each of the hypotheses in more details.

Hypothesis #0: We use the NLTK stopword list for English and found 143 unique stopwords in our data.[1] As expected, stopwords are the least location predictive group of words.[2] Among the stopwords *ain*, *wasn* and *wouldn* are among the most predictive ones. Note that *wasn't* and *wouldn't* are also in our data, but they are not as location predictive.

Hypothesis #1: We also compare words with spelling variations in British and American English, using `https://en.oxforddictionaries.com/usage/british-and-american-terms` as our data source. Overall, in our data, we found 475 words that have different spellings in British and American English.

We observe that British spellings are more predictive. For example, while *harbor* and *harbour* are mostly observed in coastal areas, *harbour* (British) is more often observed in eastern coastal regions, while *harbor* (American) is distributed more diversely. However, the difference between British and American words is not significant.

Hypothesis #2: City names and country names are often said to be more predictive of location. In this experiment, we use GeoNames[3] to find city/country names including their alternative names. We found 23,701 geonames in our data. We observe that on average, geonames are significantly more location indicative than the rest of dictionary words.

Hypothesis #3: Both metrics show that OOV words are on average more predictive of location than the dictionary words. Note that such words are among the 100K most frequent words and are not considered as random noise. We consider words not found in WordNet for OOV words. Overall, we found 31,049 dictionary words and 68,951 OOV words in our data.

Hypothesis #4: Our experiments show that hashtags are significantly more predictive than the dictionary words as well as the rest of the examined OOV words. In our data, *#1* and *#fail* are among the least predictive hashtags, while the most predictive hashtags are mainly location names and events such as *#monett* (a city name), *#disney366* and *#zipsblackout*. In our data, we have 17,131 hashtags.

Hypothesis #5: Emoticons[4] are the last group

[1] http://www.nltk.org/data.html
[2] This experiment is more of a sanity check.
[3] http://www.geonames.org/
[4] There was no emojis in our list of most frequent 100K

Synsets	Examples	After elimination Synsets	Examples
indian.n.01	yuma, muskogee	unit.n.03	usaf, sss
amerindian.n.01	yuma, muskogee,	natural_phenomenon.n.01	whiteout, earthquake
wood.n.01	hazelwood, tupelo	alcohol.n.01	homebrew, oktoberfest,
agency.n.01	usaf, sss	phenomenon.n.01	whiteout, earthquake,
extremity.n.04	terminus, skyline	occupation.n.01	engineering, internship
plant_material.n.01	hazelwood, tupelo	symbol.n.01	emmys, phd,
traveler.n.01	trespasser, tourists	region.n.01	aerospace, rooftop
person_of_color.n.01	yuma, muskogee	worker.n.01	esthetician, hairstylist
fish.n.01	sharks, marlins	implement.n.01	poker, nutcracker
administrative_unit.n.01	usaf, sss	inhabitant.n.01	peruvian, hoosiers
american.n.01	hoosiers, tarheels	organization.n.01	friendlys, usaf
geological_formation.n.01	seaside, canyon	liquid.n.01	cocktails, espresso

Table 2: Most location predictive synsets before and after eliminating the location and sport team names.

	Median distance error	Accuracy (city)	Accuracy (country)
In dictionary	860	10.85	77.93
OOV	667	14.96	79.95
Geonames	698	14.43	79.60
All	510	17.41	84.04

Table 3: Geolocation results on WORLD dataset

of OOV words in our analysis. We found 196 emoticons in our data. According to Table 1, emoticons on average are more predictive than dictionary words. Yet, they are among the least predictive ones in the group of OOV words. Our further analysis shows that *:)* and *;)* are the least predictive emoticons, while *(ˆ-ˆ)* and *=)* are among the most predictive ones showing that emoticons can also be location predictive. This is in line with the work of (Park et al., 2013), where they observed that people in Eastern countries prefer vertical emoticons (based on eye shape style), while Western countries prefer horizontal ones (based on mouth style).

Hypothesis #6: Among the words not found in dictionary, there exist non-standard words, which are typos, ad hoc abbreviations, unconventional spellings and phonetic substitutions (Han et al., 2012a), such as *2mrw* (i.e., *tomorrow*). Here, we use (Han et al., 2012a) to compare these nonstandard words with their normalized versions. Overall, we found 4,795 non-standard words, as well as their normalized version in our data.

Using entropy and KLD, we show that the normalized versions are not very location indicative, yet, the non-standard words are significantly more predictive than their normalized versions. This shows that preferred styles to write words in a non-standard way have implicit location information.

---

words.

5.2 Semantic Classes

In this section, we examine the semantic categories that are most location indicative using WordNET. For each word, we extract all the possible hypernymes. The synsets with less than 10 samples are removed. For each synset, the median entropy and KLD of the respective samples are calculated.

The synsets observed in both the top 20 synsets using entropy and the top 20 synsets using KLD are shown in Table 2. We noticed that the name of sports teams and locations are among the top categories. For example, the samples of *Wood.n.01*, such as *hazelwood* and *tupelo*, are also part of the name of locations in the United States, and *sharks* and *marlins* from *fish.n.01* are part of sports team names. Therefore, we removed the words which are part of the names of US teams using DBPedia and locations using geonames. This resulted in a different top 20 categories, which are shown under *after elimination* column. After eliminating named entities of cities, countries and sport teams, we observe that the best predictors are mostly natural phenomena, occupations, and organizations.

6 Geolocation

We also evaluated the above hypotheses in the context of a geolocation experiment using the geographically diverse more dataset, WORLD (Han et al., 2012c). The WORLD dataset covers 3,709 cities worldwide and consists of tweets from 1.4M users, where 10,000 users are held out as development set and 10,000 as test set. The task is to predict the primary location of a new user based on that person's tweet history.

We use logistic regression as classifier to predict the users location, following Rahimi et al. (2015). The results (median distance error, city accuracy and country accuracy) are shown in Table 3.

Similar to our findings in our analysis above, we see that OOV words are better features than dictionary words. Also geonames features, alone, have high performance, even better than dictionary words. The rest of the examined groups are not performing as good, individually. The combination of all words (shown as All) results in the best performance.

7 Conclusion

In this paper, we examined six hypotheses about location-specific language use. We confirmed that OOV words are more predictive of location than dictionary words. Moreover, we showed that spelling variants and hashtags are strong predictors for location. Finally, we showed that our findings are also applicable to geolocation of users around the world.

Acknowledgments

This work was supported by the Data Transparency Lab.

References

Amr Ahmed, Liangjie Hong, and Alexander J Smola. 2013. Hierarchical geographical modeling of user locations from social media posts. In *Proceedings of the 22nd international conference on World Wide Web*. ACM, pages 25–36.

Zhiyuan Cheng, James Caverlee, and Kyumin Lee. 2010. You are where you tweet: a content-based approach to geo-locating twitter users. In *Proceedings of the 19th ACM international conference on Information and knowledge management*. ACM, pages 759–768.

Lianhua Chi, Kwan Hui Lim, Nebula Alam, and Christopher J Butler. 2016. Geolocation prediction in twitter using location indicative words and textual features. *WNUT 2016* page 227.

Jacob Eisenstein, Brendan O'Connor, Noah A Smith, and Eric P Xing. 2010. A latent variable model for geographic lexical variation. In *Proceedings of the 2010 Conference on Empirical Methods in Natural Language Processing*. Association for Computational Linguistics, pages 1277–1287.

Bo Han, Paul Cook, and Timothy Baldwin. 2012a. Automatically constructing a normalisation dictionary for microblogs. In *Proceedings of the 2012 joint conference on empirical methods in natural language processing and computational natural language learning*. Association for Computational Linguistics, pages 421–432.

Bo Han, Paul Cook, and Timothy Baldwin. 2012b. Geolocation prediction in social media data by finding location indicative words. In *Proceedings of COLING*. pages 1045–1062.

Bo Han, Paul Cook, and Timothy Baldwin. 2012c. Geolocation prediction in social media data by finding location indicative words. In *Proceedings of COLING*. pages 1045–1062.

Bo Han, Paul Cook, and Timothy Baldwin. 2014. Text-based twitter user geolocation prediction. *Journal of Artificial Intelligence Research* 49:451–500.

Liangjie Hong, Amr Ahmed, Siva Gurumurthy, Alexander J Smola, and Kostas Tsioutsiouliklis. 2012. Discovering geographical topics in the twitter stream. In *Proceedings of the 21st international conference on World Wide Web*. ACM, pages 769–778.

Jaram Park, Vladimir Barash, Clay Fink, and Meeyoung Cha. 2013. Emoticon style: Interpreting differences in emoticons across cultures. In *ICWSM*.

Umashanthi Pavalanathan and Jacob Eisenstein. 2015. Confounds and consequences in geotagged twitter data. *arXiv preprint arXiv:1506.02275* .

Reid Priedhorsky, Aron Culotta, and Sara Y Del Valle. 2014. Inferring the origin locations of tweets with quantitative confidence. In *Proceedings of the 17th ACM conference on Computer supported cooperative work & social computing*. ACM, pages 1523–1536.

Afshin Rahimi, Trevor Cohn, and Timothy Baldwin. 2015. Twitter user geolocation using a unified text and network prediction model. In *Proceedings of the 53rd Annual Meeting of the Association for Computational Linguistics and the 7th International Joint Conference on Natural Language Processing of the Asian Federation of Natural Language Processing (ACL2015)*. The Association for Computational Linguistics, pages 630–636.

Stephen Roller, Michael Speriosu, Sarat Rallapalli, Benjamin Wing, and Jason Baldridge. 2012. Supervised text-based geolocation using language models on an adaptive grid. In *Proceedings of the 2012 Joint Conference on Empirical Methods in Natural Language Processing and Computational Natural Language Learning*. Association for Computational Linguistics, pages 1500–1510.

Bahar Salehi, Dirk Hovy, Eduard Hovy, and Anders
Søgaard. 2017. Huntsville, hospitals, and hockey
teams: Names can reveal your location. In *Proceedings of the 3rd Workshop on Noisy User-generated
Text (WNUT)*. Copenhagen, Denmark.

Benjamin Wing and Jason Baldridge. 2014. Hierarchical discriminative classification for text-based geolocation. In *EMNLP*. pages 336–348.

Benjamin P Wing and Jason Baldridge. 2011. Simple supervised document geolocation with geodesic
grids. In *Proceedings of the 49th Annual Meeting of
the Association for Computational Linguistics: Human Language Technologies-Volume 1*. Association
for Computational Linguistics, pages 955–964.

The Effect of Error Rate in Artificially Generated Data for Automatic Preposition and Determiner Correction

Fraser Bowen and **Jon Dehdari** and **Josef van Genabith**
University of Saarland
Deutsches Forschungsinstitut für Künstliche Intelligenz

Abstract

In this research we investigate the impact of mismatches in the density and type of error between training and test data on a neural system correcting preposition and determiner errors. We use synthetically produced training data to control error density and type, and "real" error data for testing. Our results show it is possible to combine error types, although prepositions and determiners behave differently in terms of how much error should be artificially introduced into the training data in order to get the best results.

1 Introduction

The field of Grammatical Error Correction (GEC) is currently dominated by neural translation models, specifically sequence-to-sequence translation. However, despite offering substantial improvements on the well-established statistical machine translation approach to GEC, neural networks come with their own challenges.

Firstly, neural models require a large amount of training data, however the amount of annotated learner English consisting of source (original text) and target (corrected text) is low. Models are at risk of overfitting, simply because the volume of data is not high enough. Secondly, the data that has been used up until now does not generalise very well across different test sets. This means that there has been some success in correcting errors, but only from test sets that are in some sense similar to the training data. Thirdly, it is generally unknown how erroneous the test data is, and if the training data has a different distribution of errors, it is likely that unwanted corrections will be made, or required corrections will be missed.

Currently, there is research into generating artificial data for training neural models, specifically data that resembles learner English (Cahill et al., 2013; Rozovskaya and Roth, 2010; Felice, 2016; Liu and Liu, 2016). The artificial data is generated from monolingual sentences of grammatical English by systematically introducing noise into it. This way, training data consisting of sentences with both "incorrect" and "correct" versions can be generated from monolingual data, which is easily accessible. There is also evidence that artificially generated data can generalise a GEC system better than simply using manually procured correction data (Cahill et al., 2013).

A third advantage of synthetically introducing noise into a corpus is the ability to control how much noise, and which noise, is introduced. The first main question of our research is how the amount of noise introduced into the corpus affects a neural model's behaviour at test time with respect to mismatches in error density and error type between training and test data. Artificial data lends itself to this kind of research, thanks to the control over the corpus.

Up until now, the effect of the amount of errors in the training corpus has only been explored with prepositions specifically (Cahill et al., 2013). We begin by extending this line of research to determiners. The second research question is then: how do two different types of error interact? It is quite possible that introducing many types of frequent grammatical errors one after the other would not create convincing artificial learner data, because several types of error can affect the same word, and a neural model may not be able to learn to combine them in this way.

Proceedings of the 3rd Workshop on Noisy User-generated Text, pages 68–76
Copenhagen, Denmark, September 7, 2017. ©2017 Association for Computational Linguistics

2   Related Work

Currently the best results in GEC have used neural machine translation. Yuan and Briscoe (2016) achieved the best scores using a 2-layer encoder-decoder system with attention, trained on the Cambridge Learner Corpus (CLC), a large data set of two million correction Learner English sentences. The CLC is not publicly available, which has inspired the use of automatically generated data with neural models. Liu and Liu (2016) have done exactly this with 16 different types of errors. Their success, although small compared to using manually annotated supervised revision data, has inspired our investigation into the particular effects of combining error types in an artificial corpus.

One particularly interesting approach to generating artificial data is from Cahill et al. (2013), who, focusing on preposition errors, creates confusion sets for each preposition using supervised revision data, and selects replacements at random from these probability distributions. This approach was developed from Rozovskaya and Roth (2010), who first suggested the idea of probabilistically selecting likely error candidates. Interestingly, the artificial data proved to make manually annotated data more robust, meaning that it generalised better across different types of test sets, despite the fact that the overall quality of corrections was lowered. This was confirmed by Felice (2016), who also found that this kind of probabilistic error generation increases precision, and lowers recall.

One main focus of our research is the effect of the amount of errors in the training corpus on the amount of corrections made at test time. Rozovskaya et al. (2012) identify a useful technique known as error inflation, where more errors are introduced into the training data in order to improve recall. This is further explored in our work.

3   Experimental Setup

3.1   Data

In our research, errors are systemically introduced into "correct" English data. The correct data comes from the NewsCrawl corpus in WMT-2016.[1] It is open domain, featuring a wide variety of topics and writing styles, taken from recent articles. We used 21,789,157 sentences for training, and 5,447,288 held-out sentences from the same source for a development set.

We follow the same methodology of Cahill et al. (2013) to generate noise. Specifically, supervised revision data is used to see how often particular words are corrected into specific prepositions or determiners. The revision data which is used for our research is the Lang-8 corpus, which is available for academic purposes upon request.[2] The corpus is scraped from the Lang-8 website, where crowd-sourced grammar corrections are posted for non-native speakers of English. It is arguably more reliable than Wikipedia, which contains vandalism, however, it is noticeably smaller than Wikipedia.

The process of introducing errors into the WMT data using the Lang-8 corpus is as follows:

1. Extract plain text versions of the Lang-8 corpus, consisting solely of sentences with corrections

2. Compare source sentence with corrections using an efficient *diff* algorithm.[3] Note that this often included several steps of revisions.

3. Prepare a list of all prepositions/determiners. This is taken from the tags of the WMT data retrieved from the Stanford tagger.[4]

4. Remove all sentences that do not contain a single revision involving a preposition or a determiner. Using a hand-crafted set of possible prepositions/determiners, it is determined for each sentence whether it involves a deletion (eg. "for" → "NULL"), an addition (eg. "NULL" → "the"), or a replacement (eg. "on" → "in").

5. Generate confusion sets for each preposition/determiner by listing all the deletions which are replaced by that word, and counting the frequency of each specific revision.

---

[1] http://www.statmt.org/wmt16/translation-task.html

[2] http://cl.naist.jp/nldata/lang-8
[3] http://code.google.com/p/google-diff-match-patch

[4] Using word lists has the advantage of not relying on unsupervised POS-tagging methods. However, there are certain ambiguities which are not addressed. In this research, the preposition "to" is not included, due to confusion with the infinitive particle. There are however other less frequent ambiguous cases which are included, such as "that" and "before", which can both appear as conjunctions. Future experiments would benefit from a comparison of the performance of POS tags against word lists.

From there, generate a probability distribution for each preposition/determiner.

6. Insert the target word itself into the distribution with a frequency relative to the error rate. An 80% error rate for example means that 20% of the time, the same word is selected, effectively leaving it in its "correct" form.

7. Prepositions/determiners in the WMT corpus are systemically replaced by one of the options in their respective probability distributions, selected at random by a sampler.

3.2 Experiments

Cahill et al. (2013) have made their revision data extracted from Wikipedia available for download, which is why it is appropriate to compare it to the revision data which is extracted from Lang-8. Both sets of revision data are used to create two separate confusion sets for prepositions. They are then used to create two sets of error corpora in which 20%, 40%, 60% and 80% of prepositions are altered according to the error introduction procedure detailed above.

To compare, revision data extracted from Lang-8 is also used to create error corpora containing the same amounts of prepositional error. It is worth noting that Cahill et al.'s research does not include the empty "NULL" preposition, meaning that errors in which a preposition is missing are not accounted for. By contrast, in our work we include every case in which a preposition is inserted, as well as replaced, although we do not deal with deletions. Deleting prepositions which were inserted in the revision data simply follows the same procedure as replacements, where a preposition is replaced with the null preposition. Inserting prepositions which were deleted in the revision data is much more difficult, as it is not clear where in a sentence each preposition should be. The use of context words before and after a deletion is being explored in more current research, but does not feature in these experiments. This is nevertheless a major contribution, because insertions and deletions make up a significant part of the errors. In Lang-8, for example, there were 10054 corrections of prepositions, of which 4274 were insertions, and 2657 were deletions. This means that replacements only consist of 31% percent of the errors.

We also use determiner revision data extracted from Lang-8 to create determiner errors in a sim-ilar fashion, with 20%, 40%, 60% and 80% of errors.

A final set of synthetic error data is then generated where both prepositions and determiners are introduced into the same corpus, containing 20%, 40%, 60% and 80% of both kinds of error. This is to investigate whether the GEC system is capable of dealing with two types of error at once.

3.3 Evaluation

In order to test the effects of mismatching error density and type between training and test data, each model is tested on specially created test sets with varying amounts of error in them. Cahill et al. (2013) found that the highest scores came from models both trained and tested on similar error rates. Our research aims to build on this finding.

The first test set is made from Lang-8, which is also used to create the confusion sets for the training data. Specifically, only the sentences with prepositions, determiners, and a mix of both in the revisions are used. No other types of error are included. These sentences are mixed with corrected sentences (where the revised sentence is used as both source and target) to varying degrees. In each case, 1000 sentences of erroneous data are mixed with either 4000, 1500, 666, or 250 sentences of "correct" English, also taken from Lang-8. This is in order to create test sets in which 20%, 40%, 60%, and 80% of sentences are erroneous, similar to the training data. Table 1 shows the test sets created out of the Lang-8 corpus.

The NUCLE corpus (Ng et al., 2014) was used as training and test sets for the CoNLL-2014 Shared Task (Ng et al., 2014) on GEC, and since then has been commonly used in the field for comparison with previous work. The NUCLE corpus is used in our research in order to generate test sets from a different domain, despite those test sets being smaller. Again, prepositions, determiners and a combination of both are extracted and mixed with corrected sentences from the same corpus. Due to the smaller amount of relevant errors, as many sentences containing each error as possible are taken. For prepositions, this amounts 332 sentences, for determiners, 595 sentences, and for both, 169 sentences. Table 2 shows the test sets created out of the NUCLE corpus.

For our experiments we use OpenNMT, an open-source implementation of a bidirectional

Test sets	Error type	Error Rate	Size
test-l8p20	Preposition	20%	5000
test-l8p40	Preposition	40%	2500
test-l8p60	Preposition	60%	1666
test-l8p80	Preposition	80%	1250
test-l8d20	Determiner	20%	5000
test-l8d40	Determiner	40%	2500
test-l8d60	Determiner	60%	1666
test-l8d80	Determiner	80%	1250
test-l8b20	Both	20%	5000
test-l8b40	Both	40%	2500
test-l8b60	Both	60%	1666
test-l8b80	Both	80%	1250

Table 1: Lang-8 Corpus test sets

Test sets	Error type	Error Rate	Size
test-np20	Preposition	20%	1660
test-np40	Preposition	40%	830
test-np60	Preposition	60%	553
test-np80	Preposition	80%	415
test-nd20	Determiner	20%	2975
test-nd40	Determiner	40%	1487
test-nd60	Determiner	60%	992
test-nd80	Determiner	80%	744
test-nb20	Both	20%	845
test-nb40	Both	40%	423
test-nb60	Both	60%	282
test-nb80	Both	80%	211

Table 2: NUCLE Corpus test sets

RNN encoder–decoder network with attention[5]. OpenNMT was chosen because of its ease of use, and similarity to the architecture used by the current state of the art results reported by Yuan and Briscoe (2016). The selected evaluation metric is the GLEU score, which has been shown to be the most appropriate metric for GEC (Napoles et al., 2015).

4 Results and Discussion

The first objective of our research is to see the difference between testing on Lang-8 and NUCLE test sets when trained on data containing varying error densities created using data from Lang-8. For prepositional errors, the GLEU scores of the four different models are in Table 3, and the results are plotted in Figure 4. When tested on corpora with only 20% error, the GLEU score remains the same on both test sets. However, the higher the error rate in the test set, the better the models perform on the NUCLE set in comparison with the Lang-8 set. This is surprising, seeing as the Lang-8 corpus was used to inform the process of error generation in the training set.

In the tables cited in this paper, it is expected that the highest scores will occur along the diagonal. A test set containing 20% error would be best handled by training data which also contains 20% error. Likewise with 40%, 60% and 80 %. Conversely, training data containing 80% error would not perform as well on test data containing 40% as the training data which also has 40% error. This data shows, however that this is not always the case. When testing on 80% error, the models trained on 80% error density themselves obtain – as expected – the highest score, although only slightly. Interestingly, however, the 80% models also perform better on the 40% and 60% test sets, which seems to confirm Rozovskaya et al. (2012)'s "Error Inflation" idea. This is the idea that putting more errors than needed into the training data helps the model generalise more.

One interesting observation from the data is the fact that all the models perform better on the 20% test sets. This is likely because the models are capable of recognising that a sentence need not be corrected, and doing so is simpler than finding a correction of incorrect sentences.

Testing on determiner errors revealed similar results. The results are provided in Table 4, and plotted in Figure 4. In this case, error inflation does not seem to work, as the highest scoring results for each test set is more or less the training set with the matching error density. This indicates that systems that correct determiners have different properties to those which correct prepositions.

---

[5]http://opennmt.net/

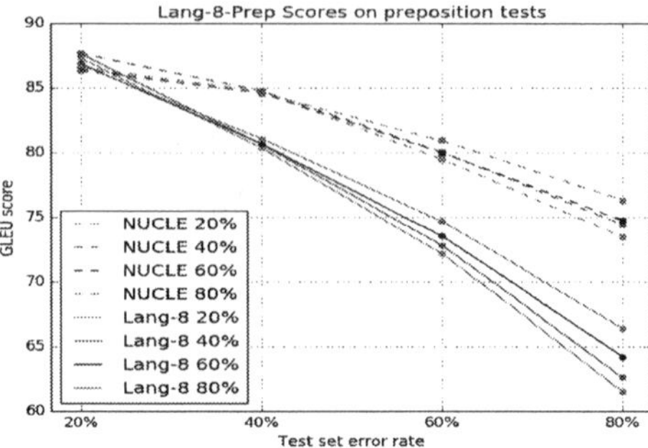

Figure 1: Plot of the data in Table 3

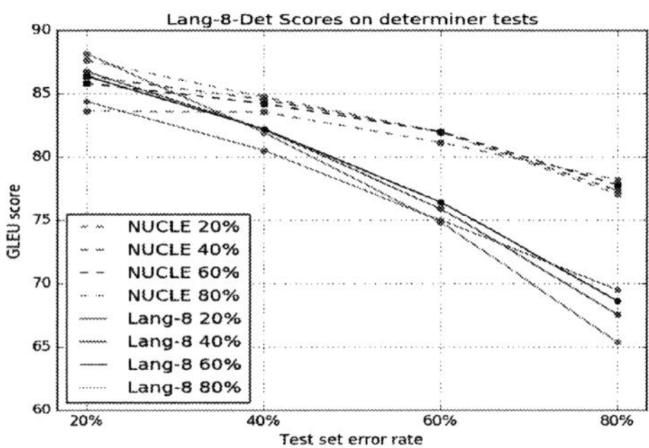

Figure 2: Plot of the data in Table 4

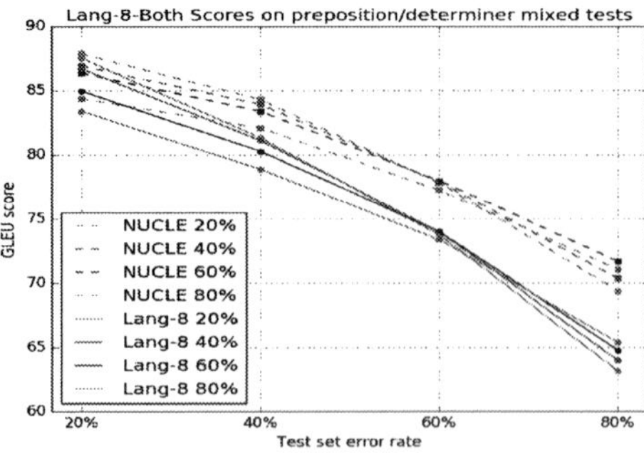

Figure 3: Plot of the data in Table 5

The results of training models on data containing a combination of both kinds of error on combined preposition and determiner test data is shown in Table 5 and Figure 4. The data is consists of slightly lower scores in general, suggesting that mixing error types does not have as high a quality of correction as single errors. Also, the NUCLE test scores in particular suffer in comparison with the singular error models, showing a failure to generalise across domains. Finally, "Error Inflation" also does not appear to work here.

These results shed doubt on the "Error Inflation" present in the preposition experiment. If it were dependent on the type of error, and prepositions were the kind which encouraged the use of "Error Inflation", then it follows that it should at least be present in the combined models. Instead of different error types subtly influencing the behaviour of the combined model in a cumulative way, the behaviour seems more random. In one case, the 20% combined model performs better on the 40% NUCLE test set than the 40% one, which suggests that reducing the amount of introduced error would make an improvement.

Table 6 and Figure 4 show how well the combined model performs on test sets with individual error types only. First of all, the scores are lower than the respective values attained by models trained on individual errors on the same test sets, but only slightly. Also, as seen in Tables 3, 4 and 5, the combined model testing on the combined test set returns lower scores than the individual models testing on their respective test sets with just one of the error types. However, the combined models' scores are better than those achieved by the individual models on the combined test sets, as shown in Table 7 and Figure 4. This indicates that the combined model is better suited for tackling both errors at once, and only a little worse at tackling individual errors than the individual error models. This is a predictable outcome, but the reduction in GLEU score suggests that combining errors in an attempt to correct all errors will generate noise, and the more error types that are covered, the less likely that they will be correctly revised at test time, which makes the idea of making an generalised corrector for all errors less feasible.

It is also worth mentioning that correcting determiners seems to result in higher scores than correcting prepositions. This could be due to the amount of possible prepositions that need to be considered compared to the determiners. Although many determiners are considered, the vast majority of the cases involve the three articles "a", "an" and "the", as well as the null determiner. This is evidence for the need to consider the variation between different errors types when generating errors.

The final research question is whether the confusion set generated from Wikipedia revisions by Cahill et al. (2013) is much different from the one generated from Lang-8. Table 8 and Figure 4 show the results of preposition models informed by Wikipedia and Lang-8 tested on Lang-8 test sets. Table 9 and Figure 4 show the results of the same models on the NUCLE test sets. As expected, the errors generated from the confusion set informed by Lang-8 performs better on the Lang-8 test sets than on the NUCLE test sets. What is interesting, however, is that the Wikipedia revisions performed significantly better not only on the NUCLE test sets, but also on the Lang-8 test sets. This is surprising, because the Wikipedia revisions are not necessarily in the same domain, whereas the Lang-8 revisions are from the same dataset. Furthermore, the Wikipedia revisions do not take insertions or deletions into account. It is clear that the amount of revisions considered makes a difference: there were 10054 Lang-8 revisions, and 303847 Wikipedia revisions, 30 times more. The small amount of Lang-8 revisions could also account for the noise identified in the Lang-8 models, but this noise is also present in the Wikipedia revisions, where "error inflation" appears to only appear sometimes and not always.

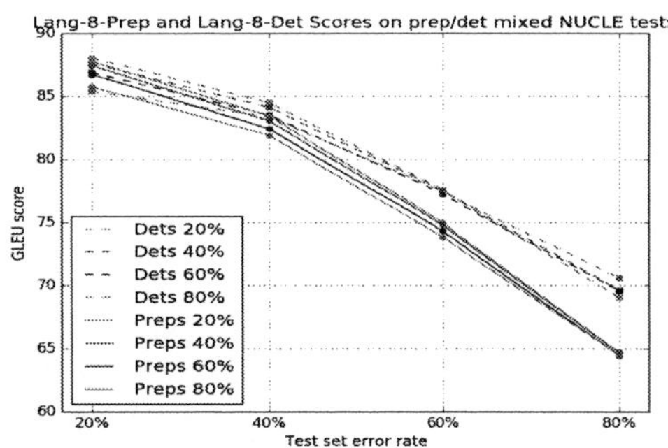

Figure 5: Plot of the data in Table 7

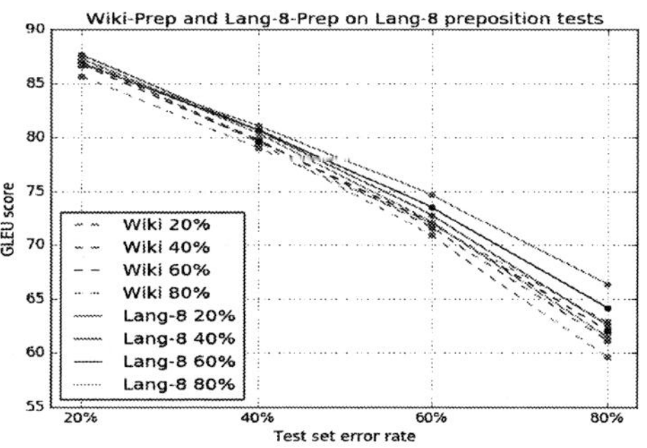

Figure 6: Plot of the data in Table 8

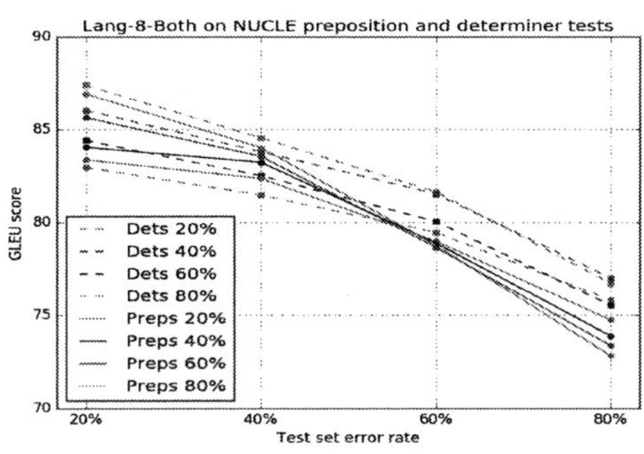

Figure 4: Plot of the data in Table 6

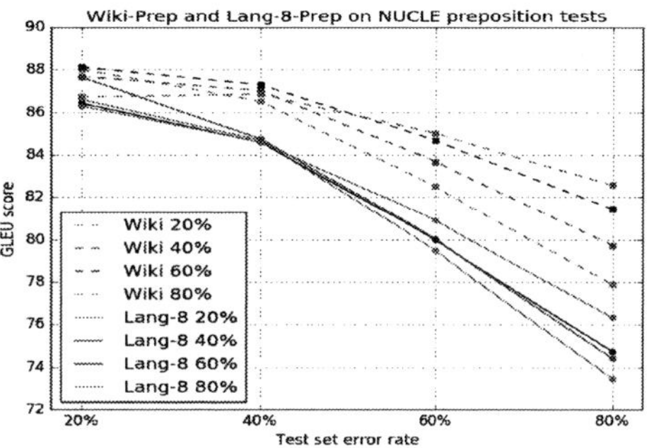

Figure 7: Plot of the data in Table 9

5 Conclusion

Our research aims to shed light on the issue of choosing how many errors to include in artificially generated erroneous data by tackling two specific error types. Results reveal some predictable outcomes, such as that it is easier to deal with test corpora which have smaller error rates, because leaving correct sentences alone is easier for the model to learn than making a good correction. Also, in most cases, there is a correlation between the error rate of the training data and the test data. However, some of the results revealed unexpected outcomes. Although it is possible that the data is noisy, the results, particularly for the prepositions, support a concept called "Error Inflation", which suggests that including more errors into the training data will lead to a higher GLEU score. This effect was not observed in the determiner and combined models, suggesting that there might be variation between different error types depending on the distribution of revisions made for that error type. It is possible to combine two error types together into one training set, and tackle two error types at once at test time, although the scores are not as high as when solving only individual errors. Also, the confusion set generated from Wikipedia revisions proved to yield better results than that generated from Lang-8, due to the significantly larger number of revisions. Finally, this research supports generating erroneous data as a valid approach to improving neural models for GEC, and informs future researchers about the effects of error rate mismatches in training and test data.

Acknowledgments

We would like to thank Joel Tetreault for his advice and experience in Automatic Error Generation, as well as Mamoru Komachi of Lang-8 for access to the Lang-8 dataset.

References

Aoife Cahill, Nitin Madnani, Joel Tetreault, and Diane Napolitano. 2013. Robust systems for preposition error correction using Wikipedia revisions. In *Proceedings of the 2013 Conference of the North American Chapter of the Association for Computational Linguistics: Human Language Technologies*. Atlanta, Georgia, pages 507–517. http://www.aclweb.org/anthology/N13-1055.

Mariano Felice. 2016. Artificial error generation for translation-based grammatical error correction. Technical Report UCAM-CL-TR-895, University of Cambridge, Computer Laboratory. http://www.cl.cam.ac.uk/techreports/UCAM-CL-TR-895.pdf.

Zhuoran Liu and Yang Liu. 2016. Exploiting unlabeled data for neural grammatical error detection. *ArXiv preprint* 1611.08987. http://arxiv.org/abs/1611.08987.

Courtney Napoles, Keisuke Sakaguchi, Matt Post, and Joel Tetreault. 2015. Ground truth for grammatical error correction metrics. In *Proceedings of the 53rd Annual Meeting of the Association for Computational Linguistics and the 7th International Joint Conference on Natural Language Processing (Volume 2: Short Papers)*. Beijing, China, pages 588–593. http://www.aclweb.org/anthology/P15-2097.

Hwee Tou Ng, Siew Mei Wu, Ted Briscoe, Christian Hadiwinoto, Raymond Hendy Susanto, and Christopher Bryant. 2014. The CoNLL-2014 shared task on grammatical error correction. In *Proceedings of the Eighteenth Conference on Computational Natural Language Learning: Shared Task*. Baltimore, Maryland, pages 1–14. http://www.aclweb.org/anthology/W14-1701.

Alla Rozovskaya and Dan Roth. 2010. Training paradigms for correcting errors in grammar and usage. In *Human Language Technologies: The 2010 Annual Conference of the North American Chapter of the Association for Computational Linguistics*. Los Angeles, California, pages 154–162. http://www.aclweb.org/anthology/N10-1018.

Alla Rozovskaya, Mark Sammons, and Dan Roth. 2012. The UI system in the HOO 2012 shared task on error correction. In *Proceedings of the Seventh Workshop on Building Educational Applications Using NLP*. Montréal, Canada, pages 272–280. http://www.aclweb.org/anthology/W12-2032.

Zheng Yuan and Ted Briscoe. 2016. Grammatical error correction using neural machine translation. In *Proceedings of the 2016 Conference of the North American Chapter of the Association for Computational Linguistics: Human Language Technologies*. San Diego, California, pages 380–386. http://www.aclweb.org/anthology/N16-1042.

A Appendix - Tables of results

Test Sets	20%	40%	60%	80%
test-l8p20	87.29	87.63	86.85	86.77
test-l8p40	80.35	80.63	80.68	81.07
test-l8p60	72.17	72.82	73.54	74.68
test-l8p80	61.51	62.60	64.21	66.39
test-np20	86.60	87.64	86.42	86.28
test-np40	84.69	84.76	84.59	84.60
test-np60	79.49	80.04	79.99	80.91
test-np80	73.48	74.43	74.75	76.34

Table 3: GLEU score according to how much **preposition** error in training data informed by Lang-8, tested on test sets with varying amounts of error from **Lang-8 and NUCLE**.

Test Sets	20%	40%	60%	80%
test-nd20	87.40	86.02	84.40	82.95
test-nd40	84.53	83.80	82.51	81.47
test-nd60	81.63	81.52	80.04	79.45
test-nd80	76.73	77.01	75.53	75.82
test-np20	86.91	85.63	84.03	83.36
test-np40	84.02	83.55	83.22	82.35
test-np60	78.75	78.64	78.88	78.99
test-np80	72.82	73.36	73.88	74.74

Table 6: GLEU score according to how much **combined** preposition and determiner error in training data informed by Lang-8, tested separately on **NUCLE** test sets with varying amounts of **determiner** error, and then **preposition** error.

Test Sets	20%	40%	60%	80%
test-l8d20	88.16	86.76	86.39	84.38
test-l8d40	81.94	82.18	82.20	80.53
test-l8d60	74.83	75.92	76.45	74.99
test-l8d80	65.36	67.54	68.61	69.49
test-nd20	87.64	86.40	85.82	83.63
test-nd40	84.74	84.53	84.22	83.53
test-nd60	81.95	81.96	81.98	81.13
test-nd80	77.08	77.36	77.79	78.20

Table 4: GLEU score according to how much **determiner** error in training data informed by Lang-8, tested on test sets with varying amounts of error from **Lang-8 and NUCLE**.

Test Sets	20%	40%	60%	80%
test-nb20	88.01	87.55	86.85	85.36
test-nb40	84.48	84.12	83.51	83.36
test-nb60	77.58	77.51	77.26	77.45
test-nb80	69.05	69.64	69.57	70.58
test-nb20	87.74	87.39	86.71	85.72
test-nb40	83.43	83.04	82.41	81.90
test-nb60	74.98	74.79	74.32	73.83
test-nb80	64.66	64.66	64.45	64.49

Table 7: GLEU score according to how much **preposition** error (first 4 rows) or **determiner** error (last 4 rows) in training data informed by Lang-8, tested on test sets with varying amounts of **combined** determiner/preposition error from NUCLE.

Test Sets	20%	40%	60%	80%
test-l8b20	87.53	86.70	84.96	83.40
test-l8b40	81.32	81.11	80.28	78.86
test-l8b60	73.74	73.99	73.99	73.37
test-l8b80	63.16	63.98	64.77	65.38
test-nb20	87.86	86.91	86.35	84.36
test-nb40	84.30	83.92	83.38	82.09
test-nb60	77.78	77.87	77.96	77.22
test-nb80	69.39	70.35	71.68	71.05

Table 5: GLEU score according to how much **combined** preposition and determiner error in training data informed by Lang-8, tested on test sets with varying amounts of error from **Lang-8 and NUCLE**.

Test Sets	20%	40%	60%	80%
test-l8p20	87.27	87.00	86.72	85.66
test-l8p40	79.52	79.78	79.67	79.03
test-l8p60	70.87	71.63	72.03	71.99
test-l8p80	59.66	61.18	62.09	62.85
test-l8p20	87.29	87.63	86.85	86.77
test-l8p40	80.35	80.63	80.68	81.07
test-l8p60	72.17	72.82	73.54	74.68
test-l8p80	61.51	62.60	64.21	66.39

Table 8: GLEU score according to how much preposition error in training data informed by **Wikipedia** (first 4 rows) and **Lang-8** (last 4 rows), tested on test sets with varying amounts of preposition error from **Lang-8**.

Test Sets	20%	40%	60%	80%
test-np20	88.01	87.68	88.12	86.72
test-np40	86.52	87.02	87.29	86.84
test-np60	82.49	83.68	84.67	85.02
test-np80	77.89	79.74	81.43	82.56
test-np20	86.60	87.64	86.42	86.28
test-np40	84.69	84.76	84.59	84.60
test-np60	79.49	80.04	79.99	80.91
test-np80	73.48	74.43	74.75	76.34

Table 9: GLEU score according to how much preposition error in training data informed by **Wikipedia** (first 4 rows) and **Lang-8** (last 4 rows), tested on test sets with varying amounts of preposition error from **NUCLE**.

An Entity Resolution Approach to Isolate Instances of Human Trafficking Online

Chirag Nagpal, Kyle Miller, Benedikt Boecking and **Artur Dubrawski**

chiragn@cs.cmu.edu, mille856@andrew.cmu.edu, boecking@andrew.cmu.edu, awd@cs.cmu.edu

Carnegie Mellon University

Abstract

Human trafficking is a challenging law enforcement problem, and traces of victims of such activity manifest as 'escort advertisements' on various online forums. Given the large, heterogeneous and noisy structure of this data, building models to predict instances of trafficking is a convoluted task. In this paper we propose an entity resolution pipeline using a notion of proxy labels, in order to extract clusters from this data with prior history of human trafficking activity. We apply this pipeline to 5M records from backpage.com and report on the performance of this approach, challenges in terms of scalability, and some significant domain specific characteristics of our resolved entities.

1 Introduction

Over the years, human trafficking has grown to be a challenging law enforcement issue. The advent of the internet has brought the problem into the public domain making it an ever greater societal concern. Prior studies (Kennedy, 2012) have leveraged computational techniques to mine online escort advertisements from classifieds websites to detect spatio-temporal patterns, by utilizing certain domain specific features of the ads. Other studies (Dubrawski et al., 2015) have utilized machine learning approaches to identify if ads are likely to be involved in human trafficking activity. Significant work has also been carried out in building large distributed systems to store and process such data, and carry out entity resolution to establish ontological relationships between various entities. (Szekely et al., 2015)

In this paper we explore the possibility of leveraging online escort data in an attempt to identify sources of advertisements, i.e. grouping related ads by the persons that generated them. We isolate such clusters of related advertisements originating from the same source and identify if these potential sources of are involved in human trafficking using prior domain knowledge.

In case of ordinary Entity Resolution schemes, each record is considered to represent a single entity. A popular approach in such scenarios is a 'merge and purge' strategy where records are compared, matched, and then merged into a single more informative record, and the individual records are deleted from the dataset. (Benjelloun et al., 2009)

While our problem can be considered a case of Entity Resolution, escort advertisements pose additional challenges as they form a noisy and unstructured dataset. For example, a single advertisement may represent more than one entity and as such can contain features belonging to more than one individual or group. We describe these idiosyncrasies of this domain in detail in the following sections. Since the advertisements are associated with multiple modalities including text, hyperlinks, images, timestamps, locations etc. in order to featurize characteristics from texts, we use a regex based information extractor constructed via the GATE framework (Cunningham, 2002). This allows us to generate certain domain specific features from our dataset such as aliases, cost, location, phone numbers, or specific URLs. We use these hand engineered features along with other generic features like text similarity, number of common images as features for our binary match function. We note that many identifying characteristics of entities like aliases, are common and shared between escorts which makes it difficult to generate exact matches over individual fea-

77

Proceedings of the 3rd Workshop on Noisy User-generated Text, pages 77–84
Copenhagen, Denmark, September 7, 2017. ©2017 Association for Computational Linguistics

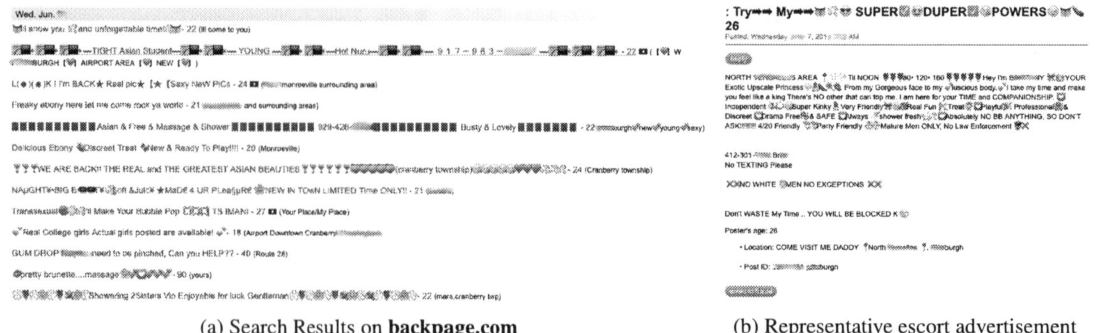

(a) Search Results on backpage.com   (b) Representative escort advertisement

Figure 1: Escort advertisements are a classic source of what can be described as noisy text. Notice the excessive use of emojis, intentional misspelling and relatively benign colloquialisms to obfuscate a more nefarious intent. Domain experts extract meaningful cues from the spatial and temporal indicators, and other linguistic markers to identify suspected trafficking activity, which further motivate the leveraging of computational approaches to support such decision making.

tures.

We proceed to leverage machine learning approaches to learn a classifier that can predict if two advertisements are from the same source, the challenge being the lack of prior knowledge of the source of advertisements. We thus depend upon a strong linking feature, in our case phone numbers, which can be used as proxy evidence for the source of the advertisements and can help us generate labels for the training and test data for a classifier. We can therefore use such strong evidence as to learn another function, which can help us generate labels for our dataset, this semi-supervised approach is described as 'surrogate learning' in (Veeramachaneni and Kondadadi, 2009). Pairwise comparisons result in an extremely high number of comparisons over the entire dataset. In order to reduce this computational burden we introduce a blocking scheme described later.

The resulting clusters are labeled according to their human trafficking relevance using prior expert knowledge. Rule learning is used to establish differences between such relevant clusters and other extracted clusters. The entire pipeline is represented by Figure 2.

2 Domain and Feature Extraction

Figure 1 is illustrative of the search results of escort advertisements and a page advertising a particular individual. The text is inundated with special characters, emojis, as well as misspelled words that are specific markers and highly informative to domain experts. The text consists of

Table 1: Performance of **TJBatchExtractor**

Feature	Precision	Recall	F_1 Score
Age	0.980	0.731	0.838
Cost	0.889	0.966	0.926
E-mail	1.000	1.000	1.000
Ethnicity	0.969	0.876	0.920
Eye Color	1.000	0.962	0.981
Hair Color	0.981	0.959	0.970
Name	0.896	0.801	0.846
Phone Number	0.998	0.995	0.997
Restriction(s)	0.949	0.812	0.875
Skin Color	0.971	0.971	0.971
URL	0.854	0.872	0.863
Height	0.978	0.962	0.970
Measurement	0.919	0.883	0.901
Weight	0.976	0.912	0.943

information regarding the escort's area of operation, phone number, any particular client preferences, and the advertised cost. We built a regular expression based feature extractor to extract this information and store it in a fixed schema, using the popular JAPE tool part of the GATE suite of NLP tools. The extractor we build for this domain, **TJBatchExtractor**, is open source and publicly available at `github.com/ autoncompute/CMU_memex`.

Table 1 lists the performance of our extraction tool on 1,000 randomly sampled escort advertisements, for the various features. Most of the features are self explanatory. (The reader is directed to (Dubrawski et al., 2015) for a complete descrip-

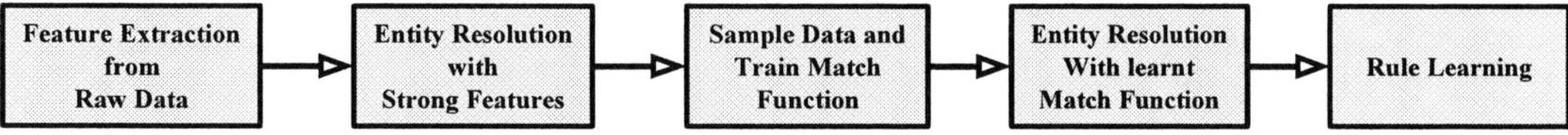

Figure 2: The proposed Entity Resolution pipeline

tion of the fields extracted.) The noisy nature, along with intentional obfuscations, especially in case of features like names results in lower performance as compared to the other extracted features.

Apart from the regular expression based features, we also extract the hashvalues of the images in the advertisements as their identifier, along with the posting date and time, and location.[1]

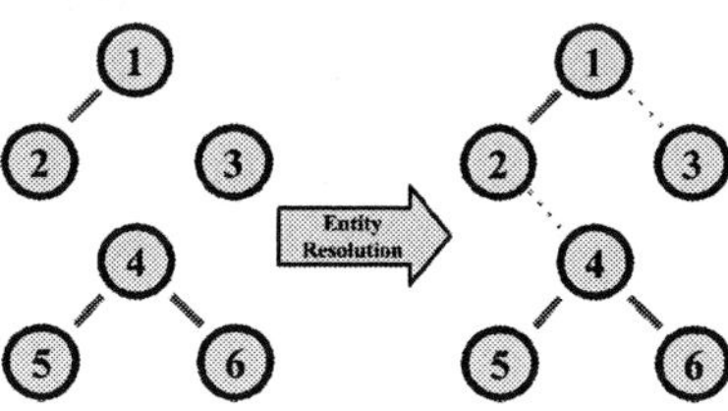

Figure 3: On applying our match function, weak links are generated for classifier scores above a certain match threshold. The strong links between nodes are represented by solid lines. Dashed lines represent the weak links generated by our classifier.

3 Entity Resolution

3.1 Definition

The trained match function can be used to represent our data as a graph where the nodes represent advertisements and edges represent the similarity between ads. We approach the problem of extracting connected components from our dataset using pairwise entity resolution. The similarity or connection between two nodes is treated as a learning problem, with training data for the problem generated by using 'proxy' labels from existing evidence of connectivity from strong features.

More formally, the problem can be considered to be to sample all connected components $\mathcal{H}_i(\mathcal{V}, \mathcal{E})$ from a graph $\mathcal{G}(\mathcal{V}, \mathcal{E})$. Here, $\mathcal{V}$, the set of vertices ($\{v_1, v_2, ..., v_n\}$) is the set of advertisements and $\mathcal{E}$, $\{(v_i, v_j), (v_j, v_k), ..., (v_k, v_l)\}$ is the set of edges between individual records, the

presence of which indicates that they represent the same entity.

We need to learn a function $M(v_i, v_j)$ such that
$$M(v_i, v_j) = \Pr((v_i, v_j) \in \mathcal{E}(\mathcal{H}_i), \forall \mathcal{H}_i \in \mathcal{H})$$

The set of strong features present in a given record can be considered to be the function '$\mathcal{S}$'. In our problem, $\mathcal{S}_v$ represents all the phone numbers associated with v.

Thus $\mathcal{S} = \bigcup \mathcal{S}_{v_i}, \forall v_i \in \mathcal{V}$. Here, $|\mathcal{S}| << |\mathcal{V}|$

Now, let us further consider the graph $\mathcal{G}^*(\mathcal{V}, \mathcal{E})$ defined on the set of vertices $\mathcal{V}$, such that $(v_i, v_j) \in \mathcal{E}(\mathcal{G}^*)$ if $|\mathcal{S}_{v_i} \cap \mathcal{S}_{v_j}| > 0$ (more simply, the graph described by strong features.)

Let $\mathcal{H}^*$ be the set of all the of connected components $\{\mathcal{H}_1^*(\mathcal{V}, \mathcal{E}), \mathcal{H}_2^*(\mathcal{V}, \mathcal{E}), ..., \mathcal{H}_n^*(\mathcal{V}, \mathcal{E})\}$ defined on the graph $\mathcal{G}^*(\mathcal{V}, \mathcal{E})$

Now, function $\mathcal{P}$ is such that for any $p_i \in \mathcal{S}$
$$\mathcal{P}(p_i) = \mathcal{V}(\mathcal{H}_k^*) \iff p_i \in \bigcup \mathcal{S}_{v_i}, \forall v_i \in \mathcal{V}(\mathcal{H}_k^*)$$

3.2 Sampling Scheme

For our classifier we need to generate a set of training examples '$\mathcal{T}$', and $\mathcal{T}_{pos}$ & $\mathcal{T}_{neg}$ are the subsets of samples labeled positive and negative.
$$\mathcal{T}_{pos} = \{F_{v_i, v_j} | v_i \in \mathcal{P}(p_i), v_j \in \mathcal{P}(p_i), \forall p_i \in S\}$$
$$\mathcal{T}_{neg} = \{F_{v_i, v_j} | v_i \in \mathcal{P}(p_i), v_j \notin \mathcal{P}(p_i), \forall p_i \in S\}$$

In order to ensure that the sampling scheme does not end up sampling near duplicate pairs, we introduce a sampling bias such that for every feature vector $F_{v_i, v_j} \in \mathcal{T}_{pos}$, $\mathcal{S}_{v_i} \cap \mathcal{S}_{v_j} = \phi$

This reduces the likelihood of sampling near-duplicates as evidenced in Figure 5, which is a histogram of jaccard similarities between the sets of unigrams of ad pairs.
$$sim(v_i, v_j) = \frac{|\text{unigrams}(v_i) \cap \text{unigrams}(v_j)|}{|\text{unigrams}(v_i) \cup \text{unigrams}(v_j)|}$$

We observe that although we do still end with some near duplicates ($sim > 0.9$), we have high number of non duplicates. ($0.1 < sim < 0.3$) which ensures robust training data for our classifier.

3.3 Training

To train our classifier we experiment with various classifiers like Logistic Regression (LR), Naive Bayes (NB) and Random Forest (RF) using

---

[1] These features are present as metadata, and do not require the use of hand engineered regular expressions.

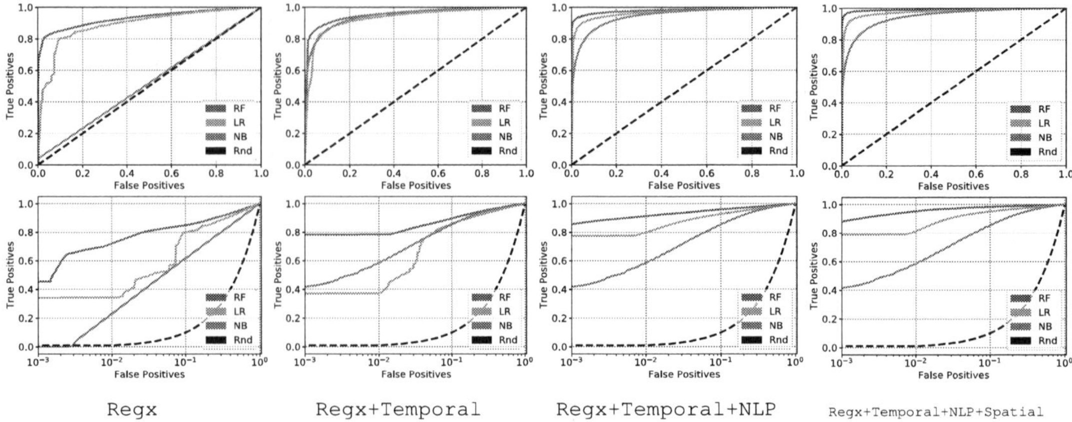

Figure 4: ROC curves for our match function trained on various feature sets. The ROC curve shows reasonably large true positive rates for extremely low false positive rates, which is a desirable behaviour of the match function.

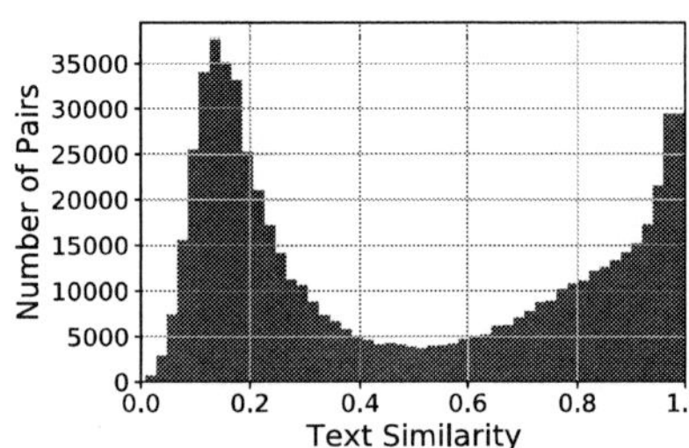

Figure 5: Text similarity for our sampling Scheme. We use Jaccard similarity between the ad unigrams as a measure of text similarity. The histogram shows that the sampling scheme results in both, a large number of near duplicates and non duplicates. Such a behavior is desired to ensure a robust match function.

Table 2: Most Informative Features

	Top 10 Features
1	Location (State)
2	Number of Special Characters
3	Longest Common Substring
4	Number of Unique Tokens
5	Time Difference
6	If Posted on Same Day
7	Presence of Ethnicity
8	Presence of Rate
9	Presence of Restrictions
10	Presence of Names

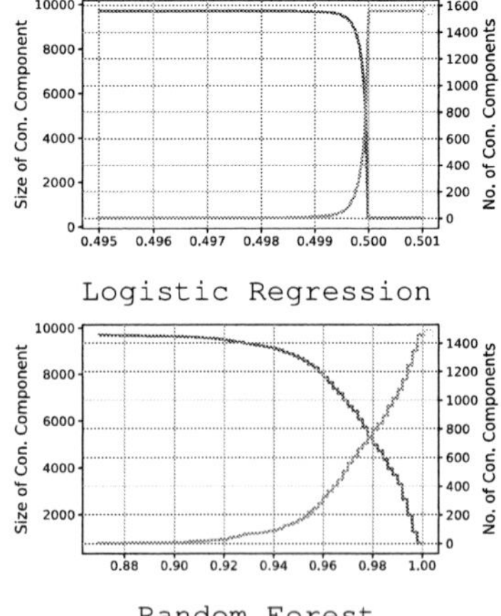

Figure 6: The plots represents the number of connected components and the size of the largest component versus the match threshold.

Scikit (Pedregosa et al., 2011). Table 2 shows the most informative features learnt by the Random Forest classifier. It is interesting to note that the most informative features include the spatial (Location), temporal (Time Difference, Posting Date) and also the linguistic (Number of Special Characters, Longest Common Substring) features. We also find that the domain specific features, extracted using regexs, prove to be informative.

The receiver operating characteristic (ROC) curves for the classifiers we tested with different feature sets are presented in Figure 4. The classifiers perform well at very low false positive rates. Such a behavior is desirable for the classifier to act as a match function, in order to generate sensible results for the downstream tasks. High false positive rates increase the number of links between our records, leading to a 'snowball effect' which results in a break-down of the downstream Entity Resolution process as evidenced in Figure 6.

In order to minimize this breakdown, we need to heuristically learn an appropriate confidence value for our classifier. This is done by carrying out the Entity Resolution process on 10,000 randomly selected records from our dataset. The value of size of the largest extracted connected component and the number of such connected components isolated is calculated for different decision thresholds of our classifier. This allows us to come up with a sensible heuristic for the confidence value.

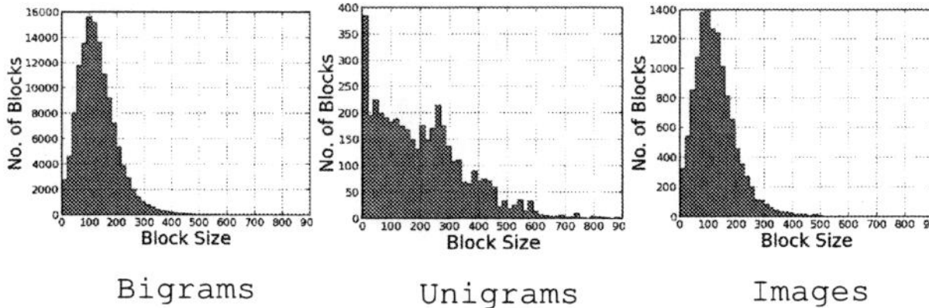

Figure 7: Blocking Scheme

3.4 Blocking Scheme

Our dataset consists of over 5 million records. Naive pairwise comparisons across the dataset makes this problem computationally intractable. In order to reduce the number of comparisons, we introduce a blocking scheme and perform exhaustive pairwise comparisons only within each block before resolving the dataset across blocks. We block the dataset on features including rare unigrams, rare bigrams and rare images. Figure 7 represents the distribution of the frequency of advertisements across the different blocking schemes.

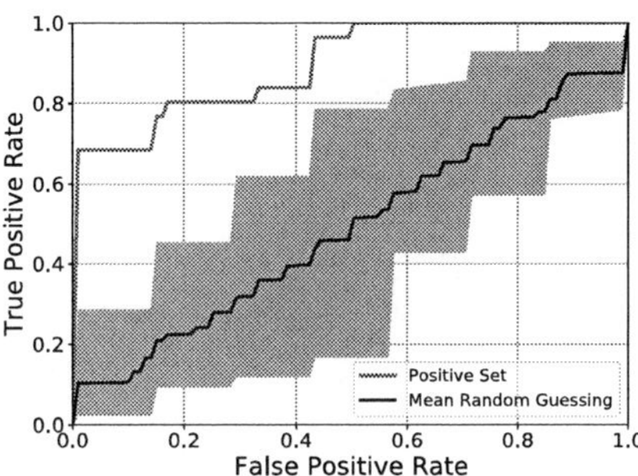

Figure 9: ROC for the connected component classifier. The black line is the positive set, while the red line is the average ROC for 100 randomly guessed predictors.

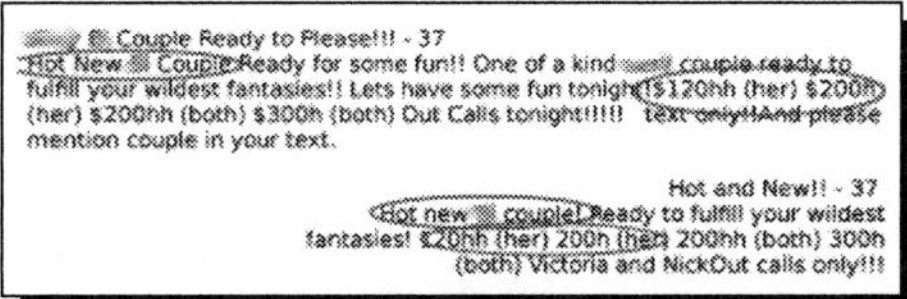

(a) This pair of ads have extremely similar textual content including use of non-latin and special characters. The ad also advertises the same individual, as strongly evidenced by the common alias, 'Paris'.

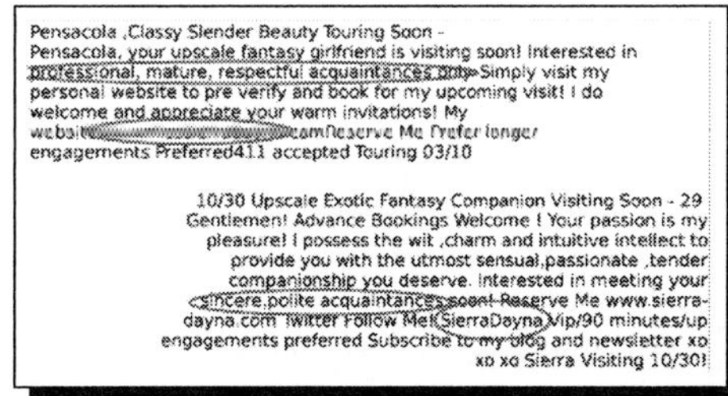

(b) The first ad here does not include any specific names of individuals. However, The strong textual similarity with the second ad and the same advertised cost, helps to match them and discover the individuals being advertised as 'Nick' and 'Victoria'.

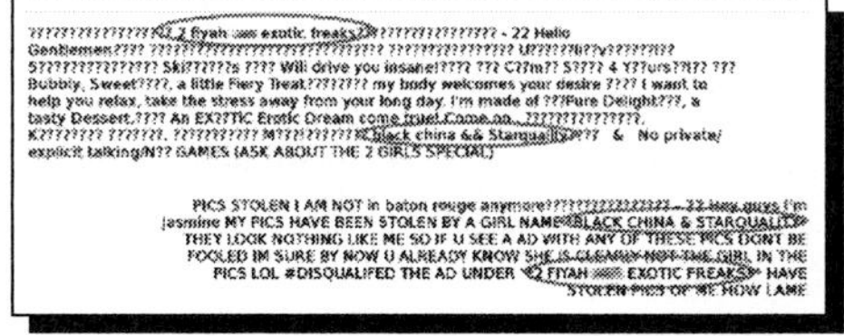

(c) While this pair is not extremely similar in terms of language, however the existence of the rare alias 'SierraDayna' in both advertisemets helps the classifier in matching them. This match can also easily be verified by the similar language structure of the pair.

(d) The first advertisement represents entities 'Black China' and 'Star Quality', while the second advertisement, reveals that the pictures used in the first advertisement are not original and belong to the author of the second ad. This example pair shows the robustness of our match function. It also reveals how complicated relationships between various ads can be.

Figure 8: Representative results of advertisement pairs matched by our classifier. In all the four cases the advertisement pairs had no phone number information (strong feature) in order to detect connections. Note that sensitive elements have been intentionally obfuscated.

Table 3: Results Of Rule Learning

Rule	Support	Ratio	Lift
Xminchars<=250, 120000<Xmaximgfrq, 3<Xmnweeks<=3.4, 4<Xmnmonths<=6.5	11	90.9%	2.67
Xminchars<=250, 120000<Xmaximgfrq 4<Xmnmonths<=6.5,	16	81.25%	2.4
Xstatesnorm<=0.03, 3.6<Xuniqimgsnorm<=5.2, 3.2<Xstdmonths	17	100.0%	2.5
Xstatesnorm<=0.03, 1.95<Xstdweeks<=2.2, 3.2<Xstdmonths	19	94.74%	2.37

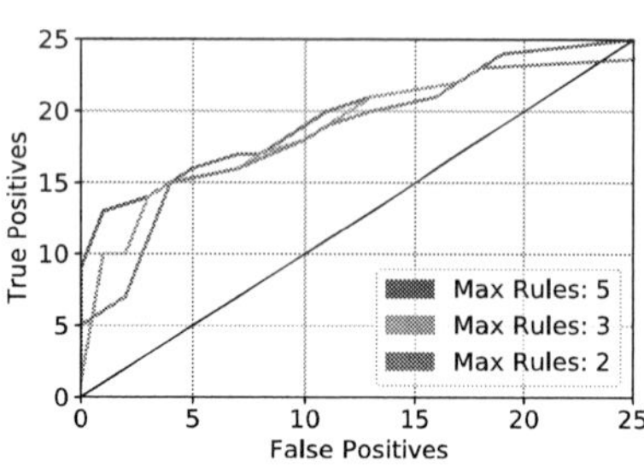

Figure 10: The figure presents PN curves for various values of the maximum rules extracted by the rule learner.

Figure 11: Representative entity isolated by our pipeline, believed to be involved in human trafficking. The nodes represent advertisements, while the edges represent links between advertisements. This entity has 802 nodes and 39,383 edges. This visualization is generated using Gephi. (Bastian et al., 2009). This entity operated in cities, across states and advertised multiple different individuals along with multiple phone numbers. This suggests a more complicated and organised activity and serves as an example of how complicated certain entities can be in this trade.

4   Rule Learning

We extract clusters and identify records that are associated with human trafficking using domain knowledge from experts. We featurize the extracted components using features like size of the cluster, the spatio-temporal characteristics, and the connectivity of the clusters. For our analysis, we consider only components with more than 300 advertisements. We then train a random forest classifier to predict if a cluster contains indicators of human trafficking. In order to establish statistical significance, we compare the ROC results of our classifier using four fold cross-validation for 100 random connected components versus the positive set. Figure 9 & Table 4 lists the performance of the classifier in terms of false positive and true positive Rate while Table 5 lists the most informative features for this classifier.

Additionally we extract rules from our feature set that help establish differences between the trafficking relevant clusters. Some of the rules with corresponding ratios and lift are given in Table 3. PN curves for Rule Learning are analogous to ROC Curves in Classification (Fürnkranz and Flach, 2005) and PN curves corresponding to various rules learnt are presented in the Figure 10. It can be observed that the features used by the rule learning to learn rules with maximum support and ratios, correspond to the ones labeled by the random forest as informative. This also serves as validation for the use of rule learning.

Table 4: Metrics for the Connected Component classifier

AUC	TPR@FPR=1%	FPR@TPR=50%
90.38%	66.6%	0.6%

Table 5: Most Informative Features

Top 5 Features	
1	Posting Months
2	Posting Weeks
3	Std-Dev. of Image Frequency
4	Norm. No. of Names
5	Norm. No. of Unique Images

5   Conclusion

In this paper we approached the problem of isolating sources of human trafficking from online escort advertisements with a pairwise Entity Resolution approach. We trained a classifier able to predict if two advertisements are from the same source using phone numbers as a strong feature which we exploit as proxy ground truth to generate training data. The resulting classifier proved to be robust, as evidenced from extremely low false positive rates. Other approaches like (Szekely et al., 2015) aim at building similar knowledge graphs using similarity score between each feature. This has some limitations. Firstly, we need labelled training data in order to train match functions to detect ontological relations. The challenge is aggravated since this approach considers each feature independently making generation of enough labelled training data for training multiple match functions an extremely complicated task.

Since we utilise existing features as proxy evidence, our approach can generate a large amount of training data without the need of any human annotation. Our approach requires just learning a single function over the entire featureset. Hence, our classifier can learn multiple complicated relations between features to predict a match, instead of the naive feature independence assumption.

We then proceeded to use this classifier in order to perform entity resolution using a heuristically learned match threshold. The resultant connected components were again featurised, and a classifier model was fit before subjecting to rule learning. On comparison with (Dubrawski et al., 2015), the connected component classifier performs a little better with higher values of the area under the ROC curve and the TPR@FPR=1% indicating a steeper ROC curve. We hypothesize that due to the entity resolution process, we are able to generate larger, more robust amount of training data which is immune to the noise in labelling and results in a stronger classifier. The learnt rules show high ratios and lift for reasonably high support as shown in Table 3. Rule learning also adds an element of interpretability to the models we built and as compared to more complex ensemble methods like Random Forests, having hard rules as classification models are preferred by domain experts to build evidence for incrimination.

6   Future Work

While our blocking scheme performs well to reduce the number of comparisons, scalability is still a significant challenge since our approach involves naive pairwise comparisons. One solution to this issue may be to design such a pipeline in a distributed environment. Another approach could be to use a computationally inexpensive technique to de-duplicate the dataset first, which would greatly help with regard to scalability.

In our approach, the ER process depends upon the heuristically learnt match threshold. Lower threshold values can significantly degrade the performance, producing extremely large connected components as a result. The possibility of treating this attribute as a learning task, would help making this approach more generic, and non domain specific.

Hashcodes of the images associated with the ads were also utilized as a feature for the match function. However, simple features like number of unique and common images etc., did not prove to be very informative. Further research is required in order to make better use of such visual data.

Acknowledgments

The authors would like to thank all staff, faculty and students who made the Robotics Institute Summer Scholars program 2015 at Carnegie Mellon University possible. This work has been partially supported by the National Institute of Justice (2013-IJ-CX-K007) and the Defense Advanced Research Projects Agency (FA8750-14-2-0244).

References

Mathieu Bastian, Sebastien Heymann, and Mathieu Jacomy. 2009. Gephi: An open source software for exploring and manipulating networks. http://www.aaai.org/ocs/index.php/ICWSM/09/paper/view/154.

Omar Benjelloun, Hector Garcia-Molina, David Menestrina, Qi Su, Steven Euijong Whang, and Jennifer Widom. 2009. Swoosh: a generic approach to entity resolution. *The VLDB JournalThe International Journal on Very Large Data Bases* 18(1):255–276.

Hamish Cunningham. 2002. Gate, a general architecture for text engineering. *Computers and the Humanities* 36(2):223–254.

Artur Dubrawski, Kyle Miller, Matthew Barnes, Benedikt Boecking, and Emily Kennedy. 2015.

Leveraging publicly available data to discern patterns of human-trafficking activity. *Journal of Human Trafficking* 1(1):65–85.

Johannes Fürnkranz and Peter A Flach. 2005. Roc nrule learningtowards a better understanding of covering algorithms. *Machine Learning* 58(1):39–77.

Emily Kennedy. 2012. Predictive patterns of sex trafficking online .

Fabian Pedregosa, Gaël Varoquaux, Alexandre Gramfort, Vincent Michel, Bertrand Thirion, Olivier Grisel, Mathieu Blondel, Peter Prettenhofer, Ron Weiss, Vincent Dubourg, Jake Vanderplas, Alexandre Passos, David Cournapeau, Matthieu Brucher, Matthieu Perrot, and Édouard Duchesnay. 2011. Scikit-learn: Machine learning in python. *J. Mach. Learn. Res.* 12:2825–2830. http://dl.acm.org/citation.cfm?id=1953048.2078195.

Pedro Szekely, Craig A. Knoblock, Jason Slepicka, Andrew Philpot, Amandeep Singh, Chengye Yin, Dipsy Kapoor, Prem Natarajan, Daniel Marcu, Kevin Knight, David Stallard, Subessware S. Karunamoorthy, Rajagopal Bojanapalli, Steven Minton, Brian Amanatullah, Todd Hughes, Mike Tamayo, David Flynt, Rachel Artiss, Shih-Fu Chang, Tao Chen, Gerald Hiebel, and Lidia Ferreira. 2015. Building and using a knowledge graph to combat human trafficking. In *Proceedings of the 14th International Semantic Web Conference (ISWC 2015)*.

Sriharsha Veeramachaneni and Ravi Kumar Kondadadi. 2009. Surrogate learning: from feature independence to semi-supervised classification. In *Proceedings of the NAACL HLT 2009 Workshop on Semi-Supervised Learning for Natural Language Processing*. Association for Computational Linguistics, pages 10–18.

Noisy Uyghur Text Normalization

Osman Tursun   **Ruket Çakıcı**
Computer Engineering Department
Middle East Technical University
Ankara Turkey
`wusiman.tuerxun, ruken@ceng.metu.edu.tr`

Abstract

Uyghur is the second largest and most actively used social media language in China. However, a non-negligible part of Uyghur text appearing in social media is unsystematically written with the Latin alphabet, and it continues to increase in size. Uyghur text in this format is incomprehensible and ambiguous even to native Uyghur speakers. In addition, Uyghur texts in this form lack the potential for any kind of advancement for the NLP tasks related to the Uyghur language. Restoring and preventing noisy Uyghur text written with unsystematic Latin alphabets will be essential to the protection of Uyghur language and improving the accuracy of Uyghur NLP tasks. To this purpose, in this work we propose and compare the noisy channel model and the neural encoder-decoder model as normalizing methods.

1 Introduction

Uyghur is an alphabetic language, whose alphabet includes 32 phones. Currently, the Uyghur is written with Perso-Arabic, Latin or Cyrillic-based scripts. The most widely used Uyghur alphabet is the modified Perso-Arabic script. However, in some situations, especially in social media, users adopt Latin letters to overcome certain limitations of the Perso-Arabic script. A major problem is that Latin letters are irregularly used as alternatives to Perso-Arabic script because mapping between Perso-Arabic script and Latin alphabet is not trivial. For example, "X", "SH" or "Ş" are all used as alternative representations for the Perso-Arabic character ش (phoneme [ʃ]). Table 1, which based on the result of a conducted survey, shows that 15 out of 32 letters have two to four alternatives. To the best of our knowledge, although unsystematic usage of Latin-based alphabets is a well-discussed problem within Uyghur society, it does not appear in the literature. As far as we know it is only described in (Duval and Janbaz, 2006) as "unsystematic transliterations". In this paper, we refer to this issue as **unsystematic usage of Latin alphabets** (UULA).

UULA problem is similar to text normalization, which has received attention recently (Sproat et al., 2001; Ikeda et al., 2016) because of a large amount of unnormalized text in the social media. In this work, with respect to the smallest text element, we divide the text normalization problem into two sub-categories: *word-based* and *character-based* normalization. The word-based normalization (Sproat et al., 2001; Ikeda et al., 2016) turns non-standard words such as slang, acronyms and phonetic substantiation into standard dictionary words. On the other hand, character-based normalization transform the raw text through substituting the irregularly used characters with proper ones. Character-level normalization includes problems such as diacritic restoration (DR) (Mihalcea and Nastase, 2002), de-ASCIIfication (Arslan, 2015) and so on.

UULA normalization is a character-level normalization, yet it is harder than other character-level normalization problems. It is a many-to-many mapping problem while most of the other types of character-level normalizations are one-to-many. As mentioned above, Table 1 shows 15 of 32 characters have 2 to 4 alternatives. Besides that, UULA texts suffer heavy ambiguity as well. For instance, if the sentence "I gave a Yuan" is written in Uyghur UULA as "Men bir koy berdim", which may mean "I gave a sheep" or "I gave a Yuan".

85

Proceedings of the 3rd Workshop on Noisy User-generated Text, pages 85–93

Table 1: Possible Latin alphabet alternatives of Uyghur Perso-Arabic alphabet.

Uyghur	ژ	ئو	ئە	ق	ئى	ئۆ	ج	ئۆ	غ	خ	ش	ه	ڭ	ئې	ۋ
Phonetics	ʒ	o	ɛ	q	i	e	t͡ʃ	ø	ʁ	χ	ʃ	h	ŋ	e	v
CTA[1]	J	O	E	Q	I	Ü	Ç	Ö	Ğ	X	Ş	H	Ñ	É	V
Alternatives	ZH, J / Z, Y	O / U	A / E	Q / K	I / E	V, U / O, Ü	Ç, Q / CH	O, U / V, Ö	G, GH / H, Ğ	X / H	X / SH, Ş	H / Y	G / NG, Ñ	E, I / Ë, É	V / W

Table 2 shows some other cases of ambiguity. In short, UULA restoration which is addressed in this paper is a non-trivial problem.

Table 2: Examples of confusion cases.

UULA	CTA(Means)
Kan	Qan(Blood) — Kan(Mine)
Soz	Söz(Word) — Soz(Stretch)
Oruk	Oruq(Thin) — Örük(Apricot)
Soyux	Söyüş(Kiss) — Soyuş(Peel off)
Kalgin	Kelgin(come) — Qalghin (stay)

UULA restoration techniques are critical to process non-standard Uyghur text and develop a new type of input method editor (IME) that automatically suggests correctly written words and thus reduce the amount of UULA text. Figure 1 and Table 3 show several real examples of the increasing amount of UULA text on social media and the Internet. In this study we aim to 1) process and standardize the UULA text on the web so that it can be used for other NLP tasks such as information retrieval 2) help to create IMEs equipped with UULA restoration techniques that will prevent the generation of more non-standard text. Furthermore, although UULA restoration is a problem specific to the Uyghur language, the result will be useful for other character-level normalization problems and may be used for languages with similar mapping issues.

(a) Video title   (b) Facebook name   (c) Chatting

Figure 1: Examples of UULA cases from social media.

The rest of the paper is organized as follows: we first talk about the background and related work in Section 2 and 3. Then, the methods for UULA

Table 3: Illustrations of examples displayed in Figure1.

Figure	UULA	CTA	Means
1a	Appigim	Apiim	My Baby
1b	Mamat irzat	Memet irzat	Uyghur Person Name
1c	Men tehi sizni uhlap kalgan ohxaydu daptiman.	Men texi sizni uxlap kalgan oxshaydu deptimen.	I thought you were sleeping.
1c	Yaki hata sual sorap kalgan ohxayman daptiman.	Yaki hata soal sorap kalgan oxshaymen deptimen.	Or I asked improper question.
1c	Yak hey. Munqiga kirip ketken.	Yak hey, munchigha kirip ketken.	Nothing happen. I was taking a bath.

restoration are described in Section 4. The experimental setup is given in Section 5 which is followed by results, and discussion. Finally, we talk about the conclusion and future work.

2 Background and Survey

2.1 Uyghur Alphabets

Uyghur is the native language of more than 15 million Uyghur people. Currently, the modern Uyghur Perso-Arabic alphabet (UPAA) is the most used and official script of Xinjiang Uyghur Autonomous regions of China. In the last century, due to cultural and political reasons (Duval and Janbaz, 2006), Uyghurs have witnessed several reforms of the Uyghur writing system. Each of them brings certain adverse effects on Uyghur culture and society such as creating generation gaps, increasing illiteracy ratio, loss of materials written in previous scripts and so on. As a result, Uyghur society tends to refuse any new alternative scripts to the currently used UPAA. Furthermore, this social atmosphere causes unsuccessful propagation of an authentic Uyghur Latin alphabet system: Uyghur Latin alphabet (ULA), which is a project by Xin-

---

[1]CTA: Common Turkic Alphabet, which is composed of 34 Latin letters.

jiang University in July 2001 (Duval and Janbaz, 2006). However, many Uyghur people have not adopted or even learned this system yet.

With the digital information age, Uyghur people, especially the young generation, are starting to use Latin letters to bypass the limitation related to the UPAA in social media and the internet. There are intrinsic and extrinsic limitations of UPAA. The intrinsic limitation is that, in many new computer programs, web pages, applications etc., UPAA suffers many problems such as unqualified display, absence of IME, and so on. On the other hand, the extrinsic limitation comes from users. Many Uyghur people are not familiar with the UPAA keyboard. Additionally, some Uyghur people consider typing with UPAA input method or switching to it from the other input methods like English as inconvenient work.

Although Uyghur people use Latin letters as an alternative to UPAA, many of them have not chosen the authentic ULA as the alternative. Before and after the announcement of ULA, both systematic and unsystematic transliterations with Latin letters were actively used. According to the survey mentioned in (Duval and Janbaz, 2006), up to 18 different systematic Latin Alphabet systems existed in 2000. These are replaced by the ULA since it is announced as the official Latin alternative of UPAA. However, UULA is still very common in spite of anti-UULA propaganda. Possible explanations can be found for this from many aspects: linguistic, social, political, and so on. These discussions are not in the scope of this paper as our goal is restoring and preventing UULA texts with the aid of an automated system.

2.2 Survey

In 2016, we conducted a small e-survey[2] about how Uyghur-speaking people use Latin alphabets when writing in Uyghur. In this survey, we included questions about the participants' favorite alphabet system and Latin-based alternatives to UPAA. Besides that, we asked them to write 10 different words or phrases given in Latin-derived alphabets they personally use (Table 5).

Among 170 attenders, 39.8% mainly used UPAA, 29.7% mainly use ULA, 30.5% use UULA. However, we also discovered that Uyghur people use different scripts in different circumstances. We discover that nearly half of the peo-

____
[2]available at http://goo.gl/forms/5Pi2vCeUr3

Table 4: Possible alternatives of corrupted characters.

Char.	Alt.	Char.	Alt.	Char.	Alt.
u	u, ö, ü	a	a, e	w	v
v	v, ö, ü	k	k, q	ch	ç
o	o, ö, ü	n	n, ñ	ng	ñ
i,	i, é	j	j, c	sh	ş
h	h, x, ğ	q	q, ç	gh	ğ
y	y, h, j	x	x, ş	zh	j
e	e, é, i	k	k, q	ë	é
g	g, ñ, ğ	z	z, j		

ple use Latin-based characters as alternatives to UPAA frequently. Nevertheless, through asking attendees to type 10 different words or sentences with Latin letters, we concluded the pattern of UULA is the one shown in Table 4. According to the table, if a sentence includes all of these characters, there will be nearly 450,000 different alternative representations of that sentence.

Table 5: Selected survey results.

Samples	Feedback
ژورنال	Jurnal, Jornal, Zhornal, Zhurnal, Zornal, Zurnal, Yornal, Yurnal
ئەقل	akil, eqil, ekil, akel
ھوقۇق	huquq, hukuk, hokok, hoqoq, hoquq, hokuk
بلەيزۈك	Bilayzuk, Belayzuk, Bilayzvk, Beleyzuk, Bileyzvk, Bileyzk, Bileyzvk, Bilayzuk, Bileyzuk
چوچۇرە	Qoqura, Chochure, Ququra, Chchre, Ququre, Qoqure, Qoqore, Chochvre, Chuchure, Qvqvra, Qoqvra, Qoqora, Chchvre, Chochore, Ququra Qoqvre, re, Chchre
مېنىڭ	Menig, Mening, Mning, Mning, Mening, Mineg, Mineng, Minig, Mining
دوغاپ	dogap, doghap, dohap, dugap, dughap, dohap, duhap
گېزىت قەغزى	gezit qeghizi, gezit kagizi, gizit qeghizi, gizit kagizi, gizit qeghizi, gizit kegizi, gizit kagizi, gezit kegizi, gzit qeghizi, gezit kagizi, gzit qeghizi, gezit qeghizi, gizit qegizi, gizit kagaz
خەيرى - خوش ھەسەن	xeyr xosh hesen, hayri hox hasan, xeyir xosh hesen, hair hox hasan, heyir hosh hesen, xeyir xosh hesen, heyir hox hesen
ھېلىقى فونتان	heliki fontan, heliqi fontan, hiliki fontan, hiliqi fontan, heliqi fontan, yiliki fontan, heliki fontan, hiliki funtan, hiliki fontan, hliqi fontan

3 Related Work

This is the first study on UULA restoration to our knowledge. However, the problem is closely related to text normalization, which is the focus of studies given in this section. With an exponential growth of noisy texts, the text normalization study has become a hot topic in NLP. In the literature, text normalization is viewed as being related to either spell-checking (Cook and Stevenson, 2009; Choudhury et al., 2007) or machine translation (Aw et al., 2006; Kobus et al., 2008; Ikeda et al., 2016). However, it is pointed out that traditional spell-checking algorithms are not very effective on some text normalization problems such as normalizing text messages like SMS, tweets, comments, etc (Pennell and Liu, 2010; Clark and Araki, 2011).

According to Kukich's early survey (Kukich, 1992) on automatic word correction, there are several types of spelling correction techniques such as minimum edit distance (Damerau, 1964), similarity key (Odell and Russell, 1918), rule-based methods (Yannakoudakis and Fawthrop, 1983), N-gram-based models (Riseman and Hanson, 1974), probabilistic (Bledsoe and Browning, 1959; Cook and Stevenson, 2009; Choudhury et al., 2007) and neural net techniques (Cherkassky and Vassilas, 1989). Among them, probabilistic models (e.g. noisy channel model) are successfully used for text normalization (Cook and Stevenson, 2009; Choudhury et al., 2007). The noisy channel model method normalizes non-standard words with the channel model and the language model, which are achieved by analyzing and processing a large corpus of noisy and formal texts.

Statistical (Aw et al., 2006), rule-based (Beaufort et al., 2010) and neural network techniques (Ikeda et al., 2016) from machine translation are used for text normalization. Since the neural machine translation (Cho et al., 2014) showed promising results, it has also been adapted to other problems such as text normalization and language correction. Xie et al. (2016) applied character-based sequence modelling with attention mechanism for language correction. The most closely related previous work to our study is Ikeda et al. (2016). They used a neural encoder-decoder model for normalizing noise in Japanese text introduced by the usage of three different writing systems. They also built a synthetic database with predefined rules for data augmentation. They compared their neural network model with rule-based methods, while we compare our neural network model with a probabilistic model.

4 Method

For UULA restoration, the aim is to recover the target sequence Y from the source sequence X. Word-based or character-based models can be used for this. In the character-based model, $X = < l_1^x, l_2^x, \ldots, l_n^x >$, $Y = < l_1^y, l_2^y, \ldots, l_n^y >$ where l_1^x is the first character of X, and n is the length of the word(s). On the other hand, for the word-based model, $X = < w_1^x, w_2^x, \ldots, w_m^x >$, $Y = < w_1^y, w_2^y, \ldots, w_m^y >$ where m is number of words in X or Y, and w is a word. For word-based restoration, we adopt the noisy channel model. Meanwhile, we use an encoder-decoder based sequence to sequence model for character-based restoration. In fact, both of models can be character or word based. In the encoder-decoder model, to reduce the input dimension, we picked the character-based solution over the word-based. However, we choose the word-based solution for the noisy channel model because of simple implementation and robust filtering with a dictionary.

4.1 Noisy Channel Model (NCM)

Noisy channel model (Church and Gale, 1991; Mays et al., 1991) is a widely applied method for spell checking. It assumes spelling mistakes were introduced while inputs were passing through a noisy communication channel. If P is the probabilistic model of the noisy channel, then the correct word w_i^y, from the dictionary V, corresponding to the word w_i^x can be found by using the following formula:

$$w_i^y = \operatorname*{argmax}_{w \in V} P(w|w_i^x) \tag{1}$$

$$= \operatorname*{argmax}_{w \in V} \frac{P(w_i^x|w)P(w)}{P(w_i^x)} \tag{2}$$

$$= \operatorname*{argmax}_{w \in V} P(w_i^x|w)P(w) \tag{3}$$

Equation 3 shows that the target word w_i^y depends on conditional probability $P(w_i^x|w)$ and prior probability $P(w)$. $P(w)$ is calculated with the language model, while $P(w_i^y|w)$ is calculated with the error model. The error model is achieved with static analysis on real error samples. Since our error samples are created synthetically, we build the error model with the same confusion table with which we generated corrupt data. Here, the confusion table is at the character-level but we need a word-level confusion table. In order to overcome this issue, we apply the Bledsoe-Browning technique (Bledsoe and Browning, 1959). It calculates the word-level confusion probability by multiplying the confusion probability of the letters as in Equation 4.

$$P(w_i^y|w_i^x) = \prod_n^i P(l_i^y|l_i^x) \qquad (4)$$

4.2 Neural Encoder-Decoder Model (NEDM)

From a different perspective, the text normalization task can be considered as a text regeneration process starting with the information extracted from noisy data. We can view text reconstruction as rewriting new text with same meaning. During generation, the text process model (encoder) extracts abstract information from un-normalized text. The generalization model (decoder) starts to generate the text once it receives information from the text processing model. The generation model is trained by maximizing the probability of the generated text, $P(Y)$. According to the chain rule, it is decomposed into:

$$P(Y) = \prod_{t=1}^M p(y_i|y_1, y_2, \ldots, y_{i-1}) \qquad (5)$$

where M is the length of the sequence, and y_i is a unit in the sequence. Therefore, we need a model that learns the conditional distributions: $p(y_i|y_1, y_2, \ldots, y_{i-1})$.

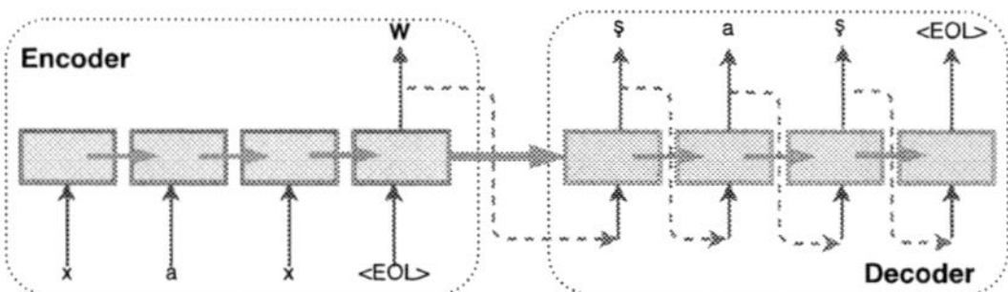

Figure 2: Encoder-decoder model.

The encoder-decoder model in (Cho et al., 2014) works in a similar fashion. It divides many-to-many mappings into many-to-one and one-to-many mappings. The encoder does a many-to-one mapping, while the decoder performs a one-to-many mapping. Both the encoder and the decoder are recurrent neural networks. One of the advantages of this model is that the encoder and the decoder are jointly trained to maximize the conditional probability, $P(Y|X)$.

$$P(Y|X) = \prod_{t=1}^M p(l_i^y|l_1^y, l_2^y, \ldots, l_{i-1}^y, X) \qquad (6)$$

As the Figure 2 and Equation 6 show, the encoder extracts abstract information W from input X, and then the decoder starts generating target text sequentially with the information that comes from the encoder and the previous time step.

5 Experiment and Results

5.1 Dataset

In the experiments, we use both synthetic and authentic data. We train/build our models with synthetic data because of limited access to the real cases and difficulties of building ground truth. Nevertheless, we conduct tests both on synthetic and real data that we have collected. [3]

5.1.1 Synthetic Data

The synthetic dataset used in our experiments is built by scrawling raw text from news websites such as "tianshannet.com", "okyan.com" and "uy-cnr.cn". In total, we collected 2GB of data for training and testing, 10 text files of different genres, each of which includes around 586 words. Note that these data are written in UPAA, while we convert them to the CTA format for convenience.

The training of the encoder-decoder model uses pairs of source and target sequences. Target sequences are collected from raw text, while source sequences are created synthetically by randomly replacing letters in the target sequence using the mapping shown in Table 4. Notice that words in synthetic UULA text may include more characters than ground-truth target words. This is caused by replacing some single letters by double letters. For example, ş to sh , ç to ch, and so on. To ensure that corresponding words in source-target pairs have the same length, we pad n "w"s at the end of a target word whose corresponding source word includes n additional letters. The reason for choosing the character "w" is that it is not in CTA. Similarly, we generate the target and source text for testing. However, for more convincing test results on synthetic data, we generated 10 different source texts for each of the target text. Testing results on each of the synthetic files are the mean of 10 cases, while the final accuracy of all synthetic data is the mean of all the results on the synthetic files.

---

[3] The Noisy Uyghur Text Dataset used in this study is freely accessible from the URL: `http://kovan.ceng.metu.edu.tr/~osman`.

5.1.2 Real Data

We collect 226 sentences (1372 words in total) from social media platforms such as "Wechat", "Facebook" and so on. For building the ground truth, we first use our model for restoration. Secondly, we restore texts manually. Finally, we apply a spell-checker for further restoring. While collecting real data and building the corresponding ground, we found that the real data has more noise than the usual UULA. We found in real data that there are various types of spelling errors, misuse of punctuation and repetitions.

5.2 Implementation Details

5.2.1 Neural Encoder-Decoder Model

We built our neural encoder-decoder model with TensorFlow (Abadi et al., 2015). Both encoder and decoder models used three layers stacked LSTMs with 256 hidden units and 256 dimension character embeddings. For training the model, the Adam optimizer with 0.0001 learning rate is applied. We trained the model in only 2 epochs with a 128 batch size. We selected the model with the best validation results on the validation set that is described below. The training process is accomplished on Tesla K40 GPU.

In this model, the length of the target and the source sequences is 30, and, instead of special tokens, blank space is placed at the beginning and the end of a sequence. Note that these sequences are constructed by grouping words in the raw text by keeping sequence length under 30. We build them as follows: First, we tokenize the text with blank space or new line character, then we append a blank space to the beginning of each token. Then, we concatenate them in order by keeping the sequence length at maximum 30. If concatenating the next word makes the current sequence length bigger than 30, then only blank spaces are appended. However, the new sequence will start from the next word. In total, we generate 63,824,760 sequences. We divide them into training, validation and testing sets in this portion: 60%, 20%, 20%.

5.2.2 Noisy Channel Model

The channel probability, in other words, the error model, in the NCM is generated according to the Table 1. For example, the probability of l_1='ş' turning into l_2='x', $p(l_2|l_1)$ is 1/3, since ş has three alternatives. We generate a 3-gram language model by running Kenlm language modeling tool (Heafield, 2011) on our collected text.

The Noisy channel model method normalizes the text word-by-word by selecting the most probable candidate from all possible candidates by ranking their probabilities. These candidates are generated with Table 1. For example, the word "xax" will have 8 candidates: "xax, şax, xex, şex, xeş, şeş, şaş, xaş", since both "x" and "a" have two alternatives. According to our experiment, on average, 1074 candidates are proposed for each word. However, we filter these candidates with the use of a dictionary. The dictionary includes all unique words from the raw text. With this dictionary filter, 1074 candidates are filtered to an average of 1.6 candidates. After filtering, a candidate is passed to the noisy channel model to find the candidate with the highest likelihood. If all candidates are filtered, then the original is kept.

5.3 Results and Analysis

The performance of two models is evaluated by conducting two tests: UULA text restoration test and the IME recommendation test. The former tests the accuracy the model on restoring documents with UULA noise. On the other hand, the latter checks a model's prediction accuracy of the word being typed. In the IME recommendation test, we conjecture that the models have limited access to previous words. Therefore, we test two models by providing a limited number of previous words to them (at most two words in IME testing). In fact, the noisy channel model always has limited access to the previous context, therefore its results are the same for two tests.

Accuracy results of the tests are calculated as in Equation 7.

$$Accuracy = \frac{\text{\# of correct words}}{\text{\# of words}} \quad (7)$$

where "correct words" means correctly recommended or restored words. We did not calculate the precision-recall value, since the recall is always equal to 1, and precision is equal to the accuracy.

From Table 6, we can see both the neural encoder-decoder model and the noisy channel model show high performance on the synthetic dataset. However, the noisy channel model is slightly better than the encoder-decoder model. Table 7 shows that both of the models are suitable for developing IME specialized for UULA restoration. However, the 2-gram noisy channel model returns the best performance. We believe that there are three possible explanations for why the NCM outperforms the NEDM on the synthetic dataset: 1) The dictionary used in NCM is very robust, it filters out almost all of the unqualified candidates. 2) The channel model used in NCM is too ideal because it is exactly calculated not generally approximated. 3) The NEDM model needs more training with synthetic data pairs.

In the real cases as Table 8 shows, the neural encoder-decoder model is slightly better than the noisy channel model. In the real dataset, some words are not included in the dictionary, therefore noisy channel model cannot restore them correctly. Besides, other factors such as spelling errors, misuse of punctuation and redundant repeating bring more challenges to the noisy channel model as compared to the neural encoder-decoder model, since the former works at word-level but the latter at character-level.

Table 6: The results of UULA restoration on synthetic dataset (Before restoration, the accuracy is *19.40 ± 0.03*).

Model	Accuracy (%)
NEDM	93.09 ± 2.21
NCM 1-gram	94.16 ± 0.08
NCM 2-gram	**94.54 ± 0.11**
NCM 3-gram	94.52 ± 0.11

Table 7: The results of IME recommendation on synthetic dataset.

N-gram	NEDM (%)	NCM (%)
1-gram	91.65	94.16
2-gram	94.38	**94.54**

Table 8: The results of UULA restoration on real noisy data (Before restoration, the accuracy is *26.14 %*).

Model	Accuracy (%)
NEDM	**65.69**
NCM 2-gram	64.95

In Tables 9, 10 and Figure 3, the qualitative results are given, where both NCM and NEDM fail to restore certain noisy words. The NCM fails in restoring a noisy word when the corresponding

Table 9: Examples of comparison of two models and the baselines on synthetic UULA texts (Underlined means the original noisy text. *Italic* means the text is erroneously restored to non-standard text. **Bold** means the text is wrongly restored to an unwanted (but in dictionary) text).

	Sentences
UULA	pütukqilek tarehiy nayayeti uzun bir kesip. qademda orda-saraylargha, yamulgha mexsus pütvkqeler qoyulğan.
Baseline	pütükçilik tarixiy nahayiti uzun bir kesip. qedimde orda-saraylarğa, yamulğa mexsus pütükçiler qoyulğan.
NCM	pütükçilik tarixiy nahayiti uzun bir kesip. **qedemde** orda-*saraylargha*, *yamulgha* mexsus *pütvkqeler* qoyulğan.
NEDM	pütükçilik tarixiy nahayiti uzun bir kesip. **qedemde** orda-saraylarğa, yamulğa mexsus pütükçiler qoyulğan.
UULA	tulum ilgerki zamanlardeki uyghurlar saparga çeqkan vaketta ozuq-tvlvk we başka lazematlik turmux buyumlerine kaqilaydehan tëriden yasalhan halta yam xundakla kadimki uygurlar eshlitip kalgan muyem qatnax korallerining biri.
Baseline	tulum ilgirki zamanlardiki uyğurlar seperge çiqqan vaqitta ozuq-tülük ve başqa lazimetlik turmuş buyumlirini qaçilaydiğan tëridin yasalğan xalta hem şundaqla qedimki uyğurlar işlitip kelgen muhim qatnaş qoralliriniñ biri.
NCM	tulum ilgirki zamanlardiki uyğurlar seperge çiqqan vaqitta ozuq-tülük ve başqa lazimetlik turmuş buyumlirini qaçilaydiğan tëridin yasalğan xalta hem şundaqla qedimki uyğurlar işlitip kelgen muhim qatnaş qoralliriniñ biri.
NEDM	tulum ilgirki zamanlardiki uyğurlar seperge çiqqan vaqitta ozuq-tülük ve başqa lazimetlik turmuş buyumlirini qaçilaydiğan tëridin yasalğan xalta hem şundaqla qedimki uyğurlar işlitip **qalğan** muhim qatnaş qoralliriniñ biri.

Table 10: Examples of comparison of two models and the baselines on real UULA texts (The text formatting has the same meaning as in Table 9).

	Sentences
UULA	nur xirkitinig adrisini bildihanlar bamu?
Baseline	nur şirkitiniñ adrésini bilidiğanlar barmu?
NCM	nur şirkitiniñ *adrisini bildihanlar bamu*?
NEDM	nur şirkitiniñ *adrisini* bildiğanlar *bamu*?
UULA	muxu hakta taklip pikir berilsa?
Baseline	muşu heqte teklip pikir bérilse?
NCM	muşu *hakta* teklip pikir bérilse?
NEDM	muşu heqte teklip pikir *birilse*?
UULA	chishliri chushup ketkuche eytiptu bichare ashiq boway
Baseline	çişliri çüşüp ketküçe éytiptu biçare aşiq bovay
NCM	çişliri çüşüp ketküçe éytiptu biçare aşiq bovay
NEDM	çişliri çüşüp *ketküçi* éytiptu biçare aşiq bovay

original word does not appear in the dictionary or has an ignorable N-gram score. Meanwhile, the NEDM model tends to map characters to popular patterns. Therefore, in a few cases, it restores noisy words to unexpected ones.

```
rusiye sün'iy hemrah xevir     ruseya sun'ey yamray haver
i özbükstanliq iqtisadşuna     e vzbikstanlek iktisadxuna
s kurtof özbékistan özini      s kurtof ozbekestan ozene
özi qamdaydiğan iqtisadiy      özi qamdaydeghan eqtesade
siyasetni yolğa qoyup, yuq     y seyasatne yolgha koyup,
iri tamojna béci arqiliq b     yukire tamojna bece arqeli
u döletniñ bazirini qoğday     q bu dölatnen bazirene kog
du. özbékistan hazir téxi      daydu. ozbekistan yazir t
dölet halqiğan, rayon bir      éxi dölet yalqiğan, rayon
gevdileşken teşkilatqa kir     ber gawdeleshkan tashkilat
iş teyyarliqini qilip bola     qa keriş teyyarlikene qele
lmidi, özbékistan gah bez      p bolalmedi, vzbikestan ga
i bir gevdileşken teşkilat     h bezi bir gewdeleşken teş
larğa kirip, gah bu teşkil     kilatlarğa kerep, gah bu t
atlardin çékinidu. özbékis     ashkilatlardin chekinidu.
tan davamliq muşu siyasetn     ozbekistan dawamleq muxu s
i yolğa qoyidu, kérimof öz     eyasetne yolha qoyedu, kar
bikistan pirézdinti bolğan     imof uzbekestan perézdent
da bu siyaset özgermesliki     i bolğanda bu seyaset özga
mumkin, dédi.                  rmesleke mumkin, dede.

rusiye sün'iy hemrah xevir     rusiye sün'iy hemrah xevir
i özbékstanliq iqtisadşuna     i öbkekstanliq iqtisdaşnu
s kurtof özbékistan özini      sa kurtof özbékistan özin
özi qamdaydiğan iqtisadiy      i özi qamdaydiğan iqtisadi
siyasetni yolğa qoyup, yuq     y siyasetni yolğa qoyup, y
iri tamojna béci arqiliq b     uqiri tamojna béci arqili
u döletniñ bazirini qoğday     q budöletniñ bazirini qoğd
du. özbékistan hazir téxi      aydu. özbékistan hazir téx
dölet halqiğan, rayon bir      i dölet halqiğan, rayon bi
gevdileşken teşkilatqa kir     r gevdileşken teşkilatqa k
iş teyyarliqini qilip bola     iriş teyyarliqini qilip bo
lmidi, özbékistan gah bez      lalmidi, özbékistan gax be
i bir gevdileşken teşkilat     zi bir gevdileşken teşkila
larğa kirip, gah bu teşkil     tlarğa kirip, gah bu eşkil
atlardin çékinidu. özbékis     atlardin çékinidu. özbékis
tan davamliq muşu siyasetn     tan davamliq muşu siyasetn
i yolğa qoyidu, kérimof öz     i yolğa qoyidu, kérimof öz
bikistan pirézdinti bolğan     békistan pirézdinti bolğan
da bu siyaset özgermeslik      da bu siyaset özgermeslik
i mumkin, dédi.                i mumkin, dédi.|
```

Figure 3: An example output of the neural encoder-decoder model on a subset of the synthetic UULA text (Top and bottom left part are the same ground truth, top right is the UULA, bottom right is the restoration. Blue highlights are differences.).

6 Conclusion and Future Work

In this work, we propose two models for normalizing Uyghur UULA texts. The noisy channel model views the problem as a spell-checking problem, while the neural encoder-decoder model views it as a machine translation problem. Both of them return highly accurate results on restoration and recommendation tasks on the synthetic dataset. However, their accuracy on real datat would benefit from further improvement. To improve their performance on the real dataset, one possible strategy is to consider other noisy factors appearing in the real dataset. In future work, we will update our models to handle other noisy elements such as spelling errors and the misuse of punctuation on the real dataset. However, we believe that it is easier to adapt the neural encoder-decoder model to the new challenges than the noisy channel model. This is because it only requires fine-tuning on extra data for different kinds of noise, while the noisy channel model requires redesigning of the model structure.

7 Acknowledgement

We gratefully acknowledge the support of NVIDIA Corporation with the donation of the Tesla K40 GPU used for this research.

References

Martín Abadi, Ashish Agarwal, Paul Barham, Eugene Brevdo, Zhifeng Chen, Craig Citro, Greg S. Corrado, Andy Davis, Jeffrey Dean, Matthieu Devin, Sanjay Ghemawat, Ian Goodfellow, Andrew Harp, Geoffrey Irving, Michael Isard, Yangqing Jia, Rafal Jozefowicz, Lukasz Kaiser, Manjunath Kudlur, Josh Levenberg, Dan Mané, Rajat Monga, Sherry Moore, Derek Murray, Chris Olah, Mike Schuster, Jonathon Shlens, Benoit Steiner, Ilya Sutskever, Kunal Talwar, Paul Tucker, Vincent Vanhoucke, Vijay Vasudevan, Fernanda Viégas, Oriol Vinyals, Pete Warden, Martin Wattenberg, Martin Wicke, Yuan Yu, and Xiaoqiang Zheng. 2015. TensorFlow: Large-scale machine learning on heterogeneous systems. Software available from tensorflow.org. http://tensorflow.org/.

Ahmet Arslan. 2015. Deasciification approach to handle diacritics in turkish information retrieval. *Information Processing & Management* .

AiTi Aw, Min Zhang, Juan Xiao, and Jian Su. 2006. A phrase-based statistical model for sms text normalization. In *Proceedings of the COLING/ACL on Main conference poster sessions.* Association for Computational Linguistics, pages 33–40.

Richard Beaufort, Sophie Roekhaut, Louise-Amélie Cougnon, and Cédrick Fairon. 2010. A hybrid rule/model-based finite-state framework for normalizing sms messages. In *Proceedings of the 48th Annual Meeting of the Association for Computational Linguistics.* Association for Computational Linguistics, pages 770–779.

Woodrow Wilson Bledsoe and Iben Browning. 1959. Pattern recognition and reading by machine. In *Papers presented at the December 1-3, 1959, eastern joint IRE-AIEE-ACM computer conference.* ACM, pages 225–232.

Vladimir Cherkassky and Nikolaos Vassilas. 1989. Performance of back propagation networks for associative database retrieval. *Int. J. Comput. Neural Net* .

Kyunghyun Cho, Bart Van Merriënboer, Caglar Gulcehre, Dzmitry Bahdanau, Fethi Bougares, Holger Schwenk, and Yoshua Bengio. 2014. Learning phrase representations using rnn encoder-decoder for statistical machine translation. *arXiv preprint arXiv:1406.1078* .

Monojit Choudhury, Rahul Saraf, Vijit Jain, Animesh Mukherjee, Sudeshna Sarkar, and Anupam Basu. 2007. Investigation and modeling of the structure of texting language. *International journal on document analysis and recognition* 10(3):157–174.

Kenneth W Church and William A Gale. 1991. Probability scoring for spelling correction. *Statistics and Computing* 1(2):93–103.

Eleanor Clark and Kenji Araki. 2011. Text normalization in social media: progress, problems and applications for a pre-processing system of casual english. *Procedia-Social and Behavioral Sciences* 27:2–11.

Paul Cook and Suzanne Stevenson. 2009. An unsupervised model for text message normalization. In *Proceedings of the workshop on computational approaches to linguistic creativity*. Association for Computational Linguistics, pages 71–78.

Fred J Damerau. 1964. A technique for computer detection and correction of spelling errors. *Communications of the ACM* 7(3):171–176.

Jean Rahman Duval and Walis Abdukerim Janbaz. 2006. An introduction to latin-script uyghur. In *Middle East & Central Asia Politics, Economics, and Society Conference*. pages 7–9.

Kenneth Heafield. 2011. Kenlm: Faster and smaller language model queries. In *Proceedings of the Sixth Workshop on Statistical Machine Translation*. Association for Computational Linguistics, pages 187–197.

Taishi Ikeda, Hiroyuki Shindo, and Yuji Matsumoto. 2016. Japanese text normalization with encoder-decoder model. *WNUT 2016* page 129.

Catherine Kobus, François Yvon, and Géraldine Damnati. 2008. Normalizing sms: are two metaphors better than one? In *Proceedings of the 22nd International Conference on Computational Linguistics-Volume 1*. Association for Computational Linguistics, pages 441–448.

Karen Kukich. 1992. Techniques for automatically correcting words in text. *ACM Computing Surveys (CSUR)* 24(4):377–439.

Eric Mays, Fred J Damerau, and Robert L Mercer. 1991. Context based spelling correction. *Information Processing & Management* 27(5):517–522.

Rada Mihalcea and Vivi Nastase. 2002. Letter level learning for language independent diacritics restoration. In *proceedings of the 6th conference on Natural language learning-Volume 20*. Association for Computational Linguistics, pages 1–7.

M Odell and R Russell. 1918. The soundex coding system. *US Patents* 1261167.

Deana L Pennell and Yang Liu. 2010. Normalization of text messages for text-to-speech. In *Acoustics Speech and Signal Processing (ICASSP), 2010 IEEE International Conference on*. IEEE, pages 4842–4845.

Edward M Riseman and Allen R Hanson. 1974. A contextual postprocessing system for error correction using binary n-grams. *IEEE Transactions on Computers* 100(5):480–493.

Richard Sproat, Alan W Black, Stanley Chen, Shankar Kumar, Mari Ostendorf, and Christopher Richards. 2001. Normalization of non-standard words. *Computer speech & language* 15(3):287–333.

Ziang Xie, Anand Avati, Naveen Arivazhagan, Dan Jurafsky, and Andrew Y Ng. 2016. Neural language correction with character-based attention. *arXiv preprint arXiv:1603.09727* .

Emmanuel J Yannakoudakis and David Fawthrop. 1983. The rules of spelling errors. *Information Processing & Management* 19(2):87–99.

Crowdsourcing Multiple Choice Science Questions

Johannes Welbl[*]
Computer Science Department
University College London
`j.welbl@cs.ucl.ac.uk`

Nelson F. Liu[*]
Paul G. Allen School of
Computer Science & Engineering
University of Washington
`nfliu@cs.washington.edu`

Matt Gardner
Allen Institute for Artificial Intelligence
`mattg@allenai.org`

Abstract

We present a novel method for obtaining high-quality, domain-targeted multiple choice questions from crowd workers. Generating these questions can be difficult without trading away originality, relevance or diversity in the answer options. Our method addresses these problems by leveraging a large corpus of domain-specific text and a small set of existing questions. It produces model suggestions for document selection and answer distractor choice which aid the human question generation process. With this method we have assembled *SciQ*, a dataset of 13.7K multiple choice science exam questions.[1] We demonstrate that the method produces in-domain questions by providing an analysis of this new dataset and by showing that humans cannot distinguish the crowdsourced questions from original questions. When using *SciQ* as additional training data to existing questions, we observe accuracy improvements on real science exams.

1 Introduction

The construction of large, high-quality datasets has been one of the main drivers of progress in NLP. The recent proliferation of datasets for textual entailment, reading comprehension and Question Answering (QA) (Bowman et al., 2015; Hermann et al., 2015; Rajpurkar et al., 2016; Hill et al., 2015; Hewlett et al., 2016; Nguyen et al., 2016) has allowed for advances on these tasks, particularly with neural models (Kadlec et al.,

2016; Dhingra et al., 2016; Sordoni et al., 2016; Seo et al., 2016). These recent datasets cover broad and general domains, but progress on these datasets has not translated into similar improvements in more targeted domains, such as science exam QA.

Science exam QA is a high-level NLP task which requires the mastery and integration of information extraction, reading comprehension and common sense reasoning (Clark et al., 2013; Clark, 2015). Consider, for example, the question *"With which force does the moon affect tidal movements of the oceans?"*. To solve it, a model must possess an abstract understanding of natural phenomena and apply it to new questions. This transfer of general and domain-specific background knowledge into new scenarios poses a formidable challenge, one which modern statistical techniques currently struggle with. In a recent Kaggle competition addressing 8th grade science questions (Schoenick et al., 2016), the highest scoring systems achieved only 60% on a multiple choice test, with retrieval-based systems far outperforming neural systems.

A major bottleneck for applying sophisticated statistical techniques to science QA is the lack of large in-domain training sets. Creating a large, multiple choice science QA dataset is challenging, since crowd workers cannot be expected to have domain expertise, and questions can lack relevance and diversity in structure and content. Furthermore, poorly chosen answer distractors in a multiple choice setting can make questions almost trivial to solve.

The first contribution of this paper is a general method for mitigating the difficulties of crowdsourcing QA data, with a particular focus on multiple choice science questions. The method is broadly similar to other recent work (Rajpurkar et al., 2016), relying mainly on showing crowd

---

[*]Work done while at the Allen Institute for Artificial Intelligence.

[1]Dataset available at `http://allenai.org/data.html`

Proceedings of the 3rd Workshop on Noisy User-generated Text, pages 94–106
Copenhagen, Denmark, September 7, 2017. ©2017 Association for Computational Linguistics

Example 1	Example 2	Example 3	Example 4
Q: What type of organism is commonly used in preparation of foods such as cheese and yogurt?	**Q:** What phenomenon makes global winds blow northeast to southwest or the reverse in the northern hemisphere and northwest to southeast or the reverse in the southern hemisphere?	**Q:** Changes from a less-ordered state to a more-ordered state (such as a liquid to a solid) are always what?	**Q:** What is the least danger-ous radioactive decay?
1) mesophilic organisms 2) protozoa 3) gymnosperms 4) viruses	1) coriolis effect 2) muon effect 3) centrifugal effect 4) tropical effect	1) exothermic 2) unbalanced 3) reactive 4) endothermic	1) alpha decay 2) beta decay 3) gamma decay 4) zeta decay
Mesophiles grow best in moderate temperature, typically between 25°C and 40°C (77°F and 104°F). Mesophiles are often found living in or on the bodies of humans or other animals. The optimal growth temperature of many pathogenic mesophiles is 37°C (98°F), the normal human body temperature. Mesophilic organisms have important uses in food preparation, including cheese, yogurt, beer and wine.	Without Coriolis Effect the global winds would blow north to south or south to north. But Coriolis makes them blow northeast to southwest or the reverse in the Northern Hemisphere. The winds blow northwest to southeast or the reverse in the southern hemisphere.	Summary Changes of state are examples of phase changes, or phase transitions. All phase changes are accompanied by changes in the energy of a system. Changes from a more-ordered state to a less-ordered state (such as a liquid to a gas) are endothermic. Changes from a less-ordered state to a more-ordered state (such as a liquid to a solid) are always exothermic. The conversion ...	All radioactive decay is dangerous to living things, but alpha decay is the least dangerous.

Figure 1: The first four *SciQ* training set examples. An instance consists of a question and 4 answer options (the correct one in green). Most instances come with the document used to formulate the question.

workers a passage of text and having them ask a question about it. However, unlike previous dataset construction tasks, we (1) need domain-relevant passages and questions, and (2) seek to create multiple choice questions, not direct-answer questions.

We use a two-step process to solve these problems, first using a noisy classifier to find relevant passages and showing several options to workers to select from when generating a question. Second, we use a model trained on real science exam questions to predict good answer distractors given a question and a correct answer. We use these predictions to aid crowd workers in transforming the question produced from the first step into a multiple choice question. Thus, with our methodology we leverage existing study texts and science questions to obtain new, relevant questions and plausible answer distractors. Consequently, the human intelligence task is shifted away from a purely *generative* task (which is slow, difficult, expensive and can lack diversity in the outcomes when repeated) and reframed in terms of a *selection*, *modification* and *validation* task (being faster, easier, cheaper and with content variability induced by the suggestions provided).

The second contribution of this paper is a dataset constructed by following this methodology. With a total budget of \$10,415, we collected 13,679 multiple choice science questions, which

we call *SciQ*. Figure 1 shows the first four training examples in *SciQ*. This dataset has a multiple choice version, where the task is to select the correct answer using whatever background information a system can find given a question and several answer options, and a direct answer version, where given a passage and a question a system must predict the span within the passage that answers the question. With experiments using recent state-of-the-art reading comprehension methods, we show that this is a useful dataset for further research. Interestingly, neural models do not beat simple information retrieval baselines on the multiple choice version of this dataset, leaving room for research on applying neural models in settings where training examples number in the tens of thousands, instead of hundreds of thousands. We also show that using *SciQ* as an additional source of training data improves performance on real 4th and 8th grade exam questions, proving that our method successfully produces useful in-domain training data.

2 Related Work

Dataset Construction. A lot of recent work has focused on constructing large datasets suitable for training neural models. QA datasets have been assembled based on Freebase (Berant et al., 2013; Bordes et al., 2015), Wikipedia articles (Yang et al., 2015; Rajpurkar et al., 2016; Hewlett et al.,

2016) and web search user queries (Nguyen et al., 2016); for reading comprehension (RC) based on news (Hermann et al., 2015; Onishi et al., 2016), children books (Hill et al., 2015) and novels (Paperno et al., 2016), and for recognizing textual entailment based on image captions (Bowman et al., 2015). We continue this line of work and construct a dataset for science exam QA. Our dataset differs from some of the aforementioned datasets in that it consists of natural language questions produced by people, instead of cloze-style questions. It also differs from prior work in that we aim at the narrower domain of science exams and in that we produce multiple choice questions, which are more difficult to generate.

Science Exam Question Answering. Existing models for multiple-choice science exam QA vary in their reasoning framework and training methodology. A set of sub-problems and solution strategies are outlined in Clark et al. (2013). The method described by Li and Clark (2015) evaluates the coherence of a scene constructed from the question enriched with background KB information, while Sachan et al. (2016) train an entailment model that derives the correct answer from background knowledge aligned with a max-margin ranker. Probabilistic reasoning approaches include Markov logic networks (Khot et al., 2015) and an integer linear program-based model that assembles proof chains over structured knowledge (Khashabi et al., 2016). The Aristo ensemble (Clark et al., 2016) combines multiple reasoning strategies with shallow statistical methods based on lexical co-occurrence and IR, which by themselves provide surprisingly strong baselines. There has not been much work applying neural networks to this task, likely because of the paucity of training data; this paper is an attempt to address this issue by constructing a much larger dataset than was previously available, and we present results of experiments using state-of-the-art reading comprehension techniques on our datasets.

Automatic Question Generation. Transforming text into questions has been tackled before, mostly for didactic purposes. Some approaches rely on syntactic transformation templates (Mitkov and Ha, 2003; Heilman and Smith, 2010), while most others generate cloze-style questions. Our first attempts at constructing a science question dataset followed these techniques. We found the methods did not produce high-

quality science questions, as there were problems with selecting relevant text, generating reasonable distractors, and formulating coherent questions.

Several similarity measures have been employed for selecting answer distractors (Mitkov et al., 2009), including measures derived from WordNet (Mitkov and Ha, 2003), thesauri (Sumita et al., 2005) and distributional context (Pino et al., 2008; Aldabe and Maritxalar, 2010). Domain-specific ontologies (Papasalouros et al., 2008), phonetic or morphological similarity (Pino and Esknazi, 2009; Correia et al., 2010), probability scores for the question context (Mostow and Jang, 2012) and context-sensitive lexical inference (Zesch and Melamud, 2014) have also been used. In contrast to the aforementioned similarity-based selection strategies, our method uses a feature-based ranker to learn plausible distractors from original questions. Several of the above heuristics are used as features in this ranking model. Feature-based distractor generation models (Sakaguchi et al., 2013) have been used in the past by Agarwal and Mannem (2011) for creating biology questions. Our model uses a random forest to rank candidates; it is agnostic towards taking cloze or humanly-generated questions, and it is learned specifically to generate distractors that resemble those in real science exam questions.

3 Creating a science exam QA dataset

In this section we present our method for crowdsourcing science exam questions. The method is a two-step process: first we present a set of candidate passages to a crowd worker, letting the worker choose one of the passages and ask a question about it. Second, another worker takes the question and answer generated in the first step and produces three distractors, aided by a model trained to predict good answer distractors. The end result is a multiple choice science question, consisting of a question q, a passage p, a correct answer a^*, and a set of distractors, or incorrect answer options, $\{a'\}$. Some example questions are shown in Figure 1. The remainder of this section elaborates on the two steps in our question generation process.

3.1 First task: producing in-domain questions

Conceiving an original question from scratch in a specialized domain is surprisingly difficult; performing the task repeatedly involves the danger of falling into specific lexical and structural patterns. To enforce diversity in question content and lexical expression, and to inspire relevant in-domain questions, we rely on a corpus of in-domain text about which crowd workers ask questions. However, not all text in a large in-domain corpus, such as a textbook, is suitable for generating questions. We use a simple filter to narrow down the selection to paragraphs likely to produce reasonable questions.

Base Corpus. Choosing a relevant, in-domain base corpus to inspire the questions is of crucial importance for the overall characteristics of the dataset. For science questions, the corpus should consist of topics covered in school exams, but not be too linguistically complex, specific, or loaded with technical detail (e.g., scientific papers). We observed that articles retrieved from web searches for science exam keywords (e.g. "animal" and "food") yield a significant proportion of commercial or otherwise irrelevant documents and did not consider this further. Articles from science-related categories in Simple Wikipedia are more targeted and factual, but often state highly specific knowledge (e.g., "Hoatzin can reach 25 inches in length and 1.78 pounds of weight.").

We chose science study textbooks as our base corpus because they are directly relevant and linguistically tailored towards a student audience. They contain verbal descriptions of general natural principles instead of highly specific example features of particular species. While the number of resources is limited, we compiled a list of 28 books from various online learning resources, including CK-12[2] and OpenStax[3], who share this material under a Creative Commons License. The books are about biology, chemistry, earth science and physics and span elementary level to college introductory material. A full list of the books we used can be found in the appendix.

Document Filter. We designed a rule-based document filter model into which individual paragraphs of the base corpus are fed. The system classifies individual sentences and accepts a paragraph if a minimum number of sentences is accepted. With a small manually annotated dataset of sentences labelled as either relevant or irrelevant, the filter was designed iteratively by adding filter rules to first improve precision and then re-

call on a held-out validation set. The final filter included lexical, grammatical, pragmatical and complexity based rules. Specifically, sentences were filtered out if they *i)* were a question or exclamation *ii)* had no verb phrase *iii)* contained modal verbs *iv)* contained imperative phrases *v)* contained demonstrative pronouns *vi)* contained personal pronouns other than third-person *vii)* began with a pronoun *viii)* contained first names *ix)* had less than 6 or more than 18 tokens or more than 2 commas *x)* contained special characters other than punctuation *xi)* had more than three tokens beginning uppercase *xii)* mentioned a graph, table or web link *xiii)* began with a discourse marker (e.g. *'Nonetheless'*) *xiv)* contained absolute wording (e.g. *'never'*, *'nothing'*, *'definitely'*) *xv)* contained instructional vocabulary (*'teacher'*, *'worksheet'*, ...).

Besides the last, these rules are all generally applicable in other domains to identify simple declarative statements in a corpus.

Question Formulation Task. To actually generate in-domain QA pairs, we presented the filtered, in-domain text to crowd workers and had them ask a question that could be answered by the presented passage. Although most undesirable paragraphs had been filtered out beforehand, a non-negligible proportion of irrelevant documents remained. To circumvent this problem, we showed each worker *three* textbook paragraphs and gave them the freedom to choose one or to reject all of them if irrelevant. Once a paragraph had been chosen, it was not reused to formulate more questions about it. We further specified desirable characteristics of science exam questions: no *yes/no* questions, not requiring further context, querying general principles rather than highly specific facts, question length between 6-30 words, answer length up to 3 words (preferring shorter), no ambiguous questions, answers clear from paragraph chosen. Examples for both desirable and undesirable questions were given, with explanations for why they were good or bad examples. Furthermore we encouraged workers to give feedback, and a contact email was provided to address upcoming questions directly; multiple crowdworkers made use of this opportunity. The task was advertised on *Amazon Mechanical Turk*, requiring *Master's* status for the crowdworkers, and paying a compensation of 0.30$ per HIT. A total of 175 workers participated in the whole crowdsourcing

---

[2] www.ck12.org
[3] www.openstax.org

project.

In 12.1% of the cases all three documents were rejected, much fewer than if a single document had been presented (assuming the same proportion of relevant documents). Thus, besides being more economical, proposing several documents reduces the risk of generating irrelevant questions and in the best case helps match a crowdworker's individual preferences.

3.2 Second task: selecting distractors

Generating convincing answer distractors is of great importance, since bad distractors can make a question trivial to solve. When writing science questions ourselves, we found that finding reasonable distractors was the most time-consuming part overall. Thus, we support the process in our crowdsourcing task with model-generated answer distractor suggestions. This primed the workers with relevant examples, and we allowed them to use the suggested distractors directly if they were good enough. We next discuss characteristics of good answer distractors, propose and evaluate a model for suggesting such distractors, and describe the crowdsourcing task that uses them.

Distractor Characteristics. Multiple choice science questions with nonsensical incorrect answer options are not interesting as a task to study, nor are they useful for training a model to do well on real science exams, as the model would not need to do any kind of science reasoning to answer the training questions correctly. The difficulty in generating a good multiple choice question, then, lies not in identifying expressions which are false answers to q, but in generating expressions which are *plausible* false answers. Concretely, besides being false answers, good distractors should thus:

- be grammatically consistent: for the question "When animals use energy, what is always produced?" a noun phrase is expected.

- be consistent with respect to abstract properties: if the correct answer belongs to a certain category (e.g., chemical elements) good distractors likely should as well.

- be consistent with the semantic context of the question: a question about animals and energy should not have *newspaper* or *bingo* as distractors.

Distractor Model Overview. We now introduce a model which generates plausible answer distrators and takes into account the above criteria. On a basic level, it ranks candidates from a large collection C of possible distractors and selects the highest scoring items. Its ranking function

$$r : (q, a^*, a') \mapsto s_{a'} \in [0, 1] \qquad (1)$$

produces a confidence score $s_{a'}$ for whether $a' \in C$ is a good distractor in the context of question q and correct answer a^*. For r we use the scoring function $s_{a'} = P(a'$ is good $\mid q, a^*)$ of a binary classifier which distinguishes plausible (good) distractors from random (bad) distractors based on features $\phi(q, a^*, a')$. For classification, we train r on actual in-domain questions with observed false answers as the plausible (good) distractors, and random expressions as negative examples, sampled in equal proportion from C. As classifier we chose a random forest (Breiman, 2001), because of its robust performance in small and mid-sized data settings and its power to incorporate nonlinear feature interactions, in contrast, e.g., to logistic regression.

Distractor Model Features. This section describes the features $\phi(q, a^*, a')$ used by the distractor ranking model. With these features, the distractor model can learn characteristics of real distractors from original questions and will suggest those distractors that it deems the most realistic for a question. The following features of question q, correct answer a^* and a tentative distractor expression a' were used:

- bags of $GloVe$ embeddings for q, a^* and a';

- an indicator for POS-tag consistency of a^* and a';

- singular/plural consistency of a^* and a';

- log. avg. word frequency in a^* and a';

- Levenshtein string edit distance between a^* and a';

- suffix consistency of a^* and a' (firing e.g. for (*regeneration, exhaustion*));

- token overlap indicators for q, a^* and a';

- token and character length for a^* and a' and similarity therein;

- indicators for numerical content in q, a^* and a' consistency therein;

- indicators for units of measure in q, a^* and a', and for co-occurrence of the same unit;

- WordNet-based hypernymy indicators between tokens in q, a^* and a', in both directions and potentially via two steps;

- indicators for 2-step connections between entities in a^* and a' via a KB based on OpenIE triples (Mausam et al., 2012) extracted from pages in Simple Wikipedia about anatomical structures;

- indicators for shared Wordnet-hyponymy of a^* and a' to one of the concepts most frequently generalising all three question distractors in the training set (e.g. *element, organ, organism*).

The intuition for the knowledge-base link and hypernymy indicator features is that they can reveal sibling structures of a^* and a' with respect to a shared property or hypernym. For example, if the correct answer a^* is *heart*, then a plausible distractor a' like *liver* would share with a^* the hyponymy relation to *organ* in WordNet.

Model Training. We first constructed a large candidate distractor set C whose items were to be ranked by the model. C contained 488,819 expressions, consisting of (1) the 400K items in the GloVe vocabulary (Pennington et al., 2014); (2) answer distractors observed in training questions; (3) a list of noun phrases from Simple Wikipedia articles about body parts; (4) a noun vocabulary of $\sim$6000 expressions extracted from primary school science texts. In examples where a^* consisted of multiple tokens, we added to C any expression that could be obtained by exchanging one unigram in a^* with another unigram from C.

The model was then trained on a set of 3705 science exam questions (4th and 8th grade) , separated into 80% training questions and 20% validation questions. Each question came with four answer options, providing three good distractor examples. We used `scikit-learn`'s implementation of random forests with default parameters. We used 500 trees and enforced at least 4 samples per tree leaf.

Distractor Model Evaluation. Our model achieved $99, 4\%$ training and $94, 2\%$ validation accuracy overall. Example predictions of the distractor model are shown in Table 1. Qualitatively, the predictions appear acceptable in most cases, though the quality is not high enough to use them directly without additional filtering by crowd workers. In many cases the distractor is semantically related, but does not have the correct type (e.g., in column 1, "nutrient" and "soil" are not elements). Some predictions are misaligned in their level of specificity (e.g. "frogs" in column 3), and multiword expressions were more likely to be unrelated or ungrammatical despite the inclusion of part of speech features. Even where the predicted distractors are not fully coherent, showing them to a crowd worker still has a positive priming effect, helping the worker generate good distractors either by providing nearly-good-enough candidates, or by forcing the worker to think why a suggestion is not a good distractor for the question.

Distractor Selection Task. To actually generate a multiple choice science question, we show the result of the first task, a (q, a^*) pair, to a crowd worker, along with the top six distractors suggested from the previously described model. The goal of this task is two-fold: (1) quality control (validating a previously generated (q, a^*) pair), and (2) validating the predicted distractors or writing new ones if necessary.

The first instruction was to judge whether the question could appear in a school science exam; questions could be marked as ungrammatical, having a false answer, being unrelated to science or requiring very specific background knowledge. The total proportion of questions passing was 92.8%.

The second instruction was to select up to two of the six suggested distractors, and to write at least one distractor by themselves such that there is a total of three. The requirement for the worker to generate one of their own distractors, instead of being allowed to select three predicted distractors, was added after an initial pilot of the task, as we found that it forced workers to engage more with the task and resulted in higher quality distractors.

We gave examples of desirable and undesirable distractors and the opportunity to provide feedback, as before. We advertised the task on *Amazon Mechanical Turk*, paying 0.2$ per HIT, again requiring AMT *Master's* status. On average, crowd workers found the predicted distractors good enough to include in the final question around half of the time, resulting in 36.1% of the distractors in the final dataset being generated by the model (because workers were only allowed to pick two predicted distractors, the theoretical maximum is 66%). Acceptance rates were higher in

Q: Compounds containing an atom of what element, bonded in a hydrocarbon framework, are classified as amines?	**Q:** Elements have orbitals that are filled with what?	**Q:** Many species use their body shape and coloration to avoid being detected by what?	**Q:** The small amount of energy input necessary for all chemical reactions to occur is called what?
A: nitrogen	**A:** electrons	**A:** predators	**A:** activation energy
oxygen (0.982)	**ions** (0.975)	**viruses** (0.912)	conversely energy (0.987)
hydrogen (0.962)	atoms (0.959)	ecosystems (0.896)	**decomposition energy** (0.984)
nutrient (0.942)	crystals (0.952)	frogs (0.896)	membrane energy (0.982)
calcium (0.938)	protons (0.951)	distances (0.8952)	motion energy (0.982)
silicon (0.938)	neutrons (0.946)	**males** (0.877)	context energy (0.981)
soil (0.9365)	**photons** (0.912)	crocodiles (0.869)	**distinct energy** (0.980)

Table 1: Selected distractor prediction model outputs. For each QA pair, the top six predictions are listed in row 3 (ranking score in parentheses). Boldfaced candidates were accepted by crowd workers.

the case of short answers, with almost none accepted for the few cases with very long answers.

The remainder of this paper will investigate properties of *SciQ*, the dataset we generated by following the methodology described in this section. We present system and human performance, and we show that *SciQ* can be used as additional training data to improve model performance on real science exams.

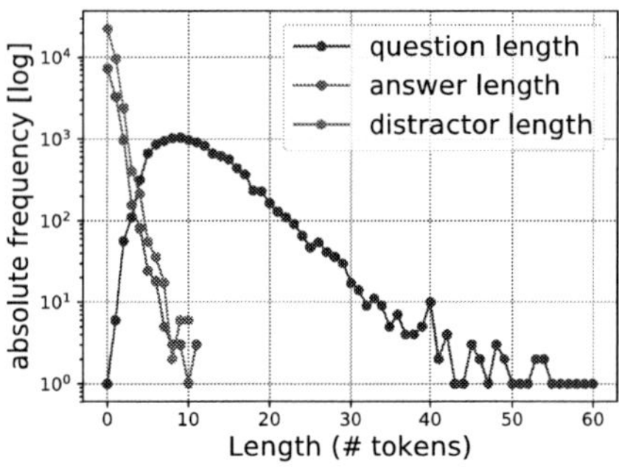

Figure 2: Total counts of question, answer and distractor length, measured in number of tokens, calculated across the training set.

Model	Accuracy
Aristo	77.4
Lucene	80.0
TableILP	31.8
AS Reader	74.1
GA Reader	73.8
Humans	87.8 ± 0.045

Table 2: Test set accuracy of existing models on the multiple choice version of *SciQ*.

3.3 Dataset properties

SciQ has a total of 13,679 multiple choice questions. We randomly shuffled this dataset and split it into training, validation and test portions, with 1000 questions in each of the validation and test portions, and the remainder in train. In Figure 2 we show the distribution of question and answer lengths in the data. For the most part, questions and answers in the dataset are relatively short, though there are some longer questions.

Each question also has an associated passage used when generating the question. Because the multiple choice question is trivial to answer when given the correct passage, the multiple choice version of *SciQ* does not include the passage; systems must retrieve their own background knowledge when answering the question. Because we have the associated passage, we additionally created a direct-answer version of *SciQ*, which has the passage and the question, but no answer options. A small percentage of the passages were obtained from unreleasable texts, so the direct answer version of *SciQ* is slightly smaller, with 10481 questions in train, 887 in dev, and 884 in test.

Qualitative Evaluation. We created a crowdsourcing task with the following setup: A person was presented with an original science exam question and a crowdsourced question. The instructions were to choose which of the two questions was more likely to be the real exam question. We randomly drew 100 original questions and 100 instances from the *SciQ* training set and presented the two options in random order. People identified the science exam question in 55% of the cases, which falls below the significance level of p=0.05 under a null hypothesis of a random guess[4].

---

[4]using normal approximation

4   SciQ Experiments

4.1   System performance

We evaluated several state-of-the-art science QA systems, reading comprehension models, and human performance on *SciQ*.

Multiple Choice Setting. We used the Aristo ensemble (Clark et al., 2016), and two of its individual components: a simple information retrieval baseline (Lucene), and a table-based integer linear programming model (TableILP), to evaluate *SciQ*. We also evaluate two competitive neural reading comprehension models: the Attention Sum Reader (AS Reader, a GRU with a pointer-attention mechanism; Kadlec et al. (2016)) and the Gated Attention Reader (GA Reader, an AS Reader with additional gated attention layers; Dhingra et al. (2016)). These reading comprehension methods require a supporting text passage to answer a question. We use the same corpus as Aristo's Lucene component to retrieve a text passage, by formulating five queries based on the question and answer[5] and then concatenating the top three results from each query into a passage. We train the reading comprehension models on the training set with hyperparameters recommended by prior work ((Onishi et al., 2016) for the AS Reader and (Dhingra et al., 2016) for the GA Reader), with early stopping on the validation data[6]. Human accuracy is estimated using a sampled subset of 650 questions, with 13 different people each answering 50 questions. When answering the questions, people were allowed to query the web, just as the systems were.

Table 2 shows the results of this evaluation. Aristo performance is slightly better on this set than on real science exams (where Aristo achieves 71.3% accuracy (Clark et al., 2016)).[7] Because TableILP uses a hand-collected set of background knowledge that does not cover the topics in *SciQ*, its performance is substantially worse here than on its original test set. Neural models perform reasonably well on this dataset, though, interestingly, they are not able to outperform a very simple information retrieval baseline, even when using exactly the same background information. This suggests that *SciQ* is a useful dataset for studying reading comprehension models in medium-data settings.

Dataset	AS Reader	GA Reader
4th grade	40.7%	37.6%
4th grade + SciQ	45.0%	45.4%
Difference	+4.3%	+7.8%
8th grade	41.2%	41.0%
8th grade + SciQ	43.0%	44.3%
Difference	+1.8%	+3.3%

Table 3: Model accuracies on real science questions validation set when trained on 4th / 8th grade exam questions alone, and when adding *SciQ*.

Direct Answer Setting. We additionally present a baseline on the direct answer version of *SciQ*. We use the Bidirectional Attention Flow model (BiDAF; Seo et al. (2016)), which recently achieved state-of-the-art results on SQuAD (Rajpurkar et al., 2016). We trained BiDAF on the training portion of *SciQ* and evaluated on the test set. BiDAF achieves a 66.7% exact match and 75.7 F1 score, which is 1.3% and 1.6% below the model's performance on SQuAD.

4.2   Using *SciQ* to answer exam questions

Our last experiment with *SciQ* shows its usefulness as training data for models that answer real science questions. We collected a corpus of 4th and 8th grade science exam questions and used the AS Reader and GA Reader to answer these questions.[8] Table 3 shows model performances when only using real science questions as training data, and when augmenting the training data with *SciQ*. By adding *SciQ*, performance for both the AS Reader and the GA Reader improves on both grade levels, in a few cases substantially. This contrasts with our earlier attempts using purely synthetic data, where we saw models overfit the synthetic data and an overall performance decrease. Our successful transfer of information from *SciQ* to real science exam questions shows that the question distribution is similar to that of real science questions.

5   Conclusion

We have presented a method for crowdsourcing the creation of multiple choice QA data, with

---

[5]The question text itself, plus each of the four answer options appended to the question text.

[6]For training and hyperparameter details, see Appendix

[7]We did not retrain the Aristo ensemble for *SciQ*; it might overly rely on TableILP, which does not perform well here.

[8]There are approx. 3200 8th grade training questions and 1200 4th grade training questions. Some of the questions come from www.allenai.org/data, some are proprietary.

a particular focus on science questions. Using this methodology, we have constructed a dataset of 13.7K science questions, called *SciQ*, which we release for future research. We have shown through baseline evaluations that this dataset is a useful research resource, both to investigate neural model performance in medium-sized data settings, and to augment training data for answering real science exam questions.

There are multiple strands for possible future work. One direction is a systematic exploration of multitask settings to best exploit this new dataset. Possible extensions for the direction of generating answer distractors could lie in the adaptation of this idea in negative sampling, e.g. in KB population. Another direction is to further bootstrap the data we obtained to improve automatic document selection, question generation and distractor prediction to generate questions fully automatically.

References

Manish Agarwal and Prashanth Mannem. 2011. Automatic gap-fill question generation from text books. In *Proceedings of the 6th Workshop on Innovative Use of NLP for Building Educational Applications*. Association for Computational Linguistics, Stroudsburg, PA, USA, IUNLPBEA '11, pages 56–64. http://dl.acm.org/citation.cfm?id=2043132.2043139.

Itziar Aldabe and Montse Maritxalar. 2010. *Automatic Distractor Generation for Domain Specific Texts*, Springer Berlin Heidelberg, Berlin, Heidelberg, pages 27–38.

Jonathan Berant, Andrew Chou, Roy Frostig, and Percy Liang. 2013. Semantic parsing on freebase from question-answer pairs. In *Proceedings of the 2013 Conference on Empirical Methods in Natural Language Processing, EMNLP 2013, 18-21 October 2013, Grand Hyatt Seattle, Seattle, Washington, USA, A meeting of SIGDAT, a Special Interest Group of the ACL*. pages 1533–1544. http://aclweb.org/anthology/D/D13/D13-1160.pdf.

Antoine Bordes, Nicolas Usunier, Sumit Chopra, and Jason Weston. 2015. Large-scale simple question answering with memory networks. *CoRR* abs/1506.02075. http://arxiv.org/abs/1506.02075.

Samuel R. Bowman, Gabor Angeli, Christopher Potts, and Christopher D. Manning. 2015. A large annotated corpus for learning natural language inference. In *Proceedings of the 2015 Conference on Empirical Methods in Natural Language Processing (EMNLP)*. Association for Computational Linguistics.

Leo Breiman. 2001. Random forests. *Machine Learning* 45(1):5–32.

Peter Clark. 2015. Elementary school science and math tests as a driver for ai: Take the aristo challenge! In *Proceedings of the Twenty-Ninth AAAI Conference on Artificial Intelligence*. AAAI Press, AAAI'15, pages 4019–4021. http://dl.acm.org/citation.cfm?id=2888116.2888274.

Peter Clark, Oren Etzioni, Tushar Khot, Ashish Sabharwal, Oyvind Tafjord, Peter Turney, and Daniel Khashabi. 2016. Combining retrieval, statistics, and inference to answer elementary science questions. In *Proceedings of the Thirtieth AAAI Conference on Artificial Intelligence*. AAAI Press, AAAI'16, pages 2580–2586. http://dl.acm.org/citation.cfm?id=3016100.3016262.

Peter Clark, Philip Harrison, and Niranjan Balasubramanian. 2013. A study of the knowledge base requirements for passing an elementary science test. In *Proceedings of the 2013 Workshop on Automated Knowledge Base Construction*. ACM, New York, NY, USA, AKBC '13, pages 37–42. https://doi.org/10.1145/2509558.2509565.

Rui Correia, Jorge Baptista, Nuno Mamede, Isabel Trancoso, and Maxine Eskenazi. 2010. Automatic generation of cloze question distractors. In *Proceedings of the Interspeech 2010 Satellite Workshop on Second Language Studies: Acquisition, Learning, Education and Technology, Waseda University, Tokyo, Japan*.

Bhuwan Dhingra, Hanxiao Liu, William W. Cohen, and Ruslan Salakhutdinov. 2016. Gated-attention readers for text comprehension. *CoRR* abs/1606.01549. http://arxiv.org/abs/1606.01549.

Michael Heilman and Noah A. Smith. 2010. Good question! statistical ranking for question generation. In *Human Language Technologies: The 2010 Annual Conference of the North American Chapter of the Association for Computational Linguistics*. Association for Computational Linguistics, Stroudsburg, PA, USA, HLT '10, pages 609–617. http://dl.acm.org/citation.cfm?id=1857999.1858085.

Karl Moritz Hermann, Tomáš Kočiský, Edward Grefenstette, Lasse Espeholt, Will Kay, Mustafa Suleyman, and Phil Blunsom. 2015. Teaching machines to read and comprehend. In *Advances in Neural Information Processing Systems (NIPS)*. http://arxiv.org/abs/1506.03340.

Daniel Hewlett, Alexandre Lacoste, Llion Jones, Illia Polosukhin, Andrew Fandrianto, Jay Han, Matthew Kelcey, and David Berthelot. 2016. Wikireading: A novel large-scale language understanding task over wikipedia. *CoRR* abs/1608.03542. http://arxiv.org/abs/1608.03542.

Felix Hill, Antoine Bordes, Sumit Chopra, and Jason Weston. 2015. The goldilocks principle: Reading children's books with explicit memory representations. *CoRR* abs/1511.02301. http://arxiv.org/abs/1511.02301.

Rudolf Kadlec, Martin Schmid, Ondrej Bajgar, and Jan Kleindienst. 2016. Text understanding with the attention sum reader network. *CoRR* abs/1603.01547. http://arxiv.org/abs/1603.01547.

Daniel Khashabi, Tushar Khot, Ashish Sabharwal, Peter Clark, Oren Etzioni, and Dan Roth. 2016. Question answering via integer programming over semi-structured knowledge. In *Proceedings of the Twenty-Fifth International Joint Conference on Artificial Intelligence, IJCAI 2016, New York, NY, USA, 9-15 July 2016*. pages 1145–1152. http://www.ijcai.org/Abstract/16/166.

Tushar Khot, Niranjan Balasubramanian, Eric Gribkoff, Ashish Sabharwal, Peter Clark, and Oren Etzioni. 2015. Exploring markov logic networks for question answering. In *Proceedings of the 2015 Conference on Empirical Methods in Natural Language Processing, EMNLP 2015, Lisbon, Portugal, September 17-21, 2015*. pages 685–694. http://aclweb.org/anthology/D/D15/D15-1080.pdf.

Yang Li and Peter Clark. 2015. Answering elementary science questions by constructing coherent scenes using background knowledge. In *EMNLP*. pages 2007–2012.

Mausam, Michael Schmitz, Robert Bart, Stephen Soderland, and Oren Etzioni. 2012. Open language learning for information extraction. In *Proceedings of the 2012 Joint Conference on Empirical Methods in Natural Language Processing and Computational Natural Language Learning*. Association for Computational Linguistics, Stroudsburg, PA, USA, EMNLP-CoNLL '12, pages 523–534. http://dl.acm.org/citation.cfm?id=2390948.2391009.

Ruslan Mitkov and Le An Ha. 2003. Computer-aided generation of multiple-choice tests. In *Proceedings of the HLT-NAACL 03 Workshop on Building Educational Applications Using Natural Language Processing - Volume 2*. Association for Computational Linguistics, Stroudsburg, PA, USA, HLT-NAACL-EDUC '03, pages 17–22. https://doi.org/10.3115/1118894.1118897.

Ruslan Mitkov, Le An Ha, Andrea Varga, and Luz Rello. 2009. Semantic similarity of distractors in multiple-choice tests: Extrinsic evaluation. In *Proceedings of the Workshop on Geometrical Models of Natural Language Semantics*. Association for Computational Linguistics, Stroudsburg, PA, USA, GEMS '09, pages 49–56. http://dl.acm.org/citation.cfm?id=1705415.1705422.

Jack Mostow and Hyeju Jang. 2012. Generating diagnostic multiple choice comprehension cloze questions. In *Proceedings of the Seventh Workshop on Building Educational Applications Using NLP*. Association for Computational Linguistics, Stroudsburg, PA, USA, pages 136–146. http://dl.acm.org/citation.cfm?id=2390384.2390401.

Tri Nguyen, Mir Rosenberg, Xia Song, Jianfeng Gao, Saurabh Tiwary, Rangan Majumder, and Li Deng. 2016. MS MARCO: A human generated machine reading comprehension dataset. *CoRR* abs/1611.09268. http://arxiv.org/abs/1611.09268.

Takeshi Onishi, Hai Wang, Mohit Bansal, Kevin Gimpel, and David A. McAllester. 2016. Who did what: A large-scale person-centered cloze dataset. In *Proceedings of the 2016 Conference on Empirical Methods in Natural Language Processing, EMNLP 2016, Austin, Texas, USA, November 1-4, 2016*. pages 2230–2235. http://aclweb.org/anthology/D/D16/D16-1241.pdf.

Andreas Papasalouros, Konstantinos Kanaris, and Konstantinos Kotis. 2008. Automatic generation of multiple choice questions from domain ontologies. In Miguel Baptista Nunes and Maggie McPherson, editors, *e-Learning*. IADIS, pages 427–434.

Denis Paperno, Germán Kruszewski, Angeliki Lazaridou, Quan Ngoc Pham, Raffaella Bernardi, Sandro Pezzelle, Marco Baroni, Gemma Boleda, and Raquel Fernández. 2016. The lambada dataset: Word prediction requiring a broad discourse context. *arXiv preprint arXiv:1606.06031* .

Jeffrey Pennington, Richard Socher, and Christopher D. Manning. 2014. Glove: Global vectors for word representation. In *Empirical Methods in Natural Language Processing (EMNLP)*. pages 1532–1543. http://www.aclweb.org/anthology/D14-1162.

Juan Pino and Maxine Esknazi. 2009. Semi-automatic generation of cloze question distractors effect of students' l1. In *SLaTE*. ISCA, pages 65–68.

Juan Pino, Michael Heilman, and Maxine Eskenazi. 2008. A Selection Strategy to Improve Cloze Question Quality. In *Proceedings of the Workshop on Intelligent Tutoring Systems for Ill-Defined Domains. 9th International Conference on Intelligent Tutoring Systems.*.

P. Rajpurkar, J. Zhang, K. Lopyrev, and P. Liang. 2016. Squad: 100,000+ questions for machine comprehension of text. In *Empirical Methods in Natural Language Processing (EMNLP)*.

Mrinmaya Sachan, Avinava Dubey, and Eric P. Xing. 2016. Science question answering using instructional materials. *CoRR* abs/1602.04375. http://arxiv.org/abs/1602.04375.

Keisuke Sakaguchi, Yuki Arase, and Mamoru Komachi. 2013. Discriminative approach to fill-in-the-blank quiz generation for language learners. In *Proceedings of the 51st Annual Meeting of the Association for Computational Linguistics, ACL 2013, 4-9 August 2013, Sofia, Bulgaria, Volume 2: Short Papers*. pages 238–242. http://aclweb.org/anthology/P/P13/P13-2043.pdf.

Carissa Schoenick, Peter Clark, Oyvind Tafjord, Peter Turney, and Oren Etzioni. 2016. Moving beyond the turing test with the allen ai science challenge. *arXiv preprint arXiv:1604.04315* .

Min Joon Seo, Aniruddha Kembhavi, Ali Farhadi, and Hannaneh Hajishirzi. 2016. Bidirectional attention flow for machine comprehension. *CoRR* abs/1611.01603. http://arxiv.org/abs/1611.01603.

Alessandro Sordoni, Phillip Bachman, and Yoshua Bengio. 2016. Iterative alternating neural attention for machine reading. *CoRR* abs/1606.02245. http://arxiv.org/abs/1606.02245.

Eiichiro Sumita, Fumiaki Sugaya, and Seiichi Yamamoto. 2005. Measuring non-native speakers' proficiency of english by using a test with automatically-generated fill-in-the-blank questions. In *Proceedings of the Second Workshop on Building Educational Applications Using NLP*. Association for Computational Linguistics, Stroudsburg, PA, USA, EdAppsNLP 05, pages 61–68. http://dl.acm.org/citation.cfm?id=1609829.1609839.

Yi Yang, Scott Wen-tau Yih, and Chris Meek. 2015. Wikiqa: A challenge dataset for open-domain question answering. ACL Association for Computational Linguistics. https://www.microsoft.com/en-us/research/publication/wikiqa-a-challenge-dataset-for-open-domain-question-answering/.

Torsten Zesch and Oren Melamud. 2014. Automatic generation of challenging distractors using context-sensitive inference rules. In *Proceedings of the Ninth Workshop on Innovative Use of NLP for Building Educational Applications, BEA@ACL 2014, June 26, 2014, Baltimore, Maryland, USA*. pages 143–148. http://aclweb.org/anthology/W/W14/W14-1817.pdf.

A   List of Study Books

The following is a list of the books we used as data source:

- OpenStax, Anatomy & Physiology. OpenStax. 25 April 2013[9]

- OpenStax, Biology. OpenStax. May 20, 2013[10]

- OpenStax, Chemistry. OpenStax. 11 March 2015[11]

- OpenStax, College Physics. OpenStax. 21 June 2012[12]

- OpenStax, Concepts of Biology. OpenStax. 25 April 2013[13]

- Biofundamentals 2.0 – by Michael Klymkowsky, University of Colorado & Melanie Cooper, Michigan State University[14]

- Earth Systems, An Earth Science Course on www.curriki.org[15]

- General Chemistry, Principles, Patterns, and Applications by Bruce Averill, Strategic Energy Security Solutions and Patricia Eldredge, R.H. Hand, LLC; Saylor Foundation[16]

- General Biology; Paul Doerder, Cleveland State University & Ralph Gibson, Cleveland State University [17]

- Introductory Chemistry by David W. Ball, Cleveland State University. Saylor Foundation [18]

- The Basics of General, Organic, and Biological Chemistry by David Ball, Cleveland State University & John Hill, University of Wisconsin & Rhonda Scott, Southern Adventist University. Saylor Foundation[19]

- Barron's New York State Grade 4 Elementary-Level Science Test, by Joyce Thornton Barry and Kathleen Cahill [20]

- Campbell Biology: Concepts & Connections by Jane B. Reece, Martha R. Taylor, Eric J. Simon, Jean L. Dickey[21]

- CK-12 Peoples Physics Book Basic [22]

- CK-12 Biology Advanced Concepts [23]

- CK-12 Biology Concepts [24]

- CK-12 Biology [25]

- CK-12 Chemistry - Basic [26]

- CK-12 Chemistry Concepts – Intermediate [27]

- CK-12 Earth Science Concepts For Middle School[28]

- CK-12 Earth Science Concepts For High School[29]

[9]Download for free at http://cnx.org/content/col11496/latest/

[10]Download for free at http://cnx.org/content/col11448/latest/

[11]Download for free at http://cnx.org/content/col11760/latest/

[12]Download for free at http://cnx.org/content/col11406/latest

[13]Download for free at http://cnx.org/content/col11487/latest

[14]https://open.umn.edu/opentextbooks/BookDetail.aspx?bookId=350

[15]http://www.curriki.org/xwiki/bin/view/Group_CLRN-OpenSourceEarthScienceCourse/

[16]https://www.saylor.org/site/textbooks/General%20Chemistry%20Principles,%20Patterns,%20and%20Applications.pdf

[17]https://upload.wikimedia.org/wikipedia/commons/4/40/GeneralBiology.pdf

[18]https://www.saylor.org/site/textbooks/Introductory%20Chemistry.pdf

[19]http://web.archive.org/web/20131024125808/http://www.saylor.org/site/textbooks/The%20Basics%20of%20General,%20Organic%20and%20Biological%20Chemistry.pdf

[20]We do not include documents from this resource in the dataset.

[21]We do not include documents from this resource in the dataset.

[22]http://www.ck12.org/book/Peoples-Physics-Book-Basic/

[23]http://www.ck12.org/book/CK-12-Biology-Advanced-Concepts/

[24]http://www.ck12.org/book/CK-12-Biology-Concepts/

[25]http://www.ck12.org/book/CK-12-Biology/

[26]http://www.ck12.org/book/CK-12-Chemistry-Basic/

[27]http://www.ck12.org/book/CK-12-Chemistry-Concepts-Intermediate/

[28]http://www.ck12.org/book/CK-12-Earth-Science-Concepts-For-Middle-School/

[29]http://www.ck12.org/book/CK-12-Earth-Science-Concepts-For-High-School/

- CK-12 Earth Science For Middle School [30]

- CK-12 Life Science Concepts For Middle School [31]

- CK-12 Life Science For Middle School [32]

- CK-12 Physical Science Concepts For Middle School[33]

- CK-12 Physical Science For Middle School [34]

- CK-12 Physics Concepts - Intermediate [35]

- CK-12 People's Physics Concepts [36]

CK-12 books were obtained under the Creative Commons Attribution-Non-Commercial 3.0 Unported (CC BY-NC 3.0) License [37].

B   Training and Implementation Details

Multiple Choice Reading Comprehension. During training of the AS Reader and GA Reader, we monitored model performance after each epoch and stopped training when the error on the validation set had increased (early stopping, with a patience of one). We set a hard limit of ten epochs, but most models reached their peak validation accuracy after the first or second epoch. Test set evaluation, when applicable, used model parameters at the epoch of their peak validation accuracy. We implemented the models in Keras, and ran them with the Theano backend on a Tesla K80 GPU.

The hyperparameters for each of the models were adopted from previous work. For the AS Reader, we use an embedding dimension of 256 and GRU hidden layer dimension of 384 (obtained

through correspondence with the authors of Onishi et al. (2016)) and use the hyperparameters reported in the original paper (Kadlec et al., 2016) for the rest. For the GA Reader, we use three gated-attention layers with the multiplicative gating mechanism. We do not use the character-level embedding features or the question-evidence common word features, but we do follow their work by using pretrained 100-dimension GloVe vectors to initialize a fixed word embedding layer. Between each gated attention layer, we apply dropout with a rate of 0.3. The other hyperparameters are the same as their original work (Dhingra et al., 2016).

Direct Answer Reading Comprehension. We implemented the Bidirectional Attention Flow model exactly as described in Seo et al. (2016) and adopted the hyperparameters used in the paper.

---

[30] `http://www.ck12.org/book/CK-12-Earth-Science-For-Middle-School/`
[31] `http://www.ck12.org/book/CK-12-Life-Science-Concepts-For-Middle-School/`
[32] `http://www.ck12.org/book/CK-12-Life-Science-For-Middle-School/`
[33] `http://www.ck12.org/book/CK-12-Physical-Science-Concepts-For-Middle-School/`
[34] `http://www.ck12.org/book/CK-12-Physical-Science-For-Middle-School/`
[35] `http://www.ck12.org/book/CK-12-Physics-Concepts-Intermediate/`
[36] `http://www.ck12.org/book/Peoples-Physics-Concepts/`
[37] `http://creativecommons.org/licenses/by-nc/3.0/`

A Text Normalisation System for Non-Standard English Words

Emma Flint[1] **Elliot Ford**[1] **Olivia Thomas**[1]
Andrew Caines[1] **Paula Buttery**[2]
[1] Department of Theoretical and Applied Linguistics
[2] Computer Laboratory
University of Cambridge, Cambridge, U.K.
{emf40|ef355|oft20|apc38|pjb48}@cam.ac.uk

Abstract

This paper investigates the problem of text normalisation; specifically, the normalisation of non-standard words (NSWs) in English. Non-standard words can be defined as those word tokens which do not have a dictionary entry, and cannot be pronounced using the usual letter-to-phoneme conversion rules; *e.g.* lbs, 99.3%, #EMNLP2017. NSWs pose a challenge to the proper functioning of text-to-speech technology, and the solution is to spell them out in such a way that they can be pronounced appropriately. We describe our four-stage normalisation system made up of components for detection, classification, division and expansion of NSWs. Performance is favourabe compared to previous work in the field (Sproat *et al.* 2001, Normalization of non-standard words), as well as state-of-the-art text-to-speech software. Further, we update Sproat *et al.*'s NSW taxonomy, and create a more customisable system where users are able to input their own abbreviations and specify into which variety of English (currently available: British or American) they wish to normalise.

1 Introduction

The transfer of surface linguistic representations between the written and spoken form is known as 'text-to-speech' (TTS) in one direction and 'automatic speech recognition' (ASR) in the other. In TTS there is a need to map word tokens to a target pronunciation, enabling synthesized speech production. Depending on the text genre, many of the word tokens will map to sound symbols in a straightforward way. For instance, the Carnegie Mellon University Pronouncing Dictionary of English[1] (CMU's PDE) lists more than 134,000 tokens and their pronunciations in ARPAbet form[2] (Table 1).

Entry	Pronunciation
AARDVARK	AA1 R D V AA2 R K
CAT	K AE1 T
MILK	M IH1 L K
PUG	P AH1 G

Table 1: Example entries from the Carnegie Mellon University Pronouncing Dictionary of English

Tokens such as these may be thought of as the 'standard' set of words – those which have been curated, and continue to be curated, for TTS and ASR.

However, there is another type of word token that does not map straightforwardly to a pronunciation, either because it is an abbreviation or acronym (1), a number (2), a date or time (3), an amount (4), an asterisked profanity (5), a url or hashtag (6), or a spelling error (7).

(1) *kHz, Rt. Hon., OED*

(2) *42, (Henry) VIII, 4/5*

(3) *15/04/1997, 2016-12-31, 09:30:01*

(4) *€500, 2000¥, 99.99%*

(5) *sh*t, f**k, *ss*

(6) http://www.abc123.com, google.com, #summer2016

(7) *anoncement, caligaphy, helko*

---

[1] http://www.speech.cs.cmu.edu/cgi-bin/cmudict
[2] http://fave.ling.upenn.edu/downloads/ARPAbet.pdf

Proceedings of the 3rd Workshop on Noisy User-generated Text, pages 107–115
Copenhagen, Denmark, September 7, 2017. ©2017 Association for Computational Linguistics

There are no entries for these examples in CMU's PDE and hence they belong in the set of 'non-standard' words (NSWs) of English.

A normalisation system should automatically detect NSWs in a given text input, identify their type, and spell them out in full such that a TTS system may produce them in a human-interpretable fashion. A successful system must also be able to deal with ambiguities present in real text; the same NSW may be pronounced in multiple ways depending on the context. For example, the number *1985* would normally be pronounced 'one thousand, nine hundred and eighty five' when used as an amount, but 'nineteen eighty five' when used as a year, and "one nine eight five" if read as a sequence of digits. Does *M8* represent the 'm eight' motorway in Scotland or is it shorthand for 'mate'?

Here we present a text normalisation system which sorts an input text into standard and non-standard words, identifies NSW types where appropriate, and expands the NSW to a form ready for speech realisation. The NSW taxonomy is founded on the seminal work by Sproat et al. (2001), with amendments to deal with (a) overlap between class identification and expansion for several classes, (b) finer classification of the numeric NSW group, and (c) developments in web language. For example, the input text below (8) would be normalised as in (9) in order to be read out appropriately by a TTS system (NSWs in bold, expansions italicised):

(8) On the **13 Feb. 2007**, **Rt. Hon.** Theresa May **MP** announced on **ITV** News that the rate of **childhod** obesity had risen from **7.3-9.6%** in just **3** years, costing the **Gov. £20m #politics**.

(9) On the *thirteenth of February two thousand and seven*, *The Right Honourable* Theresa May *M P* announced on *I T V* News that the rate of *childhood* obesity had risen from *seven point three to nine point six percent* in just *three* years, costing the *government twenty million pounds hashtag politics*.

NSW normalisation systems enable a smoother transition between the written and spoken forms of language, rather than skipping NSW tokens, or attempting pronunciations in unexpected or incorrect ways. It is a vital prerequisite for TTS and other downstream natural language processing (NLP) tasks in which technology has been developed on the basis of standard language varieties (Plank, 2016). The system means that texts from a wide range of domains may be read aloud, including newswire, parliamentary proceedings, scientific literature, microblog texts, *etc*. We have made it straightforward to opt for a specific tokenizer, or input a new dictionary of abbreviations, meaning that the system is domain-modifiable whilst still being appropriately domain-general in its foundations. We make our normalisation system publicly available as a GitHub repository[3].

2   Related Work

Sproat et al. (2001) remains the single most influential piece of work in the normalisation of NSWs. They were the first to propose a comprehensive taxonomy of NSWs, as well as various heuristics for their expansion. Prior to this, text normalisation had been given limited attention in TTS, and was attempted through the construction of specific rules appropriate for the treatment of NSWs found in the desired domain.

Sproat et al. (2001) proposed an NSW taxonomy based on four distinct domains: newswire, a recipes newsgroup, a hardware-product-specific newsgroup, and classified property advertisements. Their corpora were predominantly U.S. English and an associated set of normalisation tools was made publicly available[4]. Their work has since inspired normalisation research for different text types such as short messaging service (SMS) texts (Aw et al., 2006), email (Moore et al., 2010), and microblog texts from Twitter (Han and Baldwin, 2011). Furthermore, Roark and Sproat (2014) focused on high precision abbreviation expansion, adopting a 'do no harm' approach. We attempt to incorporate some of the normalisation steps taken in these more recent papers, as internet and SMS text has developed in idiosyncratic ways which require normalisation heuristics of their own (Eisenstein, 2013).

We adopt the taxonomy outlined in Sproat et al. (2001) and adapt it to work in a more streamlined manner, and to cope with text domains which are much more prevalent in the present day than at the time of their work – namely the Internet domain. Furthermore, although our system aims to be domain-general, we also allow users the option to input their own dictionary of abbreviations, in

---

[3]`http://github.com/EFord36/normalise`
[4]`http://festvox.org/nsw`

order to tailor towards a specific domain. A further parameter allows the user to specify whether their input variety conforms to British (BrE) or American English (AmE), improving expansion of certain ambiguous tokens, such as dates; *02/03* represents 'the second of March' in BrE, but 'the third of February' in the AmE format. In future work we can incorporate normalisation variants from other Englishes, including 'outer' and 'expanding' circle varieties (Kachru, 1992).

The publicly available resources associated with the previous work required installation of the Festival speech synthesizer[5], were only intended as a "pre-alpha" release and have not been developed since version *0.2.1* in the year 2000. Furthermore, the source code is in Scheme, whereas we release software in the more commonly-used Python programming language.

3 Our Approach to Text Normalisation

Our system is made up of separate components for the detection, classification, division and expansion of NSWs. In this section, we outline our method of normalisation by describing each of these modules in turn.

3.1 NSW detection

After the input text has been tokenised (either by the user or with our basic tokenizer), non-standard words (henceforth NSWs) are detected. This is achieved by comparison of tokens against a word list, consisting of the set of all English words in a word list corpus, the set of all alphabetic words (greater than four characters) in the Brown Corpus (Francis and Kučera, 1964), and a set of proper names. The Brown Corpus contains 1.15 million words from 500 sources, hence we deemed it to be a good representation of different genres and styles of writing, from fiction to newswire to official documents. We recognise that, as it contains texts from the 1960s and 1970s, the Brown Corpus is by now a little dated. However, its benefits include availability, practicality and coverage. Additionally, we manually add a selection of lexemes which have been coined, or come into greater usage, since the corpus was compiled, such as common technological terms.

In order to facilitate detection of NSWs, we temporarily lower-case and lemmatise the input

text (using the WordNet lemmatiser from NLTK (Bird et al., 2009)). This allows us to prevent words whose plural, inflected or capitalised form do not appear in our wordlist from being detected as NSWs. Furthermore, we exclude a number of common contractions which do not appear in our word list from NSW detection (e.g. *aren't*, *won't* and *you're*), on the basis that a normalisation system which expanded these tokens to their full forms would affect the register of the input text (*e.g.* from informal to formal), which is not the purpose of a TTS system. Single punctuation is also prevented from detection, as this provides meaningful information and is important for TTS, whereas nonsense sequences of characters should be detected, and later deleted.

To summarise, a token is detected as an NSW if it satisfies all four of the following conditions:

a. Its lower-cased form is not in the word list.

b. Its lemmatised form is not in the word list.

c. Its non-possessive form (with *'s* or *s'* removed) is not in the word list.

d. It is not single punctuation.

3.2 NSW classification

Following detection, NSWs are first classified into one of four general classes: ALPHA (for alphabetic tokens), NUMB (for numeric tokens), SPLT (for mixed tokens that require further division) or MISC (for everything else). Unlike in Sproat et al. (2001), where all NSWs are processed by a splitter, only tokens tagged as SPLT will form the input of our division algorithm. After initial classification and division of SPLT tokens, all NSWs are further classified and labelled with a specific tag to indicate how they should be expanded.

3.2.1 A modified NSW taxonomy

A summary of tags assigned to various NSW tokens can be found in Table 2, a modified version of the taxonomy developed in Sproat et al. (2001), along with a description and examples.

Although our taxonomy is largely consistent with Sproat et al. (2001), a few changes and additions have been made. Sproat and colleagues' MSPL (misspelling), FNSP (funny spelling) and ASWD (read as word) tags have been conflated into a single category WDLK (wordlike), because the effort necessary to distinguish between these tokens is

Class	Tag	Description	Examples
ALPHA	EXPN	abbreviation	*cm* (centimetres), *Dec.* (December), *addr.* (address)
	LSEQ	letter sequence	*BBC* (B B C), *U.K.* (U K)
	WDLK	word, misspelling	*beatiful* (beautiful), *slllooooow* (slow)
NUMB	NUM	cardinal number	*27* (twenty seven), *14.5* (fourteen point five), *2/3* (two thirds)
	NORD	ordinal number	*June 3* (third), *15th* (fifteenth), *Louis VI* (sixth)
	NRANGE	number range	*25-30* (twenty five to thirty)
	NTEL	telephone number	*+447892-739-562* (plus four four seven eight nine two...)
	NDIG	number as digits	*123* (one two three)
	NTIME	time	*2.45* (two forty five), *17:10* (five ten)
	NDATE	date	*19/03* (nineteenth of March), *07-07* (seventh of July)
	NADDR	address	*15 Hollybush Ave* (fifteen), *5000 Lensfield Rd.* (five thousand)
	NYER	year	*1980* (nineteen eighty), *70s* (seventies)
	MONEY	money	*£50* (fifty pounds), *100USD* (one hundred US dollars)
	PRCT	percentage	*23.5%* (twenty three point five percent)
	NSCI	scientific number	*63.2°N* (sixty three point two degrees north)
SPLT	SPLT	mixed	*ITV3* (I T V three), *500-yds* (five hundred yards)
MISC	PROF	profanity	*sh*t* (shit), *cr*p* (crap)
	URL	web address, email	*emf355@hotmail.co.uk*
	HTAG	hashtag	*#politics, #summer2016*
	NONE	not spoken	*?!*?!**

Table 2: Non-standard word taxonomy.

equal to that used in expansion, rendering it redundant. This reduces the categories defined for alphabetic tokens from four to three.

In addition, SLNT (word boundary or emphasis character, e.g. **seriously**) and PUNC (nonstandard punctuation, e.g. *?!*?!**) have been removed, as tokens previously corresponding to these tags can adequately be captured under NONE, given that all such tokens expand to nothing, emphi.e. are deleted and go unspoken. A further omission is that of the NIDE (identifier) tag in the numeric class – the distinction between this and NDIG was unclear.

Finally, we created several new tags in addition to those of Sproat and colleagues, to capture classes we believe to be both distinct and important. One major modernisation is the addition of HTAG, to reflect the growing usage of hashtags on social media platforms such as Twitter and Instagram. Such tokens are distinctive in that words are strung together without spaces or punctuation, making word boundaries (and subsequently the correct expansion) difficult to automatically determine. Additionally, NRANGE has been added to capture number ranges (e.g. *25-30, 1990-1995*), NSCI to capture scientific numbers, including coordinates, and PROF to cover profanities, which often include an asterisk as a censor.

3.2.2 Further classification of ALPHA, NUMB and MISC tokens

The purpose of the classification stage is to assign to each NSW one of the specific tags pre-

fined in our taxonomy (recall Table 2), e.g. EXPN, NRANGE, MONEY, URL etc. A separate classifier is used for each of the ALPHA, NUMB and MISC classes, which also include those NSWs retagged after the division step described below (Section 3.3). Our classification of ALPHA and NUMB tokens uses a semi-supervised label propagation algorithm, while the classification of MISC tokens is entirely rule-based.

We use a number of domain-independent features in training (13 for the ALPHA classifier, and 29 for the NUMB classifier). These look at properties of the token itself, as well as +/-2 surrounding tokens either side of the token in question. This information is important in cases where the class of the NSW is ambiguous, and its correct tag (and subsequently its expansion) can only be determined by the context. For example, a number should be tagged as an ordinal (NORD) when following or preceding a month (*e.g.* 'On *16* June...') but a cardinal (NUM) elsewhere (*e.g.* 'There were *16* people...').

Properties used in classification include –

- The length of the token.

- Case features: all upper, all lower, titlecase or mixed.

- Specific punctuation used within the token: forward slashes, hyphens, full stops, *etc.*

- The content of surrounding words, *e.g.* preceded by *on, at, from, to, etc.*

For the classification of MISC tokens, we use a

110

rule-based method, as there is no (or at least very little) ambiguity in this class compared to ALPHA and NUMB. NSWs are tagged as either HTAG (hashtag), URL (web address) or PROF (profanity) if they conform to a pre-defined regular expression pattern. For example, tokens beginning with a single # character and followed by a series of alphanumeric characters are tagged HTAG. If tokens do not match any pattern, they are tagged as NONE (and later deleted), *e.g.* a series of nonsense characters. After classification, the assigned tag is used to determine how the NSW should be expanded.

3.3 Classification and division of SPLT tokens

Many NSWs are compound words made up of distinct subcomponents, which cannot be expanded as they are, but must be broken down for further processing. Examples include mixed alphanumeric tokens, such as acronym-number compounds (*ITV3*), tokens containing mixed upper and lower case letters (*iPlayer*) and hyphenated words (*100-mile*). By classifying into ALPHA, NUMB, MISC and SPLT prior to division, single tokens that would otherwise conform to the SPLT pattern, such as dates and number ranges, are prevented from being incorrectly divided.

With a predefined list of tokens to be split, the division process is relatively straightforward; the same patterns used in the classification of SPLT tokens are used to hypothesise split points. Tokens are split by punctuation (e.g. hyphens, forward slashes), at boundaries between alphabetic and numeric characters and at boundaries between upper and lower case letters. Emphasis characters, such as asterisks, which often surround a word of importance (such as *this*), are also removed.

One ambiguous case arises in words containing a transition from upper to lower case - subtokens here could be an uppercase word followed by a lowercase word (*BBCnews*), necessitating a split after the final uppercase character, or an uppercase word followed by a titlecase words (*BBCNews*), where the split should be before the final uppercase character. For tokens matching this pattern, we deal with the ambiguity by hypothesising both split points, and checking whether the resulting word is in our word list. If neither group is in the word list, we split before the final uppercase letter as a default. This was found to be the more common pattern by Sproat *et al* (2001).

After division, each part of the SPLT token is

then retagged as ALPHA, NUMB or MISC for further classification and expansion.

3.4 NSW expansion

For the majority of NSW tokens, including all those tagged as NUMB, expansions are unambiguous, and pronunciations straightforward, once the tag is determined. Algorithms for number expansion are predominantly consistent with those in Sproat et al. (2001). However, in some cases where it was necessary to choose between multiple possible pronunciations for a single NSW, we looked at spoken data from the Spoken Wikipedia Corpus (Köhn et al., 2016) in order to make a principled, rather than arbitrary, decision. For example, for the pronunciation of years in the 2000s, we chose 'twenty thirteen' rather than 'two thousand and thirteen', based on our inspection of the corpus.

3.4.1 Unsupervised expansion of EXPN tokens

EXPN tokens are first checked against a dictionary of common abbreviations, an amended version of a list taken from the *Oxford English Dictionary*[6]. Ambiguous abbreviations in the dictionary (those with more than one possible expansion) are disambiguated in the same way as previously unknown abbreviations (see below), but their candidates are taken from the dictionary rather than generated from the word list. A second dictionary is used for common measurements, and matching NSWs are only expanded as such if the previous token is digit-based, *e.g.* 'two pounds' for *2 lb*. This stage allows us to accurately capture the most common abbreviations, whilst still being sufficiently domain-general.

For unusual EXPN tokens whose expansions are not listed in the abbreviation dictionary, we use an unsupervised method to predict the most probable expansion given the abbreviation. The algorithm first generates a list of candidate expansions for the abbreviation. These candidates are words from the word list that include the (ordered) sequence of letters in the abbreviation, either at the start of the word (as in 'address' for *addr.*), inserting any numbers of characters before the final letter ('government' for *govt.*) or inserting any number of intervening vowels ('function' for *fnctn*). This follows from observations as to how abbreviations

---

[6] `http://public.oed.com/`
`how-to-use-the-oed/abbreviations`

are most frequently formed. This list is then narrowed down by ruling out those candidates whose part-of-speech (POS) tag does not match the predicted POS tag for the abbreviation based on its syntactic context.

The final criterion for selection of an appropriate expansion uses a Corpus Lesk algorithm (Kilgarriff and Rosenzweig, 2000) to look at the overlap between the abbreviation and its possible expansions. Overlap is calculated by counting the number of words (ignoring stopwords, such as *the, at, of,* as well as the 100 most frequent words in Brown) shared by the context of the abbreviation and a signature generated for each candidate expansion, using contextual information from the Brown corpus, as well as WordNet (Fellbaum, 1998) definitions and examples. Candidates are ruled out if they overlap very little or not at all with the abbreviation. Where two candidates have equal overlap, we take the most frequent word (using frequency counts from Brown). This allows us to check that potential expansions are semantically, as well as syntactically, appropriate. As a candidate is only chosen if its character content, POS-tag and semantic context are consistent with the abbreviation, this allows us to be confident as to the accuracy of the expansion. In this way, we treat the problem of abbreviation expansion in a similar way to that of word sense disambiguation, where the task is to resolve an ambiguity between possible candidate expansions.

Since we use several criteria to predict the expansion of previously unseen abbreviations, this allows generalisation across many different domains. As a result, our method of abbreviation expansion represents a significant improvement over previous normalisation work, which was principally domain-specific.

4   Evaluation

Our normalisation system is evaluated against a gold standard corpus containing 1000 sentences taken from various websites including Wikipedia, Google News, Maths is Fun, Slate, the Urban Dictionary and the University of Cambridge. We refer to this corpus as NSW-GOLD and release it in the GitHub repository. NSW-GOLD contains 21,447 tokens in which NSWs were hand-labelled with an overall class (ALPHA, NUMB, MISC or SPLT) and a specific tag. It remains a matter of future work to add multiple gold-standard expansions for the

whole corpus, though we did so for a subset, as explained below.

Evaluation was performed for detection, classification and expansion separately. As it is possible for a word to be correctly expanded whilst being incorrectly tagged (and vice versa), we evaluate the performance of each component separately.

4.1   NSW detection

As the first stage of our normalisation system (detection) is a binary task, labelling input tokens as either NSWs or standard words, we use simple precision and recall metrics for evaluation. Precision (1) is the number of true positives (T_p) over the number of true positives plus false positives (F_p), *i.e.* the proportion of tokens labelled 'NSW' that are truly NSWs. Recall (2) is the number of true positives over the number of true positives plus the number of false negatives (F_n), *i.e.* the proportion of NSWs in NSW-GOLD that are correctly detected as such.

$$P = \frac{T_p}{T_p + F_p} \quad (1) \qquad R = \frac{T_p}{T_p + F_n} \quad (2)$$

Our evaluation for NSW detection yielded scores of 95.1% for precision and 97.4% for recall. This means that just under 3% of NSWs in NSW-GOLD went undetected but that tokens hypothesised to be NSWs were indeed NSWs 95 times out of 100. Note that we prioritize precision over recall in the detection stage, because if a word is incorrectly tagged as an NSW it should later be classified WDLK (wordlike) and expanded to itself, whereas if an NSW is not detected, it can never be expanded.

4.2   NSW classification

In order to evaluate both our overall classifier and our subclassifiers for ALPHA, NUMB and MISC tokens, we computed an accuracy score, where accuracy is the number of correctly labelled NSWs (those whose label matches that in NSW-GOLD) over the total number of NSWs. As tokens only proceed to be classified if they are tagged as NSWs, these accuracy scores do not take into account NSWs that were not detected at the initial stage, but are purely a measure of classification accuracy.

For our ALPHA classifier, accuracy was 89% (Table 3). Within the ALPHA class, performance is high for LSEQ and WDLK but lower for EXPN, reflecting the ambiguity of NSWs tagging. Some

NSW tokens, such as *LW*, could reasonably be read either as a letter sequence (LSEQ), or expanded to 'long wave' (EXPN).

For the NUMB class accuracy was found to be 89%. Whilst this performance is good, the task of assigning fine-grained labels to NSWs is much harder. Certain types, namely NUM and NYER may be tagged very accurately; others, such as, NRANGE and NTIME, are harder, whilst NTEL and NSCI were not identified at all. Improvement in identifying these NSW types remains a matter for future work. Nevertheless, in terms of expansion, provided that the NUMB class is correctly identified, many times the exact tag does not matter too much, since for several tag types the NSW will be spelled out like a number or as separate digits. This is fine for most numeric tags, and people are often willing to accept several different expansions of the same NSW, as is clear from human evaluation of expansion (next section). Moreover, this observation suggests we could collapse some of the numeric distinctions in a future review.

The SPLT class sees the lowest accuracy at 86%, which is understandable since – being of mixed content – these are inherently difficult to identify. Finally, for the MISC class accuracy was 92%. Within the MISC class, hashtags are identified without errors, but the PROF,URL,NONE types are identified less well. There are clear improvements to be made in this class in future work.

In all cases, the accuracy scores may be lower than if we had allowed for multiple tags per NSW in our evaluation, thereby reflecting the subjectivity of classification and the multi-functionality of linguistic tokens.

In Table 4 we show a confusion matrix for NSW tag types. It is apparent that errors tend to stay within class, or default to NONE (not spoken). Within the NUMB class, the NUM tag is dominant, which is tolerable as for most numeric types the expansion will be acceptable. It remains a matter for future work to improve our classifiers and add to NSW-GOLD for further evaluation.

4.3 NSW expansion – comparison to existing systems

In order to assess the accuracy of our overall system, we compared the output of our system to that of both Sproat et al. (2001)'s original system, and an online interface to the AT&T Natural Voices TTS system, which we believe to be

Class	Accuracy	Tag	Accuracy
ALPHA	0.893	EXPN	0.60
		LSEQ	0.90
		WDLK	0.92
NUMB	0.89	NUM	1.0
		NORD	0.72
		NRANGE	0.56
		NTEL	0
		NDIG	0.12
		NTIME	0.72
		NDATE	0.34
		NADDR	0.12
		NYER	0.98
		MONEY	0.80
		PRCT	0.76
		NSCI	0
SPLT	0.86	SPLT	0.86
MISC	0.92	PROF	0.66
		URL	0.48
		HTAG	1.0
		NONE	0.66

Table 3: Accuracy of NSW classification by class and tag.

derivative from Sproat and colleagues' work[7]. As Sproat et al. (2001)'s model uses training data from one of four specific domains (a recipes newsgroup, newswire, a PC-hardware newsgroup, and classified property advertisements), we evaluated against each domain separately.

For this comparison, we used a subset of 102 sentences from NSW-GOLD, selected at random. The sample contained 291 NSWs, the expansion of which were hand-annotated as either correct or incorrect in the output generated by each of the five systems. Expansions were labelled as correct if they could realistically have been produced by a human, and would be acceptable if read out by a TTS system. In the case of ambiguity, we accepted both expansions as correct, *e.g.* either 'twenty ten' or 'two thousand and ten' for the year 2010. Here, accuracy is defined as the number of correctly expanded NSWs over the total number of NSWs ($n = 291$).

Our system was found to achieve an overall accuracy of 91.4%, much higher than that of the Wizzard TTS system (75.3%), or any of the domain-specific models (see Table 5). Whilst Sproat et al. (2001)'s system is sure to perform well given data from one of their four specific domains, the inapplicability of their supervised approach to new domains was evident here. For example, when using its classified property advertisements model, the system returned incorrect expansions such as

---

[7] http://wizzardsoftware.com/ text-to-speech-sdk.php

| | Predicted labels | | | | | | | | | | | | | | | | | | | | |
| | ALPHA | | | NUMB | | | | | | | | | | | | | MISC | | | | |
Actual	EXPN	LSEQ	WDLK	NUM	NORD	NRANGE	NTEL	NDIG	NTIME	NDATE	NADDR	NYER	MONEY	PRCT	NSCI	SPLT	PROF	URL	HTAG	NONE	*n/a*
EXPN	30	12	1	0	0	0	0	0	0	0	0	0	0	0	0	0	0	0	0	7	0
LSEQ	0	45	0	0	0	0	0	0	0	0	0	0	0	0	0	0	0	0	0	0	5
WDLK	0	0	46	0	0	0	0	0	0	0	0	0	0	0	0	0	0	0	0	0	4
NUM	0	0	0	50	0	0	0	0	0	0	0	0	0	0	0	0	0	0	0	0	0
NORD	0	9	1	2	36	0	0	0	0	0	0	0	0	0	0	0	0	0	0	1	1
NRANGE	0	0	0	16	0	28	0	0	1	0	0	1	0	0	0	0	0	0	0	4	0
NTEL	0	0	0	43	0	1	0	1	0	0	0	1	0	0	0	0	0	0	0	4	0
NDIG	0	0	0	42	0	0	0	6	0	0	0	0	0	0	0	0	0	0	0	2	0
NTIME	0	0	0	14	0	0	0	0	36	0	0	0	0	0	0	0	0	0	0	0	0
NDATE	0	0	0	19	0	4	0	10	0	17	0	0	0	0	0	0	0	0	0	0	0
NADDR	0	0	0	40	2	1	0	0	0	1	6	0	0	0	0	0	0	0	0	0	0
NYER	0	0	0	1	0	0	0	0	0	0	0	49	0	0	0	0	0	0	0	0	0
MONEY	0	0	0	10	0	0	0	0	0	0	0	0	40	0	0	0	0	0	0	0	0
PRCT	0	0	0	5	0	0	0	0	0	0	0	0	0	38	0	0	0	0	0	7	0
NSCI	0	0	0	13	0	0	0	0	0	0	0	0	0	0	0	0	0	0	0	37	0
SPLT	0	0	0	3	0	0	0	0	0	0	0	0	0	0	3	43	0	1	0	0	0
PROF	0	0	0	0	0	0	0	0	0	0	0	0	0	0	0	0	33	0	0	17	0
URL	0	0	0	0	0	0	0	0	0	0	0	0	0	0	0	0	0	24	0	26	0
HTAG	0	0	0	0	0	0	0	0	0	0	0	0	0	0	0	0	0	0	50	0	0
NONE	0	1	0	0	0	0	0	0	0	0	0	0	0	0	0	0	1	0	0	33	15

Table 4: Confusion matrix for classification of NSW tags in NSW-GOLD.

| Our system | AT&T | Sproat et al. (2001) | | | |
	Natural Voices	Recipes	Hardware	News	Ads
0.914	0.753	0.460	0.536	0.601	0.574

Table 5: Cross-system comparison of NSW expansion accuracy

'kitchen H Z' for *kHz*. The total run time for our program compared to the original was also found to be significantly faster[8].

5 Conclusion and Future Work

We have presented a text normalisation system for NSWs, adopting and adapting the taxonomy designed by Sproat et al. (2001), and showed that our modular detection-classification-division-expansion system works to a high degree of accuracy across all NSW types and modules ($>$ 91%). This is an important step for TTS systems and other downstream NLP tasks. The system is made available as a GitHub repository[9] for non-commercial use under a GNU General Public License[10]. In contrast to a previous system written in Scheme (Sproat et al., 2001), the fact our system has been developed in the widely-used Python programming language makes it flexible to the unforeseen needs of other researchers. In addition, we have made it straightforward to opt for a specific tokenizer, or input a dictionary of abbreviations, meaning that the system is domain-modifiable whilst still being appropriately domain-general.

In future work, we intend to improve our system by addressing the NSW tag types for which performance was relatively poor, and by extending our taxonomy to include more tags specific to the web. We would also like to allow the generation of multiple expansions, to capture ambiguity and different pronunciation preferences. We can also further test our system against modern TTS systems available through Google Android Apps, Apple Macintosh OS, and Microsoft Office.

A further problem for normalisation is that the boundary between standard words and NSWs is not always rigid. Some words, such as proper nouns, foreign words or company names, may not have a dictionary entry (or pronunciation in the CMU), but should not (and cannot) be further expanded, thus a normalisation system would be unable to aid TTS in these cases. This is an area in

---

[8]Mean run time 1 minute 50 seconds for Sproat and colleagues' system; 22 seconds for ours, averaged over 100 runs on a Macintosh iMac with 2.7GHz Intel Core i5 processor and 8GB memory.

[9]http://github.com/EFord36/normalise

[10]https://www.gnu.org/licenses/gpl-3.0.en.html

need of further investigation and system development.

Having updated the NSW taxonomy and adopted a rule-based approach to classification, the system remains vulnerable to further macroscale shifts in language use such as that brought on by the Internet, and the kind of micro-scale non-standard neologisms which emerge (and recede) day-to-day. In future work we can therefore incorporate unsupervised methods of NSW classification and expansion, along the lines of the automatic dictionary construction method presented by Han et al. (2012), and the distributional method described by Rangarajan Sridhar (2015).

Additional areas of future interest might be in developing a 'reverse text normalisation' system for Automatic Speech Recognition (ASR) – a backwards conversion of speech into non-standard text, *e.g.* numbers. Finally, a cognitive computational investigation comparing speech production errors and NSW classification errors is a research question of general interest.

Acknowledgements

This paper reports on research supported by Cambridge English, University of Cambridge. We are thankful for support from Sidney Sussex College and Downing College, Cambridge. And we gratefully acknowledge Dimitrios Alikaniotis and Ernst for their help with this work. We thank the three reviewers for their very helpful comments and have attempted to improve the paper in line with their suggestions.

References

AiTi Aw, Min Zhang, Juan Xiao, and Jian Su. 2006. A phrase-based statistical model for sms text normalization. In *Proceedings of the COLING/ACL 2006 Main Conference Poster Session*. Association for Computational Linguistics.

Steven Bird, Edward Loper, and Ewan Klein. 2009. *Natural Language Processing with Python*. Sebastopol, CA: O'Reilly Media.

Jacob Eisenstein. 2013. What to do about bad language on the internet. In *Proceedings of NAACL-HLT 2013*. Association for Computational Linguistics.

Christiane Fellbaum, editor. 1998. *WordNet: An Electronic Lexical Database*. Cambridge, MA: MIT Press.

W. Nelson Francis and Henry Kučera. 1964. *Manual of information to accompany A Standard Corpus of Present-Day Edited American English, for use with Digital Computers*.

Bo Han and Timothy Baldwin. 2011. Lexical normalisation of short text messages: makn sens a #twitter. In *Proceedings of the 49th Annual Meeting of the Association for Computational Linguistics*. Association for Computational Linguistics.

Bo Han, Paul Cook, and Timothy Baldwin. 2012. Automatically constructing a normalisation dictionary for microblogs. In *Proceedings of the 2012 Joint Conference on Empirical Methods in Natural Language Processing and Computational Natural Language Learning*.

Braj Kachru. 1992. *The Other Tongue: English across cultures*. Chicago: University of Illinois Press.

Adam Kilgarriff and Joseph Rosenzweig. 2000. English senseval: Report and results. In *Proceedings of the Second International Conference on Language Resources and Evaluation (LREC 2000)*. European Language Resources Association (ELRA).

Arne Köhn, Florian Stegen, and Timo Baumann. 2016. Mining the spoken wikipedia for speech data and beyond. In *Proceedings of the Tenth International Conference on Language Resources and Evaluation (LREC 2016)*. European Language Resources Association (ELRA).

Stuart Moore, Sabine Buchholz, and Anna Korhonen. 2010. Annotating the enron email corpus with number senses. In *Proceedings of the Seventh International Conference on Language Resources and Evaluation (LREC'10)*. European Language Resources Association (ELRA).

Barbara Plank. 2016. What to do about non-standard (or *non-canonical*) language in NLP. In *Proceedings of the 13th Conference on Natural Language Processing (KONVENS 2016)*.

Vivek Kumar Rangarajan Sridhar. 2015. Unsupervised text normalization using distributed representations of words and phrases. In *Proceedings of the 1st Workshop on Vector Space Modeling for Natural Language Processing*.

Brian Roark and Richard Sproat. 2014. Hippocratic abbreviation expansion. In *Proceedings of the 52nd Annual Meeting of the Association for Computational Linguistics (Volume 2: Short Papers)*.

Richard Sproat, Alan Black, Stanley Chen, Shankar Kumar, Mari Ostendorf, and Christopher Richards. 2001. Normalization of non-standard words. *Computer Speech and Language* 15:287–333.

Huntsville, hospitals, and hockey teams:
Names can reveal your location

Bahar Salehi♣, Dirk Hovy♣, Eduard Hovy◇ and Anders Søgaard♣
♣Department of Computer Science, University of Copenhagen
◇School of Computer Science, Carnegie Mellon University
`bahar.salehi@gmail.com dirk.hovy@di.ku.dk`
`hovy@cmu.edu soegaard@di.ku.dk`

Abstract

Geolocation is the task of identifying a social media user's primary location, and in natural language processing, there is a growing literature on to what extent automated analysis of social media posts can help. However, not all content features are equally revealing of a user's location. In this paper, we evaluate nine name entity (NE) types. Using various metrics, we find that `GEO-LOC`, `FACILITY` and `SPORT-TEAM` are more informative for geolocation than other NE types. Using these types, we improve geolocation accuracy and reduce distance error over various famous text-based methods.

1 Introduction

Because social media such as Twitter are used in both research and industry to monitor trends and identify sudden changes in society, it is critical to be able to locate social media users. In Twitter, however, only about 1% of all tweets are geotagged, and the location specified by users in their profile is often noisy and unreliable (Cheng et al., 2010).

Geolocation is the task of identifying users' general or primary location, when this is not readily available. Accurate geolocation can improve scientific studies, as well as technologies such as event detection, recommender systems, sentiment analysis, and knowledge base population.

Since tweets contain at most 140 characters, geolocation of individual tweets is rarely feasible. Instead, most studies focus on predicting the primary location of a user by concatenating their entire tweet history. While this provides more context, it is still a noisy source with features of varying informativeness.

In this paper, we focus on named entities (NEs), a particular rich source of information, and investigate how much they can reveal about a user's primary location. Wing and Baldridge (2014) showed lists of predictive features for multiple cities, where we observe NEs among the top 20 features. This is due to the inherent localization of many NEs. E.g., top features for Los Angeles contain NEs such as names (`Irvine`, `disneyland`), parts of names (`diego`, `angeles`), and abbreviations (`UCLA`, `SoCal` (Southern California)). This observation motivates us to examine nine common NE types in social media, and their location predictiveness. Additionally, we find that using only the top three most informative types for geolocation improves accuracy and reduces the median distance error.

Contributions We study (1) the geographical informativeness of nine named entity types, and (2) explore their effect in a logistic regression model of text-based geolocation. Among the previous top text-based models, we obtain the best performance using the hidden location information of the top three NE types. This suggests that users who would like to maintain privacy should avoid using such names.

2 Related Work

Most previous studies use textual features as input. Some use KL divergence between the distribution of a users words and the words used in each region (Wing and Baldridge, 2011; Roller et al., 2012), regional topic distributions (Eisenstein et al., 2010; Ahmed et al., 2013; Hong et al., 2012), or feature selection/weighting to find words indicative of location (Priedhorsky et al., 2014; Han et al., 2012, 2014; Wing and Baldridge, 2014).

All these studies require relatively large training sets to fit the models, and can be heavily biased by

116

Proceedings of the 3rd Workshop on Noisy User-generated Text, pages 116–121
Copenhagen, Denmark, September 7, 2017. ©2017 Association for Computational Linguistics

Type	Example	%
PERSON	Barack Obama	31
GEO-LOC	Southern California	18
FACILITY	Edward theater	14
COMPANY	IBM	12
MOVIE	The town	10
BAND	pink floyd	9
PRODUCT	microsoft office	7
TV-SHOW	family guy	4
SPORT-TEAM	Eagles	2
All		55

Table 1: NE types considered in this paper and percentage of users in training set who use at least one of these NEs in their tweets.

major events during the time of collection, such as an election or a disaster. In contrast to our work, most do not consider multi-word NEs.

Only few text-based studies consider NEs, and if so, focus on location names using gazetteers like GeoNames, limiting the methods to the completeness of these gazetteers. Since they usually also use other text-based models, it is hard to determine how much location names contribute. These approaches depend on a name-disambiguation phase, using Wikipedia, DBPedia, or OpenStreetMap, since location names can refer to multiple locations (Brunsting et al., 2016).

Chi et al. (2016) explicitly study the contributions of city and country names, hashtags, and user mentionings, to geolocation. Their results suggested that a combination of city and country names, as well as hashtags, are good location predictors. Pavalanathan and Eisenstein (2015) suggest that non-standard words are more location-specific, and also, more likely to occur in geo-tagged tweets. In contrast to this paper, none of the previous works study how much various NE types reveal about the user location. Similarly, Salehi and Søgaard (2017) evaluate common hypotheses about language and location. However, they do not explicitly study named entities.

3 Resources

Data We use the WORLD dataset (Han et al., 2012), which covers 3,709 cities worldwide and consists of tweets from 1.4M users. Han et al. (2012) hold out 10,000 users as development and 10,000 as test set. For each user with at least 10 geotagged tweets, the user's location is set to be the city in which the majority of their tweets are from. We also use Han et al. (2012)'s method to extract the nearest city to a given latitude-longitude coordinate.

NER We use TwitterNLP (Ritter et al., 2011) to extract the nine most common NE types in Twitter. Table 1 shows the percentage of users in our training data who use at least one NE in their tweets. Overall, 55% of the users use at least one NE, with PERSON, GEO-LOC and FACILITY as the most popular types.

Twitter corpus In order to measure the geographical diversity of NEs, we construct a corpus from tweets posted one week before the WORLD dataset was collected (14 Sep, 2011 to 20 Sep, 2011). We remove all non-English and non-geo-tagged tweets from this corpus. This leaves us with 0.5M tweets. This corpus covers 167 countries and 2263 cities/regions around the world.[1] The most frequent countries are USA, Great Britain, Indonesia, Canada, Malaysia, Philippine and Australia, and the most frequent cities are London, Los Angeles, Chicago, Manhattan, Atlanta, Jakarta and Singapore. Using this corpus, we obtain the distribution of NEs over the cities of the world.

4 NE types and Geolocation

In Table 1, we have seen the *general distribution* of NE types, with PERSON, GEO-LOC and FACILITY as top three. In this section, we focus on the *predictiveness* of NEs (as features) for geolocation. Later, in Section 5, we will propose a method to improve geolocation by putting more emphasis on the top NEs and their hidden location information.

We conduct three experiments to quantify predictiveness of NEs. In the first, we measure the geographic distribution of each NE type, and measure their entropy. In the second experiment, we conduct feature selection via randomized logistic regression, and, in the third experiment, we establish a baseline by using majority classes for all types.

Geographic diversity We first measure the geographic distribution of each type. We extract all NEs in the WORLD training set and use the Tweet corpus to measure entropy and mean pairwise distance (in kilometers) between tweets that contain the same NEs. We compute unpredictability as entropy:

$$H(x) = -\sum_{i=1}^{n} P(x_i) \log P(x_i)$$

---

[1]We map the latitude and longitude coordinates to cities/regions based on Han et al. (2012).

	Entropy		Avg. pairwise distance	LR ↑
	city-level ↓	country-level ↓	in kilometers ↓	
GEO-LOC	**2.581**	**0.756**	**3982.077**	**0.831**
FACILITY	**2.774**	**0.798**	**4368.122**	**0.851**
SPORT-TEAM	3.002	**0.806**	**4127.404**	**0.729**
MOVIE	**2.980**	1.110	5524.074	0.492
TV-SHOW	3.090	0.906	4713.947	0.465
PERSON	3.351	1.106	5157.701	0.544
BAND	3.519	1.199	5261.419	0.535
PRODUCT	4.119	1.358	5481.787	0.498
COMPANY	5.562	1.646	5814.398	0.611

Table 2: Average geographical variation/sparsity of each NE type in Twitter and average randomized logistic regression (LR) weights. ↓ = lower values are better, ↑ = higher values are better. The top three types in each column are shown in **BOLD**.

where the entropy of NE x is measured by computing $P(x_i)$, which is the probability that x is referring to the ith city/country, based on the frequency. We measure the entropy in both city and country level, shown in Table 2.

For example, suppose *CMU* is found in four tweets from Pittsburgh and one from San Francisco, and *IBM* is found in one tweet each from Pittsburgh, San Francisco, Melbourne, and New York. In this case, the entropy for *CMU* will be lower than for *IBM*. This would indicate that *IBM* is less predictive than *CMU* for geolocation. To compute the entropy of an NE type, we average over the entropies of all NEs of that type.

The first three columns of Table 2 show that GEO-LOC and FACILITY are the least diverse location-wise. NEs of type PERSON are the most frequent NEs (see Table 1), and occur in more diverse locations. On the other hand, NEs of type SPORT-TEAM, the least frequent NEs, have low location diversity. PRODUCT and COMPANY are the least predictive types.

Feature evaluation In our second experiment, we use L_1 randomized logistic regression (Ng, 2004) on the training set to get the most predictive features. It measures how often a feature is predictive under varying conditions, by fitting hundreds of L_1-regularized models on subsets of the data. Each feature is assigned a weight between 0 and 1 based on their predictiveness. For example, the weights for countries and city names are high (on average 0.831) showing that they are very predictive. Yet, some examples of features with zero weight are *web*, *today* and *t.v.* showing that these features are not predictive at all. Table 2 (under LR column) shows the resulting prevalence for each type. These are compatible with the previous two metrics, showing GEO-LOC, FACILITY and

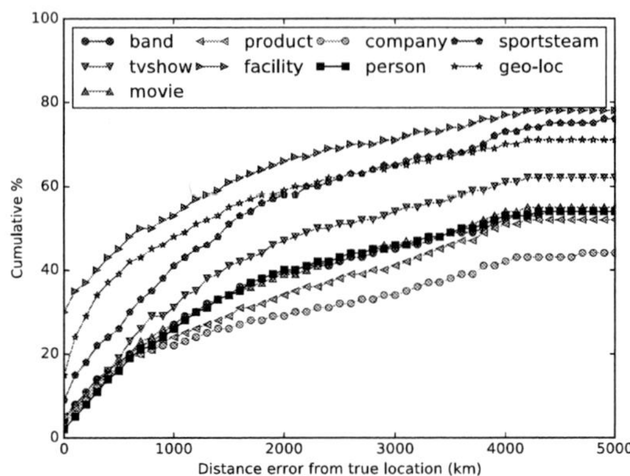

Figure 1: Distance error (test set)

SPORT-TEAM as the most predictive types.

Majority Vote Accuracy In the third experiment, we measure accuracy and distance error (in kilometers) using majority voting for each NE on the Tweet corpus. E.g., if we see *CMU* in four tweets from Pittsburgh and one tweet from San Francisco, we label the user's location as Pittsburgh. Figure 1 shows the percentage of the test set with a distance error from the true location less than K kilometers (also known as ACC@K). The three top types are again GEO-LOC, FACILITY and SPORT-TEAM, showing their higher impact on revealing the location of users.

5 NE Impact on Geolocation

Having established the informativeness of the various NE types, in this section, we examine the impact of NEs and their hidden location information for geolocation. To extract the hidden location information of each NE, we collect the locations of all tweets in our tweet corpus that contain that

Example	Me, my friend and the Eiffel tower
baseline	`Me my friend and the Eiffel tower`
Only NE	`[Eiffel tower]`
Baseline without NE	`ME my friend and the`
Our Method	`Me my friend and the Eiffel tower Paris Paris`
	`Paris Paris [Las Vegas] [Las Vegas]`

Table 3: Examples and features of methods in Section 5

Method		Accuracy			Distance	
	city$\uparrow$	country$\uparrow$	@161$\uparrow$	Median$\downarrow$	Mean$\downarrow$
Baseline	17.6	**83.6**	33.6	515	**1727**
Only NE	9.3	53.6	17.7	2186	5317
Baseline without NE	14.8	82.2	29.9	612	1885
Our Method$_{allNEs}$	17.5	83.3	33.7	520	1769
Our Method$_{top3}$	**17.8**	**83.6**	**34.0**	**495**	1735
Previous studies					
Wing and Baldridge (2014)	–	–	31.0	509	1669
Han et al. (2012)	10.3	–	24.1	646	1953

Table 4: Accuracy and distance results for various methods. – indicates no report in respective paper

NE. To divide the world into regions with roughly the same number of users, we use a k-d tree approach proposed by Roller et al. (2012). As a result, we will cover larger regions when the population density is low and vice versa. Each region is then considered as a label to train the classifiers. The approach of using k-d tree is also used in Rahimi et al. (2015); Han et al. (2012) and Wing and Baldridge (2014).

See Table 3 for an example of the following methods. All use logistic regression as classifier, following Rahimi et al. (2015).

Baseline We use (Rahimi et al., 2015)'s bag-of-words model over tweets as baseline, which is also the state-of-the-art text-based method on the publicly available WORLD dataset.

Baseline without NE Here, we remove all NEs, to observe the influence of NEs in the bag-of-words model.

Only NEs In this approach, we consider *only* NEs and discard all other words in the tweets.

Our method We consider NEs and their inherent location information in addition to the bag-of-words model. The inherent location information for each NE is extracted from our Twitter corpus.[2] Suppose, for example, that *Eiffel tower* is found in four tweets from `Paris` and two tweets from `Las Vegas`. In this case, we add `Paris` (four times) and `Las Vegas` (twice) to the input text. The

repetition is used to put more emphasis/weight based on frequency.[3] In order to measure the effectiveness of the three top NE *types* discovered in Section 4, we experiment with (1) considering all NE types (shown as **Our Method**$_{allNEs}$ in Table 4), and (2) the three most useful types (shown as **Our Method**$_{top3}$).

Evaluation metrics We use the same evaluation metrics as previous studies: accuracy depending on location granularity (city and country), accuracy within the distance of 100 miles/161km (ACC@161)[4], and median and mean error (in kilometers).

6 Results and Discussion

The results of applying each of the methods introduced in Section 5 are shown in Table 4. The baseline follows Rahimi et al. (2015), but does not use network information, to isolate the effect of NEs. They also add additional data, whereas we *only* consider the WORLD training set to be comparable with Wing and Baldridge (2014) and Han et al. (2012). Our baseline results are therefore lower than what Rahimi et al. (2015) report. Using only NEs results in a large performance drop with respect to the baseline. However, ignoring NEs (baseline-NE) also decreases the geolocation predictability by 15% (city level), indicating the importance of NEs in revealing the location of users.

Our proposed method, using all NE types

---

[2] As mentioned in Section 3, our Twitter corpus is the collection of tweets posted one week before the WORLD dataset was collected. This way we make sure that we are not training on test data.

[3] We also tried weighing features and samples according to their entropy, but we found repetition to perform better.

[4] ACC@161 measures near-miss predictions (Cheng et al., 2010)

according to their hidden location information, comes close, but does not improve over the baseline. However, when we consider only the top three NE types (GEO-LOC,FACILITY and SPORT-TEAM) from Section 4, performance increases, indicating that other NE types add noisy information.

Our error analysis shows that PERSON is very frequent, yet diverse, including politicians, athletes, and more general names. Since SPORT-TEAM is one of the most indicative types, we assume that athlete names can be useful as well. We leave this aspect for future work.

7 Conclusion

We compare the predictiveness of various named entity types for geolocation. We consider entropy, pairwise distance, feature selection weights, and the effect of the NEs on accuracy and error distance, and find that GEO-LOC, FACILITY and SPORT-TEAM are more predictive of location than other NE types.

Our results show that using the inherent localized information of NEs can improve geolocation accuracy. The results also suggest that users could obfuscate geolocation by avoiding these types.

Acknowledgments

This work was supported by the Data Transparency Lab.

References

Amr Ahmed, Liangjie Hong, and Alexander J Smola. 2013. Hierarchical geographical modeling of user locations from social media posts. In *Proceedings of the 22nd international conference on World Wide Web*. ACM, pages 25–36.

Shawn Brunsting, Hans De Sterck, Remco Dolman, and Teun van Sprundel. 2016. Geotexttagger: High-precision location tagging of textual documents using a natural language processing approach. *arXiv preprint arXiv:1601.05893* .

Zhiyuan Cheng, James Caverlee, and Kyumin Lee. 2010. You are where you tweet: a content-based approach to geo-locating twitter users. In *Proceedings of the 19th ACM international conference on Information and knowledge management*. ACM, pages 759–768.

Lianhua Chi, Kwan Hui Lim, Nebula Alam, and Christopher J Butler. 2016. Geolocation prediction in twitter using location indicative words and textual features. *WNUT 2016* page 227.

Jacob Eisenstein, Brendan O'Connor, Noah A Smith, and Eric P Xing. 2010. A latent variable model for geographic lexical variation. In *Proceedings of the 2010 Conference on Empirical Methods in Natural Language Processing*. Association for Computational Linguistics, pages 1277–1287.

Bo Han, Paul Cook, and Timothy Baldwin. 2012. Geolocation prediction in social media data by finding location indicative words. In *Proceedings of COLING*. pages 1045–1062.

Bo Han, Paul Cook, and Timothy Baldwin. 2014. Text-based twitter user geolocation prediction. *Journal of Artificial Intelligence Research* 49:451–500.

Liangjie Hong, Amr Ahmed, Siva Gurumurthy, Alexander J Smola, and Kostas Tsioutsiouliklis. 2012. Discovering geographical topics in the twitter stream. In *Proceedings of the 21st international conference on World Wide Web*. ACM, pages 769–778.

Andrew Y. Ng. 2004. Feature selection, l1 vs. l2 regularization, and rotational invariance. In *Proceedings of the Twenty-first International Conference on Machine Learning*. ICML '04, pages 78–85.

Umashanthi Pavalanathan and Jacob Eisenstein. 2015. Confounds and consequences in geotagged twitter data. *arXiv preprint arXiv:1506.02275* .

Reid Priedhorsky, Aron Culotta, and Sara Y Del Valle. 2014. Inferring the origin locations of tweets with quantitative confidence. In *Proceedings of the 17th ACM conference on Computer supported cooperative work & social computing*. ACM, pages 1523–1536.

Afshin Rahimi, Trevor Cohn, and Timothy Baldwin. 2015. Twitter user geolocation using a unified text and network prediction model. In *Proceedings of the 53rd Annual Meeting of the Association for Computational Linguistics and the 7th International Joint Conference on Natural Language Processing of the Asian Federation of Natural Language Processing (ACL2015)*. The Association for Computational Linguistics, pages 630–636.

Alan Ritter, Sam Clark, Mausam, and Oren Etzioni. 2011. Named entity recognition in tweets: An experimental study. In *EMNLP*.

Stephen Roller, Michael Speriosu, Sarat Rallapalli, Benjamin Wing, and Jason Baldridge. 2012. Supervised text-based geolocation using language models on an adaptive grid. In *Proceedings of the 2012 Joint Conference on Empirical Methods in Natural Language Processing and Computational Natural Language Learning*. Association for Computational Linguistics, pages 1500–1510.

Bahar Salehi and Anders Søgaard. 2017. Evaluating hypotheses in geolocation on a very large sample of twitter. In *Proceedings of the 3rd Workshop on Noisy User-generated Text (WNUT)*. Copenhagen, Denmark.

Benjamin Wing and Jason Baldridge. 2014. Hierarchical discriminative classification for text-based geolocation. In *EMNLP*. pages 336–348.

Benjamin P Wing and Jason Baldridge. 2011. Simple supervised document geolocation with geodesic grids. In *Proceedings of the 49th Annual Meeting of the Association for Computational Linguistics: Human Language Technologies-Volume 1*. Association for Computational Linguistics, pages 955–964.

Improving Document Clustering by Eliminating Unnatural Language

Myungha Jang[1], Jinho D. Choi[2], James Allan[1]
[1]College of Information and Computer Sciences, University of Massachusetts
[2]Department of Computer Science, Emory University
mhjang@cs.umass.edu, jinho.choi@emory.edu, allan@cs.umass.edu

Abstract

Technical documents contain a fair amount of *unnatural language*, such as tables, formulas, and pseudo-code. Unnatural language can be an important factor of confusing existing NLP tools. This paper presents an effective method of distinguishing unnatural language from natural language, and evaluates the impact of unnatural language detection on NLP tasks such as document clustering. We view this problem as an information extraction task and build a multiclass classification model identifying unnatural language components into four categories. First, we create a new annotated corpus by collecting slides and papers in various formats, PPT, PDF, and HTML, where unnatural language components are annotated into four categories. We then explore features available from plain text to build a statistical model that can handle any format as long as it is converted into plain text. Our experiments show that removing unnatural language components gives an absolute improvement in document clustering by up to 15%. Our corpus and tool are publicly available.

1 Introduction

Technical documents typically include meta components such as figures, tables, mathematical formulas, and pseudo-code to effectively communicate complex ideas and results. Let us define the term *unnatural language* as text blocks that consist of only meta components as opposed to natural language that consists of body text.

There are many effective NLP tools available as the field has been advanced. However, these tools are mostly built for input text that are natural language. As many of our tools for NLP can be badly confused by unnatural language, it is necessary to distinguish unnatural language blocks from natural language blocks, or else unnatural language blocks will cause confusion for natural language processing. Once we salvage natural language blocks from the documents, we can exploit NLP tools much better as they are intended for. This phenomenon is emphasized in technical documents that have a higher ratio of unnatural language compared to non-technical documents such as essays and novels.

Document layout analysis aiming to identify document format by classifying blocks into text, figures, and tables has been a long-studied problem (O'Gorman, 1993; Simon et al., 1997). Most previous work have focused on image-based documents, PDF and OCR formats, and used geometric analysis on the pages using the visual cues from its layout. This was a clearly important problem in many applications in NLP and IR.

This work was particularly motivated while we attempted to cluster teaching documents (e.g., lecture slides and reading materials from courses) in technical topics. We discovered that unnatural language blocks introduced significant noise for clustering, causing spurious matches between documents. For example, code consists of reserved programming keywords and variable names. Two documents can contain two very different code blocks from one another but their cosine similarity is high because they share many terms by programming convention (Figure 1). (Kohlhase and Sucan, 2006) also recognized this problem by explaining main challenges of semantic search for mathematical formula: (1) Mathematical notation is context-dependent; without human's capability to understand the formula from the context, formulas are just *noise*. (2) Identical presentations can stand for multiple distinct mathematical objects.

Proceedings of the 3rd Workshop on Noisy User-generated Text, pages 122–130
Copenhagen, Denmark, September 7, 2017. ©2017 Association for Computational Linguistics

```
int binarySearch(int[]             void merge_sort(int[] array)
array, int value, int left, int right)  if length(array) <= 1
{                                          return;

    if (left > right)                  int[] array left, right
        return -1;                     int middle = length(array)
    int middle = (left + right) / 2;   for each x in array before middle
    if (array[middle] == value)            add x to left
        return middle;                 for each x in array after or equal middle
    else if (array[middle] > value)        add x to right
        return binarySearch(array,
value, left, middle - 1);              left = merge_sort(left)
    else                               right = merge_sort(right)
        return binarySearch(array,
value, middle + 1, right);             return merge(left, right)
}
```

Figure 1: An example of how unnatural language confuses NLP tools. The left and right pseudo-code are very different, but standard NLP similarity functions such as cosine similarity can easily be confused by the terms highlighted in yellow.

This paper proposes a new approach for identifying unnatural language blocks in plain text into four types of categories: (1) TABLE (2) CODE (3) MATHEMATICAL FORMULA, and (4) MISCELLANEOUS (MISC). Text is extracted from technical documents in PDF, PPT, and HTML formats with little to no explicit visual layout information preserved. We focus on technical documents because they have a significant amount of unnatural language blocks (26.3% and 16% in our two corpora). Specifically, we focus on documents in slide formats, which have been underexplored.

We further study how removal of unnatural language improves two NLP tasks: document similarity and document clustering. Our experiments show that clustering on documents with unnatural language removed consistently showed higher accuracy on many of the settings than on original documents, with the maximum improvements up to 15% and 11% in two datasets, while it never significantly hurts the original clustering.

2 Related Work

2.1 Table Extraction

Various efforts have been made for table extraction using semi-supervised learning on the patterns of table layouts within ASCII text documents (Ng et al., 1999) web documents (Pinto et al., 2003; Lerman et al., 2001; Zanibbi et al., 2004) PDF and OCR image documents (Clark and Divvala, 2015; Liu et al., 2007). Existing techniques exploit the graphical features such as primitive geometry shapes, symbols, and lines to detect table borders. (Khusro et al., 2015) introduces and compares the state-of-the-art table extraction techniques from PDF articles. However, there does not appear to be any work that has attempted to process plain text extracted from richer formats, where table layouts are unpreserved.

2.2 Formula Extraction

Lin et al. (2011) categorized existing approaches for mathematical formulas detection by 'character-based' and 'layout-based' with respect to key features. (Chan and Yeung, 2000) provides a comprehensive survey of mathematical formula extraction using various layout features available from image-based documents. Since we have no access to layout information, character-based approaches are more relevant to our work. They use features of mathematical symbols, operators, and positions and their character sizes (Suzuki et al., 2003; Kacem et al., 2001).

2.3 Code Extraction

Tuarob et al. (2013) proposed 3 pseudo-code extraction methods: a rule based, a machine learning, and a combined method. Their rule based approach finds the presence of pseudo-code captions using keyword matching. The machine learning approach detects a box surrounding a sparse region and classifies whether the box is pseudo-code or not. They extracted four groups of features: font-style based, context based, content based, and structure based.

3 Problem Definition

Input to our task is the plain text extracted from PDF or PPT documents. The goal is to assign a class label to each line in that plain text, identifying it as natural language (regular text) or one of the

	Chinese-to-English		
	NIST05	NIST06	NIST08
L-Hiero	25.57^+	25.27^+	18.33^+
AdNN-Hiero-E	26.37	25.93	19.42
AdNN-Hiero-D	26.21	26.07	19.54

Figure 2: A table in a PDF document (left) and its text-extracted version (right). Note that it is hard to distinguish the column headings from the extracted text without its layout.

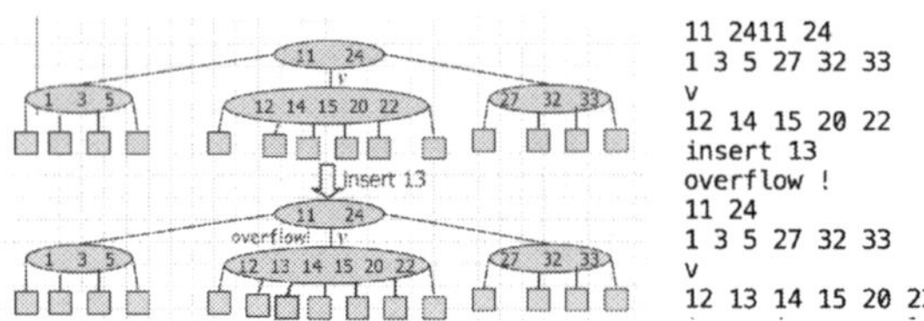

Figure 3: An example of poor text extraction. The output from Apache Tika (right) has lost its original structure. Experiments will show that document clustering is improved by removing this kind of noise labeled as MISC

four types of unnatural language block components: table, code, formula, or miscellaneous text. In this work, we focus on these four specific types because our observations lead us to believe they are the most frequently occurring components in PPT lecture slides and PDF articles. Figures are also a frequent component but we do not consider them because they are commonly pictures or drawings and cannot be easily extracted to text. In this section, we briefly discuss the characteristics of each component and challenges in their identification from the raw text.

3.1 Table

Tables are prevalent in almost every domain of technical documents. Tables are usually conveyed by its two-dimensional layout and its column and/or row headings (Khusro et al., 2015). Tables typically have multiple cells merged for layout, which makes them particularly difficult to distinguish as a table once they are converted to flat text.

3.2 Mathematical Formula

Mathematical formulas exist in two ways: isolated formulas on their own lines or as formulas embedded within a line of text. In this work, we treat both types as a formula component. Because not all math symbols can be matched to Unicode characters and because the extraction software may not convert them correctly, the extracted text tends to contain more oddly formatted or even completely wrong characters. Superscripts and subscripts are no longer distinguishable and the original visual layout (e.g., math symbols over multiple lines such as Π and $\sum$) is lost.

3.3 Code

Articles in Computer Science or related fields often contain pseudo-code or actual program code to illustrate their algorithm. We assume that even indents, one of the strong code visual cues, are not preserved in the extracted text although some extraction tool saves them, not to limit ourselves to the detailed performances of text extraction tools.

3.4 Miscellaneous Non-text (Misc.)

In addition to the components mentioned above, there are other types of unnatural language blocks that are left during conversion to text and that may provide spurious sub-topic matches between documents. To allow for those, we denote those components as miscellaneous text. One example of miscellaneous text is the text and caption that are part of the diagrams in slides. Figure 3 shows an example of miscellaneous text that lost its structure and meaning while being converted to text without the original diagram.

4 Corpus

4.1 Data Collection

We collected 1,561 lecture slides from various Computer Science and Electrical Engineering courses that are available online, and 5,898 academic papers from several years of ACL/EMNLP

Purpose	Name	Content
Classification Training	T_{SLIDES}	35 lecture slides (8,514 lines) whose components are annotated
	T_{ACL}	35 ACL papers (25,686 lines) whose components are annotated
	$T_{COMBINED}$	Combination of T_{SLIDES} and T_{ACL}
Word Embedding Training	$T_{WORD2VEC}$	1,190 lecture slides and 5,863 ACL/EMNLP papers archived over a few years that are used for training word embedding.
Clustering	C_{DSA}	128 lecture slides from 'data structure' and 'algorithm' classes
	C_{OS}	300 lecture slides from, 'operating system' classes

Table 1: Datasets used in our paper. All data are available for download at [`http://cs.umass.edu/~mhjang/publications.html`]

archive[1]. We divided the dataset for several purposes: training the classification model, training word embedding model for feature extraction, and clustering for extrinsic evaluation. The details of the dataset we used are summarized in Table 1. We make the data publicly available for download at `http://cs.umass.edu/~mhjang/publications.html`.

For classification, we constructed three datasets using two different data sources: (1) lecture slides, (2) ACL papers, and (3) a combination of both. We chose these two types of data sources because they have different ratios of unnatural language components and complement each other for coverage. Table 2 shows the ratio of the four components from each annotated dataset. For example, 1.4% of lines in T_{SLIDES} are annotated as part of table.

4.2 Text Extraction

We extracted plain text from our datasets using an open-source software package, Apache Tika. The package is available for text extraction from various formats including PDF, PPT, and HTML.

4.3 Annotation

To train a statistical model, we need ground-truth data. We created annotation guidelines for the 4 types of unnatural language components and annotated 35 lectures slides (7,943 lines) and 35 ACL papers (25,686 lines). We developed an annotation tool to support the task and also to enforce annotators to follow certain rules[2]. We hired four undergraduate annotators who have knowledge of the Computer Science domain for this task.

	TABLE	CODE	FORMULA	MISC	All
T_{SLIDES}	1.4%	14.6%	0.5%	9.8%	26.3%
T_{ACL}	4.0%	0.6%	5.0%	6.4%	16%

Table 2: % of lines by unnatural category. Both datasets have quite a bit of unnatural language (26.3% for T_{SLIDES} and 16% for T_{ACL}), though T_{ACL} has more TABLES and FORMULAS and less CODE.

5 Features

We find line-based prediction has an advantage over token-based prediction because it allows us to observe the syntactic structure of the line, how statistically common the grammar structure is, and how layout patterns compare to neighboring lines. We introduce five sets of features used to train our classifier and discuss each feature's impact on the accuracy.

5.1 N-gram (N)

Unigrams and bigrams of each line are included as features.

5.2 Parsing Features (P)

Unnatural languages are not likely to form any grammar structure. When we attempt to parse the unnatural language line, the resultant parsing tree would form unusual syntactic structure. To capture this insight, we parse each line using the dependency parser in ClearNLP (Choi and McCallum, 2013) and extract features such as the set of dependency labels, the ratio of each POS tag, and POS tags of each dependent-head pair from each parse tree.

5.3 Table String Layout (T)

Text extracted from tables loses its visual layout as a table but still preserves implicit layout through its string patterns. Tables tend to convey the same

---

[1] https://aclweb.org/anthology
[2] The guidelines and the tool are available at `http://cs.umass.edu/~mhjang/publications.html`

type of data along the same column or row. For example, if a column in a table reports numbers, it is more likely to contain numeral tokens in the same location of the lines of the table in parallel. Hence, a block of lines will more likely be a table if they share the same pattern. We encode each line by replacing each token as either S (String) or N (Numeral). We then compute the edit distance among neighboring lines weighted by language modeling probability computed from the table corpus (Equation 1, 2).

$$P_{table}(l_i) \propto P_{table}(l_i|l_{i-1})$$
$$= TableLanguageModel(l_i)\cdot$$
$$editDistance(encode(l_i), encode(l_{i-1})) \quad (1)$$

$$TableLanguageModel(l_i)$$
$$= \Pi_j^n(P(encode(t_{i,j+1})|encode(t_{i,j})) \quad (2)$$

where l_i refers to a i-th line in a document, $t_{i,j}$ refers to a j-th token in l_i.

5.4 Word Embedding Feature (E)

We train word embeddings using $T_{WORD2VEC}$ using WORD2VEC (Mikolov et al., 2013). The training corpus contained 278,719 words. Since we do a line-based prediction, we need a vector that represents the line, not each word. We consider three ways of computing a line embedding vector: (1) by averaging the vector of the words, (2) by computing a paragraph vector introduced in (Le and Mikolov, 2014), and (3) by using both.

5.5 Sequential Feature (S)

The sequential nature of the lines is also an important feature because the component most likely occurs over a block of contiguous lines. We train two models. The first model uses the annotation for the previous line's class. We then train another model using the previous line's predicted label, which is the output of the first model.

6 Classification Experiments

We use the Liblinear Support Vector Machine (SVM) (Chang and Lin, 2011) classifier for training and run 5-fold cross-validation for evaluation. To improve the robustness of structured prediction, we adopt a learning to search algorithm known as DAGGER to SVM (Ross et al., 2010). We first introduce two baselines to compare the accuracy against our statistical model.

6.1 Baselines

Since no existing work is directly applicable to our scenario, we consider two straightforward baselines.

- **Weighted Random (W-Random)**
  This assigns the random component class to each line. Instead of uniform random prediction, we made more educated guesses using the ratio of components known from the annotated dataset (Table 2).

- **Component Language Modeling (CLM)**
  Among the five language models of the five component classes (the four non-textual components and text component) generated from the annotations, we predict the component for each line by assigning the component whose language model gives the highest probability to the line.

6.2 Classification Result

We first conduct single-domain classification. Annotations within each dataset, T_{SLIDES} and T_{ACL} are split for training and testing using 5-fold cross validation scheme. Table 3 reports F1-score for prediction of the four components in the two dataset using our method as well as baselines.

	Precision	Recall	F1-score
TABLE	94.60	76.39	**84.53**
CODE	89.56	84.01	**86.69**
FORMULA	85.07	79.32	**82.10**
MISC	85.59	90.24	**87.86**
TEXT	97.76	98.79	98.27

Table 4: Multi-domain classification improves the single-domain classification in Table 3. Identification of categories with particularly low accuracy in each datasets (TABLE and FORMULA in T_{SLIDES} and CODE in T_{ACL}) are improved to be as good as the other categories.

The proposed method dramatically increased the prediction accuracies for all of the components against the baselines. CLM baseline showed the highest accuracy on CODE among the four categories in both datasets. Because pseudo-code use more controlled vocabulary (e.g., reserved words and common variable names), the language itself becomes distinctive characteristics. We also include the numbers reported by Tuarob et al. (2013)

	T_{SLIDES}				T_{ACL}			
	TABLE	CODE	FORMULA	MISC	TABLE	CODE	FORMULA	MISC
W-Random	1.69	14.62	2.82	10.57	4.15	0.62	4.44	6.08
CLM	5.41	28.62	0.00	10.47	13.10	16.45	10.32	5.18
Proposed Method	**67.89**	**90.22**	**29.09**	**89.63**	**86.58**	**63.70**	**80.98**	**87.63**
PC-CB (Tuarob et al., 2013)	N/A	75.95	N/A	N/A	N/A	75.95	N/A	N/A

Table 3: Single-domain Classification Result in F1-score: Proposed method is much better than baselines for classifying unnatural language. Note that we borrowed the F1-score reported on their dataset for reference. The number is not directly comparable to other numbers since the datasets are different.

for comparison. Since their dataset was 258 PDF scholarly articles, T_{ACL} is more a comparable dataset than T_{SLIDES}, but our training set is much smaller than their dataset. However, their number reported on Table 3 is not directly comparable to other numbers because the numbers are on different datasets.

In T_{SLIDES}, the classification F1-score for FORMULA is relatively low as 29.09% compared to the other components in the same dataset, and also compared to the FORMULA prediction in T_{ACL} (80.98%). This is due to too small amount of training data (only 0.5% of FORMULA in T_{ACL}), which is overcome in T_{SLIDES} that contain 5% of FORMULA training data (refer to Table 2).

In the proposed method, classification of CODE and MISC was significantly improved in T_{SLIDES} (around 90%), while that of TABLE and FORMULA was improved in T_{ACL} (over 80%). This shows the complementary nature between the two datasets, which suggests that a combination of both, $T_{combined}$, would further improve classification performance. Table 4 shows the multi-domain classification result using $T_{combined}$, in which all four categories are identified with an F1-score higher than 80%.

6.3 Feature Analysis

We conducted feature analysis to understand the impact of single feature and their combination. We started from single features and incrementally combined them to observe the performance (Figure 5). Features are added in a greedy fashion such that a feature that gives the higher accuracy when used alone is added first.

We first compare the three ways of computing sentence vector features mentioned in Section 5 (Figure 4). When we experiment with only embedding features, averaging word vectors performed 9-12 times better than paragraph vectors. When

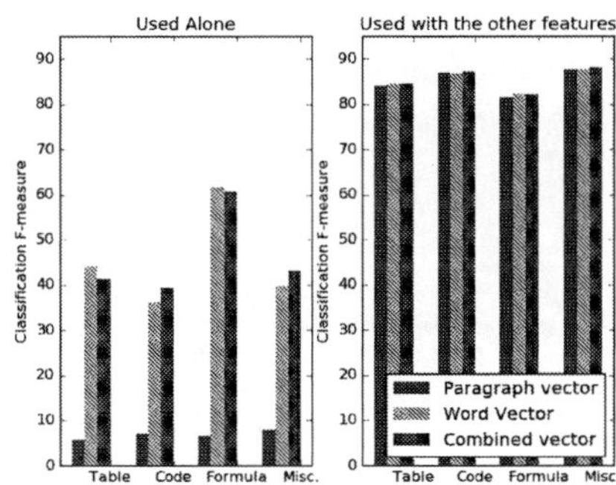

Figure 4: Three ways of computing sentence embedding vector

both features were used, there are some gains in CODE and MISC but losses in TABLE and FORMULA. However, when we experiment with all the other features in addition to embedding features, losses were covered by the other features such that combined vectors give overall the highest performances.

N-gram (N) features was the most powerful feature with 68% of F1-score when used alone. The next useful features are parsing feature (P), table layout (T), and embedding features (E) in order for TABLE, while embedding vectors were more effective than parsing feature for CODE (Figure 5).

7 Removal Effects of Unnatural Language on NLP tools

We observe how removal of unnatural language from documents affects the performance of two NLP tools: document similarity and document clustering. For the set of experiments, we prepared a gold standard clustering for each dataset, C_{DSA} and C_{OS}.

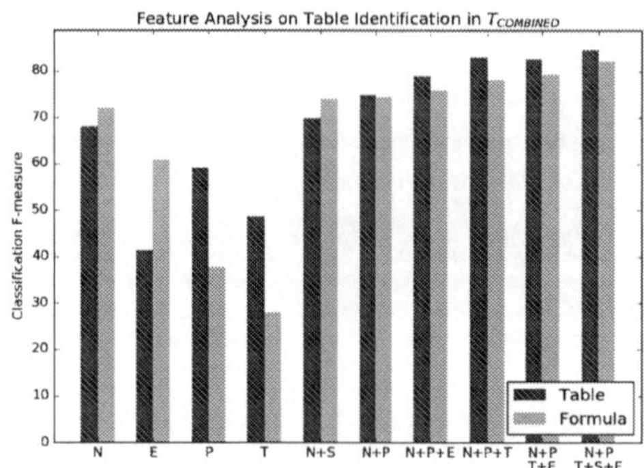

Figure 5: Feature analysis for TABLE and FOR-MULA identification in $T_{combined}$. N: N-gram, E: Embedding, P: Parsing, T: Table String Layout, S: Sequential.

7.1 Document Similarity

If two documents are similar, they must be topically relevant to each other. A good similarity measure should reflect that; two topically relevant documents should have a high similarity score. To test whether the computed similarity reflects the actual topic relevance better once the unnatural language is removed, we conduct regression analysis.

We convert the gold standard clustering to pairwise binary relevance. If two documents are in the same ground-truth cluster, they are relevant, and otherwise irrelevant. We then fit a log-linear model in R for predicting binary relevance from the cosine similarity of document pairs.

Regression models fitted in R are evaluated using AIC (Akaike, 1974). The AIC is a measure used as a means for model selection, which measures the relative quality of statistical models learned from the given data. When AIC is smaller, the fit is better and the complexity of the model is smaller since it requires fewer parameters. Table 5 shows that AIC was reduced by 53 and 118 respectively on the models trained with documents whose unnatural language blocks are removed, compared to the original documents. Since AIC does not provide a test for a model, AIC does not suggest anything about the quality of the model in an absolute sense, but relative quality. From this result, we can conclude that cosine similarity can fit a better model that predicts documents' topic relevance with significance after unnatural language blocks have been removed.

	AIC($D_{original}$)	AIC($D_{removed}$)	Improvement
C_{DSA}	-40975	-41028	-53
C_{OS}	-61404	-61522	-118

Table 5: The statistical model is trained better with documents whose unnatural language categories are removed ($D_{removed}$) than the model with the original documents ($D_{original}$) in both datasets. *Smaller* AIC scores imply *better* models.

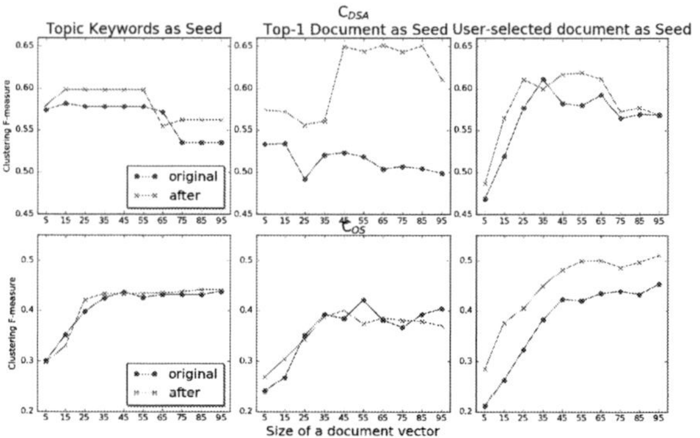

Figure 6: Clustering result on two datasets, C_{DSA} (top) and C_{OS} (bottom). X axis referes to the the size of document vector K, which controls the top-K TF-IDF terms included from documents. Y axis: Clustering F1-score.

7.2 Document Clustering

Comparing general clustering performance on two document sets is tricky because clustering performance varies by many factors, e.g., clustering algorithm, similarity function, document representation, and parameters. To make a safe claim that clustering quality of one set of documents is better than the other, clustering on one set should consistently outperform the other under many different settings. To validate this, we perform clustering experiments with multiple settings such as different document vector size and and initialization schemes.

In this experiment, we consider seeded K-means clustering algorithm (Basu et al., 2002) for teaching documents. In our application scenario, users initially submit a topic list (e.g., syllabus) of the course. Then lecture slides are grouped into the given topic cluster. Depending on users' interaction level, we consider a semi-interactive scenario where users only provide a topic list, and a fully-interactive setting where users not only provide a topic list but also provide an answer document for each topic cluster, further specifying the intended topic.

Input: Set of document vectors D = $\{d_1, ...d_n\}$, $d_i \in R^T$, set of seed vectors S = $\{s_1, ...s_k\}$, user-provided topic keywords vector T = $\{t_1, ...t_k\}$

Result: Disjoint K partitioning of D into $C_{l=1}^k$

Seed Initialization:

if *Topic-keywords seeding* **then**
| $s_i = t_i$

if *Top-1 document seeding* **then**
| $s_i = d_j$,
| $argmax_j(\text{COSINESIMILARITY}(t_i, d_j))$

if *User-selected document seeding* **then**
| $s_i = \text{DOCSELECTEDBYUSER}(t_i)$

while *convergence* **do**
| K-means clustering document selection
| process

Algorithm 1: Seeded K-means with User Interaction

In a semi-interactive setting, topic keywords are sparse seeds as they usually consist of two or three words. Therefore, we expand the topic keywords by finding the top-1 document retrieved from the keywords and use it as a seed. For experiments, we simulate the fully-interactive setting; instead of having an actual user to pick an answer document, we use an answer document randomly chosen from a gold cluster. The seeded K-means clustering algorithm with three interactive seeding schemes is described in Algorithm 1.

A simulated setting is more realistic when the selected document is suggested to the user as the top or near-top choice. In our dataset, 60% of the selected documents were ranked in top 10 in C_{DSA}, and 13% of the selected documents were ranked in top 10 in C_{OS}, which implies that the simulated setting in C_{DSA} was more realistic than in C_{DSA}. For top-1 document seeding, 64% and 78% of document seeds matched with the gold standard in C_{DSA} and C_{OS}, respectively.

Figure 6 shows the clustering result of original documents ($D_{original}$) and documents whose unnatural language blocks are removed ($D_{removed}$), with three different seeding schemes over two lecture slide datasets. In C_{DSA}, $D_{removed}$ consistently outperformed with all three seeding schemes. The clustering performed the best with $D_{removed}$ when top-1 document was used as a seed. Overall, in C_{DSA}, clustering was improved 94% of the time with the maximum absolute gain of 14.7% and the average absolute gain of 4.6%. The average

absolute loss was 0.8% when 6% of the time the removal of unnatural language made the clustering worse. In C_{OS}, clustering was improved 73% of the times with the maximum absolute gain of 11.4% and the average absolute gain of 3.9%. The average absolute loss was 1.7%. Our results suggest that removal of unnatural language blocks can significantly improve clustering most of the times with a bigger gain than occasional losses.

8 Conclusion

In this paper, we argued that unnatural language should be distinguished from natural language in technical documents for NLP tools to work effectively. We presented an approach to the identification of four types of unnatural language blocks from plain text, which is not dependent on document format. The proposed method extracts five sets of line-based textual features, and had an F1-score that was above 82% for the four categories of unnatural language. We showed how existing NLP tools can work better on documents if we remove unnatural language from documents. Specifically, we demonstrated removing unnatural language improved document clustering in many settings by up to 15% and 11% at best, while not significantly hurting the original clustering in any setting.

Acknowledgments

This work was supported in part by the Center for Intelligent Information Retrieval and in part by NSF grant #IIS-1217281. Any opinions, findings and conclusions or recommendations expressed in this material are those of the authors and do not necessarily reflect those of the sponsor.

References

Hirotugu Akaike. 1974. A new look at the statistical model identification. *Automatic Control, IEEE Transactions on*, 19(6):716–723.

Sugato Basu, Arindam Banerjee, and Raymond J. Mooney. 2002. Semi-supervised clustering by seeding. In *Proceedings of the Nineteenth International Conference on Machine Learning*, ICML '02, pages 27–34, San Francisco, CA, USA. Morgan Kaufmann Publishers Inc.

Kam-Fai Chan and Dit-Yan Yeung. 2000. Mathematical expression recognition: A survey.

Chih-Chung Chang and Chih-Jen Lin. 2011. LIB-SVM: A library for support vector machines. *ACM Transactions on Intelligent Systems and Technology*, 2:27:1–27:27.

Jinho D. Choi and Andrew McCallum. 2013. Transition-based dependency parsing with selectional branching. In *Proceedings of the 51st Annual Meeting of the Association for Computational Linguistics*, ACL'13, pages 1052–1062.

Christopher Clark and Santosh Divvala. 2015. Looking beyond text: Extracting figures, tables and captions from computer science papers. In *AAAI Workshops*.

Afef Kacem, Abdel Belaïd, and Mohamed Ben Ahmed. 2001. Automatic extraction of printed mathematical formulas using fuzzy logic and propagation of context. *IJDAR*, 4(2):97–108.

Shah Khusro, Asima Latif, and Irfan Ullah. 2015. On methods and tools of table detection, extraction and annotation in pdf documents. *J. Inf. Sci.*, 41(1):41–57.

Michael Kohlhase and Ioan Sucan. 2006. A search engine for mathematical formulae. In *AISC*, volume 4120 of *Lecture Notes in Computer Science*, pages 241–253. Springer.

Quoc V. Le and Tomas Mikolov. 2014. Distributed representations of sentences and documents. *CoRR*, abs/1405.4053.

Kristina Lerman, Craig Knoblock, and Steven Minton. 2001. Automatic data extraction from lists and tables in web sources. In *In Proceedings of the workshop on Advances in Text Extraction and Mining (IJCAI-2001), Menlo Park*. AAAI Press.

Xiaoyan Lin, Liangcai Gao, Zhi Tang, Xiaofan Lin, and Xuan Hu. 2011. Mathematical Formula Identification in PDF Documents. In *International Conference on Document Analysis and Recognition*, ICDAR, pages 1419–1423.

Ying Liu, Kun Bai, Prasenjit Mitra, and C. Lee Giles. 2007. TableSeer: automatic table metadata extraction and searching in digital libraries. In *Joint Conference on Digital Library*, JCDL, pages 91–100.

Tomas Mikolov, Kai Chen, Greg Corrado, and Jeffrey Dean. 2013. Efficient estimation of word representations in vector space. *CoRR*, abs/1301.3781.

Hwee Tou Ng, Chung Yong Lim, and Jessica Li Teng Koo. 1999. Learning to recognize tables in free text. In *Proceedings of the 37th Annual Meeting of the Association for Computational Linguistics on Computational Linguistics*, ACL '99, pages 443–450, Stroudsburg, PA, USA. Association for Computational Linguistics.

L. O'Gorman. 1993. The document spectrum for page layout analysis. *IEEE Trans. Pattern Anal. Mach. Intell.*, 15(11):1162–1173.

David Pinto, Andrew McCallum, Xing Wei, and W. Bruce Croft. 2003. Table extraction using conditional random fields. In *Proceedings of the 26th Annual International ACM SIGIR Conference on Research and Development in Informaion Retrieval*, SIGIR '03, pages 235–242, New York, NY, USA. ACM.

Stéphane Ross, Geoffrey J. Gordon, and J. Andrew Bagnell. 2010. No-regret reductions for imitation learning and structured prediction. *CoRR*, abs/1011.0686.

Anikó Simon, Jean-Christophe Pret, and A. Peter Johnson. 1997. A fast algorithm for bottom-up document layout analysis. *IEEE Trans. Pattern Anal. Mach. Intell.*, 19(3):273–277.

Masakazu Suzuki, Fumikazu Tamari, Ryoji Fukuda, Seiichi Uchida, and Toshihiro Kanahori. 2003. Infty- an integrated ocr system for mathematical documents. In *Proceedings of ACM Symposium on Document Engineering 2003*, pages 95–104. ACM Press.

Suppawong Tuarob, Sumit Bhatia, Prasenjit Mitra, and C. Lee Giles. 2013. Automatic detection of pseudocodes in scholarly documents using machine learning. In *Proceedings of the 2013 12th International Conference on Document Analysis and Recognition*, ICDAR '13, pages 738–742, Washington, DC, USA. IEEE Computer Society.

Richard Zanibbi, Dorothea Blostein, and R. Cordy. 2004. A survey of table recognition: Models, observations, transformations, and inferences. *Int. J. Doc. Anal. Recognit.*, 7(1):1–16.

Lithium NLP: A System for Rich Information Extraction from Noisy User Generated Text on Social Media

Preeti Bhargava and **Nemanja Spasojevic** and **Guoning Hu**

Lithium Technologies | Klout

San Francisco, CA

`preeti.bhargava, nemanja.spasojevic, guoning.hu@lithium.com`

Abstract

In this paper, we describe the Lithium Natural Language Processing (NLP) system - a resource-constrained, high-throughput and language-agnostic system for information extraction from noisy user generated text on social media. Lithium NLP extracts a rich set of information including entities, topics, hashtags and sentiment from text. We discuss several real world applications of the system currently incorporated in Lithium products. We also compare our system with existing commercial and academic NLP systems in terms of performance, information extracted and languages supported. We show that Lithium NLP is at par with and in some cases, outperforms state-of-the-art commercial NLP systems.

1 Introduction

Social media has become one of the major means for communication and content production. As a result, industrial systems that possess the capability to process rich user generated content from social media platform have several real-world applications. Furthermore, due to the content style, size and heterogeneity of information (e.g. text, emoticons, hashtags etc.) available on social media, novel NLP techniques and systems that are designed specifically for such content and can potentially integrate or learn information from different sources are highly useful and applicable.

However, NLP on social media data can be significantly complex and challenging due to several reasons:

- **Noisy unnormalized data** - Social media data is much more informal than traditional text and less consistent in language in terms of style, tone etc. It involves heavy usage of slang, jargons, emoticons, or abbreviations which usually do not follow formal grammatical rules. Hence, novel NLP techniques need to be developed for such content.

- **Multi-lingual content** - Social media data poses an additional challenge to NLP practitioners because the user generated content on them is often multi-lingual. Hence, any NLP system processing real world data from the web should be able to support multiple languages in order to be practical and applicable.

- **Large scale datasets** - State-of-the-art NLP systems should be able to work on large scale datasets such as social media data, often involving millions of documents. Moreover, these systems need to have low resource consumption in order to scale to such datasets in a finite amount of time. In addition, in order to be applicable and practical, they should be able to run on off-the-shelf commodity machines.

- **Rich set of information** - In order to be cost-efficient, state-of-the-art NLP systems need to be exhaustive in terms of information extracted[1] from social media text. This includes extracting entities of different types (such as professional titles, sports, activities etc.) in addition to just named entities (such as persons, organizations, locations etc.), inferring

---

[1] `https://en.wikipedia.org/wiki/Information_extraction`

131

Proceedings of the 3rd Workshop on Noisy User-generated Text, pages 131–139

Copenhagen, Denmark, September 7, 2017. ©2017 Association for Computational Linguistics

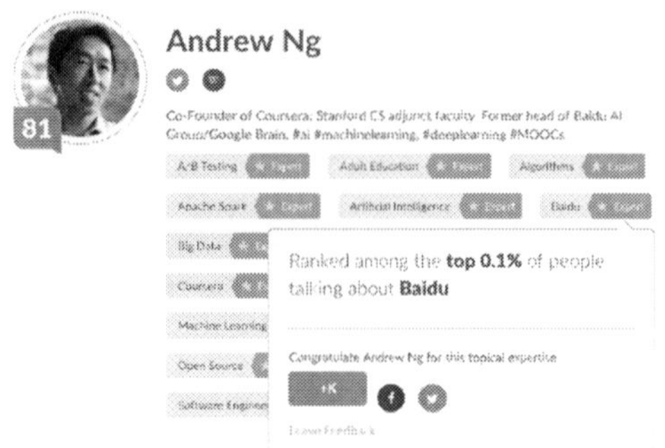

Figure 1: A user's inferred expertise topics

Figure 2: Content Personalization

fine-grained and coarse-grained subject matter topics (sports, politics, healthcare, basketball), text sentiment, hashtags, emoticons etc.

In this paper, we present the Lithium NLP[2] system which addresses these challenges. It is a resource-constrained, high-throughput and language-agnostic system for information extraction from noisy user generated text such as that available on social media. It is capable of extracting a rich set of information including entities, topics, hashtags and sentiment. Lithium NLP currently supports multiple languages including Arabic, English, French, German, Italian and Spanish. It supports large scale data from several social media platforms such as Twitter, Facebook, Linkedin, etc. by processing about $500M$ new social media messages, and $0.5M$ socially relevant URLs shared daily. Since it employs statistical NLP techniques, it uses the large scale of the data to help overcome the noisiness.

Lithium NLP is currently incorporated in several Lithium products. It enables consumer products like Klout[3] - a platform which integrates users' data from multiple social networks such as Twitter, Facebook, Instagram, Linkedin, GooglePlus, Youtube, and Foursquare, in order to measure their online social influence via the *Klout Score*[4] (Rao et al., 2015). On Klout, it is used to model users' topics of interest (Spasojevic et al., 2014) and expertise (Spasojevic et al., 2016) by building their topical profiles. Figure 1 shows

an example of a user's topics of expertise, as inferred on Klout. Currently, we build topical profiles for more than $600M$ users. These profiles are further used to recommend personalized content to these users by matching their topics of interest or expertise with content topics as this leads to better user engagement. An example of content personalization is shown in Figure 2. The user scores and topics are also available via the GNIP PowerTrack API[5].

Lithium NLP also enables enterprise products such as Lithium's social media management tools[6] - Lithium Reach and Lithium Response. It is used to analyze $20+M$ new daily engagements across Lithium's 400+ communities[7]. In the past, a version of Lithium NLP had been used to enable user targeting applications such as Klout Perks[8] (influencer reward platform), Cinch[9] (Q&A app), and Who-To-Follow recommendations. These involved selecting a group of users for targeting based on given topics and other filtering criteria.

2 Knowledge Base

Our Knowledge Base (KB) consists of about 1 million Freebase machine ids for entities that were chosen from a subset of all Freebase entities that map to Wikipedia entities. We prefer to use Freebase rather than Wikipedia as our KB since in Freebase, the same id represents a unique entity across multiple languages. Due to limited resources and usefulness of the enti-

---

[2]A screencast video demonstrating the system is available at https://youtu.be/U-o6Efh6TZc

[3]https://klout.com

[4]https://klout.com/corp/score

[5]http://support.gnip.com/enrichments/klout.html

[6]https://www.lithium.com/products/social-media-management/

[7]https://www.lithium.com/products/online-communities/

[8]https://goo.gl/vtZDqE#Klout_Perks

[9]https://goo.gl/CLcx9p#Cinch

ties, our KB contains approximately 1 million most important entities from among all the Freebase entities. This gives us a good balance between coverage and relevance of entities for processing common social media text. Section 3.1 explains how entity importance is calculated, which enables us to rank the top 1 million Freebase entities.

In addition to the KB entities, we also employ two special entities: **NIL** and **MISC**. **NIL** entity indicates that there is no entity associated with the mention, eg. mention 'the' within the sentence may link to entity **NIL**. This entity is useful especially when it comes to dealing with stop words and false positives. **MISC** indicates that the mention links to an entity which is outside the selected entity set in our KB.

3 System Overview

Figure 3 shows a high level overview of the Lithium NLP system. It has two phases:

3.1 Offline Resource Generation

In this phase, we generate several dictionaries that capture language models, probabilities and relations across entities and topics, by leveraging various multi-lingual data sources. Some of these dictionaries are derived using our DAWT[10] data set (Spasojevic et al., 2017) that consists of densely annotated wikipedia pages across multiple languages. It is 4.8 times denser than Wikipedia and is designed to be exhaustive across several domains.

The dictionaries generated from the DAWT dataset are:

- **Mention-Entity Co-occurrence** - This dictionary captures the prior probability that a mention M_i refers to an entity E_j (including **NIL** and **MISC**) within the DAWT dataset and is equivalent to the cooccurrence probability of the mention and the entity:

$$\frac{count(M_i \to E_j)}{count(M_i)}$$

  For instance, mention *Michael Jordan* can link to **Michael Jordan (Professor)** or **Michael Jordan (Basketball player)**

with different prior probabilities. Moreover, we generate a separate dictionary for each language.

- **Entity-Entity Co-occurrence** - This dictionary captures co-occurrence frequencies among entities by counting all the entities that simultaneously appear within a sliding window of 50 tokens. Moreover, this data is accumulated across all languages and is language independent in order to capture better relations and create a smaller memory footprint when supporting additional languages. Also, for each entity, we consider only the top 30 co-occurring entities which have at least 10 or more co-occurrences across all supported languages. For instance, entity **Michael Jordan (Basketball player)** co-occurs with entities **Basketball**, **NBA** etc. while entity **Michael Jordan (Professor)** co-occurs with entities **Machine Learning**, **Artificial Intelligence**, **UC Berkeley** etc.

We also generate additional dictionaries:

- **Entity Importance** - The entity importance score (Bhattacharyya and Spasojevic, 2017) is derived as a global score identifying how important an extracted entity is for a casual observer. This score is calculated using linear regression with features capturing popularity within Wikipedia links, and importance of the entity within Freebase. We used signals such as Wiki page rank, Wiki and Freebase incoming and outgoing links, and type descriptors within our KB etc.

- **Topic Parents** - This dictionary contains the parent topics for each topic in the Klout Topic Ontology [11] (KTO) - a manually curated ontology built to capture social media users' interests and expertise scores, in different topics, across multiple social networks. As of April 2017, it consists of roughly 8,030 topic nodes and 13,441 edges encoding hierarchical relationships among them.

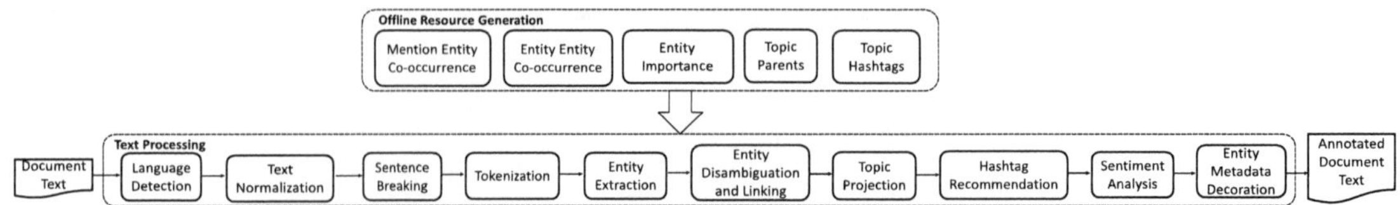

Figure 3: Overview of the Lithium NLP pipeline

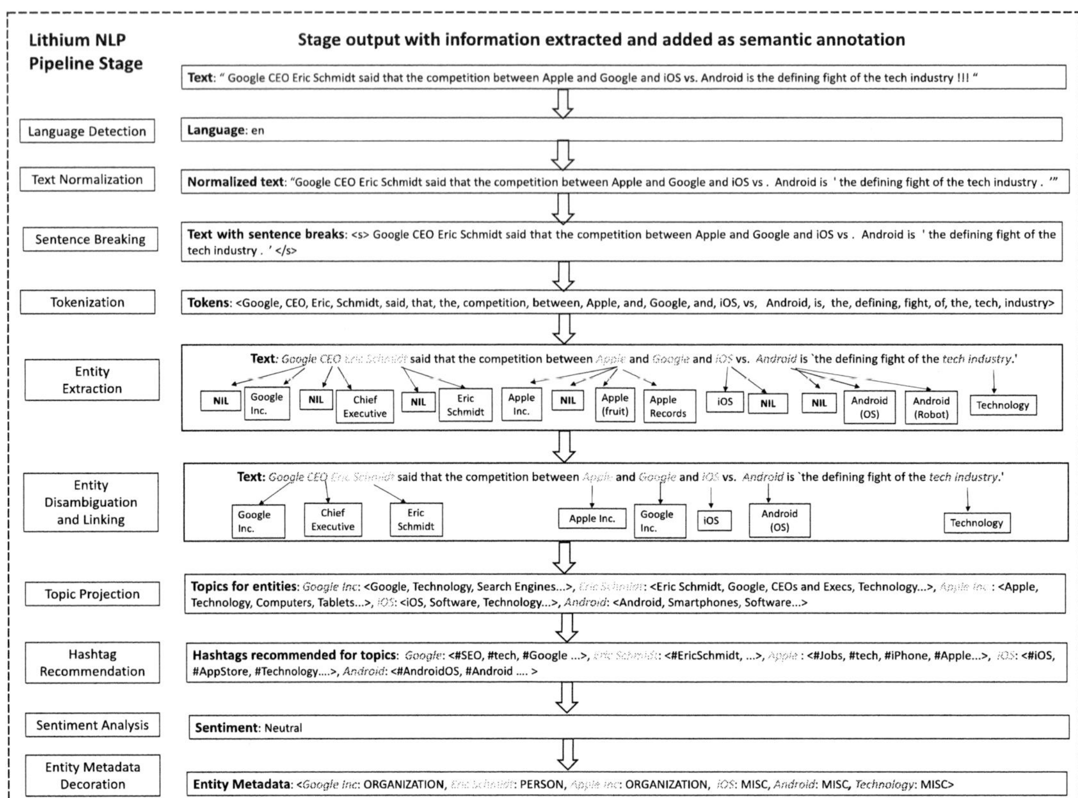

Figure 4: An example demonstrating the information extracted and added as semantic annotation at each stage of the Lithium NLP pipeline (best viewed in color)

- **Topic Hashtags** - This dictionary contains hashtags recommended for topics in KTO. We determine the hashtags via co-occurrence counts of topics and hashtags, importance, recency and popularity of hashtags as well popularity of topics.

3.2 Text Processing

In the Lithium NLP system, an input text document is stored as a Protocol Buffers[12] message. The Text Processing phase of the system processes the input text document through several stages and the information (entities,

topics etc.) extracted at every stage is added as a semantic annotation to the text. Not all annotations are added to a document, the Lithium NLP API (explained in Section 3.3) allows a client application to select specific annotations. However, certain annotations such as language and tokens are prerequisites for later stages.

The Text Processing pipeline stages are:

- **Language Detection** - This stage detects the language of the input document using an open source language detector[13]. This detector employs a naive Bayesian

---

[12]https://developers.google.com/
protocol-buffers/

[13]https://github.com/shuyo/
language-detection

filter which uses character, spellings and script as features to classify language and estimate its probability. It has a precision of 99% for 49 languages.

- **Text Normalization** - This stage normalizes the text by escaping unescaped characters and replacing special characters (e.g. diacritical marks) based on the detected language. It replaces non-ASCII punctuations and hyphens with spaces, multiple spaces with single space, converts accents to regular characters etc.

- **Sentence Breaking** - This stage breaks the normalized text into sentences using Java Text API[14]. It can distinguish sentence breakers from other marks, such as periods within numbers and abbreviations, according to the detected language.

- **Tokenization** - This stage converts each sentence into a sequence of tokens via the Lucene Standard Tokenizer[15] for all languages and the Lucene Smart Chinese Analyzer[16] for Chinese.

- **Entity Extraction** - This stage extracts mentions in each sentence using the Mention Entity Co-occurrence dictionary generated offline (Section 3.1). A mention may contain a single token or several consecutive tokens, but a token can belong to at most one mention.

  To make this task computationally efficient, we apply a simple greedy strategy that analyzes windows of n-grams (n $\in$ [1,6]) and extracts the longest mention found in each window. For each extracted mention, we generate multiple candidate entities. For instance, mention *Android* can link to candidate entities **Android (OS)** or **Android (Robot)**.

- **Entity Disambiguation and Linking (EDL)** - This stage disambiguates and links an entity mention to the correct candidate entity in our KB (Bhargava et al., 2017). It uses several features obtained from the dictionaries generated offline (Section 3.1). These include context-independent features, such as mention-entity co-occurrence, mention-entity Jaccard similarity and entity importance, and context-dependent features such as entity entity co-occurrence and entity topic semantic similarity. It employs machine learning models, such as decision trees and logistic regression, generated using these features to correctly disambiguate a mention and link to the corresponding entity. This stage has a precision of 63%, recall of 87% and an F-score of 73% when tested on an in-house dataset.

- **Topic Projection** - In this stage, we associate each entity in our KB to upto 10 most relevant topics in KTO. For instance, entity **Android (OS)** will be associated with the topics such as *Smartphones*, *Software* etc.

  We use a weighted ensemble of several semi-supervised models that employ entity co-occurrences, GloVe (Pennington et al., 2014) word vectors, Freebase hierarchical relationships and Wikipedia in order to propagate topic labels. A complete description of this algorithm is beyond the scope of this paper.

- **Hashtag Recommendation** - In this stage, we annotate the text with hashtags recommended based on the topics associated with the text in Topic Projection. This uses the Topic Hashtags dictionary generated offline (Section 3.1)

- **Sentiment Analysis** - In this stage, we determine the sentiment of the text (positive, negative or neutral) via lexicons and term counting with negation handling (Spasojevic and Rao, 2015). For this, we used several lexicons of positive and negative words (including SentiWordNet (Baccianella et al., 2010; Esuli and Sebastiani, 2007) and AFINN (Nielsen, 2011)) as well as emoticons. We compute the sentiment score as

---

[14]https://docs.oracle.com/javase/7/docs/api/java/text/BreakIterator.html

[15]http://lucene.apache.org/core/4_5_0/analyzers-common/org/apache/lucene/analysis/standard/StandardTokenizer.html

[16]https://lucene.apache.org/core/4_5_0/analyzers-smartcn/org/apache/lucene/analysis/cn/smart/SmartChineseAnalyzer.html

$$\frac{W_{Pos} - W_{Neg}}{\text{Log(Total \# of words in text)} + \epsilon}$$

where W_{Pos} is the weighted strength of positive words and emoticons, W_{Neg} is the weighted strength of negative words and emoticons in the text and ϵ is a smoothing constant. If the score is positive and above a certain threshold, the text is classified as 'Positive'. If it is below a certain threshold, the text is classified as 'Negative'. If it lies within the boundary between 'Positive' and 'Negative' classes, the text is classified as 'Neutral'.

To handle negations, we use a *lookback window*. Every time, we encounter a word from our sentiment lexicons, we look back at a window of size 3 to see if any negation words precede it and negate the weight of the sentiment word. Overall, this stage has a precision of 47%, recall of 48% and an F-score of 46% when tested on an in-house dataset.

- **Entity Metadata Decoration** - In this stage, we add the entity metadata such as its type (Person, Organization, Location, Film, Event, Book) and Location (Population, Time Zone, Latitude/Longitude).

Figure 4 demonstrates how the Lithium NLP pipeline processes a sample text *"Google CEO Eric Schmidt said that the competition between Apple and Google and iOS vs. Android is 'the defining fight of the tech industry'."* and adds the annotations at every stage.

3.3 REST API

The Lithium NLP system provides a REST API via which client applications can send a text document as request and receive the annotated text as JSON response. A snippet of an annotated response (which is in our text proto format[17]) received through the API is shown in Listing 1. Note that the disambiguated entities are also linked to their Freebase ids and Wikipedia links.

---

[17]https://github.com/klout/opendata/blob/master/wiki_annotation/Text.proto

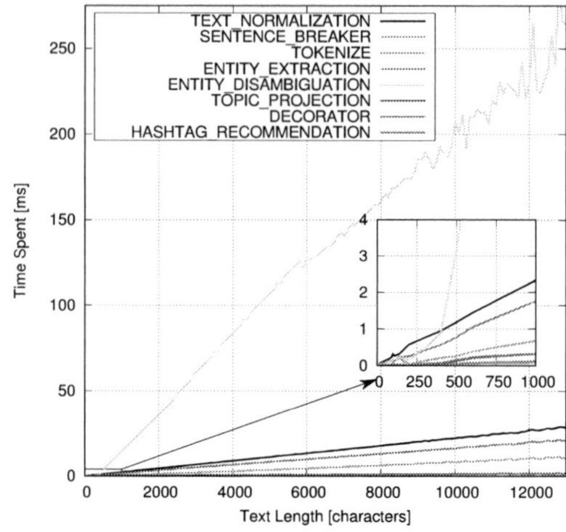

Figure 5: Lithium NLP performance per processing stage (best viewed in color)

Listing 1: JSON of annotated text summary


```
{
  "text": "Vlade Divac Serbian NBA player
      used to play for LA Lakers.",
  "language": "en",
  "annotation_summary": [{
      "type": "ENTITY",
      "annotation_identifier": [{
          "id_str": "01vpr3",
          "id_url": "https://en.wikipedia.org
              /wiki/Vlade_Divac",
          "score": 0.9456,
          "type": "PERSON"
      }, {
          "id_str": "05jvx",
          "id_url": "https://en.wikipedia.org
              /wiki/NBA",
          "score": 0.8496,
          "type": "ORGANIZATION"
      }, ...
      }]
  },
  {
    "type": "KLOUT_TOPIC",
    "annotation_identifier": [{
      "id_str": "6467710261455026125",
      "id_readable": "nba",
      "score": 0.7582
    }, {
      "id_str": "8311852403596174326",
      "id_readable": "los-angeles-lakers",
      "score": 0.66974
    }, {
      "id_str": "8582816108322807207",
      "id_readable": "basketball",
      "score": 0.5445
    }, ...]
  },
  {
    "type": "HASHTAG",
    "annotation_identifier": [{
      "id_str": "NBA",
      "score": 54285.7515
    }, {
      "id_str": "NBAPlayoffs",
      "score": 28685.6006
    }, ...]
  }],
  "sentiment": 0.0
}
```

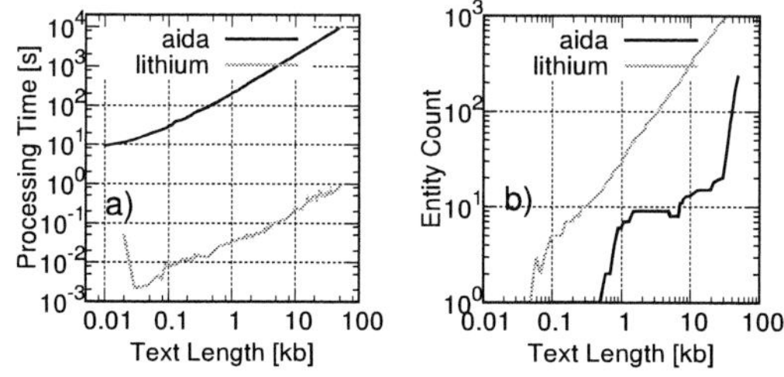

Figure 6: AIDA vs. Lithium NLP Comparison on **a)** Text processing runtime **b)** Extracted entity count (best viewed in color)

3.4 Performance

Figure 5 shows the computational performance per processing stage of the Lithium NLP system. The overall processing speed is about 22ms per 1kb of text. As shown, the time taken by the system is a linear function of text size. The EDL stage takes about 80% of the processing time.

4 Comparison with existing NLP systems

Currently, due to limited resources at our end and also due to inherent differences in the Knowledge Base (Freebase vs Wikipedia and others), test dataset, and types of information extracted (entities, topics, hashtags etc.), a direct comparison of the Lithium NLP system's performance (in terms of precision, recall and f-score) with existing academic and commercial systems such as Google Cloud NL API[18], Open Calais[19], Alchemy API[20], Stanford CoreNLP[21] (Manning et al., 2014), Ambiverse/AIDA[22] (Nguyen et al., 2014) and Twitter NLP[23] (Ritter et al., 2011, 2012) is not possible. Hence, we compare our system with some of them on a different set of metrics.

4.1 Comparison on runtime and entity density

We compare the runtime of Lithium NLP and AIDA across various text sizes. As shown in Figure 6, Lithium NLP is on an average 40,000

times faster than AIDA whose slow runtime can be attributed mainly to Stanford NER. In addition to speed, we also compare the number of entities extracted per kb of text. As shown, Lithium NLP extracts about 2.8 times more entities than AIDA.

4.2 Comparison on information extracted

Table 1 compares the types of information extracted by Lithium NLP system with existing systems. In this comparison, we explicitly differentiate between named entities (Person, Location etc.) and other entity types (Sports, Activities) as well as fine-grained topics (Basketball) and coarse-grained topics (Sports) to demonstrate the rich set of information extracted by Lithium NLP. As evident, most other systems do not provide the rich set of semantic annotations that Lithium NLP provides. A majority of the systems focus on recognizing named entities and types with only a few focusing on sentiment and coarse-grained topics as well. In contrast, Lithium NLP extracts, disambiguates and links named and other entities, extracts subject matter topics, recommends hashtags and also infers the sentiment of the text.

4.3 Comparison on languages

Table 2 compares the languages supported by the Lithium NLP system with existing systems. As evident, Lithium supports 6 different languages which is at par and in some cases, more than existing systems.

5 Conclusion and Future Work

In this paper, we described the Lithium NLP system - a resource-constrained, high-throughput and language-agnostic system for information extraction from noisy user generated text on social media. Lithium NLP extracts a rich set of information including entities, topics, hashtags and sentiment from text. We discussed several real world applications of the system currently incorporated in Lithium products. We also compared our system with existing commercial and academic NLP systems in terms of performance, information extracted and languages supported. We showed that Lithium NLP is at par with and in some

---

[18] https://cloud.google.com/natural-language/
[19] http://www.opencalais.com/opencalais-demo/
[20] https://alchemy-language-demo.mybluemix.net/
[21] http://corenlp.run/
[22] https://www.ambiverse.com/
[23] https://github.com/aritter/twitter_nlp

	Lithium NLP	Google NL	Open Calais	Alchemy API	Stanford CoreNLP	Ambiverse	Twitter NLP
Named Entities	X	X	X	X	X	X	X
Other Entities	X	X	X	X	X		
Topics (fine-grained)	X						
Topics (coarse-grained)	X		X	X			
Hashtags	X						
Document Sentiment	X			X	X		
Entity level Sentiment		X		X			
Entity types	X	X	X	X	X	X	X
Relationships			X	X	X		
Events							X

Table 1: Comparison of information extracted by Lithium NLP with existing NLP systems

	Lithium NLP	Google NL	Open Calais	Alchemy API	Stanford CoreNLP	Ambiverse	Twitter NLP
Supported Languages	Arabic, English, French, German, Italian, Spanish	Chinese, English, French, German, Italian, Japanese, Korean, Portugese, Spanish	English, French, Spanish	English, French, German, Italian, Portuguese, Russian, Spanish, Swedish	Arabic, Chinese, English, French, German, Spanish	English, German, Spanish, Chinese	English

Table 2: Comparison of languages supported by Lithium NLP with existing NLP systems

cases, outperforms state-of-the-art commercial NLP systems.

In future, we plan to extend the capabilities of Lithium NLP to include entity level sentiment as well. We also hope to collaborate actively with academia and open up the Lithium NLP API to academic institutions.

Acknowledgements

The authors would like to thank Prantik Bhattacharya, Adithya Rao and Sarah Ellinger for their contributions to the Lithium NLP system. They would also like to thank Mike Ottinger and Armin Broubakarian for their help with building the Lithium NLP UI and demo.

References

Stefano Baccianella, Andrea Esuli, and Fabrizio Sebastiani. 2010. Sentiwordnet 3.0: An enhanced lexical resource for sentiment analysis and opinion mining. In *LREC*, volume 10, pages 2200–2204.

Preeti Bhargava, Nemanja Spasojevic, and Guoning Hu. 2017. High-throughput and language-agnostic entity disambiguation and linking on user generated data. In *Proceedings of WWW 2017 workshop on Linked Data on the Web*.

Prantik Bhattacharyya and Nemanja Spasojevic. 2017. Global entity ranking across multiple languages. In *Companion Proceedings of the WWW*, pages 761 – 762.

Andrea Esuli and Fabrizio Sebastiani. 2007. Sentiwordnet: A high-coverage lexical resource for opinion mining. *Evaluation*, pages 1–26.

Christopher D Manning, Mihai Surdeanu, John Bauer, Jenny Rose Finkel, Steven Bethard, and David McClosky. 2014. The stanford corenlp natural language processing toolkit. In *ACL (System Demonstrations)*, pages 55–60.

Dat Ba Nguyen, Johannes Hoffart, Martin Theobald, and Gerhard Weikum. 2014. Aida-light: High-throughput named-entity disambiguation. In *LDOW'14*.

Finn Årup Nielsen. 2011. A new anew: Evaluation of a word list for sentiment analysis in microblogs. *arXiv preprint arXiv:1103.2903*.

Jeffrey Pennington, Richard Socher, and Christopher D Manning. 2014. Glove: Global vectors for word representation. In *Proceedings of EMNLP*, pages 1532 – 1543.

Adithya Rao, Nemanja Spasojevic, Zhisheng Li, and Trevor Dsouza. 2015. Klout score: Measuring influence across multiple social networks. In *IEEE Intl. Conf. on Big Data*.

Alan Ritter, Mausam Clark, Sam, and Oren Etzioni. 2011. Named entity recognition in tweets: an experimental study. In *Empirical Methods in Natural Language Processing*.

Alan Ritter, Mausam, Oren Etzioni, and Sam Clark. 2012. Open domain event extraction from twitter. In *KDD*.

Nemanja Spasojevic, Preeti Bhargava, and Guoning Hu. 2017. Dawt: Densely annotated wikipedia texts across multiple languages. In *Companion Proceedings of WWW*, pages 1655 – 1662.

Nemanja Spasojevic, Prantik Bhattacharyya, and Adithya Rao. 2016. Mining half a billion topical experts across multiple social networks. *Social Network Analysis and Mining*, 6(1):1–14.

Nemanja Spasojevic and Adithya Rao. 2015. Identifying actionable messages on social media. In *IEEE International Conference on Big Data*, IEEE BigData '15.

Nemanja Spasojevic, Jinyun Yan, Adithya Rao, and Prantik Bhattacharyya. 2014. Lasta: Large scale topic assignment on multiple social networks. In *Proc. of ACM KDD*, pages 1809 – 1818.

Results of the WNUT2017 Shared Task on
Novel and Emerging Entity Recognition

Leon Derczynski
University of Sheffield
S1 4DP, UK
leon.d@shef.ac.uk

Eric Nichols
Honda Research Institute
Saitama, Japan
e.nichols@jp.honda-ri.com

Marieke van Erp
VU University Amsterdam
Amsterdam, Netherlands
marieke.van.erp@vu.nl

Nut Limsopatham
Accenture
Dublin, Ireland
nut.limsopatham@gmail.com

Abstract

This shared task focuses on identifying unusual, previously-unseen entities in the context of emerging discussions. Named entities form the basis of many modern approaches to other tasks (like event clustering and summarization), but recall on them is a real problem in noisy text - even among annotators. This drop tends to be due to novel entities and surface forms. Take for example the tweet "so.. kktny in 30 mins?!" – even human experts find the entity *kktny* hard to detect and resolve. The goal of this task is to provide a definition of emerging and of rare entities, and based on that, also datasets for detecting these entities. The task as described in this paper evaluated the ability of participating entries to detect and classify novel and emerging named entities in noisy text.

1 Introduction

Named Entity Recognition (NER) is the task of finding in text special, unique names for specific concepts. For example, in "Going to San Diego", "San Diego" refers to a specific instance of a location; compare with "Going to the city", where the destination isn't named, but rather a generic city.

NER is sometimes described as a solved task due to high reported scores on well-known datasets, but in fact the systems that achieve these scores tend to fail on rarer or previously-unseen entities, making the majority of their performance score up from well-known, well-formed, unsurprising entities (Augenstein et al., 2017). This leaves them ill-equipped to handle NER in new environments (Derczynski et al., 2015). As new named entities are guaranteed to continuously emerge and gradually replace the older ones, it is important to be able to handle this change. This paper gives data and metrics for evaluating the ability of systems to detect and classify novel, emerging, singleton named entities in noisy text, including the results of seven systems participating in the WNUT 2017 shared task on the topic.

One approach to tackle rare and emerging entities would be to continuously create new training data, allow systems to learn the updates and newer surface forms. However, this involves a sustained expense in annotation costs. Another solution is to develop systems that are less sensitive to change, and can handle rare and emerging entity types with ease. This is a route to sustainable NER approaches, pushing systems to generalise well. It is this second approach that the WNUT17 shared task focuses on.

2 Task Definition

With the novel and emerging entities recognition task, we aim to establish a new benchmark dataset and current state-of-the-art for the recognition of entities in the long tail. Most language expressions form a Zipfian distribution (Zipf, 1949; Montemurro, 2001) wherein a small number of very frequent observations occur and a very long tail of less frequent observations. Our research community's benchmark datasets, representing only a small sample of all language expressions, often follow a similar distribution if a standard sample is taken. Recently, an awareness of the limitations of current evaluation datasets has risen (Hovy et al., 2006; van Erp et al., 2016; Postma et al., 2016). Due to this bias and the way many NLP ap-

Proceedings of the 3rd Workshop on Noisy User-generated Text, pages 140–147
Copenhagen, Denmark, September 7, 2017. ©2017 Association for Computational Linguistics

proaches work internally (i.e. through deriving a model from the training data that often incorporates frequency information) many NLP systems are predisposed towards the high-frequency observations and less so to low-frequency or unknown observations. This is clearly exhibited in the fact that many NLP systems' scores drop when presented with data that is different in type or distribution from the data it was trained on (Augenstein et al., 2017).

We aim to contribute to mitigating the problem of limited datasets through this shared task, for which we have annotated and made available 2,295 texts taken from three different sources (Reddit, Twitter, YouTube, and StackExchange comments) that focus on entities that are emerging (i.e. not present in data from n years ago) and rare (i.e. not present more than k times in our data).

3 Data

To focus the task on emerging and rare entities, we set out to assemble a dataset where very few surface forms occur in regular training data and very few surface forms occur more than once. Ideally, none of the surface forms would be shared between the training data and test data, but this was too ambitious in the time available.

3.1 Sources and Selection

In this section, we detail the dataset creation.

Training data – Following the WNUT15 task (Baldwin et al., 2015), the dataset from earlier Twitter NER exercises (Ritter et al., 2011) comprised this task's training data. This dataset is made up of 1,000 annotated tweets, totaling 65,124 tokens.

Development and test data – Whilst Twitter is a rich source for noisy user-generated data, we also sought to include texts that were longer than 140 characters as these exhibit different writing styles and characteristics. To align some of the development and test data with the training data, we included Twitter as a source, but additional comments were mined from Reddit, YouTube and StackExchange. These sources were chosen because they are large and samples can be mined along different dimensions such as texts from/about geospecific areas, and about particular topics and events. Furthermore, the terms of use

of the sources allowed us to download, store and distribute the data.

Reddit Documents were drawn from comments[1] from various English-speaking subreddits over January-March 2017. These were selected based on volume, for a variety of regions and granularities. For example, country- and city-level subreddits were included, as well as non-geospecific forums like `/r/restaurants`. The full list used was:

Global: politics worldnews news sports soccer restaurants

Anglosphere, low-traffic: bahamas belize Bermuda botswana virginislands Guam isleofman jamaica TrinidadandTobago

Anglosphere, high-traffic: usa unitedkingdom canada ireland newzealand australia southafrica

Cities: cincinnati seattle leeds bristol vancouver calgary cork galway wellington sydney perth johannesburg montegobay

To ensure that comments would be likely to include named entities, the data was preempted (Derczynski and Bontcheva, 2015) using proper nouns as an entity-bearing signal. Documents were filtered to include only those between 20 and 400 characters in length, split into sentences, and tagged with the NLTK (Bird, 2006) and Stanford CoreNLP (Manning et al., 2014) (using the GATE English Twitter model (Cunningham et al., 2012; Derczynski et al., 2013)) POS taggers. Only sentences with at least one word that was tagged as NNP by both taggers were kept.

YouTube The corpus includes YouTube comments. These are drawn from the all-time top 100 videos across all categories, within certain parts of the anglosphere (specifically the US, the US, Canada, Ireland, New Zealand, Australia, Jamaica, Botswana, South Africa and Singapore) during April 2017. One hundred top-level comments were drawn from each video. Non-English comments were removed with `langid.py` (Lui and Baldwin, 2012). Finally, in an attempt to cut out trite comments and diatribes, comments were filtered for length: min 10, max 200 characters.

Twitter The twitter samples were drawn from time periods matching recent natural disasters, specifically the Rigopiano avalanche and the Palm Sunday shootings. This was intended to select

---

[1]The raw data can be downloaded from `https://files.pushshift.io/reddit/comments/`.

content about emerging events, that may contain highly-specific and novel toponyms. Content was taken from an archive of the Twitter streaming API, processed to extract English-language documents using `langid.py`, and two-kenized (O'Connor et al., 2010).

StackExchange Another set of user-generated contents were drawn from StackExchange[2]. In particular, title posts and comments, which were posted between January-May 2017 and also associated to five topics (including movies, politics, physics, scifi and security) were downloaded from archive.org[3]. From these title posts and comments, 400 samples were uniformly drawn for each topic. Note that title posts and comments that are shorter than 20 characters or longer than 500 characters were excluded, in order to keep the task feasible but still challenging. On average the length of title posts and comments is 118.73 with a standard deviation of 100.89.

Note that the data is of mixed domains, and that the proportions of the mixture are not the same in dev and test data. This is intended to provide a maximally adverse machine learning environment. The underlying goal is to improve NER in a novel and emerging situation, where there is a high degree of drift. This challenges systems to generalise as best they can, instead of e.g. memorising or relying on stable context- or sub-word-level cues. Additionally, we know that entities mentioned vary over time, as does the linguistic context in which entities are situated (Derczynski et al., 2016). Changing the particular variant of noisy, user-generated text somewhat between partitions helps create this environment, high in diversity, and helps represent the constant variation found in the wild.

3.2 Preprocessing

Candidate development and test data was filtered for common entities. To ensure that all entities in the development and test data were novel, surface forms marked as entities in the training data were gathered into a blacklist. Any texts containing any of these surface forms were excluded from the final data.

Texts were tokenized using twokenizer and processed through GATE (Cunningham et al., 2012)

---

[2]`https://stackexchange.com`
[3]`https://archive.org/download/`
`stackexchange`

for crowdsourcing. The corpus was *not* screened for obscenity and potentially offensive content.

3.3 Data Splits

The development data was taken from YouTube. The test split was drawn from the remaining sources.

3.4 Annotation Guidelines

Various named entity annotation schemes are available for named entity annotation (cf. CoNLL (Sang, 2002), ACE (LDC, 2005), MSM (Rizzo et al., 2016)). Based on these, we annotate the following entity types:

1. `person`
2. `location` (including GPE, facility)
3. `corporation`
4. `product` (tangible goods, or well-defined services)
5. `creative-work` (song, movie, book and so on)
6. `group` (subsuming music band, sports team, and non-corporate organisations)

The following guidelines were used for each class.

`person` – Names of people (e.g. *Virginia Wade*). Don't mark people that don't have their own name. Include punctuation in the middle of names. Fictional people can be included, as long as they're referred to by name (e.g. *Harry Potter*).

`location` – Names that are locations (e.g. *France*). Don't mark locations that don't have their own name. Include punctuation in the middle of names. Fictional locations can be included, as long as they're referred to by name (e.g. *Hogwarts*).

`corporation` – Names of corporations (e.g. *Google*). Don't mark locations that don't have their own name. Include punctuation in the middle of names.

`product` – Name of products (e.g. *iPhone*). Don't mark products that don't have their own name. Include punctuation in the middle of names. Fictional products can be included, as long as they're referred to by name (e.g. *Everlasting Gobstopper*). It's got to be something you can touch, and it's got to be the official name.

Metric	Dev	Test
Documents	1,008	1,287
Tokens	15,734	23,394
Entities	835	1,040
person	470	414
location	74	139
corporation	34	70
product	114	127
creative-work	104	140
group	39	150

Table 1: The emerging entity dataset statistics

creative-work – Names of creative works (e.g. *Bohemian Rhapsody*). Include punctuation in the middle of names. The work should be created by a human, and referred to by its specific name.

group – Names of groups (e.g. *Nirvana, San Diego Padres*). Don't mark groups that don't have a specific, unique name, or companies (which should be marked corporation).

3.5 Annotation

Once selected and preprocessed, annotations were taken from the crowd. The GATE crowdsourcing plugin (Bontcheva et al., 2014) provided effective mediation with CrowdFlower for this. Three annotators were allocated per document/sentence, and all sentences were multiply annotated. Annotators were selected from the UK, USA, Australia, New Zealand, Ireland, Canada, Jamaica and Botswana. Once gathered, crowd annotations were processed using max-recall automatic adjudication, which has proven effective for social media text (Derczynski et al., 2016). The authors performed a final manual annotation over the resulting corpus, to compensate for crowd noise.

3.6 Statistics

The dataset dimensions are given in Table 1. The test partition was slightly larger than the development data, which we hope provides greater resolution on this more critical part.

4 Evaluation

The shared task evaluates against two measures. In addition to classical entity-level precision, recall and their harmonic mean, F1, surface forms found in the emerging entities task are also evaluated. The set of unique surface forms in the gold data and the submission are compared, and their precision, recall and F1 are measured as well. This latter measure measures how good systems are at correctly recognizing a diverse range of entities, rather than just the very frequent surface forms.

For example, the classical measure would reward a system that always recognizes *London* accurately, and so such a system would get a high score on a corpus where 50% of the Location entities are just *London*. The second measure, though, would reward *London* just once, regardless of how many times it appeared in the text.

These two measures are denoted F1 (entity) and F1 (surface).

Surface forms should also be given the right class. For example, finding *London* as an entity is useful, but not if it's recognized as a product. Therefore, when computing surface F1, the units used for evaluation are $\langle surface form, entity type \rangle$ tuples. This favors a certain kind of system construction; for example, the tuple formulation assumes that systems are doing joint recognition and typing, instead of the two in distinct stages. However, our goal is to evaluate performance of systems after both named entity recognition and typing, so it fits well in this use case.

5 Results

Results of the evaluation are given in Table 2. Note that surface recognition performance is often lower than entity recognition performance, suggesting that the entities being missed are those that are rarer, and so don't count towards entity F1 as much. We also see that NER in novel, emerging settings remains hard, reinforcing earlier findings that NE systems do not generalize well, especially in this environment (Augenstein et al., 2017).

6 Analysis

To gain insights into the difficult and less difficult parts of the task, we did a qualitative analysis of the outputs of the different systems. We see the most systems have no problems with entities that consist of common English names (e.g. "Lynda", "Becky"). However, when (part of) a name is also a common word (e.g. "Andrew Little", "Donald Duck"), we see that some systems only identify "Andrew" or "Donald" as part of the name. Furthermore, some systems erroneously tag words such as "swift" as entities, probably due to a bias towards 'Taylor Swift' in many current datasets.

Team	F1 (entity)	F1 (surface)
Arcada (Jansson and Liu, 2017)	39.98	37.77
Drexel-CCI (Williams and Santia, 2017)	26.30	25.26
FLYTXT (Sikdar and Gambäck, 2017)	38.35	36.31
MIC-CIS	37.06	34.25
SJTU-Adapt (Lin et al., 2017)	40.42	37.62
SpinningBytes (von Däniken and Cieliebak, 2017)	40.78	39.33
UH-RiTUAL (Aguilar et al., 2017)	**41.86**	**40.24**

Table 2: Results of the emerging entity extraction task.

Locations that contain elements that are also common in person names present an obstacle for the participating systems, for example in the detection of "Smith Tower" or "Crystal Palace" where "Smith" and "Crystal" are sometimes recognised as person names.

Names originating from other languages such as "Leyonhjelm" or "Zlatan" for persons or "Sonmarg" and "Mahazgund" for locations often present problems for the systems. "Mahagzund" is for example classified as corporation, group or person or "other" (no entity) whilst it refers to a village in Kashmir region of India.

`Corporation` and `creative work` were generally a difficult classes for the systems to predict. For `corporation`, this may be partly due to confusion between the corporation and group and product classes, as well as the fact that sometimes the corporation name is used to indicate a headquarters. For example "Amazon" on its own would in most cases be deemed a corporation in our gold standard, but in "Amazon Web Services" it is part of a product name. The 'White House' can both be a location and a corporation, which requires the systems to distinguish between subtle contextual differences in use of the term.

The difficulty in detecting entities of class `creative-work` can often be explained by the fact that these entities contain person names (e.g. "Grimm") , common words (e.g. "Demolition Man", "Rogue One") and can be quite long (e.g. "Miss Peregrine's Home for Peculiar Children").

Annotation still remains hard; some entities in the corpus, if we co-opt Kripke's "rigid designator" (Kripke, 1972) to define that role, are hard to fit into a single category. There were also other types of entity in the data; we did not attempt to define a comprehensive classification schema. The shortness of texts often makes disambiguation hard, too, as the spatial, temporal, conversational and topical context which a human reader relies on to interpret texts are all hidden under this model of annotation.

Twitter accounts can also fall into a number of different classes, and rather than instruct annotators on this, we left behavior up to them. Much prior work has avoided assigning tags to these (Ritter et al., 2011; Liu et al., 2011) though accounts often represent not only a person, also organizations, regions, buildings and so on. Therefore, much of our data carries these labels on Twitter account names, where the annotator has specified it.

7 Related Work

Named entity recognition has a long standing tradition of shared tasks, with the most prominent being the multilingual named entity recognition tasks organised at CoNLL in 2002 and 2003 (Sang, 2002; Tjong Kim Sang and Meulder, 2003). However, these, as well as follow-up tasks such as ACE (LDC, 2005) focused on formal and relatively clean texts such as newswire. This remains a difficult task, especially with the addition of the OntoNotes dataset, with modern work still pushing forward the state of the art (Chiu and Nichols, 2016).

Since 2011, Twitter has been gaining attention as a rich source for information extraction challenges such as (Ritter et al., 2011) and the Making Sense of Microposts challenge series starting in 2013 (Rizzo et al., 2017).

Emerging entities have received some attention entity linking approaches (Hoffart et al., 2014; far, 2016; NIST, 2017). In particular for entity linking, identifying whether an entity is present in a knowledge base to prevent an erroneous link from being created is a key problem.

Rare entities are an even less researched problem. Recasens et al. (2013) attempt to identify entity mentions that occur only once within a discourse to improve co-reference resolution. In (Jin et al., 2014), a system is presented that is focused on linking low frequent entities.

In the previous two WNUTs there has been attention for named entity recognition in noisy user-generated data in the form of a shared task on Named Entity Recognition in Twitter (Baldwin et al., 2015; Strauss et al., 2016). However, in those tasks, the dataset consisted of a random sample from a particular period without a particular focus on rare or emerging entities.

8 Conclusion

We have presented the setup and results of the WNUT2017 Shared Task on Novel and Emerging Entity Recognition. For this task, we created a new benchmark dataset consisting of 1,008 development and 1,287 test documents containing nearly 2,000 entity mentions. The documents were chosen in such a way that they contained mostly rare and novel entities of the types `person`, `location`, `corporation`, `product`, `creative-work` and `group`. The results of the seven systems that participated in this task show that entity recognition on these entities indeed is more difficult than on high frequent entities commonly found in named entity recognition challenges. More work in this area is thus needed and this shared task is only a small start. Going forward, datasets like this may be extended, possibly also with other entity classes for particular domains. Furthermore, we hope that more NLP tasks take up the challenge of creating more diverse benchmark datasets to expand our coverage of rare and novel language use.

Finally, the task is very tough. These are low figures for named entity recognition, and the surface form capture was even harder, reinforcing earlier findings that systems are failing to generalise successfully, instead profiting from frequently repeated entities in regular contexts. This is not working for noisy text, not Tweets, but broadly.

Acknowledgments

We thanks the participants for their enjoyable collaboration and for joining in this new task. This research received support from the European Commission's Horizon 2020 funding programme under grant agreement 687847, COMRADES. Leon Derczynski thanks the University of California San Diego for facilities provided during this research. Marieke van Erp acknowledges that the research for this paper was made possible by the CLARIAH-CORE project financed by NWO.

References

2016. *On Emerging Entity Detection*.

Gustavo Aguilar, Suraj Maharjan, Adrian Pastor López Monroy, and Thamar Solorio. 2017. A Multi-task Approach for Named Entity Recognition in Social Media Data. In *Proceedings of the 3rd Workshop on Noisy, User-generated Text (W-NUT) at EMNLP*. ACL.

Isabelle Augenstein, Leon Derczynski, and Kalina Bontcheva. 2017. Generalisation in Named Entity Recognition: A Quantitative Analysis. *Computer Speech & Language* .

Timothy Baldwin, Young-Bum Kim, Marie Catherine De Marneffe, Alan Ritter, Bo Han, and Wei Xu. 2015. Shared tasks of the 2015 workshop on noisy user-generated text: Twitter lexical normalization and named entity recognition. *ACL-IJCNLP* 126:2015.

Steven Bird. 2006. NLTK: the natural language toolkit. In *Proceedings of the COLING/ACL on Interactive presentation sessions*. Association for Computational Linguistics, pages 69–72.

Kalina Bontcheva, Ian Roberts, Leon Derczynski, and Dominic Paul Rout. 2014. The GATE Crowdsourcing Plugin: Crowdsourcing Annotated Corpora Made Easy. In *EACL*. pages 97–100.

Jason PC Chiu and Eric Nichols. 2016. Named Entity Recognition with Bidirectional LSTM-CNNs. *Transactions of the Association for Computational Linguistics* 4:357–370.

Hamish Cunningham, Diana Maynard, Kalina Bontcheva, Valentin Tablan, Niraj Aswani, Ian Roberts, Genevieve Gorrell, Adam Funk, Angus Roberts, Danica Damljanovic, et al. 2012. Developing language processing components with gate version 8 (a user guide). *University of Sheffield, UK, Web: http://gate.ac.uk/sale/tao/index.html* .

Leon Derczynski and Kalina Bontcheva. 2015. Efficient named entity annotation through pre-empting. In *International Conference Recent Advances in Natural Language Processing, RANLP*. Association for Computational Linguistics, volume 2015, pages 123–130.

Leon Derczynski, Kalina Bontcheva, and Ian Roberts. 2016. Broad Twitter Corpus: A Diverse Named Entity Recognition Resource. In *In Proc. of the Intl Conference on Computational Linguistics (COLING)*. pages 161–172.

Leon Derczynski, Diana Maynard, Giuseppe Rizzo, Marieke van Erp, Genevieve Gorrell, Raphaël Troncy, Johann Petrak, and Kalina Bontcheva. 2015. Analysis of named entity recognition and linking for tweets. *Information Processing & Management* 51(2):32–49.

Leon Derczynski, Alan Ritter, Sam Clark, and Kalina Bontcheva. 2013. Twitter Part-of-Speech Tagging for All: Overcoming Sparse and Noisy Data. In *RANLP*. pages 198–206.

Johannes Hoffart, Yasemin Altun, and Gerhard Weikum. 2014. Discovering emerging entities with ambiguous names. In *Proceedings of the 23rd international conference on World wide web*. pages 385–396.

Eduard Hovy, Mitchell Marcus, Martha Palmer, Lance Ramshaw, and Ralph Weischedel. 2006. Ontonotes: The 90% solution. In *Proceedings of the Human Language Technology Conference of the NAACL, Companion Volume: Short Papers*. Association for Computational Linguistics, New York City, USA, pages 57–60.

Patrick Jansson and Shuhua Liu. 2017. Distributed Representation, LDA Topic Modelling and Deep Learning for Emerging Named Entity Recognition from Social Media. In *Proceedings of the 3rd Workshop on Noisy, User-generated Text (W-NUT) at EMNLP*. ACL.

Yuzhe Jin, Emre Kcman, Kuansan Wang, and Ricky Loynd. 2014. Entity linking at the tail: sparse signals, unknown entities, and phrase models. In *Proceedings of the 7th ACM international conference on Web search and data mining*. pages 453–462.

Saul A Kripke. 1972. Naming and necessity. In *Semantics of natural language*, Springer, pages 253–355.

LDC. 2005. *ACE (Automatic Content Extraction) English Annotation Guidelines for Entities version 5.6.1*. Linguistic Data Consortium.

Bill Y. Lin, Frank Xu, Zhiyi Luo, and Kenny Zhu. 2017. Multi-channel BiLSTM-CRF Model for Emerging Named Entity Recognition in Social Media. In *Proceedings of the 3rd Workshop on Noisy, User-generated Text (W-NUT) at EMNLP*. ACL.

Xiaohua Liu, Shaodian Zhang, Furu Wei, and Ming Zhou. 2011. Recognizing named entities in tweets. In *Proceedings of the 49th Annual Meeting of the Association for Computational Linguistics: Human Language Technologies-Volume 1*. Association for Computational Linguistics, pages 359–367.

Marco Lui and Timothy Baldwin. 2012. langid.py: An off-the-shelf language identification tool. In *Proceedings of the ACL 2012 system demonstrations*. Association for Computational Linguistics, pages 25–30.

Christopher D Manning, Mihai Surdeanu, John Bauer, Jenny Rose Finkel, Steven Bethard, and David McClosky. 2014. The Stanford CoreNLP natural language processing toolkit. In *ACL (System Demonstrations)*. pages 55–60.

Marcelo A Montemurro. 2001. Beyond the Zipf–Mandelbrot law in quantitative linguistics. *Physica A: Statistical Mechanics and its Applications* 300(3):567–578.

NIST. 2017. Tac kbp2017 entity discovery and linking pilot on 10 low-resource languages. Technical report, NIST.

Brendan O'Connor, Michel Krieger, and David Ahn. 2010. Tweetmotif: Exploratory search and topic summarization for twitter. In *Proceedings of ICWSM-2010 (demo track)*.

Marten Postma, Filip Ilievski, Piek Vossen, and Marieke van Erp. 2016. Moving away from semantic overfitting in disambiguation datasets. In *Proceedings of EMNLP 2016's UBLP (Uphill Battles in Language Processing) workshop*.

Marta Recasens, Marie-Catherine de Marneffe, and Christopher Potts. 2013. The life and death of discourse entities: Identifying singleton mentions. In *HLT-NAACL*. pages 627–633.

Alan Ritter, Sam Clark, Mausam, and Oren Etzioni. 2011. Named entity recognition in tweets: An experimental study. In *Proc. of Empirical Methods for Natural Language Processing (EMNLP)*. Edinburgh, UK.

Giuseppe Rizzo, Bianca Pereira, Andrea Varga, Marieke van Erp, and Amparo Elizabeth Cano Basave. 2017. Lessons learnt from the Named Entity rEcognition and Linking (NEEL) challenge series. *Semantic Web Journal* .

Giuseppe Rizzo, Marieke van Erp, Julien Plu, and Raphaël Troncy. 2016. Making sense of microposts (#microposts2016) named entity recognition and linking (neel) challenge. In *Proceedings of the 6th Workshop on 'Making Sense of Microposts' colocated with the 25th International World Wide Web Conference (WWW 2016)*.

Erik F. Tjong Kim Sang. 2002. Introduction to the conll-2002 shared task: Language-independent named entity recognition. In *Proceedings of CoNLL-2002*. Taipei, Taiwan.

Utpal Kumar Sikdar and Björn Gambäck. 2017. A Feature-based Ensemble Approach to Recognition of Emerging and Rare Named Entities. In *Proceedings of the 3rd Workshop on Noisy, User-generated Text (W-NUT) at EMNLP*. ACL.

Benjamin Strauss, Bethany E Toma, Alan Ritter, Marie-Catherine de Marneffe, and Wei Xu. 2016. Results of the wnut16 named entity recognition shared task. *WNUT 2016* page 138.

Erik F. Tjong Kim Sang and Fien De Meulder. 2003. Introduction to the CoNLL-2003 Shared Task: Language-Independent Named Entity Recognition. In *Proceedings of CoNLL-2003*. Edmonton, Canada, pages 142–147.

Marieke van Erp, Pablo Mendes, Heiko Paulheim, Filip Ilievski, Julien Plu, Giuseppe Rizzo, and Joerg Waitelonis. 2016. Evaluating entity linking: An analysis of current benchmark datasets and a roadmap for doing a better job. In *Proceedings of LREC 2016*.

Pius von Däniken and Mark Cieliebak. 2017. Transfer Learning and Sentence Level Features for Named Entity Recognition on Tweets . In *Proceedings of the 3rd Workshop on Noisy, User-generated Text (W-NUT) at EMNLP*. ACL.

Jake Williams and Giovanni Santia. 2017. Context-Sensitive Recognition for Emerging and Rare Entities. In *Proceedings of the 3rd Workshop on Noisy, User-generated Text (W-NUT) at EMNLP*. ACL.

George Kingsley Zipf. 1949. *Human behavior and the principle of least effort*. Addison-Wesley Press.

A Multi-task Approach for Named Entity Recognition in Social Media Data

Gustavo Aguilar, Suraj Maharjan, A. Pastor López-Monroy and **Thamar Solorio**
Department of Computer Science
University of Houston
Houston, TX 77204-3010
{gaguilaralas, smaharjan2, alopezmonroy, tsolorio}@uh.edu

Abstract

Named Entity Recognition for social media data is challenging because of its inherent noisiness. In addition to improper grammatical structures, it contains spelling inconsistencies and numerous informal abbreviations. We propose a novel multi-task approach by employing a more general secondary task of Named Entity (NE) segmentation together with the primary task of fine-grained NE categorization. The multi-task neural network architecture learns higher order feature representations from word and character sequences along with basic Part-of-Speech tags and gazetteer information. This neural network acts as a feature extractor to feed a Conditional Random Fields classifier. We were able to obtain the first position in the 3rd Workshop on Noisy User-generated Text (WNUT-2017) with a 41.86% entity F1-score and a 40.24% surface F1-score.

1 Introduction

Named Entity Recognition (NER) aims at identifying different types of entities, such as people names, companies, location, etc., within a given text. This information is useful for higher-level Natural Language Processing (NLP) applications such as information extraction, summarization, and data mining (Chen et al., 2004; Banko et al., 2007; Aramaki et al., 2009). Learning Named Entities (NEs) from social media is a challenging task mainly because (i) entities usually represent a small part of limited annotated data which makes the task hard to generalize, and (ii) they do not follow strict rules (Ritter et al., 2011; Li et al., 2012).

This paper describes a multi-task neural network that aims at generalizing the underneath rules of emerging NEs in user-generated text. In addition to the main category classification task, we employ an auxiliary but related secondary task called NE segmentation (i.e. a binary classification of whether a given token is a NE or not). We use both tasks to jointly train the network. More specifically, the model captures word shapes and some orthographic features at the character level by using a Convolutional Neural Network (CNN). For contextual and syntactical information at the word level, such as word and Part-of-Speech (POS) embeddings, the model implements a Bidirectional Long-Short Term Memory (BLSTM) architecture. Finally, to cover well-known entities, the model uses a dense representation of gazetteers. Once the network is trained, we use it as a feature extractor to feed a Conditional Random Fields (CRF) classifier. The CRF classifier jointly predicts the most likely sequence of labels giving better results than the network itself.

With respect to the participants of the shared task, our approach achieved the best results in both categories: 41.86% F1-score for entities, and 40.24% F1-score for surface forms. The data for this shared task is provided by Derczynski et al. (2017).

2 Related Work

Traditional NER systems use hand-crafted features, gazetteers and other external resources to perform well (Ratinov and Roth, 2009). Luo et al. (2015) obtain state-of-the-art results by relying on heavily hand-crafted features, which are expensive to develop and maintain. Recently, many studies have outperformed traditional NER systems by applying neural network architectures. For instance, Lample et al. (2016) use a bidirectional LSTM-

Proceedings of the 3rd Workshop on Noisy User-generated Text, pages 148–153
Copenhagen, Denmark, September 7, 2017. ©2017 Association for Computational Linguistics

CRF architecture. They obtain a state-of-the-art performance without relying on hand-crafted features. Limsopatham and Collier (2016), who achieved the first place on WNUT-2016 shared task, use a BLSTM neural network to leverage orthographic features. We use a similar approach but we employ CNN and BLSTM in parallel instead of forwarding the CNN output to the BLSTM. Nevertheless, our main contribution resides on Multi-Task Learning (MTL) and a combination of POS tags and gazetteers representation to feed the network.

Recently, MTL has gained significant attention. Researchers have tried to correlate the success of MTL with label entropy, regularizers, training data size, and other aspects (Martínez Alonso and Plank, 2017; Bingel and Søgaard, 2017). For instance, Collobert and Weston (2008) use a multi-task network for different NLP tasks and show that the multi-task setting improves generality among shared tasks. In this paper, we take advantage of the multi-task setting by adding a more general secondary task, NE segmentation, along with the primary NE categorization task.

3 Methodology

This section describes our system[1] in three parts: feature representation, model description[2], and sequential inference.

3.1 Feature Representation

We select features to represent the most relevant aspects of the data for the task. The features are divided into three categories: character, word, and lexicons.

Character representation: we use an orthographic encoder similar to that of Limsopatham and Collier (2016) to encapsulate capitalization, punctuation, word shape, and other orthographic features. The only difference is that we handle non-ASCII characters. For instance, the sentence *"3rd Workshop !"* becomes *"ncc Cccccccc p"* as we map numbers to 'n', letters to 'c' (or 'C' if capitalized), and punctuation marks to 'p'. Non-ASCII characters are mapped to 'x'. This encoded representation reduces the sparsity of character features and allows us to focus on word shapes

and punctuation patterns. Once we have an encoded word, we represent each character with a 30-dimensional vector (Ma and Hovy, 2016). We account for a maximum length of 20 characters[3] per word, applying post padding on shorter words and truncating longer words.

Word representation: we have two different representations at the word level. The first one uses pre-trained word embeddings trained on 400 million tweets representing each word with 400 dimensions (Godin et al., 2015)[4]. The second one uses Part-of-Speech tags generated by the CMU Twitter POS tagger (Owoputi et al., 2013). The POS tag embeddings are represented by 100-dimensional vectors. In order to capture contextual information, we account for a context window of 3 tokens on both words and POS tags, where the target token is in the middle of the window.

We randomly initialize both the character features and the POS tag vectors using a uniform distribution in the range $\left[-\sqrt{\frac{3}{dim}}, +\sqrt{\frac{3}{dim}} \right]$, where dim is the dimension of the vectors from each feature representation (He et al., 2015).

Lexical representation: we use gazetteers provided by Mishra and Diesner (2016) to help the model improve its precision for well-known entities. For each word we create a binary vector of 6 dimensions (one dimension per class). Each of the vector dimensions is set to one if the word appears in the gazetteers of the related class.

3.2 Model Description

Character level CNN: we use a CNN architecture to learn word shapes and some orthographic features at the character level representation (see Figure 1). The characters are embedded into a $\mathbb{R}^{d \times l}$ dimensional space, where d is the dimension of the features per character and l is the maximum length of characters per word. Then, we take the character embeddings and apply 2-stacked convolutional layers. Following Zhou et al. (2015), we perform a *global average pooling*[5] instead of the widely used *max pooling* operation. Finally, the result is passed to a fully-connected layer using a Rectifier Linear Unit (ReLU) activation function, which yields the character-based representation of

---

[1] https://github.com/tavo91/NER-WNUT17

[2] The neural network is implemented using Keras (https://github.com/fchollet/keras) and Theano as backend (http://deeplearning.net/software/theano/).

[3] Different lengths do not improve results

[4] http://www.fredericgodin.com/software

[5] Zhou et al. (2015) empirically showed that *global average pooling* captured more extensive information from the feature maps than *max pooling*.

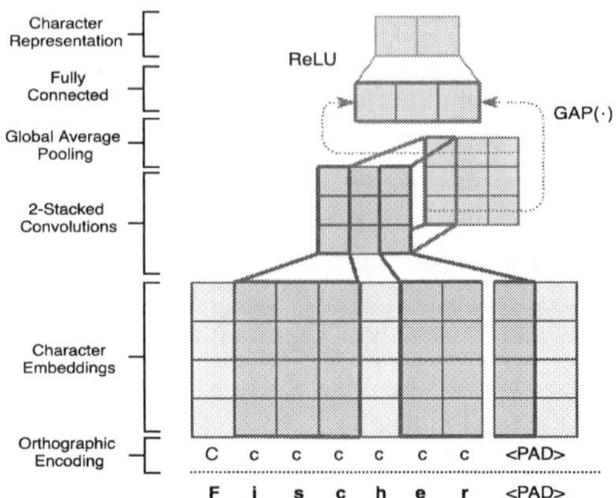

Figure 1: Orthographic character-based representation of a word (green) using a CNN with 2-stacked convolutional layers. The first layer takes the input from embeddings (red) while the second layer (blue) takes the input from the first convolutional layer. Global Average Pooling is applied after the second convolutional layer.

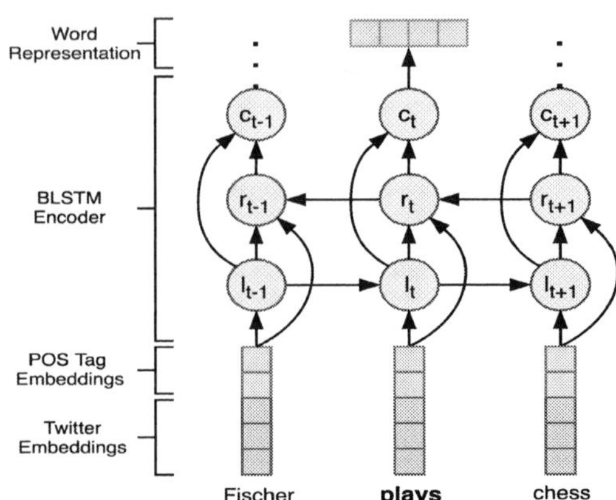

Figure 2: Word representation of POS-tag embeddings (blue) and Twitter word embeddings (red) using a BLSTM neural network.

a word. The resulting vector is used as input for the rest of the network.

Word level BLSTM: we use a Bidirectional LSTM (Dyer et al., 2015) to learn the contextual information of a sequence of words as described in Figure 2. Word embeddings are initialized with pre-trained Twitter word embeddings from a Skip-gram model (Godin et al., 2015) using word2vec (Mikolov et al., 2013). Additionally, we use POS tag embeddings, which are randomly initialized using a uniform distribution. The model receives the concatenation of both POS tags and Twitter word embeddings. The BLSTM layer extracts the features from both forward and backward directions and concatenates the resulting vectors from each direction ($[\vec{h}; \overleftarrow{h}]$). Following Ma and Hovy (2016), we use 100 neurons per direction. The resulting vector is used as input for the rest of the network.

Lexicon network: we take the lexical representation vectors of the input words and feed them into a fully-connected layer. We use 32 neurons on this layer and a ReLU activation function. Then, the resulting vector is used as input for the rest of the network.

Multi-task network: we create a unified model to predict the NE segmentation and NE categorization tasks simultaneously. Typically, the additional task acts as a regularizer to generalize the model (Goodfellow et al., 2016; Collobert and Weston, 2008). The concatenation of character, word and lexical vectors is fed into the NE segmentation

and categorization tasks. We use a single-neuron layer with a sigmoid activation function for the secondary NE segmentation task, whereas for the primary NE categorization task, we employ a 13-neuron[6] layer with a softmax activation function. Finally, we add the losses from both tasks and feed the total loss backward during training.

3.3 Sequential Inference

The multi-task network predicts probabilities for each token in the input sentence individually. Thus, those individual probabilities do not account for sequential information. We exploit the sequential information by using a Conditional Random Fields[7] classifier over those probabilities. This allows us to jointly predict the most likely sequence of labels for a given sentence instead of performing a word-by-word prediction. More specifically, we take the weights learned by the multi-task neural network and use them as features for the CRF classifier (see Figure 3). Taking weights from the common dense layer captures both of the segmentation and categorization features.

4 Experimental Settings

We preprocess all the datasets by replacing the URLs with the token <URL> before performing any experiment. Additionally, we use half of development set as validation and the other half as evaluation.

---

[6] Using BIO encoding, each of the 6 classes will have a *begin* and *inside* version (e.g. B-product, I-product).

[7] Python CRF-Suite library: `https://github.com/scrapinghub/python-crfsuite`

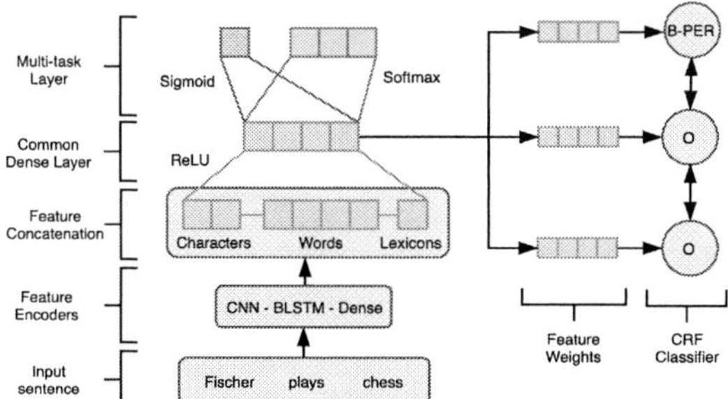

Figure 3: Overall system design. First, the system embeds a sentence into a high-dimensional space and uses CNN, BLSTM, and dense encoders to extract features. Then, it concatenates the resulting vectors of each encoder and performs multi-task. The top left single-node layer represents segmentation (red) while the top right three-node layer represents categorization (blue). Finally, a CRF classifier uses the weights of the common dense layer to perform a sequential classification.

Classes	Precision (%)	Recall (%)	F1 (%)
corporation	35.71	29.41	32.26
creative-work	60.00	5.26	9.68
group	30.00	12.00	17.14
location	65.71	56.10	60.53
person	83.98	62.04	71.36
product	39.29	15.71	22.45
Entity	72.16	43.30	54.12
Surface	68.38	95.05	79.54

Table 1: This table shows the results from the CRF classifier at the class level. The classification is conducted using the development set as both validation and evaluation.

Classes	Precision (%)	Recall (%)	F1 (%)
corporation	31.91	22.73	26.55
creative-work	36.67	7.75	12.79
group	41.79	16.97	24.14
location	56.92	49.33	52.86
person	70.72	50.12	58.66
product	30.77	9.45	14.46
Entity	57.54	32.90	41.86
Surface	56.31	31.31	40.24

Table 2: This table shows the final results of our submission. The hardest class to predict for is *creative-work*, while the easiest is *person*.

Regarding the network hyper-parameters, in the case of the CNN, we set the kernel size to 3 on both convolutional layers. We also use the same number of filters on both layers: 64. Increasing the number of filters and the number of convolutional layers yields worse results, and it takes significantly more time. In the case of the BLSTM architecture, we add dropout layers before and after the Bidirectional LSTM layers with dropout rates of 0.5. The dropout layers allow the network to reduce overfitting (Srivastava et al., 2014). We also tried using a batch normalization layer instead of dropouts, but the experiment yielded worse results. The training of the whole neural network is conducted using a batch size of 500 samples, and 150 epochs. Additionally, we compile the model using the AdaMax optimizer (Kingma and Ba, 2014). Accuracy and F1-score are used as evaluation metrics.

For sequential inference, the CRF classifier uses L-BFGS as a training algorithm with L1 and L2 regularization. The penalties for L1 and L2 are 1.0 and $1.0e^{-3}$, respectively.

5   Results and Discussion

We compare the results of the multi-task neural network itself and the CRF classifier on each of our experiments. The latter one always shows the best results, which emphasizes the importance of sequential information. The results of the CRF, using the development set, are in Table 1.

Moreover, the addition of a secondary task allows the CRF to use more relevant features from the network improving its results from a F1-score of 52.42% to 54.12%. Our finding that a multi-task architecture is generally preferable over the single task architecture is consistent with prior research (Søgaard and Goldberg, 2016; Collobert and Weston, 2008; Attia et al., 2016; Maharjan et al., 2017).

We also study the relevance of our features by performing multiple experiments with the same architecture and different combinations of features. For instance, removing gazetteers from the model drops the results from 54.12% to 52.69%. Similarly, removing POS tags gives worse results (51.12%). Among many combinations, the feature set presented in Section 3.1 yields the best results.

The final results of our submission to the WNUT-2017 shared task are shown in Table 2. Our approach obtains the best results for the *person* and *location* categories. It is less effective for *corporation*, and the most difficult categories for our system are *creative-work* and *product*. Our intuition is that the latter two classes are the most difficult to predict for because they grow faster and have less restrictive patterns than the rest. For instance, products can have any type of letters or numbers in their names, or in the case of creative works, as many words as their titles can hold (e.g.

Participants	F1 - E (%)	F1 - SF (%)
MIC-CIS	37.06	34.25
Arcada	39.98	37.77
Drexel-CCI	26.30	25.26
SJTU-Adapt	40.42	37.62
FLYTXT	38.35	36.31
SpinningBytes	40.78	39.33
UH-RiTUAL	**41.86**	**40.24**

Table 3: The scores of all the participants in the WNUT-2017 shared task. The metrics of the shared task are entity and surface form F1-scores. Our results are highlighted.

name of movies, books, songs, etc.).

Regarding the shared-task metrics, our approach achieves a 41.86% F1-score for entities and 40.24% for surface forms. Table 3 shows that our system yields similar results to the other participants on both metrics. In general, the final scores are low which states the difficulty of the task and that the problem is far from being solved.

6 Error Analysis

By evaluating the errors made by the CRF classifier, we find that the NE boundaries are a problem. For instance, when a NE is preceded by an article starting with a capitalized letter, the model includes the article as if it were part of the NE. This behavior may be caused by the capitalization features captured by the CNN network. Similarly, if a NE is followed by a conjunction and another NE, the classifier tends to join both NEs as if the conjunction were part of a single unified entity. Another common problem shown by the classifier is that fully-capitalized NEs are disregarded most of the time. This pattern may be related to the switch of domains in the training and testing phases. For instance, some Twitter informal abbreviations[8] may appear fully-capitalized but they do not represent NEs, whereas in Reddit and Stack Overflow fully-capitalized words are more likely to describe NEs.

7 Conclusion

We show that our multi-task neural network is capable of extracting relevant features from noisy user-generated text. We also show that a CRF classifier can boost the neural network results because it uses the whole sentence to predict the most likely set of labels. Additionally, our approach emphasizes the importance of POS tags in

conjunction with gazetteers for NER tasks. Twitter word embeddings and orthographic character embeddings are also relevant for the task.

Finally, our ongoing work aims at improving these results by getting a better understanding of the strengths and weaknesses of our model. We also plan to evaluate the current system in related tasks where noise and emerging NEs are prevalent.

References

Eiji Aramaki, Yasuhide Miura, Masatsugu Tonoike, Tomoko Ohkuma, Hiroshi Mashuichi, and Kazuhiko Ohe. 2009. TEXT2TABLE: Medical Text Summarization System based on Named Entity Recognition and Modality Identification. In *Proceedings of the Workshop on Current Trends in Biomedical Natural Language Processing*, BioNLP '09, pages 185–192, Stroudsburg, PA, USA. Association for Computational Linguistics.

Mohammed Attia, Suraj Maharjan, Younes Samih, Laura Kallmeyer, and Thamar Solorio. 2016. CogALex-V Shared Task: GHHH - Detecting Semantic Relations via Word Embeddings. In *Proceedings of the 5th Workshop on Cognitive Aspects of the Lexicon (CogALex - V)*, pages 86–91, Osaka, Japan. The COLING 2016 Organizing Committee.

Michele Banko, Michael J. Cafarella, Stephen Soderland, Matt Broadhead, and Oren Etzioni. 2007. Open Information Extraction from the Web. In *Proceedings of the 20th International Joint Conference on Artificial Intelligence*, IJCAI'07, pages 2670–2676, San Francisco, CA, USA. Morgan Kaufmann Publishers Inc.

Joachim Bingel and Anders Søgaard. 2017. Identifying beneficial task relations for multi-task learning in deep neural networks. In *Proceedings of the 15th Conference of the European Chapter of the Association for Computational Linguistics: Volume 2, Short Papers*, pages 164–169, Valencia, Spain. Association for Computational Linguistics.

Hsinchun Chen, Wingyan Chung, Jennifer Jie Xu, Gang Wang, Yi Qin, and Michael Chau. 2004. Crime Data Mining: A General Framework and Some Examples. *Computer*, 37(4):50–56.

Ronan Collobert and Jason Weston. 2008. A Unified Architecture for Natural Language Processing: Deep Neural Networks with Multitask Learning. In *Proceedings of the 25th International Conference on Machine Learning*, ICML '08, pages 160–167, New York, NY, USA. ACM.

Leon Derczynski, Eric Nichols, Marieke van Erp, and Nut Limsopatham. 2017. Results of the WNUT2017 Shared Task on Novel and Emerging Entity Recognition. In *Proceedings of the 3rd Workshop on Noisy, User-generated Text (W-NUT) at EMNLP*. ACL.

---

[8] E.g. *LOL* is an informal social media expression that stands for *Laughing Out Loud*, which is not an NE.

Chris Dyer, Miguel Ballesteros, Wang Ling, Austin Matthews, and Noah A. Smith. 2015. Transition-Based Dependency Parsing with Stack Long Short-Term Memory. *CoRR*, abs/1505.08075.

Fréderic Godin, Baptist Vandersmissen, Wesley De Neve, and Rik Van de Walle. 2015. Multimedia Lab @ ACL WNUT NER Shared Task: Named Entity Recognition for Twitter Microposts using Distributed Word Representations. In *Proceedings of the Workshop on Noisy User-generated Text*, pages 146–153, Beijing, China. Association for Computational Linguistics.

Ian Goodfellow, Yoshua Bengio, and Aaron Courville. 2016. *Deep Learning*. MIT Press. http://www.deeplearningbook.org.

Kaiming He, Xiangyu Zhang, Shaoqing Ren, and Jian Sun. 2015. Delving Deep into Rectifiers: Surpassing Human-Level Performance on ImageNet Classification. *CoRR*, abs/1502.01852.

Diederik P. Kingma and Jimmy Ba. 2014. Adam: A method for stochastic optimization. *CoRR*, abs/1412.6980.

Guillaume Lample, Miguel Ballesteros, Sandeep Subramanian, Kazuya Kawakami, and Chris Dyer. 2016. Neural Architectures for Named Entity Recognition. *CoRR*, abs/1603.01360.

Chenliang Li, Jianshu Weng, Qi He, Yuxia Yao, Anwitaman Datta, Aixin Sun, and Bu-Sung Lee. 2012. TwiNER: Named Entity Recognition in Targeted Twitter Stream. In *Proceedings of the 35th International ACM SIGIR Conference on Research and Development in Information Retrieval*, SIGIR '12, pages 721–730, New York, NY, USA. ACM.

Nut Limsopatham and Nigel Collier. 2016. Bidirectional LSTM for Named Entity Recognition in Twitter Messages. In *Proceedings of the 2nd Workshop on Noisy User-generated Text (WNUT)*, pages 145–152, Osaka, Japan. The COLING 2016 Organizing Committee.

Gang Luo, Xiaojiang Huang, Chin-Yew Lin, and Zaiqing Nie. 2015. Joint Entity Recognition and Disambiguation. In *Proceedings of the 2015 Conference on Empirical Methods in Natural Language Processing*, pages 879–888, Lisbon, Portugal. Association for Computational Linguistics.

Xuezhe Ma and Eduard H. Hovy. 2016. End-to-end Sequence Labeling via Bi-directional LSTM-CNNs-CRF. *CoRR*, abs/1603.01354.

Suraj Maharjan, John Arevalo, Manuel Montes, Fabio A. González, and Thamar Solorio. 2017. A Multi-task Approach to Predict Likability of Books. In *Proceedings of the 15th Conference of the European Chapter of the Association for Computational Linguistics: Volume 1, Long Papers*, pages 1217–1227, Valencia, Spain. Association for Computational Linguistics.

Héctor Martínez Alonso and Barbara Plank. 2017. When is multitask learning effective? Semantic sequence prediction under varying data conditions. In *Proceedings of the 15th Conference of the European Chapter of the Association for Computational Linguistics: Volume 1, Long Papers*, pages 44–53, Valencia, Spain. Association for Computational Linguistics.

Tomas Mikolov, Kai Chen, Greg Corrado, and Jeffrey Dean. 2013. Efficient Estimation of Word Representations in Vector Space. *CoRR*, abs/1301.3781.

Shubhanshu Mishra and Jana Diesner. 2016. Semi-supervised Named Entity Recognition in noisy-text. In *Proceedings of the 2nd Workshop on Noisy User-generated Text (WNUT)*, pages 203–212, Osaka, Japan. The COLING 2016 Organizing Committee.

Olutobi Owoputi, Brendan O'Connor, Chris Dyer, Kevin Gimpel, Nathan Schneider, and Noah A. Smith. 2013. Improved Part-of-Speech Tagging for Online Conversational Text with Word Clusters. In *Proceedings of the 2013 Conference of the North American Chapter of the Association for Computational Linguistics: Human Language Technologies*, pages 380–390, Atlanta, Georgia. Association for Computational Linguistics.

Lev Ratinov and Dan Roth. 2009. Design Challenges and Misconceptions in Named Entity Recognition. In *Proceedings of the Thirteenth Conference on Computational Natural Language Learning*, CoNLL '09, pages 147–155, Stroudsburg, PA, USA. Association for Computational Linguistics.

Alan Ritter, Sam Clark, Mausam, and Oren Etzioni. 2011. Named Entity Recognition in Tweets: An Experimental Study. In *Proceedings of the Conference on Empirical Methods in Natural Language Processing*, EMNLP '11, pages 1524–1534, Stroudsburg, PA, USA. Association for Computational Linguistics.

Anders Søgaard and Yoav Goldberg. 2016. Deep multi-task learning with low level tasks supervised at lower layers. In *Proceedings of the 54th Annual Meeting of the Association for Computational Linguistics (Volume 2: Short Papers)*, pages 231–235, Berlin, Germany. Association for Computational Linguistics.

Nitish Srivastava, Geoffrey Hinton, Alex Krizhevsky, Ilya Sutskever, and Ruslan Salakhutdinov. 2014. Dropout: A Simple Way to Prevent Neural Networks from Overfitting. *J. Mach. Learn. Res.*, 15(1):1929–1958.

Bolei Zhou, Aditya Khosla, Àgata Lapedriza, Aude Oliva, and Antonio Torralba. 2015. Learning Deep Features for Discriminative Localization. *CoRR*, abs/1512.04150.

Distributed Representation, LDA Topic Modelling and Deep Learning for Emerging Named Entity Recognition from Social Media

Patrick Jansson and **Shuhua Liu**
Arcada University of Applied Sciences
Jan-Magnus Janssonin aukio 1, 00560 Helsinki, Finland
{patrick.jansson, shuhua.liu}@arcada.fi

Abstract

This paper reports our participation in the W-NUT 2017 shared task on emerging and rare entity recognition from user generated noisy text such as tweets, online reviews and forum discussions. To accomplish this challenging task, we explore an approach that combines LDA topic modelling with deep learning on word level and character level embeddings. The LDA topic modelling generates topic representation for each tweet which is used as a feature for each word in the tweet. The deep learning components consist of two-layer bidirectional LSTM and a CRF output layer. Our submitted result performed at 39.98 (F1) on entity and 37.77 on surface forms. Our new experiments after submission reached a best performance of 41.81 on entity and 40.57 on surface forms.

1 Introduction

The shared task Emerging and Rare Entity Recognition at the 3rd Workshop on Noisy User-generated Text (W-NUT 2017) takes on the challenge of identifying unusual, previously-unseen entities in noisy texts such as tweets, online reviews and other social discussions (http://noisy-text.github.io/2017/emerging-rare-entities.html). The emergent nature of novel named entities in user generated content and the often very creative natural of their surface forms make the task of automatic detection of such entities particularly difficult. To address such challenges, the shared task

organizer prepared training, development and test datasets and provided to the participants. The datasets try to "resemble turbulent data containing few repeated entities, drawn from rapidly-changing text types or sources of non-mainstream entities". Results from the shared task are evaluated using F1 measures on the entities and surface forms found in the test data. It rewards systems at correctly detecting a diverse range of entities rather than only the frequent ones.

Inspired by the work of Limsopatham and Collier (2016, winner of w-nut 2016 shared task on Named Entity Recognition in Twitter), Chiu and Nichols (2016), and Huang et al (2015), we approached this shared task with bidirectional LSTM models (Long Short Term Memory recurrent neural network model) enhanced by CRF output layer, using both character-level and word-level embeddings as inputs. In addition, different from the study of Limsopatham and Collier (2016), we didn't make use of orthographic features of characters but tried to incorporate POS tags as well as document topics extracted from LDA topic modelling as optional inputs to the modelling process. The LDA topic modelling generates topic representation for each tweet which is used as a feature for each word in the tweet.

Our submitted result performed at 39.98 (F1) on entity and 37.77 (F1) on surface forms, using 10% of the combined training and development set for validation. After submission, we continued with more experiments, using data combining the training set and development set in training process, with ground truth available that helps the selection of the results. Our best result reached a performance of 41.81 on entity and 40.57 on surface forms.

Proceedings of the 3rd Workshop on Noisy User-generated Text, pages 154–159
Copenhagen, Denmark, September 7, 2017. ©2017 Association for Computational Linguistics

2 Data and Preprocessing

The shared task datasets consist of a training set, a development set and a test set. Basic statistics of each data set in shown in Table 1. The shared task focuses on discovering 6 types of target entities and surface forms of: Corporation, Creative-Work, Group, Location, Person and Product (Derczynski et al, 2017).

Entities all

	Training	Dev	Test
# tweets/posts	3394	1009	1287
Tokens total	62730	15733	23394
Entities total	3160	1250	1740
Corporation	267	46	88
Creative-work	346	238	360
Group	414	64	235
Location	793	107	244
Person	995	587	560
Product	345	208	253

Surface

	Training	Dev	Test
Corporation	180	44	79
Creative-work	259	203	292
Group	343	60	188
Location	589	99	174
Person	742	484	476
Product	284	184	200
	2397	1074	1409

Table 1: Dataset overview

In counting surface forms, every "word-label" combination has to be unique and letter case sensitive. When the same word appears twice but as different entities both are counted.

For the stop words removing, we utilized the Stopwords ISO (https://github.com/stopwords-iso/stopwords-en) list. The cutoff value for infrequent terms is set as one when applying LDA modelling.

3 Emerging and Rare Entity Detection from Social Media: Framework and Methods

Our approach to emerging and rare entity detection from social media is illustrated in Figure 1. Our methodology framework consists of the following components: (1) character-level embeddings and bidirectional LSTM modeling; (2) word level embeddings and bidirectional LSTM modelling; (3) LDA topic modelling, POS tags enhanced bidirectional LSTM; (4) fully connected layers, and (5) a CRF (Conditional Random Fields) output layer.

3.1 Character-level Representation

Character-level information was found to be valuable input for named entity recognition from social media (Limsopatham and Collier, 2016; Vosoughi et al, 2016). Chiu and Nichols (2015) found that modelling both the character-level and word-level embeddings within a neural network for named entity recognition helps improve the performance.

In our system, each character is represented as an N dimensional embedding which is learned and adjusted during the training process. The character level representations will then be merged into one M dimensional (50d-200d seems to work well) representation for each word. Character capitalization is kept.

We used 20-dimensional embeddings to represent each character. To learn character-level representations for each word we use a bidirectional LSTM to create a 200-dimensional representation for each word.

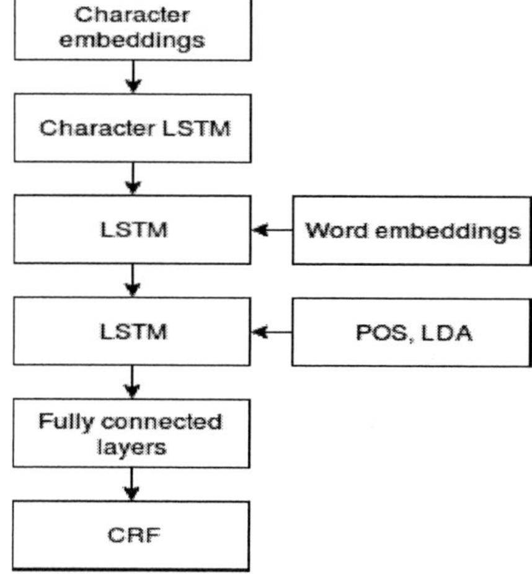

Figure 1: Methodology Framework

3.2 Word Embeddings

Word embeddings are distributed representation of words that offers continuous representations of words and text features such as the linguistic context of words (Mikolv et al, 2013a,

2013b). Word embeddings are the current norm for many text applications as they are found to be able to accurately capture not only syntactic regularities but also (local) semantic regularities of words and phrases (Mikolv et al, 2013a, Hasen et al, 2015; Limsopatham and Collier, 2016; Vosoughi et al, 2016).

Estimation of the word vectors is done using various types of model architectures trained on large corpora. Word2vec (Mikolv et al, 2013a, 2013b) and GloVe (Pennington et al, 2014) are two widely used efficient model architectures and algorithms for learning high quality continuous vector representations of words from huge data sets with billions of words. They have been used to train and create word embeddings that can be applied directly by other applications.

Considering our target source and based on some primitive test, we choose to use 200-dimensional GloVe pre-trained embeddings (Pennington et al, 2014), which was trained on a Twitter corpus with 27 billion tokens and a vocabulary size of 1.2 million.

3.3 POS Tagging

Part of Speech is also an important indicator of named entities, which we would like to include in our model (Huang et al, 2015). GATE Twitter POS tagger (https://gate.ac.uk/wiki/twitter-postagger.html) is used to assign POS tags for each word. POS tags is represented as 50-dimensional trainable embedding.

3.4 LDA Topic Modelling

Topic modeling offers a powerful means for finding hidden thematic structure in large text collections. In topic models, topics are defined as a distribution over a fixed vocabulary of terms and documents are defined as a distribution over topics. LDA topic modeling and its variations represent the most popular methods (Blei et al, 2003; Blei, 2012).

We consider the topic composition of each Tweet or social media post an important indicator of subject domain context, which can be used to complement the local linguistic context of word vector. We make use of topic representation for each tweet derived from LDA modelling as a feature for each word in the Tweet.

We applied the online LDA method by Hoffman et al (2010), implemented in Genism (https://radimrehurek.com/gensim/models/ldamodel.html). It can handily analyze massive document collections or document streams.

When generate topic models, all the three datasets are combined into one corpus, and each entry is treated as a separate document. Each document is cleaned and preprocessed, which includes removing stop-words, punctuation and infrequent terms. An LDA model of 250 topics was trained and used for our system that generated submitted results. Using the model, we get a document level topic for each document, the topic value is then assigned to each word in the document. We also use the model to get a topic for each word in the documents. If the probability that a document or a word belongs to a topic is, the same for each topic, a special token is assigned to it instead of a topic. Each topic token is then assigned to a 250-dimensional embedding, embeddings for document and word-level topics are initialized separately.

3.5 Two-Layer Bidirectional LSTM

Bidirectional LSTM has been shown effective for modelling social media sentences (Huang et al., 2015; Dyer et al., 2015; Limsopatham and Collier, 2016). To learn deep neural models for named entity recognition we adopted a two-layer bidirectional LSTM, followed by two fully connected layers, and a Conditional Random Field (CRF) as an output layer where we maximize the joint likelihood.

For the first LSTM layer, we concatenate the 200-dimensional GloVe word embeddings and the 200-dimensional embeddings for character level representation. For the second layer, we concatenate the output of the first layer with the POS-feature embeddings and LDA-feature embeddings. The LSTM output dimensions are 256 for the first layer and 512 for the second layer.

After the second LSTM layer, we use two fully connected layers at each time step, and feed this representation into the CRF output-layer. The dimensions of the fully connected layers are 128 and 64 for the first and second layer respectively.

Between each layer in the network we applied dropout and batch normalization (Ioffe and Szregedy, 2015). A dropout rate of 0.25 is used for the first two layers of the network (the Character LSTM and the character + word LSTM). For all the other layers of the network, a dropout rate of 0.5 is used.

The fully connected layers are extra hidden layers before the CRF output layer, which allow the models to learn higher level representations without adding complexity through an extra compositional layer (Rei and Yannakoudakis, 2016).

Conditional random field (CRF) has shown to be one of the most effective methods for named entity recognition in general and in social media (Lafferty et al., 2001; McCallum and Li, 2003; Baldwin et al., 2015; Limsopatham and Collier, 2016). It also helped our system to gain performance in recognizing emerging entities and surface forms.

The deep neural model was implemented using Keras with a TensorFlow backend and Keras community contributions for the CRF implementation. One model is trained for both entity and surface form recognition. Any feature can be included or excluded as needed when running the model.

4   Experiments and Results

In this section, we report two sets of experiments and results. Results from the 1st set of experiments were submitted to the shared task organizer for evaluation. The 2nd set of experiments are done after the submission. Using the ground truth released by the organizer we evaluated the results directly by ourselves. The ground truth being available also helps us in identifying the best model.

4.1   1st Set of Experiments and Submitted Results

To train the model, the training set and the dev sets are merged, of which 10% (in terms of size, about half of the original dev set) are used for validation. We used a batch size of 32 for training, and the RMSprop optimizer with an initial leaning rate of 0.001. The results are shown in Table 2. The results from all participating systems are presented in Table 3 (Derczynski, et al, 2017).

The overall performance of our system reached 39.98 on entities and 37.77 on surface forms. The performance on Person and Location types of entities and surface forms are comparatively better, with F1 score at 55,88 and 47,38 respectively for entities, and F1 score at 53.30 and 42.80 for their surface forms. The system is less effective on identifying Corporation, Product, Creative-work and Group types of entities and surface forms, especially disappointing in terms of recall. For Creative-work and Product type entities, recall only reached 9.86% and 11.02% respectively.

	Accuracy	Precision	Recall	FB1
Entities	94.03%	47.40%	34.57%	39.98
Surface forms		44.94%	32.57%	37.77
	Entity types	Precision	Recall	FB1
	Corporation	19.05%	18.18%	18.60
	Creative-work	31.82%	9.86%	15.05
	Group	38.36%	16.97%	23.53
	Location	44.00%	51.33%	47.38
	Person	58.91%	53.15%	55.88
	Product	31.11%	11.02%	16.28
	Surface forms	Precision	Recall	FB1
	Corporation	20.37%	18.33%	19.30
	Creative-work	32.56%	10.29%	15.64
	Group	35.29%	17.02%	22.97
	Location	39.73%	46.40%	42.80
	Person	56.38%	50.53%	53.30
	Product	31.82%	11.97%	17.39

Table 2: Our submitted results

Team	F (entity)	F (surface)
MIC-CIS	37.06	34.25
Arcada	39.98	37.77
Drexel-CCI	26.30	25.26
SJTU-Adapt	40.42	37.62
FLYTXT	38.35	36.31
SpinningBytes	40.78	39.33
UH Ritual	41.86	40.24

Table 3: Submitted results, all participants

4.2   2nd Set of Experiments and Updated Results

After submission, we continued our modelling work with new training strategies. In terms of the data, all samples of the training set and dev set are used for training the model, which is then directly applied to test set. We also experimented more with different options of the number of topics in LDA topic modelling. We found that incorporating LDA features does have a positive effect on the performance. We used models with topic counts in the range of 20, 50, 150, 250, 350, 450. The results (FB1 value for entity and surface forms) are illustrated in Table 4. The scores are maxima out of two runs of experiments, where each run goes through all the topic counts.

# Topics	0	20	50	150
Entity	40.63	40.63	41.48	**41.81**
Surface	38.06	38.95	39.68	**40.57**
# Topics	250	350	450	
Entity	41.78	41.66	40.95	
Surface	39.90	39.48	39.29	

Table 4: Performance variation related with number of topics for LDA modelling

When topic number set as 150, breakdown of the performance shows that the system performed best for the more difficult entity types and surface forms, as is shown in Table 5. For Creative-work and Product type entities, recall reached 15.49% and 14.96% respectively. For their surface forms, recall reached 16.18% and 16.24% respectively.

	Accuracy	Precision	Recall	FB1
Entities	94.10%	50.86%	35.50%	41.81
Surface forms		49.55%	34.35%	40.57
	Entity types	Precision	Recall	FB1
	Corporation	31.71%	19.70%	24.30
	Creative-work	37.29%	15.49%	21.89
	Group	40.62%	15.76%	22.71
	Location	49.09%	54.00%	51.43
	Person	61.16%	51.75%	56.06
	Product	31.15%	14.96%	20.21
	Surface forms	Precision	Recall	FB1
	Corporation	31.43%	18.33%	23.16
	Creative-work	37.93%	16.18%	22.68
	Group	40.32%	17.73%	24.63
	Location	47.14%	52.80%	49.81
	Person	60.06%	49.20%	54.09
	Product	32.20%	16.24%	21.59

Table 5: Performance on different types of entities, number of topics for LDA modelling = 150

5 Discussion and Conclusion

In this paper, we reported our participation in the W-NUT 2017 shared task on emerging and rare entity recognition from user generated noisy text. We described our system that leverages the power of LDA topic modelling, POS tags, character-level and word-level embeddings, bidirectional LTSM and CRF. The LDA topic modelling generates topic representation for each tweet or social media post. The deep learning model consists of two-layer bidirectional LSTM, two fully connected layers and a CRF output layer. We make use of topic representation for each tweet derived from LDA modelling as a feature for each word in a tweet or post. The topic composition of each post offers a certain subject domain context that could complement the local linguistic context of word embeddings.

We reported two sets of experiments and results. Results from the 1st set of experiments were submitted to the shared task organizer for evaluation. Our submitted results performed at 39.98 (F1) on entities and 37.77 (F1) on surface forms.

The 2nd set of experiments are done as follow up study after the submission, adopting a different training strategy. Using the ground truth released by the organizer we evaluated the results directly by ourselves. The ground truth being available helped us to identify the best model.

We experimented more with different options of the number of topics in LDA topic modelling. We found that incorporating LDA features does have a positive effect on the performance. The new results reached a best performance of 41.81 on entities and 40.57 on surface forms, with the number of topics set as 150. When the number of topics is set the same as for our submitted results (i.e. 250), the new results showed performance gain as well, reached 41.78 on entities and 39.90 on surface forms.

For future work, it would be interesting to train the LDA model on a larger corpus, to hopefully find a more accurate subject domain context for each tweet or post. It would be useful as well to explore the effects of alternative word embeddings such as fasttext. It would also be interesting to apply our system in identifying city event related entities and surface forms from other social media data.

Acknowledgements

This work is part of the DIGILENS-HKI project on mining community knowledge from social media (http://rdi.arcada.fi/katumetro-digilens-hki). We thank and gratefully acknowledge funding from Helsinki Region Urban Research Program (http://www.helsinki.fi/kaupunkitutkimus/) and Arcada Foundation (tuf.arcada.fi).

References

Blei D, A. Ng and M. I. Jordan. 2003. Latent Dirichlet Allocation. Advances in Neural Information Processing Systems. Pages 601-608.

Blei D. 2012. Probabilistic Topic Models. Communications of the ACM, 55(4):77-84.

Benjamin Strauss, Bethany E. Toma, Alan Ritter, Marie Catherine de Marneffe, and Wei Xu. 2016. Results of the wnut16 named entity recognition shared task. In Proceedings of the Workshop on Noisy User-generated Text (WNUT 2016), Osaka, Japan.

Baldwin Timothy, Young-Bum Kim, Marie Catherine de Marneffe, Alan Ritter, Bo Han, and Wei Xu. 2015. Shared tasks of the 2015 workshop on noisy user-generated text: Twitter lexical normalization and named entity recognition. ACL-IJCNLP, 126:2015.

Chiu Jason P. C., Eric Nichols, Named Entity Recognition with Bidirectional LSTM-CNNs, TACL2016

Derczynski Leon, Diana Maynard, Giuseppe Rizzo, Marieke van Erp, Genevieve Gorrell, Raphael Troncy, Johann Petrak, and Kalina Bontcheva. 2015. Analysis of named entity recognition and linking for tweets. Information Processing & Management, 51(2):32–49.

Derczynski Leon, Eric Nichols, Marieke van Erp, Nut Limsopatham, Results of the WNUT2017 Shared Task on Novel and Emerging Entity Recognition, in Proceedings of the 3rd Workshop on Noisy, User-generated Text, 2017

Dyer Chris, Miguel Ballesteros, Wang Ling, Austin Matthews, and Noah A Smith. 2015. Transition-based dependency parsing with stack long short-term memory. arXiv preprint arXiv:1505.08075.

Godin Frederic, Baptist Vandersmissen, Wesley De Neve and Rik Vande Walle. 2015. Multimedialab@acl w-nut shared task: Named entity recognition for twitter micro posts using distributed word representations. ACL-IJCNLP 2015, page 146.

Hasan Sadid A., Yuan Ling, Joey Liu, Oladimeji Farri, Exploiting Neural Embeddings for Social Media Data Analysis. TREC 2015

Hoffman M, D. Blei and F. Bach. 2010. Online learning for Latent Dirichlet Allocation. Advances in Neural Information Processing Systems 23, 856-864.

Huang Zhiheng, Wei Xu, Kai Yu, Bidirectional LSTM-CRF Models for Sequence Tagging, ArXiv2015

Lafferty John, Andrew McCallum, and Fernando Pereira. 2001. Conditional random fields: Probabilistic models for segmenting and labeling sequence data. In Proceedings of the eighteenth international conference on machine learning, ICML, volume 1, pages 282–289.

Ioffe Sergey, Szregedy Christian, Batch Normalization: Accelerating Deep Network Training by Reducing Internal Covariate Shift, ArXiv2015

Limsopatham Nut, Nigel Collier, Bidirectional LSTM for Named Entity Recognition in Twitter Messages, 2016

McCallum Andrew and Wei Li. 2003. Early results for named entity recognition with conditional random fields, feature induction and web-enhanced lexicons. In Proceedings of the seventh conference on Natural language learning at HLT-NAACL 2003-Volume 4, pages 188–191. Association for Computational Linguistics.

Mikolov Tomas, Kai Chen, Greg Corrado, and Jeffrey Dean. 2013. Efficient Estimation of Word Representations in Vector Space. In Proceedings of Workshop at ICLR, 2013.

Mikolov Tomas, Ilya Sutskever, Kai Chen, Greg Corrado, and Jeffrey Dean. 2013. Distributed Representations of Words and Phrases and their Compositionality. In Proceedings of NIPS, 2013

Pennington Jeffrey, Richard Socher, and Christopher D Manning. 2014. GloVe: Global vectors for word representation. In EMNLP, pages 1532–1543.

Vosoughi Soroush, Prashanth Vijayaraghavan, Deb Roy, Tweet2Vec: Learning Tweet Embeddings Using Character-level CNN-LSTM Encoder-Decoder, Proceedings of SIGIR 2016, July 17-21, 2016, Pisa, Italy

Zhang Xiang, Junbo Zhao, Yann LeCun. Character-level Convolutional Networks for Text Classification. Advances in Neural Information Processing Systems 28 (NIPS 2015). Poster. Datasets. Code. Errata.

Marek Rei and Helen Yannakoudakis, "Compositional Sequence Labeling Models for Error Detection in Learner Writing", Proceedings of the 54th Annual Meeting of the Association for Computational Linguistics, pages 1181–1191, Berlin, Germany, August 7-12, 2016.

Multi-channel BiLSTM-CRF Model for
Emerging Named Entity Recognition in Social Media

Bill Y. Lin[*] and **Frank F. Xu**[*] and **Zhiyi Luo** and **Kenny Q. Zhu**

Shanghai Jiao Tong University

Shanghai, China

{yuchenlin, frankxu, jessherlock}@sjtu.edu.cn, kzhu@cs.sjtu.edu.cn

Abstract

In this paper, we present our multi-channel neural architecture for recognizing emerging named entity in social media messages, which we applied in the *Novel and Emerging Named Entity Recognition* shared task at the EMNLP 2017 Workshop on Noisy User-generated Text (W-NUT). We propose a novel approach, which incorporates comprehensive word representations with multi-channel information and Conditional Random Fields (CRF) into a traditional Bidirectional Long Short-Term Memory (BiLSTM) neural network without using any additional hand-crafted features such as gazetteers. In comparison with other systems participating in the shared task, our system won the 3rd place in terms of the average of two evaluation metrics.

1 Introduction

Named entity recognition (NER) is one of the first and most important steps in Information Extraction pipelines. Generally, it is to identify mentions of entities (persons, locations, organizations, etc.) within unstructured text. However, the diverse and noisy nature of user-generated content as well as the emerging entities with novel surface forms make NER in social media messages more challenging.

The first challenge brought by user-generated content is its unique characteristics: short, noisy and informal. For instance, tweets are typically short since the number of characters is restricted to 140 and people indeed tend to pose short messages even in social media without such restric-

tions, such as YouTube comments and Reddit. [1] Hence, the contextual information in a sentence is very limited. Apart from that, the use of colloquial language makes it more difficult for existing NER approaches to be reused, which mainly focus on a general domain and formal text (Baldwin et al., 2015; Derczynski et al., 2015).

Another challenge of NER in noisy text is the fact that there are large amounts of emerging named entities and rare surface forms among the user-generated text, which tend to be tougher to detect (Augenstein et al., 2017) and recall thus is a significant problem (Derczynski et al., 2015). By way of example, the surface form *"kktny"*, in the tweet *"so.. kktny in 30 mins?"*, actually refers to a new TV series called *"Kourtney and Kim Take New York"*, which even human experts found hard to recognize. Additionally, it is quite often that netizens mention entities using rare morphs as surface forms. For example, *"black mamba"*, the name for a venomous snake, is actually a morph that Kobe Bryant created for himself for his aggressiveness in playing basketball games (Zhang et al., 2015). Such morphs and rare surface forms are also very difficult to detect and classify.

The goal of this paper is to present our system participating in the *Novel and Emerging Named Entity Recognition* shared task at the EMNLP 2017 Workshop on Noisy User-generated Text (W-NUT 2017), which aims for NER in such noisy user-generated text. We investigate a multi-channel BiLSTM-CRF neural network model in our participating system, which is described in Section 3. The details of our implementation are in presented in Section 4, where we also present some conclusion from our experiments.

---

[*] The two authors made equal contributions.

[1] The average length of the sentences in this shared task is about 20 tokens per sentence.

Proceedings of the 3rd Workshop on Noisy User-generated Text, pages 160–165

Copenhagen, Denmark, September 7, 2017. ©2017 Association for Computational Linguistics

2   Problem Definition

The NER is a classic sequence labeling problem, in which we are given a sentence, in the form of a sequence of tokens $\mathbf{w} = (w_1, w_2, ..., w_n)$, and we are required to output a sequence of token labels $\mathbf{y} = (y_1, y_2, ..., y_n)$. In this specific task, we use the standard BIO2 annotation, and each named entity chunk are classified into 6 categories, namely Person, Location (including GPE, facility), Corporation, Consumer good (tangible goods, or well-defined services), Creative work (song, movie, book, and so on) and Group (subsuming music band, sports team, and non-corporate organizations).

3   Approach

In this section, we will first introduce the overview of our proposed model and then present each part of the model in detail.

3.1   Overview

Figure 1 shows the overall structure of our proposed model, instead of solely using the original pretrained word embeddings as the final word representations, we construct a comprehensive word representation for each word in the input sentence. This comprehensive word representations contain the character-level sub-word information, the original pretrained word embeddings and multiple syntactical features. Then, we feed them into a Bidirectional LSTM layer, and thus we have a hidden state for each word. The hidden states are considered as the feature vectors of the words by the final CRF layer, from which we can decode the final predicted tag sequence for the input sentence.

3.2   Comprehensive Word Representations

In this subsection, we present our proposed comprehensive word representations. We first build character-level word representations from the embeddings of every character in each word using a bidirectional LSTM. Then we further incorporate the final word representation with the embedding of the syntactical information of each token, such as the part-of-speech tag, the dependency role, the word position in the sentence and the head position. Finally, we combine the original word embeddings with the above two parts to obtain the final comprehensive word representations.

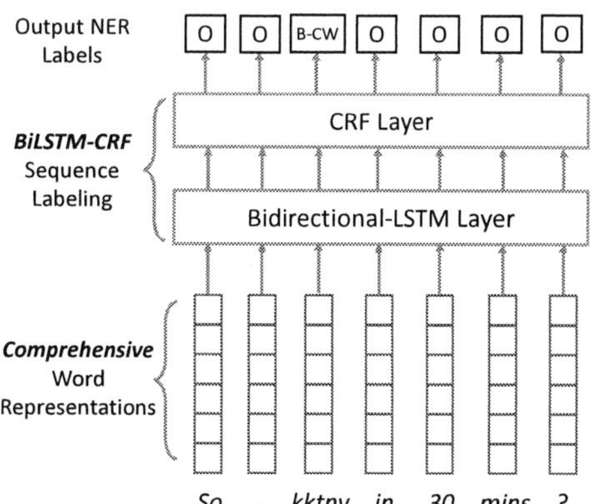

Figure 1: Overview of our approach.

3.2.1   Character-level Word Representations

In noisy user-generated text analysis, sub-word (character-level) information is much more important than that in normal text analysis for two main reasons: 1) People are more likely to use novel abbreviations and morphs to mention entities, which are often out of vocabulary and only occur a few times. Thus, solely using the original word-level word embedding as features to represent words is not adequate to capture the characteristics of such mentions. 2) Another reason why we have to pay more attention to character-level word representation for noisy text is that it is can capture the orthographic or morphological information of both formal words and Internet slang.

There are two main network structures to make use of character embeddings: one is CNN (Ma and Hovy, 2016) and the other is BiLSTM(Lample et al., 2016). BiLSTM turns to be better in our experiment on development dataset. Thus, we follow Lample et al. (2016) to build a BiLSTM network to encode the characters in each token as Figure 2 shows. We finally concatenate the forward embedding and backward embedding to the final character-level word representation.

3.2.2   Syntactical Word Representations

We argue that the syntactical information, such as POS tags and dependency roles, should also be explicitly considered as contextual features of each token in the sentence.

TweetNLP and TweeboParser (Owoputi et al., 2013; Kong et al., 2014) are two popular software to generate such syntactical tags for each token given a tweet. Given the nature of the noisy tweet text, a new set of POS tags and dependency

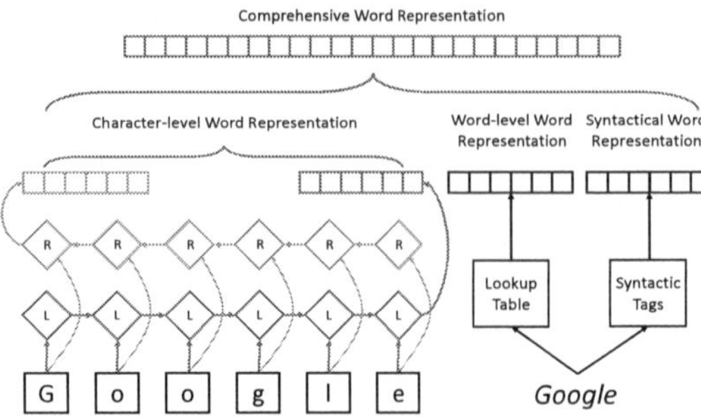

Figure 2: Illustration of comprehensive word representations.

trees are used in the tool, called Tweebank (Gimpel et al., 2011). See Table 1 for an example POS tagging. Since a tweet often contains more than one utterance, the output of TweeboParser will often be a multi-rooted graph over the tweet.

Word position embedding are included as well as it is widely used in other similar tasks, like relation classification (Xu et al., 2016). Also, head position embeddings are taken into account while calculating these embedding vectors to further enrich the dependency information. It tries to exclude these tokens from the parse tree, resulting a head index of -1.

After calculating all 4 types of embedding vectors (POS tags, dependency roles, word positions, head positions) for every tokens, we concatenate them to form a syntactical word representation.

Token	so	..	kktny	in	30	mins	?
POS	R	,	N	P	$	N	,
Position	1	2	3	4	5	6	7
Head	0	-1	0	3	6	4	-1

Table 1: Example of POS tagging for tweets.

3.2.3 Combination with Word-level Word Representations

After obtaining the above two additional word representations, we combine them with the original word-level word representations, which are just traditional word embeddings.

To sum up, our comprehensive word representations are the concatenation of three parts: 1) character-level word representations, 2) syntactical word representation and 3) original pretrained word embeddings.

3.3 BiLSTM Layer

LSTM based networks are proven to be effective in sequence labeling problem for they have access to both past and the future contexts. Whereas, hidden states in unidirectional LSTMs only takes information from the past, which may be adequate to classify the sentiment is a shortcoming for labeling each token. Bidirectional LSTMs enable the hidden states to capture both historical and future context information and then to label a token.

Mathematically, the input of this BiLSTM layer is a sequence of comprehensive word representations (vectors) for the tokens of the input sentence, denoted as $(\mathbf{x_1}, \mathbf{x_2}, ..., \mathbf{x_n})$. The output of this BiLSTM layer is a sequence of the hidden states for each input word vectors, denoted as $(\mathbf{h_1}, \mathbf{h_2}, ..., \mathbf{h_n})$. Each final hidden state is the concatenation of the forward $\overleftarrow{\mathbf{h_i}}$ and backward $\overrightarrow{\mathbf{h_i}}$ hidden states. We know that

$$\overleftarrow{\mathbf{h_i}} = \text{lstm}(\mathbf{x_i}, \overleftarrow{\mathbf{h_{i-1}}}) \, , \, \overrightarrow{\mathbf{h_i}} = \text{lstm}(\mathbf{x_i}, \overrightarrow{\mathbf{h_{i+1}}})$$

$$\mathbf{h_i} = \left[\, \overleftarrow{\mathbf{h_i}} \, ; \, \overrightarrow{\mathbf{h_i}} \, \right]$$

3.4 CRF Layer

It is almost always beneficial to consider the correlations between the current label and neighboring labels since there are many syntactical constrains in natural language sentences. For example, I-PERSON will never follow a B-GROUP. If we simply feed the above mentioned hidden states independently to a Softmax layer to predict the labels, then such constrains will not be more likely to be broken. Linear-chain Conditional Random Field is the most popular way to control the structure prediction and its basic idea is to use a series of potential function to approximate the conditional probability of the output label sequence given the input word sequence.

Formally, we take the above sequence of hidden states $\mathbf{h} = (\mathbf{h_1}, \mathbf{h_2}, ..., \mathbf{h_n})$ as our input to the CRF layer, and its output is our final prediction label sequence $\mathbf{y} = (y_1, y_2, ..., y_n)$, where y_i is in the set of all possible labels. We denote $\mathcal{Y}(\mathbf{h})$ as the set of all possible label sequences. Then we derive the conditional probability of the output sequence given the input hidden state sequence is

$$p(\mathbf{y}|\mathbf{h}; \mathbf{W}, \mathbf{b}) = \frac{\prod_{i=1}^{n} \exp(\mathbf{W}_{y_{i-1}, y_i}^T \mathbf{h} + \mathbf{b}_{y_{i-1}, y_i})}{\sum_{\mathbf{y}' \in \mathcal{Y}(\mathbf{h})} \prod_{i=1}^{n} \exp(\mathbf{W}_{y'_{i-1}, y'_i}^T \mathbf{h} + \mathbf{b}_{y'_{i-1}, y'_i})}$$

, where $\mathbf{W}$ and $\mathbf{b}$ are the two weight matrices and the subscription indicates that we extract the weight vector for the given label pair (y_{i-1}, y_i).

To train the CRF layer, we use the classic maximum conditional likelihood estimation to train our model. The final log-likelihood with respect to the weight matrices is

$$L(\mathbf{W}, \mathbf{b}) = \sum_{(\mathbf{h_i}, \mathbf{y_i})} \log p(\mathbf{y_i} | \mathbf{h_i}; \mathbf{W}, \mathbf{b})$$

Finally, we adopt the Viterbi algorithm for training the CRF layer and the decoding the optimal output sequence $\mathbf{y}^*$.

4 Experiments

In this section, we discuss the implementation details of our system such as hyper parameter tuning and the initialization of our model parameters. [2]

4.1 Parameter Initialization

For word-level word representation (i.e. the lookup table), we utilize the pretrained word embeddings[3] from GloVe(Pennington et al., 2014). For all out-of-vocabulary words, we assign their embeddings by randomly sampling from range $\left[-\sqrt{\frac{3}{\dim}}, +\sqrt{\frac{3}{\dim}}\right]$, where dim is the dimension of word embeddings, suggested by He et al.(2015). The random initialization of character embeddings are in the same way. We randomly initialize the weight matrices $\mathbf{W}$ and $\mathbf{b}$ with uniform samples from $\left[-\sqrt{\frac{6}{r+c}}, +\sqrt{\frac{6}{r+c}}\right]$, r and c are the number of the rows and columns, following Glorot and Bengio(2010). The weight matrices in LSTM are initialized in the same work while all LSTM hidden states are initialized to be zero except for the bias for the forget gate is initialized to be 1.0 , following Jozefowicz et al.(2015).

4.2 Hyper Parameter Tuning

We tuned the dimension of word-level embeddings from {50, **100**, 200}, character embeddings from {10, **25**, 50}, character BiLSTM hidden states (i.e. the character level word representation) from {20, **50**, 100}. We finally choose the bold ones. The dimension of part-of-speech tags, dependecny roles, word positions and head positions are all 5.

As for learning method, we compare the traditional SGD and Adam (Kingma and Ba, 2014). We found that Adam performs always better than SGD, and we tune the learning rate form {1e-2,**1e-3**,1e-4}.

4.3 Results

To evaluate the effectiveness of each feature in our model, we do the feature ablation experiments and the results are shown in Table 2.

Features	F1 (entity)	F1 (surface form)
Word	37.16	34.15
Char(LSTM)+Word	38.24	37.21
POS+Char(LSTM)+Word	40.01	37.57
Syntactical+Char(CNN)+Word	40.12	37.52
Syntactical+Char(LSTM)+Word	**40.42**	**37.62**

Table 2: Feature Ablation

In comparison with other participants, the results are shown in Table 3.

Team	F1 (entity)	F1 (surface form)
Drexel-CCI	26.30	25.26
MIC-CIS	37.06	34.25
FLYTXT	38.35	36.31
Arcada	39.98	37.77
Ours	**40.42**	**37.62**
SpinningBytes	40.78	39.33
UH-RiTUAL	**41.86**	**40.24**

Table 3: Result comparison

5 Related Work

Conditional random field (CRF) is a most effective approaches (Lafferty et al., 2001; McCallum and Li, 2003) for NER and other sequence labeling tasks and it achieved the state-of-the-art performance previously in Twitter NER (Baldwin et al., 2015). Whereas, it often needs lots of hand-craft features. More recently, Huang et al. (2015) introduced a similar but more complex model based on BiLSTM, which also considers hand-crafted features. Lample et al. (2016) further introduced using BiLSTM to incorporate character-level word representation. Whereas, Ma and Hovy (2016) replace the BiLSTM to CNN to build the character-level word representation. Limsopatham and Collier (2016), used similar model and achieved the best performance in the last shared task (Strauss et al., 2016). Based on the previous work, our system take more syntactical information into account, such as part-of-speech tags, dependency roles, token positions and head positions, which are proven to be effective.

---

[2]The detailed description of the evaluation metric and the dataset are shown in `http://noisy-text.github.io/2017/emerging-rare-entities.html`

[3]`http://nlp.stanford.edu/data/glove.twitter.27B.zip`

6 Conclusion

In this paper, we present a novel multi-channel BiLSTM-CRF model for emerging named entity recognition in social media messages. We find that BiLST-CRF architecture with our proposed comprehensive word representations built from multiple information are effective to overcome the noisy and short nature of social media messages.

References

Isabelle Augenstein, Leon Derczynski, and Kalina Bontcheva. 2017. Generalisation in named entity recognition: A quantitative analysis. *Computer Speech & Language* 44:61–83.

Timothy Baldwin, Young-Bum Kim, Marie Catherine De Marneffe, Alan Ritter, Bo Han, and Wei Xu. 2015. Shared tasks of the 2015 workshop on noisy user-generated text: Twitter lexical normalization and named entity recognition. *ACL-IJCNLP* 126:2015.

Leon Derczynski, Diana Maynard, Giuseppe Rizzo, Marieke van Erp, Genevieve Gorrell, Raphaël Troncy, Johann Petrak, and Kalina Bontcheva. 2015. Analysis of named entity recognition and linking for tweets. *Information Processing & Management* 51(2):32–49.

Kevin Gimpel, Nathan Schneider, Brendan O'Connor, Dipanjan Das, Daniel Mills, Jacob Eisenstein, Michael Heilman, Dani Yogatama, Jeffrey Flanigan, and Noah A Smith. 2011. Part-of-speech tagging for twitter: Annotation, features, and experiments. In *Proceedings of the 49th Annual Meeting of the Association for Computational Linguistics: Human Language Technologies: short papers-Volume 2*. Association for Computational Linguistics, pages 42–47.

Xavier Glorot and Yoshua Bengio. 2010. Understanding the difficulty of training deep feedforward neural networks. In *Proceedings of the Thirteenth International Conference on Artificial Intelligence and Statistics, AISTATS 2010, Chia Laguna Resort, Sardinia, Italy, May 13-15, 2010*. pages 249–256.

Kaiming He, Xiangyu Zhang, Shaoqing Ren, and Jian Sun. 2015. Delving deep into rectifiers: Surpassing human-level performance on imagenet classification. In *2015 IEEE International Conference on Computer Vision, ICCV 2015, Santiago, Chile, December 7-13, 2015*. pages 1026–1034.

Zhiheng Huang, Wei Xu, and Kai Yu. 2015. Bidirectional LSTM-CRF models for sequence tagging. *CoRR* abs/1508.01991.

Rafal Józefowicz, Wojciech Zaremba, and Ilya Sutskever. 2015. An empirical exploration of recurrent network architectures. In *Proceedings of the 32nd International Conference on Machine Learning, ICML 2015, Lille, France, 6-11 July 2015*. pages 2342–2350.

Diederik Kingma and Jimmy Ba. 2014. Adam: A method for stochastic optimization. *arXiv preprint arXiv:1412.6980* .

Lingpeng Kong, Nathan Schneider, Swabha Swayamdipta, Archna Bhatia, Chris Dyer, and Noah A Smith. 2014. A dependency parser for tweets .

John D. Lafferty, Andrew McCallum, and Fernando C. N. Pereira. 2001. Conditional random fields: Probabilistic models for segmenting and labeling sequence data. In *Proceedings of the Eighteenth International Conference on Machine Learning (ICML 2001), Williams College, Williamstown, MA, USA, June 28 - July 1, 2001*. pages 282–289.

Guillaume Lample, Miguel Ballesteros, Sandeep Subramanian, Kazuya Kawakami, and Chris Dyer. 2016. Neural architectures for named entity recognition. In *NAACL HLT 2016, The 2016 Conference of the North American Chapter of the Association for Computational Linguistics: Human Language Technologies, San Diego California, USA, June 12-17, 2016*. pages 260–270.

Nut Limsopatham and Nigel Collier. 2016. Bidirectional lstm for named entity recognition in twitter messages.

Xuezhe Ma and Eduard H. Hovy. 2016. End-to-end sequence labeling via bi-directional lstm-cnns-crf. In *Proceedings of the 54th Annual Meeting of the Association for Computational Linguistics, ACL 2016, August 7-12, 2016, Berlin, Germany, Volume 1: Long Papers*.

Andrew McCallum and Wei Li. 2003. Early results for named entity recognition with conditional random fields, feature induction and web-enhanced lexicons. In *Proceedings of the Seventh Conference on Natural Language Learning, CoNLL 2003, Held in cooperation with HLT-NAACL 2003, Edmonton, Canada, May 31 - June 1, 2003*. pages 188–191. http://aclweb.org/anthology/W/W03/W03-0430.pdf.

Olutobi Owoputi, Brendan O'Connor, Chris Dyer, Kevin Gimpel, Nathan Schneider, and Noah A Smith. 2013. Improved part-of-speech tagging for online conversational text with word clusters. Association for Computational Linguistics.

Jeffrey Pennington, Richard Socher, and Christopher D. Manning. 2014. Glove: Global vectors for word representation. In *EMNLP*.

Benjamin Strauss, Bethany E. Toma, Alan Ritter, Marie-Catherine de Marneffe, and Wei Xu. 2016. Results of the wnut16 named entity recognition shared task.

Yan Xu, Ran Jia, Lili Mou, Ge Li, Yunchuan Chen, Yangyang Lu, and Zhi Jin. 2016. Improved relation classification by deep recurrent neural networks with data augmentation. *arXiv preprint arXiv:1601.03651* .

Boliang Zhang, Hongzhao Huang, Xiaoman Pan, Sujian Li, Chin-Yew Lin, Heng Ji, Kevin Knight, Zhen Wen, Yizhou Sun, Jiawei Han, and Bülent Yener. 2015. Context-aware entity morph decoding. In *Proceedings of the 53rd Annual Meeting of the Association for Computational Linguistics and the 7th International Joint Conference on Natural Language Processing of the Asian Federation of Natural Language Processing, ACL 2015, July 26-31, 2015, Beijing, China, Volume 1: Long Papers.* pages 586–595.

Transfer Learning and Sentence Level Features for Named Entity Recognition on Tweets

Pius von Däniken

SpinningBytes AG

Mark Cieliebak

ZHAW

Abstract

We present our system for the WNUT 2017 Named Entity Recognition challenge on Twitter data. We describe two modifications of a basic neural network architecture for sequence tagging. First, we show how we exploit additional labeled data, where the Named Entity tags differ from the target task. Then, we propose a way to incorporate sentence level features. Our system uses both methods and ranked second for entity level annotations, achieving an F1-score of 40.78, and second for surface form annotations, achieving an F1-score of 39.33.

1 Introduction

Named Entity Recognition (NER) is an important Natural Language Processing task. Its goal is to tag entities such as names of people and locations in text. State-of-the-art systems can achieve F1-scores of up to 92 points on English news texts (Chiu and Nichols, 2015). Achieving good performance on more complex domains such as user generated texts on social media is still a hard problem. The best system submitted for the WNUT 2016 shared task achieved an F1-score of 52.41 on English Twitter data (Strauss et al., 2016).

In this work, we present our submission for the WNUT 2017 shared task on "Novel and Emerging Entity Recognition" (Derczynski et al., 2017). We extend a basic neural network architecture for sequence tagging (Chiu and Nichols, 2015; Collobert et al., 2011) by incorporating sentence level feature vectors and exploiting additional labeled data for transfer learning. We build on and take inspiration from recent work from (Falkner et al.,

2017; Sileo et al., 2017) on NER for French Twitter data (Lopez et al., 2017).

Our submitted solution reached an F1-score of 41.76 for entity level annotations and 57.98 on surface form annotations. This places us second on entity level annotations, where the best system achieved an F1-score of 41.90, and fourth on surface form annotations, where the best system achieved an F1-score of 66.59.

2 System Description

Our solution is based on a sequence labeling system that uses a bidirectional LSTM (Hochreiter and Schmidhuber, 1997) which extracts features for training a Conditional Random Field (Sutton and McCallum, 2012). We apply a transfer learning approach, since previous research has shown that this can improve sequence labeling systems (Yang et al., 2017). More precisely, we modify the base system to allow for joint training on the WNUT 2016 corpus (Strauss et al., 2016), which uses a different tag set than our target task. In addition, we extend the system to incorporate sentence level feature vectors. All these methods are combined to build the system that we used for our submission to the WNUT 2017 shared task. Figure 1 shows an overview of the different architectures, which are described in detail in the following sections.

2.1 Basic Sequence Labeling System

Figure 1a shows an overview of our base system. We use a bidirectional Long Short Term Memory network (LSTM) (Hochreiter and Schmidhuber, 1997) to learn the potential function for a linear chain Conditional Random Field (CRF) (Sutton and McCallum, 2012) to predict a sequence of Named Entity tags $y_{1:T}$ from a sequence of feature vectors $x_{1:T}$. This is based on an architecture previously used in (Chiu and Nichols, 2015), which

Proceedings of the 3rd Workshop on Noisy User-generated Text, pages 166–171
Copenhagen, Denmark, September 7, 2017. ©2017 Association for Computational Linguistics

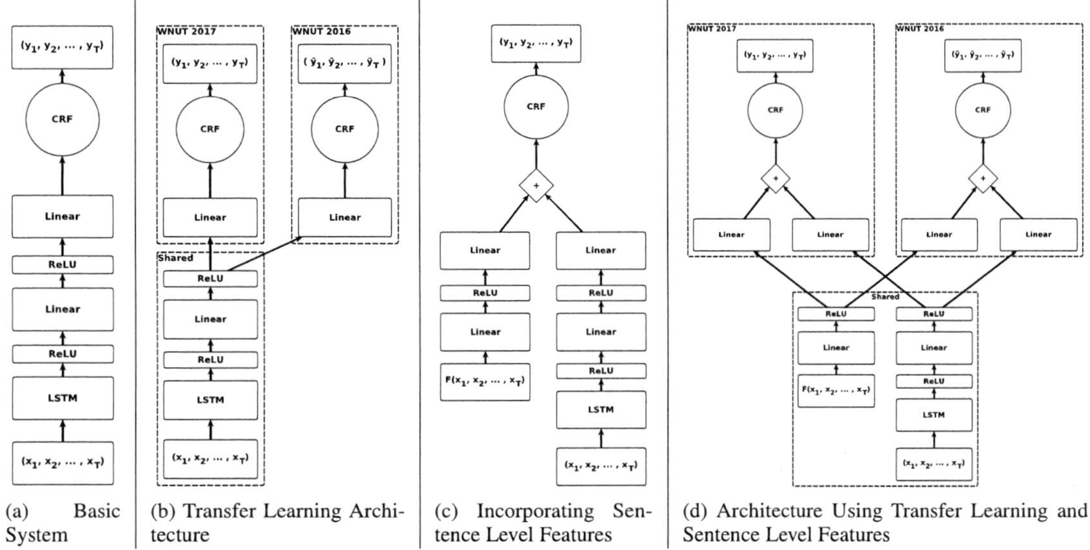

(a) Basic System   (b) Transfer Learning Architecture   (c) Incorporating Sentence Level Features   (d) Architecture Using Transfer Learning and Sentence Level Features

Figure 1: Overview Of The Different Network Architectures Used

achieved state-of-the-art performance for Named Entity Recognition on the English CoNLL 2003 data set (Tjong Kim Sang and De Meulder, 2003).

Bidirectional LSTM: For every word in w_t in a given input sentence $w_{1:T}$, we first compute a feature vector x_t, which is the concatenation of all the word level features described in Section 2.5. The sequence of feature vectors $x_{1:T}$ is then fed to a bidirectional LSTM. The output of both the forward and backward LSTM are concatenated to get $o_{1:T}$, which get passed through a Rectified Linear Unit, ($ReLU$) (Nair and Hinton, 2010). Every $o_t \in o_{1:T}$ then gets passed through a fully connected feed-forward network with one hidden layer and $ReLU$ activation: $s_t = W_2 \, relu(W_1 o_t + b_1) + b_2$. Let N_{tags} be the number of possible NER-tags, d_o the dimension of o_t and d_h the dimension of the hidden layer. The resulting vector $s_t \in \mathbb{R}^{N_{tags}}$ represents a score for every possible tag y at time step t. The values $W_1 \in \mathbb{R}^{d_h \times d_o}$, $b_1 \in \mathbb{R}^{d_h}$, $W_2 \in \mathbb{R}^{N_{tags} \times d_h}$ and $b_2 \in \mathbb{R}^{N_{tags}}$ are weights of the feed-forward network.

Conditional Random Field: A linear chain CRF models the conditional probability of an output sequence $y_{1:T}$ given an input sequence $x_{1:T}$ as:

$$p\left(y_{1:T}|x_{1:T}\right) = \frac{1}{Z(x_{1:T})} \prod_{t=1}^{T} e^{\phi(y_{t-1},y_t,x_{1:T},t,\Theta)} \quad (1)$$

where $Z\left(x_{1:T}\right)$ is a normalization constant:

$$Z\left(x_{1:T}\right) = \sum_{\forall y_{1:T}} \prod_{t=1}^{T} e^{\phi(y_{t-1},y_t,x_{1:T},t,\Theta)} \quad (2)$$

ϕ is a potential function parametrized by a set of parameters Θ. In our case we use:

$$\phi\left(y_{t-1}, y_t, x_{1:T}, t, \Theta = \{\theta, A\}\right) = \\ s_{\theta,y_t,t}\left(x_{1:T}\right) + A_{y_{t-1},y_t} \quad (3)$$

Let θ be the parameters of the network described above. Then $s_{\theta,y_t,t}\left(x_{1:T}\right)$ is the score that the network parametrized by θ outputs for tag y_t at time step t given the input sequence $x_{1:T}$. $A \in \mathbb{R}^{N_{tags} \times N_{tags}}$ is a matrix such that $A_{i,j}$ is the score of transitioning from tag i to tag j.

Training: During training we try to maximize the likelihood of the true tag sequence $y_{1:T}$ given the input feature vectors $x_{1:T}$. We use the Adam (Kingma and Ba, 2014) algorithm to optimize the parameters $\Theta = \{\theta, A\}$. Additionally we perform gradient clipping (Pascanu et al., 2012) and apply dropout (Srivastava et al., 2014) to the LSTM outputs $o_{1:T}$. The neural network parameters θ are randomly initialized from a normal distribution with mean zero and variance according to (Glorot and Bengio, 2010) (normal Glorot initialization). The transition scores A are initialized from a uniform distribution with mean zero and variance according to (Glorot and Bengio, 2010), (uniform Glorot initialization).

167

2.2 Transfer Learning

In this setting we use the WNUT 2016 corpus (Strauss et al., 2016) as an additional source of labeled data. The idea is to train the upper layers of the neural network on both datasets to improve its generalization ability. It was shown in (Yang et al., 2017) that this can improve the system performance. Figure 1b gives an overview of our transfer learning architecture.

Modified Architecture: We share all network layers except for the last linear projection to get separate tag scores for each data set:

$$s_t^{2016} = W_2^{2016} relu(W_1 o_t + b_1) + b_2^{2016}$$
$$s_t^{2017} = W_2^{2017} relu(W_1 o_t + b_1) + b_2^{2017} \quad (4)$$

The resulting tag scores get fed to separate CRFs, which have separate transition matrices A^{2016} and A^{2017}.

Training: During training we alternately use a batch from each dataset and backpropagate the loss of the corresponding CRF.

2.3 Incorporating Sentence Level Features

Figure 1c shows how we include sentence level features into our architecture. In this setting we take an additional feature vector $f_{sent} = F(x_{1:T}) \in \mathbb{R}^{d_{sent}}$ for each input sentence $x_{1:T}$.

Modified Architecture: We use an additional feed-forward network to extract tag scores $s_{sent} \in \mathbb{R}^{N_{tags}}$ from the sentence feature vector f_{sent}:

$$s_{sent} = W_{2,sent} \, relu\left(W_{1,sent} f_{sent} + b_{1,sent}\right) + b_{2,sent}$$

The dimensions used are: $W_{1,sent} \in \mathbb{R}^{d_{h,sent} \times d_{sent}}$, $b_{1,sent} \in \mathbb{R}^{d_{h,sent}}$, $W_{2,sent} \in \mathbb{R}^{N_{tags} \times d_{h,sent}}$ and $b_{2,sent} \in \mathbb{R}^{N_{tags}}$. The value $d_{h,sent}$ is the dimension of the hidden layer of the feed-forward network. Let $s_{1:T,word}$ be the scores that the basic network described in Section 2.1 outputs for sequence $x_{1:T}$. To get the final scores $s_{1:T}$ fed to the CRF we add s_{sent} to every $s_{t,word} \in s_{1:T,word}$: $s_t = s_{sent} + s_{t,word}$.

2.4 Combined System

The combined system adds the sentence level features to the transfer learning architecture. We share all layers except the linear projections to tag scores for both sentence features and word features in a manner analogous to Sections 2.2 and 2.3. The resulting architecture is shown in Figure 1d.

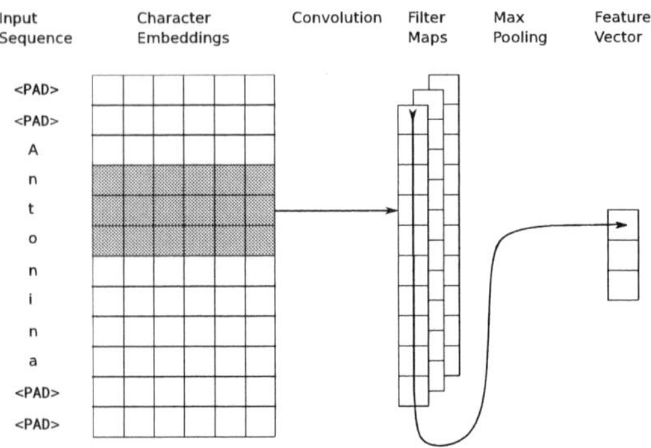

Figure 2: Neural Network used to extract character level features

2.5 Features

Word Embeddings: We use the FastText (Bojanowski et al., 2016) library to compute word embeddings. We train the model on a corpus of 200 million tweets and all tweets from the WNUT 2016 and WNUT 2017 corpora. The vocabulary contains all words occurring at least 10 times. Other parameters use the default values set by the library [1]. In particular, the size of the context window is set to 5 and the embedding dimension is 100.

This results in an embedding matrix $E_{word} \in \mathbb{R}^{N_{vocab} \times 100}$, where N_{vocab} is the number of unique tokens in the WNUT 2016 and WNUT 2017 corpora. FastText predicts embedding vectors for words that were out-of-vocabulary during training by considering character n-grams of the word. The embedding matrix E_{word} is not updated during training.

Word Capitalization Features: Following (Chiu and Nichols, 2015) we add explicit capitalization features, since capitalization information is lost during word embedding lookups. The 6 feature options are: *all capitalized, uppercase initial, all lower cased, mixed capitalization, emoji* and *other*. An embedding matrix $E_{wordCap} \in \mathbb{R}^{6 \times d_{wordCap}}$ is used to feed these features to the network and updated during training via backpropagation. $E_{wordCap}$ is initialized using normal Glorot initialization.

Character Convolution Features: A convolutional neural network is used to extract additional character level features. Its architecture is shown in Figure 2. First, we add special padding tokens

---

[1] https://github.com/facebookresearch/fastText

168

on both sides of the character sequence w, to extend it to a target length, $l_{w,max}$. If there is an odd number of paddings, the additional padding is added on the right. For sequences longer than $l_{w,max}$, only the first $l_{w,max}$ characters are used. An embedding matrix $E_{char} \in \mathbb{R}^{N_c \times d_c}$ maps characters to $\mathbb{R}^{d_c}$ vectors. N_c is the number of unique characters in the dataset with the addition of the padding token.

Using E_{char}, we embed the padded sequence w and get $C_w \in \mathbb{R}^{l_{w,max} \times d_c}$. A set of m convolution filters $\in \mathbb{R}^{d_c \times h}$ is then applied to C_w. This results in m feature maps $M_i \in \mathbb{R}^{l_{w,max}-h+1}$, which are passed through a $ReLU$ activation. The final feature vector $F \in \mathbb{R}^m$ is attained by max pooling, such that $F_i = \max M_i$.

The embedding matrix is initialized using uniform Glorot initialization. The m convolution filters are initialized using normal Glorot initialization.

Character Capitalization Convolution Features: Analogous to the word capitalization features, we use additional character capitalization features. The feature options are: *upper*, *lower*, *punctuation*, *numeric* and *other*. We apply a neural network with the same architecture as described above to extract the final character capitalization feature vector.

Sentence Embeddings: In (Pagliardini et al., 2017) the authors introduce sent2vec, a new method for computing sentence embeddings. They show that these embeddings provide improved performance for several downstream tasks.

To train the sent2vec model, we use the same training set as the one used for word embeddings and we use default values for all the model parameters[2]. In particular, the resulting sentence feature vectors are in $\mathbb{R}^{100}$.

3 Experiments

We implemented the system described in Section 2.4 using the Tensorflow framework [3].

We monitored the systems performance during training and aborted experiments that had an F1-score of less than 40 after two epochs (evaluated on the development set). We let successful experiments run for the full 6 epochs (cf. Section 3.2). For the submission to WNUT 2017, we ran 6 successful experiments and submitted the one which

Parameter	Value
$l_{w,max}$	30
N_{tags} WNUT 2016	21
N_{tags} WNUT 2017	13
$d_{wordCap}$	6
d_c	15
LSTM hidden units	64
$d_{h,word}$	128
$d_{h,sent}$	128
m	10
h	3
Dropout rate	0.3
Learning Rate	0.003
Gradient Clip Norm	2
Batch size	100
Number of epochs	6

Table 1: Model Parameters

had the highest entity level F1-score on the development set.

3.1 Preprocessing

Tokenization: Since the WNUT 2016 and WNUT 2017 corpora are in the CoNLL format, they are already tokenized. To tokenize the additional tweets used for training word and sentence embeddings (cf. Section 2.5), we use the Twitter tokenizer provided by the Python NLTK library [4].

Token Substitution: We perform some simple pattern-based token substitutions. To normalize Twitter user handles, we substitute every word starting with an @ character by a special user token. Similarly, all words starting with the prefix *http* are replaced by a url token. Finally, for words longer than one character, we remove up to one initial # character.

3.2 Model Parameters

Table 1 shows the parameters used for training the model.

3.3 Experiments Performed After The Submission

Following the submission, we conducted additional experiments to investigate the influence of the transfer learning approach and sent2vec features on the system performance.

---

[2]https://github.com/epfml/sent2vec
[3]https://www.tensorflow.org/

[4]http://www.nltk.org/api/nltk.tokenize.html#module-nltk.tokenize.casual

	Precision (%)		Recall (%)		F1	
	Mean	Stddev	Mean	Stddev	Mean	Stddev
Surface Forms	45.55	0.47	34.94	0.87	39.54	0.55
Entities Overall	47.23	0.55	36.33	0.83	41.06	0.52
Corporation	8.81	0.99	10.86	1.62	9.70	1.14
Creative Work	22.41	2.55	11.03	1.50	14.73	1.73
Group	39.27	7.47	9.49	2.20	15.13	2.86
Location	58.55	2.88	47.11	1.79	52.12	0.66
Person	57.82	1.60	63.60	1.10	60.55	0.84
Product	22.47	2.17	7.87	1.93	11.60	2.38

Table 2: Aggregated performance of all experiments, run before the submission, evaluated on the test set

	Precision (%)	Recall (%)	F1
Surface Forms	45.47	34.66	39.33
Entities Overall	47.09	35.96	40.78
Corporation	8.24	11.67	9.66
Creative Work	21.92	11.76	15.31
Group	31.71	9.22	14.29
Location	58.95	44.80	50.91
Person	57.67	61.97	59.74
Product	20.00	5.13	8.16

Table 3: Performance of the submitted annotations evaluated on the test set

For each of the 4 systems described in Section 2, we ran 6 experiments. We use the same parameters as shown in Section 3.2.

4 Results

Table 2 shows precision, recall and F1-score of our system. We compute the mean and standard deviations over the 6 successful experiments we considered for submission (cf. Section 3). Table 3 shows the breakdown of the performance of the annotations we submitted for the WNUT 2017 shared task.

Table 4 shows the performance of the different subsystems proposed in Section 2. We report the mean and standard deviation over the 6 experiments we performed after submission, for every system.

All reported scores were computed using the evaluation script provided by the task organizers.

5 Discussion

From table 4 we can see that using sent2vec features increases precision and decreases recall slightly, leading to an overall lower performance compared to the basic system. The transfer learning system shows a more substantial decrease in precision and increase in recall and overall per-

forms best out of the 4 systems. Combination of the two approaches is counterproductive and outperforms the basic system only slightly.

During training we observed that restarting experiments as described in Section 3 was only necessary when using sent2vec features.

One weakness of our transfer learning setting is that the two datasets we used have almost identical samples and only differ in their annotations. The WNUT 2016 corpus uses 10 entity classes: *company*, *facility*, *Geo location*, *movie*, *music artist*, *other*, *person*, *product*, *sports team*, and *TV show*. Further work is needed to study the effect of using an unrelated data set for transfer learning.

6 Conclusion

We described a deep learning approach for Named Entity Recognition on Twitter data, which extends a basic neural network for sequence tagging by using sentence level features and transfer learning. Our approach achieved 2nd place at the WNUT 2017 shared task for Named Entity Recognition, obtaining an F1-score of 40.78.

For future work, we plan to explore the power of transfer learning for NER in more depth. For instance, it would be interesting to see how annotated NER data for other languages or other text types affects the system performance.

References

Piotr Bojanowski, Edouard Grave, Armand Joulin, and Tomas Mikolov. 2016. Enriching word vectors with subword information. *ArXiv e-prints* https://arxiv.org/abs/1607.04606.

Jason P. C. Chiu and Eric Nichols. 2015. Named Entity Recognition with Bidirectional LSTM-CNNs. *ArXiv e-prints* https://arxiv.org/abs/1511.08308.

Ronan Collobert, Jason Weston, Léon Bottou, Michael Karlen, Koray Kavukcuoglu, and Pavel Kuksa. 2011. Natural language processing (almost) from scratch. *Journal of Machine Learning Research* 12:2493–2537.

Leon Derczynski, Eric Nichols, Marieke van Erp, and Nut Limsopatham. 2017. Results of the WNUT2017 Shared Task on Novel and Emerging Entity Recognition. In *Proceedings of the 3rd Workshop on Noisy, User-generated Text (W-NUT) at EMNLP*. ACL.

Nicole Falkner, Stefano Dolce, Pius von Däniken, and Mark Cieliebak. 2017. Swiss Chocolate at CAp 2017 NER challenge: Partially annotated data and

	Entities						Surface Forms					
	Precision (%)		Recall (%)		F1		Precision (%)		Recall (%)		F1	
	Mean	Stddev	Mean	Stddev	Mean	Stddev	Mean	Stddev	Mean	Stddev	Mean	Stddev
Basic System	58.77	3.72	32.47	1.23	41.74	0.70	56.53	3.80	30.75	1.37	39.73	0.71
Transfer Learning	48.17	1.34	**37.55**	1.43	**42.16**	0.52	46.31	1.31	**35.86**	1.51	**40.38**	0.62
Sent2Vec Features	**59.51**	1.73	30.91	0.52	40.67	0.41	**57.30**	1.98	29.20	0.58	38.66	0.46
Combined System	50.41	3.19	36.04	2.10	41.88	0.69	48.60	3.00	34.50	2.36	40.20	0.99

Table 4: Performance of the different subsystems evaluated on the test set, after the submission

transfer learning. Conférence sur l'Apprentissage Automatique.

Xavier Glorot and Yoshua Bengio. 2010. Understanding the difficulty of training deep feedforward neural networks. In *Proceedings of the Thirteenth International Conference on Artificial Intelligence and Statistics*. PMLR, Chia Laguna Resort, Italy, volume 9 of *Proceedings of Machine Learning Research*, pages 249–256.

Sepp Hochreiter and Jürgen Schmidhuber. 1997. Long short-term memory. *Neural Comput.* 9(8):1735–1780.

Diederik P. Kingma and Jimmy Ba. 2014. Adam: A Method for Stochastic Optimization. *ArXiv e-prints* https://arxiv.org/abs/1412.6980.

Cdric Lopez, Ioannis Partalas, Georgios Balikas, Nadia Derbas, Amlie Martin, Coralie Reutenauer, Frdrique Segond, and Massih-Reza Amini. 2017. French named entity recognition in twitter challenge. Technical report.

Vinod Nair and Geoffrey E. Hinton. 2010. Rectified linear units improve restricted boltzmann machines. In *Proceedings of the 27th International Conference on Machine Learning (ICML-10)*. Omnipress, pages 807–814.

Matteo Pagliardini, Prakhar Gupta, and Martin Jaggi. 2017. Unsupervised Learning of Sentence Embeddings using Compositional n-Gram Features. *ArXiv e-prints* https://arxiv.org/abs/1703.02507.

Razvan Pascanu, Tomas Mikolov, and Yoshua Bengio. 2012. On the difficulty of training Recurrent Neural Networks. *ArXiv e-prints* https://arxiv.org/abs/1211.5063.

Damien Sileo, Camille Pradel, Philippe Muller, and Tim Van de Cruys. 2017. Synapse at CAp 2017 NER challenge: Fasttext crf. Conférence sur l'Apprentissage Automatique.

Nitish Srivastava, Geoffrey Hinton, Alex Krizhevsky, Ilya Sutskever, and Ruslan Salakhutdinov. 2014. Dropout: A simple way to prevent neural networks from overfitting. *J. Mach. Learn. Res.* 15(1):1929–1958.

Benjamin Strauss, Bethany E. Toma, Alan Ritter, Marie-Catherine de Marneffe, and Wei Xu. 2016. Results of the WNUT16 named entity recognition shared task. In *The 2nd Workshop on Noisy User-generated Text*. pages 138–144.

Charles Sutton and Andrew McCallum. 2012. An introduction to conditional random fields. *Found. Trends Mach. Learn.* 4(4):267–373.

Erik F. Tjong Kim Sang and Fien De Meulder. 2003. Introduction to the CoNLL-2003 shared task: Language-independent named entity recognition. In *Proceedings of the Seventh Conference on Natural Language Learning at HLT-NAACL 2003 - Volume 4*. Association for Computational Linguistics, Stroudsburg, PA, USA, CONLL '03, pages 142–147.

Zhilin Yang, Ruslan Salakhutdinov, and William W. Cohen. 2017. Transfer Learning for Sequence Tagging with Hierarchical Recurrent Networks. *ArXiv e-prints* https://arxiv.org/abs/1703.06345.

Context-Sensitive Recognition for Emerging and Rare Entities

Jake Ryland Williams and **Giovanni C. Santia**
College of Computing and Informatics, Drexel University
30 North 33rd Street, Philadelphia PA, 19104
`{jw3477,gs495}@drexel.edu`

Abstract

We present a novel named entity recognition (NER) system, and its participation in the Emerging and Rare Entity Recognition shared task, hosted at the 2017 EMNLP Workshop on Noisy User Generated Text (W-NUT). With a specialized evaluation highlighting performance on rare, and sparsely-occurring named entities, this task provided an excellent opportunity to build out a newly-developed statistical algorithm and benchmark it against the state-of-the-art. Powered by flexible context features of word forms, our system's capacity for identifying never-before-seen entities made it well suited for the task. Since the system was only developed to recognize a limited number of named entity types, its performance was lower overall. However, performance was competitive on the categories trained, indicating potential for future development.

1   Introduction

NER is a common foundational step for many pipelines that rely on natural language processing (NLP). The main goal is the identification of mentions of entities (e.g., persons or locations). As a pre-processing task for unstructured text, NER may, for example, provide index keywords for information retrieval systems (Tjong Kim Sang and De Meulder, 2003), or topic-rich features for machine learning (ML) applications (Kumaran and Allan, 2004; Vavliakis et al., 2013). Effective approaches to NER have long utilized conditional random fields (Lafferty et al., 2001), support vector machines (McCallum and Li, 2003), and perceptrons (Settles, 2004; Ju et al., 2011; Luo et al., 2015). In addition to relying on face-value, gold-standard data, systems may benefit from a variety of other data representations and sources (Strauss et al., 2016), including gazetteers, word classes (e.g, Brown clusters), orthographic features, and grammatical relations between types of words, such as part of speech. Large-scale annotated resources for NER have also been developed in semi-supervised fashions, constructed from online encyclopedias (Nothman et al., 2008, 2012) and refined by crowdsourcing (Bos et al., 2017).

While NER systems have been in development for some time, their applicability to noisy-text domains (i.e., unedited, user-generated content) is somewhat limited. This is a multi-faceted problem (Derczynski et al., 2015), involving grammatical inconsistency and rapidly-shifting domains, requiring specialized algorithms. While progress has been made through annotation and specialized systems development (Ritter et al., 2011), there are still large gains to be made for this domain (Augenstein et al., 2017), which is highlighted well by both the shared task at the W-NUT this year (Strauss et al., 2016), and that of the previous year.

Adaptation to the task domain's wide-range of writing styles and abundant grammatical inconsistencies presents the need for algorithmic flexibility. These properties make precision loss an issue, and the presence of rare and emerging entities makes recall an extreme challenge, too. Our participation in the present shared task relies on a novel approach: utilizing flexible "contexts" as features - derived from token forms - alone. We rely upon these features for their capacity to relate to never-before-seen tokens as potential entities, and incorporate them into a statistical model that can handle both gold-standard data and large, lexical resources.

Proceedings of the 3rd Workshop on Noisy User-generated Text, pages 172–176
Copenhagen, Denmark, September 7, 2017. ©2017 Association for Computational Linguistics

2 Approach

2.1 Shared Task Data

We began our approach by scoping the task data set composition. There were 6 named entity types: corporation, creative work, group, location, person, and product, which were a mapping down from 10 in the 2016 W-NUT Twitter NER Shared Task. A decomposition of the current shared task data (see Tab. 1) exhibits several important features. The proportion of unique entities out of all increased from about 80% to 90% from the training to the development and test sets. However, the training, development, and test sets all exhibited internal stability in the proportions of unique numbers for each type of named entity. In other words, no named entity type dropped out of proportion when considering unique forms. However, the focus on rare entities resulted in large increases in the percentage of the data occupied by the person category. These proportions and the availability of large-scale gazetteer data highlighted this type for the initial focus of our model's development.

2.2 System Design

2.2.1 Previous Work

Context models are conditional statistical models whose features are derived from the structural patterns surrounding or within written language. We refer to context models that rely on exterior information as **external** context models, and those that rely on interior information as **internal** context models. For example, word-level context models applied to the text: "Out to lunch in New York City." might place the entity "New York City" in the external context "Out to lunch in *.", or the internal context "New York *" (in each case reserving * as a wildcard).

Context models trace their roots to Shannon (1948), but have likewise seen recent attention (Piantadosi et al., 2011). They have been applied to both patterns of character appearance and word appearance, with the majority of attention directed towards word patterns and external models. In recent work by Williams et al. (2015a), an internal context model was used to identify missing multi-word dictionary entries. We utilize this model here, but apply it at the character level so as to be able to identify both single snd multi-word named entities.

2.2.2 Context-Sensitive NER

We represent a token, w, by its sequence of n characters:

$$w = (l_1, l_2, \cdots, l_n),$$

and define its set of 2^{n-1} contexts, C_w by the corresponding removal patterns of contiguous subsequences. The context, $c_{i \cdots j} \in C_w$, defined by the removal of characters i through j is:

$$c_{i \cdots j} = (l_1, \cdots, l_{i-1}, *, \cdots, *, l_{j+1}, \cdots, l_n).$$

Despite execution at the sub-word level, this is precisely the same construction as in Williams et al. (2015a), which was used to compute likelihoods of dictionary definition.

For a given word, weighting across its contexts is accomplished as in Williams et al. (2015a), induced by a partition process (Williams et al., 2015b). However instead of dictionary definition, we use the context conditional probabilities to determine the likelihoods of named entity tags. For any word, w, and positive tag, t (e.g., B-location, I-person, B-group, etc.), a computed likelihood, $L(t|C_w)$, can be interpreted as "the likelihood of drawing a t-tagged word from the contexts of w". Note that these likelihoods can be non-zero for words that were not present in training, and are higher for words that are similar to tagged words. For example, if $w_1 = $ *Larry*, $w_2 = $ *Harry*, and only w_1 appeared in a gold standard, with tag $t = $ B-person, $L(t|C_{w_2})$ would be elevated.

2.2.3 Entity Recognition

To handle entities composed of multiple words, e.g., $(w_1, w_2, \cdots, w_k)$, we assess a potential entity's membership to a particular type, e.g., "location", via the harmonic mean, $\overline{L}(t_1, t_2, \cdots, t_k|w_1, w_2, \cdots, w_k)$, of their component-word likelihood values, such that only the first word has the B-version tag (t_1) and all others have the I-version. A candidate is accepted if its likelihood mean is above a thresholds value, which is determined in optimization (see Sec. 4).

2.2.4 Conflict Resolution

A given word may fall within multiple predicted entities, both of different types and lengths. To resolve potential conflicts between predicted entities we establish precedence by accepting 1) predictions appearing first, over 2) longer predictions, over 3) predictions of higher likelihood.

Category	Training		Development		Test	
	Total (%)	Unique (%)	Total (%)	Unique (%)	Total (%)	Unique (%)
Corporation	221 (11.19)	140 (8.73)	34 (4.07)	32 (4.29)	69 (6.63)	63 (6.82)
Creative Work	140 (7.09)	127 (7.92)	105 (12.57)	101 (13.54)	141 (13.54)	135 (14.61)
Group	264 (13.37)	231 (14.4)	39 (4.67)	38 (5.09)	151 (14.51)	131 (14.18)
Location	538 (27.75)	434 (27.06)	74 (8.86)	68 (9.12)	138 (13.26)	114 (12.34)
Person	660 (33.42)	546 (34.04)	469 (56.17)	398 (53.35)	441 (39.77)	363 (39.29)
Product	142 (7.19)	126 (7.86)	114 (13.65)	109 (14.61)	128 (12.3)	118 (12.77)
All	1975	1604	835	746	1041	924

Table 1: Description of shared-task data. Each of the **Training**, **Development**, and **Test** data are broken down by types of named entities (**Corporation** , **Creative Work**, **Group**, **Location**, **Person**, and **Product**), with counts and percents for the **Unique** and **Total** named entity forms present, in addition to total numbers of **All** named entities present.

3   Materials

3.1   Gold-Standard Data

In addition to the gold-standard data provided for the shared task (see Sec. 2.1 and Tab. 1) we utilize 1) all components of the W-NUT 2016 Twitter NER shared task (Strauss et al., 2016), 2) all components of the 2003 CONLL NER shared task (Tjong Kim Sang and De Meulder, 2003), 3) the WikiNER annotations (Nothman et al., 2008, 2012), and 4) the Groningen Meaning Bank (Bos et al., 2017). Each corpus required mapping its entity types to the six 2017 shared task types, and for data sets (2), (3), and (4), only mappings for the location and person types were deemed appropriate (geo-loc, facility, and loc to location, and per to person). However for data set (1), additional mappings were accepted from tvshow and movie to creative-work, sportsteam to group, and company to corporation.

3.2   Supplemental Lexica

To extend model training to as many forms as possible, supplemental lexica were incorporated from the gazetteer materials provided alongside the gold data from the W-NUT 2016 Twitter NER shared task. Only several gazetteers were incorporated into the final model: automotive.model and business.consumer_product for the product type; firstname.5k, lastname.5000, people.family_name, and people.person.filtered for the person type; and location.country for the location type. Each entry in a given gazetteer was treated as a weighted instance of its named entity type. Weights offset the extreme size of gazetteers in comparison to the gold standard data, and were determined as follows. For a given entity type, let x be the number of typed named entities in the gold standard training data, and y be the number of gazetteer entries. The type's gazetteer entries were then incor-porated with weight x/y, and all O-tagged tokens were counted with weight 2.

4   Optimization

Model development consisted of training on the gold-standard training data (see Sec. 2.1), in addition to the external gold standards (see Sec. 3.1), and the supplemental lexica (see Sec. 3.2). With the trained model, optimization was performed with respect to the development data set, which notably had a disproportionate representation of person entities. We determined thresholds for each of the entity types through separate optimizations. Given the brief timeline, these were conducted adaptively, optimizing thresholds for by-type F_1 values, honing in by step sizes of 0.1, 0.01, and finally 0.001. Note that the optimization procedure exhibited no predictive power on entity types creating work and corporation, leading us to restrain our model from predicting those types. After final threshold parameters were determined, a final combined model (see Sec. 2.2.4) was allowed to train additionally on the development data set before being applied to the final test data set.

5   Results

To understand our model's performance in the context of other systems, we provide a fine-grained system evaluation across the entity types (see Tab. 2). This follows the specialized shared-task evaluation method, focusing on precision, recall, and F_1 with respect to unique named entity surface forms. On the primary categories in which our model made predictions (location and person), our model's performance was reasonably competitive, with high levels of precision. At location, our system outperformed two other models by overall F_1, and was in range of the other models with respect to the person type. For all other entity types,

Category	Arcada	Drexel-CCI	FLYTXT	MIC-CIS	SJTU-Adapt	SpinningBytes	UH Ritual
Precision							
Corporation	20.37	0	25.00	12.86	26.67	10.59	38.89
Creative Work	37.21	0	33.33	23.64	60.00	26.03	35.71
Group	35.29	0	26.47	25.00	31.65	31.71	39.34
Location	39.04	58.21	33.33	36.21	34.48	61.05	52.34
Person	54.90	49.58	61.15	46.76	64.83	55.94	68.46
Product	25.00	25.00	16.67	18.03	21.15	16.67	28.21
All	43.93	50.64	43.52	36.82	46.36	45.33	55.18
Recall							
Corporation	32.83	0	12.70	14.29	19.05	14.29	22.22
Creative Work	11.85	0	12.59	9.63	2.22	14.07	7.41
Group	18.32	0	13.85	20.61	19.08	9.92	18.32
Location	49.57	33.91	44.35	54.78	52.17	50.43	48.70
Person	50.82	32.42	49.73	45.60	51.65	62.09	48.90
Product	9.32	0.85	6.78	9.32	9.32	4.24	9.32
All	32.83	17.06	30.45	31.21	32.29	35.64	31.64
F1							
Corporation	18.80	0	16.84	13.53	22.22	12.16	28.28
Creative Work	17.98	0	18.28	13.68	4.29	18.27	12.27
Group	24.12	0	17.09	26.87	23.81	15.12	25.00
Location	43.68	42.86	38.06	43.60	41.52	55.24	50.45
Person	52.78	39.2	54.85	46.18	57.49	58.85	57.05
Product	13.58	1.64	9.64	12.29	12.94	6.76	14.01
All	37.58	25.53	35.83	33.78	38.06.86	39.90	40.22

Table 2: Shared-task results. All precision, recall, and F_1 values are computed with respect to unique entity forms, in accordance with the task specific evaluation.

our system performed poorly (although no predictions were made for the corporation and creative work categories). Notably, the only categories at which other teams performed consistently well were the person and location categories, with the main observation being low recall, rarely above 20%.

6 Discussion

For this shared task we developed and evaluated a novel NER algorithm that relies only on features derived from word forms. Despite having the lowest task evaluation scores, this model exhibited competitive performance at two of the largest categories. These two categories (person and location) had significant external data availabile (both gold standards and supplemental lexica), and exhibited the most promise during model optimization. The system's ability to perform competitively at these entity types appears to suggest that increased performance at the other types may be possible with the availability of other, category-specific and large-scale external resources.

We note that our model's optimization exhibited an extreme lack of predictive power at the corporation and creative work categories, which, in addition to being affected by sparsity, may have also been affected by the lack of acceptable mappings from the external gold-standard resources into these categories. While lexical data were weighted to good effect (increased performance), the coverage of gold standard data only over the person and location entity types may have negatively impacted our system's ability to predict other types. Thus, a potential improvement for prediction of these types might be accomplished by applying a similar weighting scheme to the external gold-standard data. This leaves us with avenues for improvement, along with competitive, task-specific scores at the person and location categories; all of this, while relying on features derived only from word forms, points toward value in the continued development of context-sensitive NER for rare and emerging entities.

Acknowledgments

The authors thank the shared-task organizers for their efforts in running this event, the anonymous reviewers for their thoughtful comments, and greatfully acknowledge support from the Drexel University College of Computing and Informatics and Department of Information Science.

References

Isabelle Augenstein, Leon Derczynski, and Kalina Bontcheva. 2017. Generalisation in named entity recognition: A quantitative analysis. *Computer Speech & Language* 44:61–83. https://doi.org/https://doi.org/10.1016/j.csl.2017.01.012.

Johan Bos, Valerio Basile, Kilian Evang, Noortje J. Venhuizen, and Johannes Bjerva. 2017. *The Groningen Meaning Bank*, Springer Netherlands, Dordrecht, pages 463–496. https://doi.org/10.1007/978-94-024-0881-2_18.

Leon Derczynski, Diana Maynard, Giuseppe Rizzo, Marieke van Erp, Genevieve Gorrell, Raphal Troncy, Johann Petrak, and Kalina Bontcheva. 2015. Analysis of named entity recognition and linking for tweets. *Information Processing & Management* 51(2):32 – 49. https://doi.org/http://dx.doi.org/10.1016/j.ipm.2014.10.006.

Zhenfei Ju, Jian Wang, and Fei Zhu. 2011. Named entity recognition from biomedical text using svm. In *Bioinformatics and Biomedical Engineering,(iCBBE) 2011 5th International Conference on*. IEEE, pages 1–4.

Giridhar Kumaran and James Allan. 2004. Text classification and named entities for new event detection. In *Proceedings of the 27th Annual International ACM SIGIR Conference on Research and Development in Information Retrieval*. ACM, New York, NY, USA, SIGIR '04, pages 297–304. https://doi.org/10.1145/1008992.1009044.

John Lafferty, Andrew McCallum, and Fernando Pereira. 2001. Conditional random fields: Probabilistic models for segmenting and labeling sequence data. In *Proceedings of International Conference on Machine Learning (ICML)*. pages 282–289.

Gang Luo, Xiaojiang Huang, Chin-Yew Lin, and Zaiqing Nie. 2015. Joint named entity recognition and disambiguation. In *Proc. EMNLP*. pages 879–880.

Andrew McCallum and Wei Li. 2003. Early results for named entity recognition with conditional random fields, feature induction and web-enhanced lexicons. In *Proceedings of the Seventh Conference on Natural Language Learning at HLT-NAACL 2003 - Volume 4*. Association for Computational Linguistics, Stroudsburg, PA, USA, CONLL '03, pages 188–191. https://doi.org/10.3115/1119176.1119206.

Joel Nothman, James R. Curran, and Tara Murphy. 2008. Transforming wikipedia into named entity training data. In *In Proceedings of the Australasian Language Technology Association Workshop 2008*. pages 124–132.

Joel Nothman, Nicky Ringland, Will Radford, Tara Murphy, and James R. Curran. 2012. Learning multilingual named entity recognition from Wikipedia. *Artificial Intelligence* 194:151–175. https://doi.org/10.1016/j.artint.2012.03.006.

S. T. Piantadosi, H. Tily, and E. Gibson. 2011. Word lengths are optimized for efficient communication. *Proceedings of the National Academy of Sciences* 108(9):3526. http://colala.bcs.rochester.edu/papers/PNAS-2011-Piantadosi-1012551108.pdf.

Alan Ritter, Sam Clark, Mausam, and Oren Etzioni. 2011. Named entity recognition in tweets: An experimental study. In *Proceedings of the Conference on Empirical Methods in Natural Language Processing*. Association for Computational Linguistics, Stroudsburg, PA, USA, EMNLP '11, pages 1524–1534. http://dl.acm.org/citation.cfm?id=2145432.2145595.

Burr Settles. 2004. Biomedical named entity recognition using conditional random fields and rich feature sets. In *Proceedings of the International Joint Workshop on Natural Language Processing in Biomedicine and Its Applications*. Association for Computational Linguistics, Stroudsburg, PA, USA, JNLPBA '04, pages 104–107. http://dl.acm.org/citation.cfm?id=1567594.1567618.

Claude E. Shannon. 1948. A mathematical theory of communication. *Bell system technical journal* 27.

Benjamin Strauss, Bethany Toma, Alan Ritter, Marie-Catherine de Marneffe, and Wei Xu. 2016. Results of the wnut16 named entity recognition shared task. In *Proceedings of the 2nd Workshop on Noisy User-generated Text (WNUT)*. The COLING 2016 Organizing Committee, Osaka, Japan, pages 138–144. http://aclweb.org/anthology/W16-3919.

Erik F. Tjong Kim Sang and Fien De Meulder. 2003. Introduction to the conll-2003 shared task: Language-independent named entity recognition. In *Proceedings of the Seventh Conference on Natural Language Learning at HLT-NAACL 2003 - Volume 4*. Association for Computational Linguistics, Stroudsburg, PA, USA, CONLL '03, pages 142–147. https://doi.org/10.3115/1119176.1119195.

Konstantinos N. Vavliakis, Andreas L. Symeonidis, and Pericles A. Mitkas. 2013. Event identification in web social media through named entity recognition and topic modeling. *Data Knowl. Eng.* 88:1–24. https://doi.org/10.1016/j.datak.2013.08.006.

Jake Ryland Williams, Eric M. Clark, James P. Bagrow, Christopher M. Danforth, and Peter Sheridan Dodds. 2015a. Identifying missing dictionary entries with frequency-conserving context models. *Phys. Rev. E* 92:042808. https://doi.org/10.1103/PhysRevE.92.042808.

Jake Ryland Williams, Paul R. Lessard, Suma Desu, Eric M. Clark, James P. Bagrow, Christopher M. Danforth, and Peter Sheridan Dodds. 2015b. Zipf's law holds for phrases, not words. *Nature Scientific Reports* 5:12209.

A Feature-based Ensemble Approach to
Recognition of Emerging and Rare Named Entities

Utpal Kumar Sikdar
R & D Department
Flytxt
Trivandrum, Kerala, India
utpal.sikdar@flytxt.com

Björn Gambäck
Department of Computer Science
Norwegian University of Science and Technology
Trondheim, Norway
gamback@ntnu.no

Abstract

Detecting previously unseen named entities in text is a challenging task. The paper describes how three initial classifier models were built using Conditional Random Fields (CRFs), Support Vector Machines (SVMs) and a Long Short-Term Memory (LSTM) recurrent neural network. The outputs of these three classifiers were then used as features to train another CRF classifier working as an ensemble.

5-fold cross-validation based on training and development data for the emerging and rare named entity recognition shared task showed precision, recall and F_1-score of 66.87%, 46.75% and 54.97%, respectively. For surface form evaluation, the CRF ensemble-based system achieved precision, recall and F_1 scores of 65.18%, 45.20% and 53.30%. When applied to unseen test data, the model reached 47.92% precision, 31.97% recall and 38.55% F_1-score for entity level evaluation, with the corresponding surface form evaluation values of 44.91%, 30.47% and 36.31%.

1 Introduction

The recognition of named entities is inherently complicated by the fact that new names emerge constantly and productively. This is particularly true for social media text and for other texts that are written in a more informal manner, where the issue is further complicated by a higher degree of misspellings as well as different types of unconventional spellings; on social media such as Twitter, abbreviated forms of words are common, as are merging of multiple words, special symbols and characters inserted into the words, etc.

Several approaches to Twitter named entity extraction have been explored, but it is still a challenging task due to noisiness of the texts. Liu et al. (2011) proposed a semi-supervised learning framework to identify Twitter names, using a k-Nearest Neighbors (kNN) approach to label names and taking these labels as an input feature to a Conditional Random Fields (CRF) classifier, achieving almost 80% accuracy on their own annotated data. Ritter et al. (2011) proposed a supervised model based on Labeled LDA (Ramage et al., 2009), and also showed part-of-speech and chunk information to be important components in Twitter named identification. Li et al. (2012) introduced an unsupervised Twitter named entity extraction strategy based on dynamic programming.

The present work addresses emerging and rare entity recognition. The first Twitter named entity shared task was organized at the ACL 2015 workshop on noisy user-generated text (Baldwin et al., 2015), with two subtasks: Twitter named entity identification and classification of those named entities into ten different types. Of the eight systems participating in the first workshop, the best (Yamada et al., 2015) achieved an F_1 score of 70.63% for Twitter name identification and 56.41% for classification, by combining supervised machine learning with high quality knowledge obtained from several open knowledge bases such as Wikipedia. Another team, (Akhtar et al., 2015) used a strategy based on differential evolution, getting F_1 scores of 56.81% for the identification task and 39.84% for classification.

A second shared task on Twitter Named Entity recognition was organized at COLING in 2016 (Strauss et al., 2016). The best placed system (Limsopatham and Collier, 2016) used a bi-directional LSTM (Long Short-Term Memory) neural network model, and achieved 52.41% and 65.89% F_1-scores on entity level and segmentation

Proceedings of the 3rd Workshop on Noisy User-generated Text, pages 177–181
Copenhagen, Denmark, September 7, 2017. ©2017 Association for Computational Linguistics

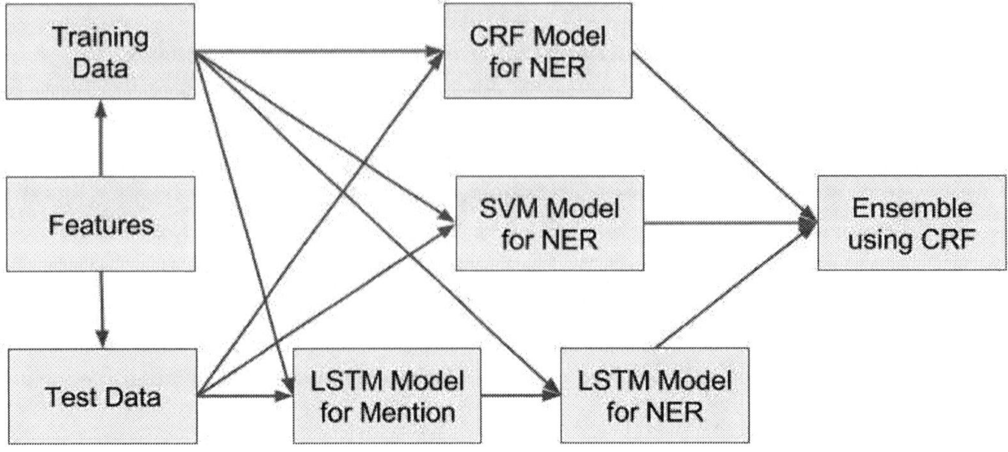

Figure 1: Overall system architecture

level evaluation, respectively. A system based on Conditional Random Fields (CRFs) and a range of features (Sikdar and Gambäck, 2016) achieved the best recall at segmentation level evaluation, and the second best F_1-score (63.22%).

A related shared task on Twitter named entity recognition and linking (NEEL) to the DBpedia database was held in conjunction with the 2016 WWW conference (Cano et al., 2016). Five teams particpated, with the best system (Waitelonis and Sack, 2016) achieving recall, precision and F-scores of 49.4%, 45.3% and 47.3%. In that system, each token was mapped to gazetteers developed from DBpedia. Tokens that were not nouns or did not match stop words were discarded.

The present paper outlines an ensemble-based machine learning approach to the identification and classification of rare and emerging named entities. Here the classification categories are Person, Location, Corporation, Product, Creativework and Group. A Conditional Random Fields (Lafferty et al., 2001) classifier was trained using the outputs from three other classifiers as features, with those classifiers in turn being built using three different learning strategies: CRFs, Support Vector Machines (SVMs), and a deep learning based Long Short-Term Memory (LSTM) recurrent neural network. The rest of the paper is organized as follows: The named entity identification methodology and the different features used are introduced in Section 2. Results are presented and discussed in Section 3, while Section 4 addresses future work and concludes.

2 Name Recognition Methodology

The named entity recognition method is divided into two steps. In the first step, three classifiers are built to recognize named entities using different features from the unstructured text. In the second step, the outputs from the three classifiers are considered as three features and used to train a CRF classifier working as an ensemble learner, to produce the final named entity recognition. The system architecture is shown in Figure 1.

2.1 CRF-based Named Entity Recognition

The Conditional Random Fields Named Entity Recognition model was implemented using the C++ based CRF++ package[1], which allows for fast training by utilizing L-BFGS (Liu and Nocedal, 1989), a limited memory quasi-Newton algorithm for large scale numerical optimization. The CRF classifier was trained with L2 regularization and a range of features:
- local context (-3 to +2)[2],
- part-of-speech information,
- chunk information,
- suffix and prefix characters (-4, +4), and
- word frequency,

together with a number of Boolean flags, namely, is-word-length $<$ 5, is-followed-by-special-character ('@' or '#'), is-stop-word, is-all-upper-case, is-all-digit, is-alpha-and-digit-together, and is-last-word.

---

[1]https://taku910.github.io/crfpp/
[2]Here '-' and '+' indicate the number of preceding and following words in the context window, respectively.

2.2 SVM-based Named Entity Recognition

Since Support Vector Machines previously have
been successfully utilized to recognize named entities in formal text, e.g. by Isozaki and Kazawa
(2002), a classifier was built using the C++ based
SVM package Yamcha[3] with polynomial kernel
and default settings. The same features as for the
CRF model were used to train the SVMs.

2.3 LSTM-based Named Entity Recognition

The proposed deep learning based name entity
recognition model consists of two Long Short-
Term Memory recurrent neural network (Hochreiter and Schmidhuber, 1997), a model which was
also successfully used by Lample et al. (2016) to
achieve state-of-the-art named entity recognition
results in formal texts. The first LSTM identifies
the boundaries of a named entity (called mention)
and this mention is then used as one of the features
for named entity recognition in the second LSTM.

For identifying mentions, two binary features, is-start-with-capital-letter and is-all-upper-
case, were extracted together with the following:

- word shape-1, a length 6 one-hot vector containing the following six binary flags: upper
case, lower case, digit, '@' symbol, '#' symbol, and other characters,

- word shape-2, a length 39 one-hot vector consisting of the 26 letters of the English alphabet converted to lower case, together with the
ten digits, the two symbols '@' and '#', and
one spot for other characters, and

- a word2vec pre-trained vector of length 150,
Tweets were collected from the W-NUT 2016
shared task,[4] the 2016 NEEL challenge,[5] and
the W-NUT 2017 workshop datasets to build the
word2vec model (Mikolov et al., 2013a,b). The
skip-gram approach was used with negative sampling and a context window of 5. All features were
then concatenated into one vector and fed to the
first LSTM network for mention recognition.

After a mention had been identified, it was used
as one of the features for recognition of named
entities in the second LSTM model, which as
features together with word-shape-1 and word-
shape-2 (as above) utilized three Boolean flags
(is-mention, is-start-with-capital-letter, and is-all-
upper-case), and GloVe (Pennington et al., 2014),

---

[3]http://chasen.org/~taku/software/yamcha/
[4]http://noisy-text.github.io/2016/
[5]http://microposts2016.seas.upenn.edu/
  challenge.html

Data set	tweets	named entities
Training	3,394	1,975
Development	1,009	833
Test	1,287	1,041

Table 1: Twitter dataset statistics

a pre-trained Twitter word vector (here a GloVe
vector of dimension 100 was selected).

These features were concatenated to train an
LSTM model for 50 epochs with a batch size of
256. The network was set up as consisting of two
hidden layers with 256 hidden units.

2.4 A Named Entity Recognition Ensemble

In the second step, the outputs of the above three
classifiers were considered as input features to a
CRF classifier, which was trained using these three
features together with the previous and next two
context words. Note that this final CRF classifier
being used a selector in the ensemble thus does not
cover all features of the CRF classifier described
above (Section 2.1), but only utilizes the context
and the three classifiers' outputs as features.

An ensemble based on using majority voting
was also tested, which selected the output of one
of the classifiers at random, in case they all produced different outputs. The results of the voting-
based ensemble improved on the CRF and SVM
models, but turned out worse than the LSTM
model. However, the ensemble using a Conditional Random Field model to select among the
classifier outputs improved results over the board.

3 Experiments

The experiments were based on the datasets provided by the organizers of the W-NUT 2017
shared task on emerging and rare named entity
recognition (Derczynski et al., 2017). The statistics of the datasets are shown in Table 1.

3.1 Results

For the experiments, the development data was
merged with the training data, and a 5-fold cross-
validation was executed. The CRF-based classifier model produced the precision, recall and F_1
values of 51.79%, 45.51% and 48.31%, respectively. The LSTM model performed better when
compared to the CRF-based model with respect to
recall and F_1-score, achieving precision, recall and

System	Entity			Surface form		
	Precision	Recall	F_1-score	Precision	Recall	F_1-score
CRF	51.79	45.51	48.31	47.25	42.02	44.48
SVM	48.99	44.87	46.65	44.56	41.64	43.05
LSTM	51.58	51.33	51.37	47.21	47.94	47.57
Ensemble	66.87	46.75	54.97	65.18	45.20	53.30

Table 2: 5-fold cross-validated results on combined development and training data

System	Entity			Surface form		
	Precision	Recall	F_1-score	Precision	Recall	F_1-score
CRF	40.75	28.17	33.32	38.53	27.43	32.05
SVM	34.46	29.38	31.72	32.58	28.69	30.51
LSTM	39.83	30.86	34.78	37.52	29.11	32.78
Ensemble	47.92	31.97	38.55	44.91	30.47	36.31

Table 3: Performance on the unseen test data (5-fold cross-validated)

F_1 values of 51.58%, 51.33% and 51.37%. However, as shown in Table 2, the CRF-ensemble approach outperformed all the other models with respect to F_1-score. For surface evaluation, a similar behaviour could be observed, with the ensemble model achieving the highest F_1-score at 53.30%.

The different classifiers were also applied to the unseen test data and produced similar results after 5-fold cross-validation, with the ensemble approach achieving the best F_1-score compared to all other models, as can be seen in Table 3. The CRF ensemble's named entity precision, recall and F_1-score on the test data were 47.92%, 31.97% and 38.55%, respectively. For surface form evaluation, the ensemble system achieved 44.91% precision, 30.47% recall and 36.31% F_1-score.

Table 4 compares our results (FLYTXT) to the other systems participating in the shared task, with the FLYTXT ensemble-based system placing in 5th position in the final ranking on both named entity and surface form evaluation.

3.2 Error Analysis

The system suffers from poor recall, with the model only finding 720 of 1079 named entities in the test data. The system also classified many identified named entities wrongly, and in total correctly identified 345 named entities. This may be due to almost all named entities present in the test data being unknown and fairly dissimilar to the ones appearing in the training data.

4 Conclusion

This paper has proposed an ensemble-based system for Twitter named entity identification and classification. A range of different features was developed to extract Twitter names from the tweets. Three initial classifiers were built, one for CRF-based named entity extraction, one utilizing SVMs, and one based on a deep learner (LSTM). The ensemble utilized a CRF classifier taking the output of the other three models as input.

In the future, we will analyse the errors in more detail and aim to use external resources (e.g., DBpedia and Wikipedia) to reduce the misclassification of the tokens, as well as to identify more entities from the tweets. We will also try to generate more models and later ensemble these model to improve the system performance.

Team	Entity	Surface form
UH-RiTUAL	41.86	40.24
SpinningBytes	40.78	39.33
SJTU-Adapt	40.42	37.62
Arcada	39.98	37.77
FLYTXT	38.35	36.31
MIC-CIS	37.06	34.25
Drexel-CCI	26.30	25.26

Table 4: Comparison of system results (F_1 scores)

References

Md Shad Akhtar, Utpal Kumar Sikdar, and Asif Ekbal. 2015. IITP: Multiobjective differential evolution based Twitter named entity recognition. In (Xu et al., 2015), pages 106–110.

Timothy Baldwin, Marie Catherine de Marneffe, Bo Han, Young-Bum Kim, Alan Ritter, and Wei Xu. 2015. Shared tasks of the 2015 workshop on noisy user-generated text: Twitter lexical normalization and named entity recognition. In (Xu et al., 2015), pages 126–135.

Amparo E. Cano, Daniel Preoţiuc-Pietro, Danica Radovanović, Katrin Weller, and Aba-Sah Dadzie. 2016. #Microposts2016 — 6th workshop on 'making sense of microposts'. In *Proceedings of the 25th World Wide Web Conference (WWW'16)*. ACM, Montréal, Canada, pages 1041–1042.

Leon Derczynski, Eric Nichols, Marieke van Erp, and Nut Limsopatham. 2017. Results of the WNUT2017 shared task on novel and emerging entity recognition. In *Proceedings of the 3rd Workshop on Noisy, User-generated Text*. ACL, EMNLP 2017, Copenhagen, Denmark.

Bo Han, Alan Ritter, Leon Derczynski, Wei Xu, and Timothy Baldwin, editors. 2016. *Proceedings of the 2nd Workshop on Noisy User-generated Text*. ACL, 26th COLING, Osaka, Japan.

Sepp Hochreiter and Jürgen Schmidhuber. 1997. Long short-term memory. *Neural Computation* 9(8):1735–1780.

Hideki Isozaki and Hideto Kazawa. 2002. Efficient support vector classifiers for named entity recognition. In *Proceedings of the 19th International Conference on Computational linguistics*. ACL, Taipei, Taiwan, volume 1. Paper 54.

John Lafferty, Andrew McCallum, and Fernando C.N. Pereira. 2001. Conditional Random Fields: Probabilistic models for segmenting and labeling sequence data. In *Proceedings of the 18th International Conference on Machine Learning*. IMIS, Williamstown, MA, USA, pages 282–289.

Guillaume Lample, Miguel Ballesteros, Sandeep Subramanian, Kazuya Kawakami, and Chris Dyer. 2016. Neural architectures for named entity recognition. In *Proceedings of the 15th Annual Conference of the North American Chapter of the Association for Computational Linguistics*. ACL, San Diego, CA, USA, pages 260–270.

Chenliang Li, Jianshu Weng, Qi He, Yuxia Yao, Anwitaman Datta, Aixin Sun, and Bu-Sung Lee. 2012. TwiNER: Named entity recognition in targeted Twitter stream. In *Proceedings of the 35th International ACM SIGIR Conference on Research and Development in Information Retrieval*. ACM, Portland, OR, USA, pages 721–730.

Nut Limsopatham and Nigel Collier. 2016. Bidirectional LSTM for named entity recognition in Twitter messages. In (Han et al., 2016), pages 145–152.

Dong C. Liu and Jorge Nocedal. 1989. On the limited memory BFGS method for large scale optimization. *Mathematical Programming* 45(1):503–528.

Xiaohua Liu, Shaodian Zhang, Furu Wei, and Ming Zhou. 2011. Recognizing named entities in tweets. In *Proceedings of the 49th Annual Meeting of the Association for Computational Linguistics*. ACL, Portland, OR, USA, pages 359–367.

Tomas Mikolov, Kai Chen, Greg Corrado, and Jeffrey Dean. 2013a. Efficient estimation of word representations in vector space. *CoRR* abs/1301.3781.

Tomas Mikolov, Ilya Sutskever, Kai Chen, Greg Corrado, and Jeffrey Dean. 2013b. Distributed representations of words and phrases and their compositionality. In *Advances in Neural Information Processing Systems 26 (NIPS 2013)*. Curran Associates, Red Hook, NY, USA, pages 3111–3119.

Jeffrey Pennington, Richard Socher, and Christopher D. Manning. 2014. Glove: Global vectors for word representation. In *The 2014 Conference on Empirical Methods in Natural Language Processing*. ACL, Doha, Qatar, pages 1532–1543.

Daniel Ramage, David Hall, Ramesh Nallapati, and Christopher D. Manning. 2009. Labeled LDA: A supervised topic model for credit attribution in multi-labeled corpora. In *Proceedings of the 2009 Conference on Empirical Methods in Natural Language Processing*. ACL, Singapore, pages 248–256.

Alan Ritter, Sam Clark, Mausam, and Oren Etzioni. 2011. Named entity recognition in tweets: An experimental study. In *Proceedings of the 2011 Conference on Empirical Methods in Natural Language Processing*. ACL, Edinburgh, Scotland, UK, pages 1524–1534.

Utpal Kumar Sikdar and Björn Gambäck. 2016. Feature-rich Twitter named entity recognition and classification. In (Han et al., 2016), pages 164–170.

Benjamin Strauss, Bethany E. Toma, Alan Ritter, Marie Catherine de Marneffe, and Wei Xu. 2016. Results of the WNUT16 named entity recognition shared task. In (Han et al., 2016), pages 138–144.

Jörg Waitelonis and Harald Sack. 2016. Named entity linking in #tweets with KEA. In *Proceedings of 6th Workshop on Making Sense of Microposts*. CEUR, Montréal, Canada, pages 61–63.

Wei Xu, Bo Han, and Alan Ritter, editors. 2015. *Proceedings of the ACL 2015 Workshop on Noisy User-generated Text*. Beijing, China.

Ikuya Yamada, Hideaki Takeda, and Yoshiyasu Takefuji. 2015. Enhancing named entity recognition in Twitter messages using entity linking. In (Xu et al., 2015), pages 136–140.

Association for Computational Linguistics
209 N. Eighth Street
Stroudsburg, Pennsylvania 18360

ISBN 978-1-5108-4753-8